CU00921802

FROM PARCHM

From Parchment to Practice explores the problems that arise when a new constitution has been adopted. All new constitutions must manage tension between two forces: aspirations for social and political transformation on the one hand and demands for preservation of old interests and institutions on the other. The period following the initial adoption of a new constitution is the conceptual, temporal, and institutional bridge between the past and future. It is the moment when the transformative and the preservative forces in constitutional design can come into the sharpest conflict. Through a series of case studies, this volume analyses the variable nature of these type of conflicts – and the diverse means through which they are mediated, whether successfully or not.

Tom Ginsburg is Leo Spitz Professor of International Law at the University of Chicago and a Research Professor at the American Bar Foundation. He also co-directs the Comparative Constitutions Project, an NSF-funded dataset cataloging the world's constitutions since 1789. He is the author of several books, including *How to Save a Constitutional Democracy* (with Aziz Huq, 2018), *Comparative Constitutional Law* (with Rosalind Dixon, 2011), and *The Endurance of National Constitutions* (with Zachary Elkins and James Melton, 2009).

Aziz Z. Huq is Frank and Bernice Greenberg Professor of Law at the University of Chicago, where he teaches and researches in constitutional law. He is the author of *How to Save a Constitutional Democracy* (with Tom Ginsburg, 2018). His scholarship has won awards from the Association of American Law Schools, and has been published in leading legal and peer-reviewed journals. Previously, Huq was Director of the Liberty and National Security Project of the Brennan Center for Justice, and a Senior Consultant Analyst for the International Crisis Group.

COMPARATIVE CONSTITUTIONAL LAW AND POLICY

Series Editors

Tom Ginsburg *University of Chicago*
Zachary Elkins *University of Texas at Austin*
Ran Hirschl *University of Toronto*

Comparative constitutional law is an intellectually vibrant field that encompasses an increasingly broad array of approaches and methodologies. This series collects analytically innovative and empirically grounded work from scholars of comparative constitutionalism across academic disciplines. Books in the series include theoretically informed studies of single constitutional jurisdictions, comparative studies of constitutional law and institutions, and edited collections of original essays that respond to challenging theoretical and empirical questions in the field.

Books in the Series

The Failure of Popular Constitution Making in Turkey: Regressing Towards Constitutional Autocracy
Edited by Felix Petersen and Zeynep Yanasmayan

A Qualified Hope: The Indian Supreme Court and Progressive Social Change
Edited by Gerald N. Rosenberg, Sudhir Krishnaswamy, and Shishir Bail

Constitutions in Times of Financial Crisis
Edited by Tom Ginsburg, Mark D. Rosen, and Georg Vanberg

Reconstructing Rights: Courts, Parties, and Equality Rights in India, South Africa, and the United States
Stephan Stohler

Constitution-Making and Transnational Legal Order
Edited by Tom Ginsburg, Terence C. Halliday, and Gregory Shaffer

Hybrid Constitutionalism
Eric C. Ip

The Politico-Legal Dynamics of Judicial Review
Thenuis Roux

The Invisible Constitution in Comparative Perspective
Edited by Rosalind Dixon and Adrienne Stone

Constitutional Courts in Asia: A Comparative Perspective
Edited by Albert H. Y. Chen and Andrew Harding

Judicial Review in Norway
Anine Kierulf

From Parchment to Practice

IMPLEMENTING NEW CONSTITUTIONS

Edited by

TOM GINSBURG
University of Chicago

AZIZ Z. HUQ
University of Chicago

CAMBRIDGE
UNIVERSITY PRESS

University Printing House, Cambridge CB2 8BS, United Kingdom

One Liberty Plaza, 20th Floor, New York, NY 10006, USA

477 Williamstown Road, Port Melbourne, VIC 3207, Australia

314–321, 3rd Floor, Plot 3, Splendor Forum, Jasola District Centre, New Delhi – 110025, India

79 Anson Road, #06–04/06, Singapore 079906

Cambridge University Press is part of the University of Cambridge.

It furthers the University's mission by disseminating knowledge in the pursuit of education, learning, and research at the highest international levels of excellence.

www.cambridge.org
Information on this title: www.cambridge.org/9781108487733
DOI: 10.1017/9781108767859

First published 2020

Printed in the United Kingdom by TJ International Ltd. Padstow Cornwall

A catalogue record for this publication is available from the British Library.

Library of Congress Cataloging-in-Publication Data
NAMES: From Parchment to Practice: Implementing New Constitutions (Conference) (2017 : University of Chicago Law School) | Ginsburg, Tom, editor. | Huq, Aziz Z., editor. | University of Chicago. Law School, sponsoring body.
TITLE: From parchment to practice : implementing new constitutions / edited by Tom Ginsburg, University of Chicago; Aziz Z. Huq, University of Chicago
DESCRIPTION: Cambridge, United Kingdom ; New York, NY, USA : Cambridge University Press, 2020. | SERIES: Comparative constitutional law and policy | Includes index.
IDENTIFIERS: LCCN 2019037627 (print) | LCCN 2019037628 (ebook) | ISBN 9781108487733 (hardback) | ISBN 9781108738026 (paperback) | ISBN 9781108767859 (epub)
SUBJECTS: LCSH: Constitutional law–Congresses. | New democracies–Congresses.
CLASSIFICATION: LCC K3165.A6 F76 2017 (print) | LCC K3165.A6 (ebook) | DDC 342–dc23
LC record available at https://lccn.loc.gov/2019037627
LC ebook record available at https://lccn.loc.gov/2019037628

ISBN 978-1-108-48773-3 Hardback
ISBN 978-1-108-73802-6 Paperback

Contents

Figures

Figures

Tables

Tables

Contributors

Daniel Abebe is Vice Provost and the Harold J. and Marion F. Green Professor of Law at the University of Chicago.

Eric Alston is Scholar in Residence, Finance Division, Faculty Director, Hernando de Soto Capital Markets Program, Leeds School of Business, University of Colorado Boulder.

Melissa Crouch is an Associate Professor in law at the University of New South Wales, Sydney, Australia.

Rosalind Dixon is Professor of Law at the University of New South Wales, Sydney, Australia, and President of the International Society of Constitutional Law.

Claudia Flores is Clinical Professor and Director of the Human Rights Clinic at the University of Chicago Law School.

James Thuo Gathii is the Wing-Tat Lee Chair in International Law and Professor at Loyola University, Chicago.

Tom Ginsburg is the Leo Spitz Professor of International Law at the University of Chicago, and a Research Professor at the American Bar Foundation.

Diego González is Assistant Professor of Constitutional Law at University of Colombia in Bogota, Colombia, and a Deputy Justice at the Constitutional Court of Colombia.

Aziz Z. Huq is Frank and Bernice Greenberg Professor of Law at the University of Chicago, where he teaches and researches in constitutional law.

Madhav Khosla is an Associate Professor of Political Science at Ashoka University, the Ambedkar Visiting Associate Professor of Law at Columbia University, and a Junior Fellow at the Harvard Society of Fellows.

Sanford Levinson is the W. St. John Garwood and W. St. John Garwood, Jr. Centennial Chair of Law at the University of Texas Law School.

Theunis Roux is Professor of Law at the University of New South Wales, Sydney, Australia. He is a former Secretary-General of the International Association of Constitutional Law (IACL).

Susan H. Williams is Walter W. Foskett Professor of Law and the Co-Director of the Center for Constitutional Democracy at Indiana University, Bloomington.

1

Introduction

From Parchment to Practice

Tom Ginsburg and Aziz Z. Huq[*]

It is getting to be harder to run a constitution than to frame one.

Woodrow Wilson, 1887

This book concerns a set of problems that arise from the distinctive conceptual and practical tension in the first period after a new constitution has been adopted. We shall argue that at a very general level, a new constitution must manage a balance or tension between two forces. These are aspirations for *transformation* and demands for *preservation* through entrenchment.[1] The first period, as we will elaborate, is the conceptual, temporal, and institutional bridge between the past and future. It is the moment when the transformative and the preservative vectors of constitutional design can come into the sharpest conflict. The variable nature of these conflicts – and the diverse means through which they are mediated, whether successfully or less successfully – is the focus of both this introduction and, in different ways, the chapters that follow.

The term "constitution" can be defined in many ways, and it is worth clarifying the scope of the book's inquiry before proceeding. We are focused here on written documents that specify the terms of central governing institutions and individual rights. This is not to understand constitutions as solely a function of their written terms, or to ignore the sociopolitical, economic, and cultural contexts in which they are written.[2] But it is to take the project of crafting and ratifying a new text as a

[*] Thanks to Eric Alston, Rosalind Dixon, Richard McAdams, and the conference participants in the "Parchment to Practice" event for valuable feedback.

[1] For a different version of these two concepts, see Reva B. Siegel, "'The Rule of Love': Wife Beating as Prerogative and Privacy." *Yale Law Journal* 105: 2117, 2178–87 (1996).

[2] On the importance of such context in comparative constitutional studies more generally, see Ran Hirschl, *Comparative Matters: The Renaissance of Comparative Constitutional Law.* New York: Cambridge University Press, 2014.

paradigmatic point of departure for the institutional articulation of new political arrangements that are fairly characterized as "constitutional" in character.

We can usefully start with the transformative aspect of constitution-making and implementation. Constitutions are often audacious blueprints for social and political change. They are crafted to inspire and motivate a new polity, and adopted at moments of high optimism in the possibility of change.[3] As Jon Elster has underscored, constitutions might reflect aspirations, but the expression of those aspirations may be possible only within and because of background social and political crises that have upset the historical equilibrium.[4] This then leads to the creation of a new order, in which a constitution is the template. Transformation is a costly proposition. It involves elections, the creation or restructuring of an executive, and institutional checks on the new leviathan in the form of courts, independent commissions, and civil society institutions. In a territorially extended state, it can require the creation of new administrative apparatus, such as new local courts, government bodies, or new police and security forces. If a new constitution is to persevere, both officials within the state and citizens subject to their rules must view the state as a reasonably legitimate one, acquire habits of obedience to its rules, and adopt favorable dispositions toward both the state and their fellow citizens. As we shall explain in this chapter, mere convergence on common understandings of what counts as a constitutional violation may not be sufficient to engender sustained compliance. On this point, we diverge from one of the prominent theories in the literature, which emphasizes coordination on common understandings as a necessary condition for constitutional implementation; while it is surely necessary, it is not sufficient.

At least in a post-war world wherein talk of individual rights is pervasive, constitution-making means that the state, so as to be minimally normatively defensible and sociologically legitimate, must take some steps to promote, respect, and protect the new rights and duties contained in the new constitution. In many instances, both the state and citizenry must develop some effective mechanisms for accountability. Failures in navigating national political conflicts or in delivering essential social services can undermine the creation of necessary social trust.[5] All this takes time and effort. The latter makes sense only if it is anticipated that a constitution will be transformative of the larger social or institutional fabric.

But consider the other side of the coin – the preservative character of constitutions. To begin with, constitutions are, of course, just pieces of paper at their

---

[3]   Mauricio Garcia-Villegas, "Law as Hope: Constitutions, Courts, and Social Change in Latin America." *Florida Journal of International Law* 16: 133 (2004); Eric Alston, "Ecuador's 2008 Constitution: The Political Economy of Securing an Aspirational Social Contract." *Constitutional Studies* 3: 69–99 (2018).

[4]   Jon Elster, "Constitution-Making and Violence." *Journal of Legal Analysis* 4 (1): 7–39 (2012).

[5]   See Aziz Z. Huq, "Constitutionalism, Legitimacy, and Public Order: A South African Case Study," in *Constitutional Triumphs, Constitutional Disappointments*, ed. Rosalind Dixon and Theunis Roux. Cambridge: Cambridge University Press, 2017, 388–405.

inception, the moment they come into force. In translating paper into practice, and in setting up institutions and changing beliefs, forces of resistance will surely be encountered. Getting a constitution up and running entails some measure of accommodation of existing patterns of political power, institutional development, and socioeconomic arrangements. Even in situations of dramatic upheavals, some elements of the prior political and social order are likely to linger and to set their face against disadvantaging change. A constitution that fails entirely to accommodate them – that is, one that fails to preserve what key members of the constitution-making coalition perceive as valuable and important – has a questionable future.

More generally, a constitution may be adopted to prevent change that would otherwise occur, or to lock in benefits for the most powerful political and economic actors in a society. A large body of literature on constitution-making characterizes such organic documents as deals struck among these powerful actors. This theme is especially prominent in the treatments of judicial review, for example by Ginsburg in his earlier work, as we shall see in this chapter.[6] In American constitutional scholarship, this position is most closely associated with the progressive historian Charles Beard, who contended that the 1787 Constitution was designed to facilitate the retention of wealth by, and the transfer of wealth to, a small minority of propertied men.[7] Common to these theories is the assumption that those who engage in constitution-making are self-interested actors, unwilling to sacrifice much or any of their material and political status for ideological ends. Such rational, self-interested actors will not reach a deal that undermines or redistributes their power in the aggregate. Short-term concessions may be made, but only to avoid subsequent, larger losses. This self-interested group of framers, if they reach a mutually beneficial bargain, will want to preserve their bargain going forward. If there is no mutually beneficial (i.e. Pareto superior) deal to be struck, then we would not expect to see a new constitution emerge. It follows from this analysis that constitutions will tend in whole or part to be preservative in character.

This tension between transformation and preservation evidences itself in several different ways. At the same time, it can be mediated through many devices and strategies. So it is best thought of as a tension rather than a fatal flaw. But it is also a tension that is predictably most acute at the moment just after a constitution's

---

[6] See Ran Hirschl, "The Political Origins of the New Constitutionalism." *Indiana Journal of Global Legal Studies* 11 (1): 71–108 (2004); Ran Hirschl, *Towards Juristocracy: The Origins and Consequences of the New Constitutionalism.* Cambridge, MA: Harvard University Press, 2009; Tom Ginsburg, *Judicial Review in New Democracies: Constitutional Courts in Asian Cases.* Cambridge: Cambridge University Press, 2003. See also J. Mark Ramseyer, "The Puzzling (In) Dependence of Courts: A Comparative Approach." *The Journal of Legal Studies* 23 (2): 721–47 (1994).

[7] Charles A. Beard, *An Economic Interpretation of the Constitution of the United States.* New York: Simon and Schuster, 2012. For a more recent account that blends Beardian themes with a focus on ideological issues, and sheer contingency, see Michael J. Klarman, *The Framers' Coup: The Making of the United States Constitution.* Oxford: Oxford University Press, 2016.

creation. We call this *the first period*. This is the period in which there is likely to be the greatest gap between the aspiration recorded on parchment and the actuality of political practice. Of course, constitutions must navigate problems of institutionalization and legitimation without regard to their age. The US Constitution is the world's oldest, and hence continues to face questions about the legitimacy and fairness of basic representational elements, such as the electoral college. But new constitutions face an especially sharp version of these difficulties, for there is likely neither deeply shared understanding of legal norms that can serve as coordinating focal points beyond the bare text nor any internalized norms of deference and legality oriented toward that text. Institutions have yet to arise in which politicians are trained and socialized, leading to the internalization of constitutional norms and commitments. No cadre of bureaucrats, for example, will have vested stakes in the maintenance of stable governance instruments. Both the constitutive and regulative elements of the constitutional order are at this instant likely to be fragile, awaiting subsequent reinforcement. Any errors or internal conflicts in the constitutional design, moreover, may not yet have been identified and instead are most likely to be uncovered by the initial acts of politicians and officials working through the new constitution's machinery.

There is abundant evidence for these propositions in the world of national constitutions, which are notoriously fragile, short-lived, and often divorced from actual practice. Figure 1.1 presents data from the Comparative Constitutions Project (CCP), showing a distribution of constitutional duration at the time of collapse. As these data make apparent, the modal age of constitutional death is one year; more than 15 percent have died by that moment.[8] Some of these are by design, in cases in which the constitution is interim or meant to be replaced. But even excluding interim constitutions from the calculus does not change the basic shape of the distribution. The data's leftward skew suggests some caution is appropriate before embracing an expansively aspirational view of constitution-making. It further hints at a distinctive problem of institutionalization and legitimation in the first period of a constitution's history. And surely it picks out empirically a phenomenon that calls out for analysis.

The CCP data also provide a measure of the different ways in which the tension between the transformative and the preservative is mediated in practice. The data contain a measure of the similarity between one constitution and the document that immediately replaces it. We use an overall similarity index, aggregating subtopics into a single measure. That measure, to be clear, does not wholly capture the

---

[8]   The Comparative Constitutions Project uses the country-year as the unit of analysis, and credits a constitution to the year it was adopted. It counts the lifespan as lasting from the year of adoption until the year of replacement. In an extreme case, a constitution adopted in January of one year and replaced in December of the following year would be counted as lasting a year. These kinds of noisy variations cut both ways. A constitution adopted in December and replaced the next month would also be counted as lasting a year.

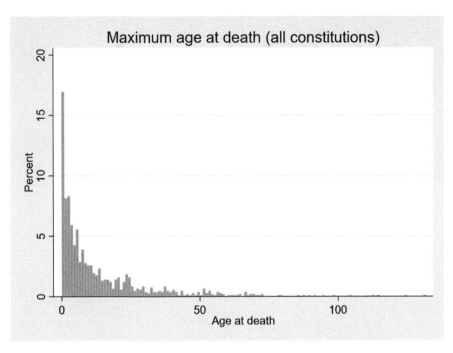

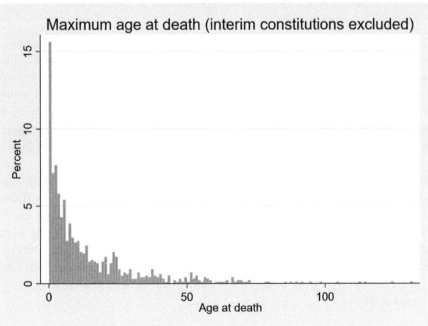

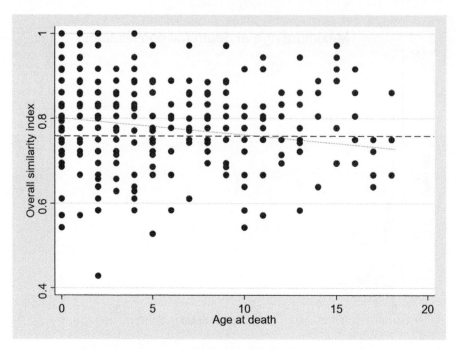

FIGURE 1.2 Similarity of constitutions with predecessor, by age (n = 640)

transformation/preservation dynamic we focus on here – a constitution, for example, may accommodate and entrench distributions of social and economic power that are not registered in prior constitutional language through the design of electoral arrangements or the way in which subnational governance is carved up. Nevertheless, Figure 1.2 usefully illustrates the fact that constitutions display a range of approaches in balancing the tension between transformation and preservation. It provides an index of similarity with the previous constitution, by age of constitutional death, for all constitutions up to the median predicted lifespan of nineteen years. The dashed line indicates the median similarity across all such constitutions, which tends to be higher than it would be between any two randomly drawn constitutions.[9] The dotted line provides the fitted line or trend. As one can see, by this measure constitutions that die in the first period tend to be slightly more conservative (in the sense of requiring less change from the prior constitutional baseline) than those that die later. Perhaps then the marginally more significant risk of the first period is being insufficiently transformative, or of hewing too close to the status quo.

---

[9] Zachary Elkins, Tom Ginsburg, and James Melton, *The Endurance of National Constitutions.* New York: Cambridge University Press, 2009.

The relationships illustrated in Figures 1.1 and 1.2, we should emphasize, are correlational rather than causal. For example, it may be that a conservative attitude to constitutional change in relation to a prior constitution indicates a failure to agree to new terms in a constitution. That bargaining failure, which is reflected in the stickiness of the text from one constitutional regime to the next, directly leads to a breakdown in political compromises and constitutional death: The actual text, however, wise or unwise, would have only an epiphenomenal role in this dynamic.

In the balance of this introduction, we therefore set out a theoretical and practical agenda for the study of what we will characterize as *the first-period problem.* Our first aim in what follows is to unpack in more detail the various theoretical claims sketched previously in this chapter. Our second aim is to sketch a general framework for thinking about the first-period problem through a common analytic device in studies of constitutional design. This is the analogy of a constitution to a contract among the most powerful social formations (or factions) in a polity. We emphasize at the inception that the contract analogy is just that – it is an analogy that captures one way of thinking about the complex social, economic, legal, cultural, ideological, and political matrix from which constitutional success (however understood) or failure emerges. It is not the only way of evaluating constitutional choice; nor does it necessarily provide a morally compelling standpoint for evaluating such choices. Nevertheless, understanding constitutions as contracts provides a perspective on the incentives and actions of powerful actors at a constitution's framing moment. As a result, it may cast light on the kinds of problems likely to arise in the first period, and the repertoire of institutional solutions available for their mitigation. We conclude by summarizing and reflecting on the case studies contained in the balance of the book, in light of the framework laid out here.

1.1 ORIGINS OF THE FIRST-PERIOD PROBLEM

A written constitution generally describes the basic political institutions of a polity, explains how those institutions are to be created and then renewed on an ongoing basis (e.g. through election, sortition, or hereditary transmission), and circumscribes the power of those institutions in various ways. So described, a constitution can play one of several functions, including defining a political community, protecting rights, and making government possible.[10] It is also the case that such documents are signals on the international plane, and hence one of the first acts of new states.[11] But whatever its foundational architecture, its inward or outward-regarding character, and whatever mix of ends it pursues, a constitution is generally intended to be efficacious. So-called sham constitutions do exist. But they do not represent the

---

[10] Tom Ginsburg and Aziz Z. Huq, "Introduction," in *Assessing Constitutional Performance*, ed. Tom Ginsburg and Aziz Z. Huq. New York: Cambridge University Press, 2016, 3–35.

[11] Mark Tushnet, "Constitution-Making: An Introduction," *Texas Law Review* 91: 1983 (2012).

modal case. As a result, they are peripheral to the questions we aim to frame and pursue in this volume.[12]

As noted previously, to be effective, a constitution must navigate between the competing demands for transformation and continuity. This dichotomous pressure not only influences the design of many constitutions, but shapes the extent and manner in which the design on paper is immediately translated into a new set of ongoing, efficacious institutions – defined as the "rule[s] of the game in a society or, more formally, are the humanly devised constraints that shape human interaction."[13]

It is rarely the case that a constitution will merely codify the status quo ante; to the contrary, constitutions are often intended to transform the status quo. Outside of the context of imposed regimes, such as that embodied in Japan's postwar constitution, a constitution tends to require costly negotiation.[14] The process of creating a constitution may involve a collective body, such as a legislature or a constituent assembly, allocating time to "arguing and bargaining" over new entitlements.[15] In the contemporary era, more elaborate processes of public canvassing and consultation are increasingly perceived as necessary legitimating steps in constitution-making.[16] And it is easy for Americans to forget in retrospect, but the enterprise of national constitution-making entails political risk, sometimes under conditions of great uncertainty, that may not materialize into political benefits.[17] All this entails transaction costs, which would hardly be worth incurring unless there was some potential positive improvement to be obtained. Whether their goals are ideological or material, or some mix of the two, dominant actors in a given polity are unlikely to expend effort and capital (either financial or political) without the possibility of some change.

---

[12] For a useful study, see David S. Law and Mila Versteeg, "Sham Constitutions." *California Law Review* 101: 863 (2013); see Walter F. Murphy, "Constitutions, Constitutionalism, and Democracy," in *Constitutionalism and Democracy: Transitions in the Contemporary World*, ed. Douglas Greenberg, et al. New York: Oxford University Press, 1993, 3, 8–9.

[13] Douglass C. North, *Institutions, Institutional Change and Economic Performance*. Cambridge: Cambridge University Press, 1990, 3.

[14] Charles L. Kades, "The American Role in Revising Japan's Imperial Constitution." *Political Science Quarterly* 104 (2): 215–47 (1989); see also Roy Moore and Donald L. Robinson, *Partners for Democracy: Crafting the New Japanese State*. New York: Oxford University Press, 2004.

[15] Jon Elster, "Arguing and Bargaining in Two Constituent Assemblies." *University of Pennsylvania Journal of Constitutional Law* 2: 345 (1999). On the choice between legislatures and constituent assemblies, see Jon Elster, "Legislatures as Constituent Assemblies," in *Constitutionalism: New Challenges – European Law from a Nordic Perspective*, ed. Joakim Nergelius. Leiden: Brill, 2006, 41–70.

[16] For contrasting views, see Yash Ghai and Guido Galli, "Constitution-Building Processes and Democratization: Lessons Learned." *Democracy, Conflict, and Human Security: Further Readings* (2006): 232–49, and Tom Ginsburg, Zachary Elkins, and Justin Blount, "Does the Process of Constitution-Making Matter?" *Annual Review of Law and Social Science* 5: 201–23 (2009).

[17] This is a theme in Klarman's account of the American constitutional founding, and is a lesson of Lin-Manuel Miranda's popular musical *Hamilton*.

In some instances, change entails an escape from a violent or unstable status quo. Constitutions are often adopted after violent crises such as wars, revolutions, or the fall of empires that have undermined or destroyed previously regnant political orders.[18] Change – in the sense of the fashioning of new institutions – is thus an obvious, pressing, need. In other contexts, however, the institutional status quo may evince a continuing measure of durability, along with sufficient flaws, such that constitution-making may be plausible but hardly unavoidable. The 1958 Constitution of the Fifth French Republic is one such constitution created in conditions of perceived political "crisis" that might well not have required a new organic document, had there been relatively minor changes in the underlying political dynamics.[19] Constitutions created under such conditions are similarly unlikely to be merely preservative of the status quo. The fact of change may itself catalyze new expectations and demands on the part of political actors that disturb the status quo, generating new forms of state-building or new challenges to state preservation.

Change is also embedded in constitutions that are principally economic or ideological projects. For example, Douglass North and Barry Weingast's well-known account of the quasi-constitutional settlement that flowed from England's Glorious Revolution focused on the relation between new constraints on the monarchy's fiscal and taxing authority and its access to international credit markets. In their view, change to constitutional institutions is motivated by economic pressure.[20] Constitutions can also be ideological projects intended to instantiate, or at least further, a normative account of state–society relations such as liberalism, Islamism, Bolivarianism, or neoliberalism.[21] The increasingly common inclusion of human rights language in postwar constitutions is yet another example of an ideological project,[22]

---

[18] Jennifer Widner, "Constitution Writing in Post-Conflict Settings: An Overview." *William & Mary Law Review* 49: 1513 (2007). For a postimperial example, see Adrien Katherine Wing and Ozan O. Varol, "Is Secularism Possible in a Majority-Muslim Country: The Turkish Example." *Texas International Law Journal* 42: 1 (2006).

[19] Carl J. Friedrich, "The New French Constitution in Political and Historical Perspective." *Harvard Law Review* 72 (5): 801–37 (1959).

[20] Douglass C. North and Barry R. Weingast, "Constitutions and Commitment: The Evolution of Institutions Governing Public Choice in Seventeenth-Century England." *Journal of Economic History* 49 (4): 803–32 (1989).

[21] On the relation of Islamism and constitutional design, see Nathan J. Brown, *Constitutions in a Nonconstitutional World: Arab Basic Laws and the Prospects for Accountable Government.* New York: SUNY Press, 2012. On the concept of neoliberal constitutionalism, see Jedediah Purdy, "Neoliberal Constitutionalism: Lochnerism for a New Economy." *Law & Contemporary Problems* 77: 195 (2014). On NeoBolivarianism, see Alston, note 3.

[22] Zachary Elkins, Tom Ginsburg, and Beth A. Simmons, "Getting to Rights: Treaty Ratification, Constitutional Convergence, and Human Rights Practice." *Harvard International Law Journal* 54: 61–95 (2013); Colin J. Beck, Gili S. Drori, and John W. Meyer, "World Influences on Human Rights Language in Constitutions: A Cross-National Study." *International Sociology* 27 (4): 483–501 (2012).

even if it not always recognized as such.[23] Like their economically motivated counter-parts, ideologically driven constitutions are intended to be transformative on the ground. They are not intended to be cheap talk, even if they are not always as efficacious as their proponents might have hoped.[24]

A final reason for underscoring the role of change in constitutional transform-ations concerns the sources of stability. An influential approach to theorizing consti-tutional stability underscores the possibility of text serving as a "focal point" for citizens seeking to coordinate their expectations and actions. If citizens agree on what counts as a violation of the constitutional order, they can coordinate enforce-ment efforts and deter governmental transgressions[25] Setting aside important ques-tions about the inevitable ambiguity of constitutional text and the dearth of citizen knowledge of the constitution (both of which might prevent the emergence of a focal point), it is unclear why we should expect focal solutions to be stable over time.

At the moment of inception, a constitution provides a solution that is superior to the status quo for all veto players. This fact will be stable so long as there are no changes to the economic, social, or geopolitical environment that produce a situation in which one veto player prefers noncompliance or a change to the constitutional agreement. But under changed conditions, mere understandings enabled by focal points will be unable to elicit compliance with the constitution. Rather, some amount of internalization – achieved through socialization, habitu-ation, or even fear – may instead be necessary to ensure continued compliance.[26]

The transformative character of constitutions abides in uneasy tension, and sometimes in potentially outright conflict, with the necessarily preservative character of those same documents. The backward-looking, status-quo favoring character of the modal constitution is a function of several political and technical dynamics.

First, the so-called strategic accounts of constitutional review, developed by Ginsburg and Ran Hirschl among others, argue that some features of a new consti-tution are motivated by the drafters' desire to preserve their interests. Dixon and Ginsburg go on to typologize these interests as coming in several kinds: personal, political, and policy.[27] Sometimes drafters will be concerned with their own welfare or personal safety, as in cases of democratization from authoritarian rule. In other cases, they may wish to preserve their party's interest in holding power. Finally, they

---

[23] The leading critique of human rights qua ideology now comes from the left. Samuel Moyn, *The Last Utopia*. Cambridge, MA: Harvard University Press, 2010.

[24] See, e.g., Adam S. Chilton and Mila Versteeg, "The Failure of Constitutional Torture Prohib-itions." *The Journal of Legal Studies* 44 (2): 417–52 (2012).

[25] Sonia Mittal and Barry R. Weingast, "Constitutional Stability and the Deferential Court." *University of Pennsylvania Journal of Constitutional Law* 13: 337 (2010).

[26] We are grateful to Richard McAdams for discussion on this point.

[27] Rosalind Dixon and Tom Ginsburg, "The Forms and Limits of Constitutions as Political Insurance." *International Journal of Constitutional Law* 15: 988–1012 (2017); see also Brad Epperly, "The Provision of Insurance? Judicial Independence and the Post-Tenure Fate of Leaders." *Journal of Law and Courts* 1 (2): 247–78 (2013).

may simply be concerned with locking in policies through entrenchment in a constitution. Whatever the motive, constitutions must reflect the interests of those drafting them to some degree, and will thus have a preservative dimension except in situations of total revolution.

Second, more mundane forces can lend a preservative bias to new constitutions. There is, most glaringly, the simple fact that adopting a constitution with a completely new suite of institutions is simply costly. The more that is changed, the higher a new constitution's implementation costs will be. A central problem for new constitutions, therefore, is persuading individuals, political factions, and social formations to expend the necessary resources to get constitutional institutions up and running in the first instance.[28]

The new constitution, moreover, might incorporate extant institutions and legal norms in ways that have an essentially backward-looking orientation. Especially when adopted in the wake of violent crisis, a new constitutional dispensation may require a marshaling of all remaining institutional resources, however flawed they might be. For example, the 2001 Bonn Agreement and the 2004 Constitution both provided seemingly new institutional arrangements for Afghanistan. Yet both effectively revived and tracked local and national administrative and judicial structures first created in the late 1970s by the Marxist government – the last administration that exercised effective control over the whole of the nation's territory in a way that allowed the fashioning of a national bureaucracy.[29] Even absent crisis, it may be too costly to reimagine wholesale the commercial, civil, criminal, and domestic laws of a polity. Because these subconstitutional regimes commonly intersect with, and inform, constitutional law, their persistence lends yet another preservative tilt to a new constitutional order. In the American context, for example, it has been argued that elements of the British common law operate as backdrop elements of the 1787 document, in some instances subverting and negating the semantic force of the constitutional text.[30] The powers of the national legislature to debate without executive interference and to elicit information, for example, are in large part shaped by pre-Revolutionary British practice and only partially specified in the constitution's text.[31] The immunities of states in federal and state tribunals, or the extent of similar immunities for Native American tribes from suit, are key determinants of the measure of constitutional remedies, and are derived from understandings (whether correct or not) of pre-ratification law.[32]

---

[28] Aziz Z. Huq, "The Function of Article V." *University of Pennsylvania Law Review* 162: 1165–1236 (2013).

[29] International Crisis Group, "Afghanistan's Flawed Constitutional Process," 2002.

[30] Stephen E. Sachs, "Constitutional Backdrops." *George Washington Law Review* 80: 1813 (2011).

[31] Josh Chafetz, "Congress's Constitution." *University of Pennsylvania Law Review* 160: 715 (2011).

[32] Daniel J. Meltzer, "The Seminole Decision and State Sovereign Immunity." *Supreme Court Review* 1996: 1–65 (1996): Theresa R. Wilson, "Nations within a Nation: The Evolution of Tribal Immunity." *American Indian Law Review* 24: 99–128 (1999).

Finally, it is important to underscore that transformation and conservation are not strictly a binary. Indeed, the very impetus for constitutional change might also paradoxically be a result of elite efforts to shore up their authority precisely through some limited species of transformation. This possibility is illuminated by Acemoglu and Robinson's well-known theory of democratic transitions. Their account stresses the role of franchise extension as a concession by extant elites to potentially democratic masses that threaten violent revolution.[33] A certain degree of constitutional change is permitted (and perhaps even required to render elite promises credible and hence durable), but the effect of such change is to preserve other elements of the social order against redistributive policy or regime change. Under these conditions, the relationship between social change and preservation is not a strict trade-off, since fidelity to some dynamics envisaged under a constitution might require flexibility and change along other margins. Rather the question is *what* changes – and who loses out as a result.

More generally, it is possible to imagine a range of ways in which impulses toward transformation and conservation can be reconciled. Most simply, different elements of a constitution might pursue transformative and preservative ends. Alternatively, the different elements of a constitution might operate in different temporal cycles. For example, a constitution might contain rights that operated not as immediate constraints on a new government, but rather as promissory notes. These would be capable of redemption only over time and by dint of efforts of mobilized social groups.[34] In Sanford Levinson's insightful formulation, the "constitution of settlement" and the "constitution of legal conversation" may unfold in different time frames so as to alleviate, perhaps inadvertently, the transformation/conservation tension.[35]

Alternatively, it is possible to imagine constitutional drafters pursuing a strategy of partial or issue-specific deferral as a means of defusing conflict. For example, the US Constitution does not, rather notoriously, contain any explicit reference to slavery, notwithstanding several implicit references to slaves for the purposes of apportionment, extradition, and international commercial regulation. One way in which the issue was explicitly deferred was in permitting the national legislature to prohibit the "Migration or Importation" of slaves but only from 1808 onward. Because all individual states had by then prohibited the international slave trade, in part out of a self-interested fear of contagion from the Caribbean slave revolts, it was a

[33] Daron Acemoglu and James A. Robinson, "Why Did the West Extend the Franchise? Democracy, Inequality, and Growth in Historical Perspective." *Quarterly Journal of Economics* 115 (4): 1167–1199 (2000); see also Daron Acemoglu and James A. Robinson, "A Theory of Political Transitions." *American Economic Review* 938–963 (2001).

[34] Michael C. Dorf, "The Aspirational Constitution." *George Washington Law Review* 77: 1631 (2008).

[35] Sanford Levinson, "Do Constitutions Have a Point? Reflections on 'Parchment Barriers' and Preambles." *Social Philosophy and Policy* 28 (1): 150–178 (2011).

strategic deferral that can be said to have "worked" in the sense of mitigating conflict.[36] One of us has suggested that deferral is a solution to expected decision costs that arise in democratic constitutional drafting of the kind discussed previously, or alternatively reflects a concern of error costs flowing from entrenched constitutional choices without sufficient information about downstream effects.[37]

Notwithstanding this point, the general point we wish to stress is that a constitution stands at the nexus of two vectors bearing upon the institutional status quo – one that pushes toward transformation and the other that tends toward conservation. As Figure 1.1 suggested, it seems that the tension between these vectors is sharpest in the first period after a constitution's adoption.

The problem of constitutional efficacy, of course, does not ever evaporate entirely after the first period. Even mature constitutions confront the question of why officials vested with state authority obey obligations under the law and limits on the lawful exercise of their authorities. Rational choice theorists have purported to find in these questions deep puzzles,[38] and express skepticism about whether officials in fact do obey the law absent some adverse political cost.[39] This first period problem is nevertheless distinctive from this "parchment barrier" problem in two ways.

To begin with, the first period problem is less about law's regulative elements and more about its constitutive force.[40] The question is often whether powerful actors will accept and employ the institutional structures embodied in a new constitutional text. Although questions of the abuse of power are not entirely absent, they are often eclipsed in importance by other kinds of failures. Especially where new institutions are relatively thinly staffed and under-resourced, the potential for abusive capture is reduced. As a corollary, the risk that forces outside the new state (such as militias or external international actors) mobilize to take advantage of institutional weakness may be graver than in later periods.[41]

Second, the difficulty of the "parchment barrier" puzzle is, in part, a function of disciplinary perspective. Sociologically oriented scholars have observed that in

---

[36] Gerald L. Neuman, "The Lost Century of American Immigration Law (1776–1875)." *Columbia Law Review* 93: 1833, 1878 (1993). There was, however, a campaign to reopen the international slave trade after 1808. Ronald T. Takaki, *A Pro-Slavery Crusade: The Agitation to Reopen the African Slave Trade*. New York: Free Press, 1971.

[37] Rosalind Dixon and Tom Ginsburg, "Deciding Not to Decide: Deferral in Constitutional Design." *International Journal of Constitutional Law* 9: 636 (2011).

[38] Daryl J. Levinson, "Parchment and Politics: The Positive Puzzle of Constitutional Commitment." *Harvard Law Review* 657–746 (2011).

[39] Frederick Schauer, "The Political Risks (If Any) of Breaking the Law." *Journal of Legal Analysis* 4 (1): 83–101 (2012).

[40] On the distinction between constitutive and regulative rules, see John R. Searle, *The Construction of Social Reality*. New York: Simon & Schuster, 1995.

[41] For example, in the early American republic, fears of how European great powers might divide and conquer the several states were powerful. Jason Mazzone, "The Security Constitution." *UCLA Law Review* 53: 29 (2015).

mature polities, characterized by stable formal institutions, legal norms tend to be internalized even when there are obvious political and material gains to be held from their abuse.[42] The difficulties of modeling constitutionalism in rational choice terms, they imply, is a function of arbitrary limitations on what counts as possible motives within the standard rational choice model. Given the role of socialization and internalization of legal norms in generating constitutional efficacy in mature constitutions, it should not surprise that the tension between transformation and preservation is commonly most acute in the first period. For it is then that officials are least socialized, when the habits and routines of formal institutions have yet to settle, and where the uncertainties about the meaning of constitutional and legal provisions are most likely to be substantial. To the extent one believes them ever to be adequate for constitutional stability, the dynamics of what Barry Weingast and Sonia Mittal have called "self-enforcing" constitutionalism are least likely to have crystallized in the first period.[43] Whether or not this problem is different in kind from that of constitutional fidelity in mature constitutional context, it is certainly different in magnitude.

Although we do not offer a precise definition of the "first period" here – leaving the term open to interpretation in the case studies in light of local circumstances – different ways of theorizing a distinction between the first period and what follows can be inferred from our basic analytic template. First, the first period might be defined in terms of the observed hazard rate for constitutions in general. The data in Figure 1.1, for example, might suggest a cut off at five years, or perhaps even one year. A second definition might instead turn on key institutional junctures, such as the first or second national election after the constitution's adoption, or the closing of the transitional period as defined by the constitution itself in its transitional period. A third definition of the first period might focus on key personnel: for example, how long are the specific figures involved in the drafting of a constitution involved in its management? As Alison LaCroix has explained, in the United States, national politicians through then-Vice President Martin Van Buren would correspond with James Madison as the last living constitutional framer, seeking guidance on the document's meaning more than thirty years after ratification.[44] Complicating matters, Rosalind Dixon has observed that drafters in Hungary, Indonesia, Colombia, and South Africa have gone on to join constitutional courts, where they could

[42] Richard H. Fallon Jr., "Constitutional Constraints." *California Law Review* 975–1037 (2009); Aziz Z. Huq, "Binding the Executive (by Law or by Politics)." *University of Chicago Law Review* 79 (2): 777–826 (2012).

[43] Sonia Mittal and Barry R. Weingast, "Self-Enforcing Constitutions: With an Application to Democratic Stability in America's First Century." *Journal of Law, Economics, & Organization* 29 (2): 278–302 (2011).

[44] Alison L. LaCroix, "The Interbellum Constitution: Federalism in the Long Founding Moment." *Stanford Law Review* 67: 397, 426 (2015).

interpret or extend their own earlier words.[45] The first period, on this view, would endure as long as the specific personnel involved in the founding moment remain active in political life.

A fourth possibility turns on the internalization of constitutional rules as guiding norms by officials under what H. L. A. Hart called the internal point of view.[46] From this perspective, the first period is over when officials have by and large acquired a habit of obedience to a new constitution. Such sociological legitimation of a constitution might be a function of habit and repetition, sunk costs, or socialization and training. But once such habits are widespread, the fundamental questions of whether and why a constitution persists become easier to answer, as there is a clear Hartian rule of recognition. Although firm data is missing, we suspect that psychological internalization requires more than the five or ten years during which the risk of constitutional failure is very high. This suggests either that socialization into new constitutional rules can be a rapid process or (more likely) that constitutions can persist even in the absence of thorough internalization. Some constitutional orders might stay in the first period for a very long time from this perspective.

Finally, one might focus on the distinct policy problems that preoccupy a first generation of constitutional implementers; it is only when those policy problems are addressed or ameliorated, so that a new set of challenges comes into focus, that one can meaningfully talk of a transition from a first to a second period. The first period is defined, in this view, by the first major problem or drama that the constitution is designed to address.[47]

1.2 MODELING THE FIRST PERIOD PROBLEM WITH A CONTRACTING ANALOGY

If the first period of a constitution's life is characterized by competing pressures toward transformation and preservation, how might we understand the ensuing conflicts and tensions? We start the discussion of this point with a now-common analogy that is drawn between constitutions on the one hand and long-term, relational contracts on the other hand.[48]

Constitutions can be usefully modeled as contracts in two different ways. First, a constitution's text embodies a deal between powerful national-level interest groups, each of whom can threaten to exit (whether by secession or through finding alternative negotiating partners) from the deal.[49] Second, a constitution, in addition

---

[45] Rosalind Dixon, "Constitutional Design Two Ways: Constitutional Drafters as Judges." *Virginia Journal of International Law* 57: 1–41 (2017).

[46] H. L. Hart, *The Concept of Law*. Cambridge University Press 3rd ed. 2012.

[47] See Gargarella, "When Is a Constitution Doing Well? The Alberdian Test in the Americas."

[48] For examples of the analogy, see Elkins et al., 2009; Huq, *Article V*.

[49] Daniel Sutter, "Enforcing Constitutional Constraints." *Constitutional Political Economy* 8 (2): 139–50 (1997); Philippe Aghion and Patrick Bolton. "Incomplete Social Contracts." *Journal of the European Economic Association* 1 (1): 38–67 (2003)

to satisfying elites, must also generate a *modus operandi* between elites and the population. Hence, in the political philosophy literature starting with John Locke, the polity is described as resulting upon a "compact" through the agreement of citizens with the aim of "mutual preservation of . . . lives, liberties, and estates."[50] Constitutions can thus be understood as a sort of double compact, reflecting a deal among the people or peoples in a state, and also among the politically powerful.[51] Whatever metaphor is taken, the constitution as compact has a *durable* and *relational* quality. Like a more familiar and workaday contract between a supplier and a manufacturer of goods, it entails iterative cooperative interactions by all parties in order for the contractual ambitions to be realized.

Such constitutional bargains are struck in a wide range of circumstances and take a wide variety of forms, emphasizing one or the other aspect of the double compact. For instance, they might involve an elite pact, in which a transition to democracy is negotiated among leaders without any popular or large-scale input. This was the case in mid-1970s Spain, which we will discuss briefly later in the chapter. A constitutional bargain can also emerge from negotiations among the members of a confederated system and yield an arrangement of discrete state units joining together under a constitution systematically reflecting the states' interests (as was the case in the United States). Finally, it can be a post-revolutionary negotiation as in Tunisia or the roundtable talks of Eastern Europe, with varying degrees of political pluralism and popular involvement. Bargaining settings are hence myriad. But all involve a negotiation about the key future institutions of a society, and how disparate elites and the publics they represent will live together.

Drawing from the contracting literature, we can isolate two general sources of constitutional crisis or failure during the first period. We call these *deficits of drafting* and *deficits of implementation*; each has internal subcategories. Both reflect the immanent conflict between those factions and groups that benefit from transformation, and those that seek a conservation of the status quo ante.

1.2.1 *Deficits of Drafting*

To start, constitutions are akin to long-term, relational contracts in that they are necessarily *incomplete*, in the sense that the contracting parties have not written down or anticipated solutions to all possible future contingencies, or because it has simply failed to address a vital question of constitutional design.[52] An example of

---

[50] John Locke, "Of Civil Government," in *Two Treatises of Government and a Letter Concerning Toleration*, ed. Ian Shapiro. 2003, 142, 155.

[51] See Sujit Choudhry, "Post-Arab Awakening Constitutionalism: Revolution, Retrenchment or Renovation?" paper presented at World Bank, January 29, 2014; see also Sujit Choudhry and Tom Ginsburg, *Introduction*, in *Constitution-Making*. Edward Elgar, 2017.

[52] On the economic theory of relational contracts, see Oliver Hart and John Moore, "Foundations of Incomplete Contracts." *Review of Economic Studies* 66 (1): 115–138 (1999). The former

failing to address contingencies might be the US drafters' failure to anticipate that the cotton gin would lead to demand for the expansion of slavery to feed the industrialized textile industry. An example of the second is failing to articulate mechanisms for constitutional interpretation. The US Constitution, for example, fails to address the rather important question of which institution should have the final word when resolving constitutional ambiguities. The result is a seemingly endless tussle over the scope and legitimacy of judicial review, the role of other branches' constitutional judgment, and the influence of popular conceptions of constitutional norms. Constitutional incompleteness of either sort arises for three reasons that roughly parallel problems that arise in the commercial contracting context – reasons we call these diverse forms *deficits of drafting*.[53] The three deficits of drafting are time, knowledge, and agreement.

Start with time. Any negotiation is bounded in terms of time allocated to it, and time constraints are especially important when it comes to constitutional negotiations. Constitutions are typically, though not always, adopted in moments of high political drama, perhaps even violent crisis.[54] Often there are upstream constraints that limit the amount of time available to drafters – deadlines that are exogenously fixed and cannot be evaded. These constraints may be helpful to facilitate agreement, as they put pressure on parties to come to agreement. But they also bound the negotiation and prevent the parties from spelling out a complete set of arrangements, and so the constitutional bargain will of necessity be incomplete. Negotiators may focus only on the largest, most salient issues, leaving more minor ones unresolved. Time pressures contribute to the introduction of structural mistakes in the constitutional text, seeding pitfalls for the immediate post-constitution-making period.

A second deficit of drafting relates to knowledge. In the parlance of contract theorists, there is a problem of incomplete information. For those theorists, information is modeled as a public good that will predictably be produced at suboptimal levels.[55] We think this is not quite the problem in the constitutional context. Instead, it seems likely that information relevant to the constitutional bargain may only be revealed *after* the document's adoption, leaving constitution-makers to negotiate on the basis of their best predictions of what will happen. Moreover, constitutions tend to be designed to hedge against known risks. But the universe of relevant risks is defined by drafters' past experiences. Constitutions will accordingly tend to address

---

is called "insufficient state contingency" in the contracting literature, while the latter is called "obligational incompleteness." On the distinction between the two forms of incompleteness, see Ian Ayres and Robert Gertner. "Strategic Contractual Inefficiency and the Optimal Choice of Legal Rules." *Yale Law Journal* 101 (4): 729–773 (1992).

[53] Huq, "Article V."

[54] Elster, "Constitutions and Violence."

[55] Jean Tirole, "Incomplete Contracts: Where Do We Stand?" *Econometrica* 67 (4): 741–81 (1999).

the known risks while leaving the polity vulnerable to risks that have yet to materialize (even if they might in some sense be predictable).[56] Compounding the problem
further, many major questions about how the constitution will actually operate
cannot be known (unless, that is, a new constitution is characterized by de minimus
change in relation to the old constitution). These might include questions of how
new institutions will actually function; how the relevant domestic or the international environment will change; or what people will demand of their leaders.
Indeed, it is arguable that constitutions are sufficiently complex systems that merely
avoiding endogenous conflicts that can unravel the system as a whole is a large task,
and hence an appropriate metric of constitutional success.[57]

It is worth noting that one reason we use the term knowledge rather than the
more conventional concept of information is that the science of constitutional
design remains nascent. Even if the problems of incompleteness could be solved
in the sense that negotiators can perfectly predict what will happen, there is still a
choice of institutions that must be made. We have imperfect knowledge about how
institutions interact with their environments to produce outcomes. This is a kind of
epistemic problem, related to fit, and might lead constitution-makers to choose the
wrong institution to resolve a problem they all wish to solve, even if they have access
to all otherwise available information.

A third deficit of drafting falls out from the task of reaching a durable agreement.
Contract theory focuses on multiple strategic barriers to reaching agreement,
including "holdout" problems, where one side refuses to give in, in the hopes of
getting a better deal. Besides the problem of incomplete information, Elkins et al.
argue that there can be a significant problem of hidden information in the process of
constitutional bargaining.[58] They describe a situation in which one party has information that it is reluctant to reveal to the other, and this reluctance might prevent
agreement entirely. Particularly relevant for our analysis, hidden information possessed by one faction of a constitutional deal raises particular challenges in the first
period of constitutional performance. Suppose, for example, an ethnic group in a
remote mountainous region knows that it has a population much larger than is
apparent to others during constitutional negotiations. Counterparties in the constitutional negotiation may prefer an electoral system that might turn out to advantage
the group. But this will only become apparent after a post-constitutional census.
Once the census is held, the counter-parties might find that they are going to have
less power than anticipated, and might in an extreme case simply refuse to hold the
post-constitutional election.

---

[56] On this and related risks of precautionary constitutionalism, see Adrian Vermeule, "Precautionary Principles in Constitutional Law." *Journal of Legal Analysis* 4 (1): 181–222 (2012).

[57] As, indeed, one of has argued. Aziz Z. Huq, "Hippocratic Constitutional Design," in Ginsburg
and Huq, *Assessing Constitutional Performance.*

[58] Elkins et al., *Endurance of National Constitutions.*

1.2.2 *Deficits of Implementation*

Contract theory suggests a second genre of problems can arise, problems we call *deficits of implementation*. The theory of incomplete long-term contracts has identified two ways in which efforts to realize such a contract can go awry. The first is that parties can fail to make the threshold or ongoing investments necessary to keep the contractual relationship durable, for example by shading on their obligations under the deal.[59] The second is that that they can exploit the investments made by other parties to the deal in order to extract surplus rents from the contract through what is known as "post-contractual opportunistic behavior."[60] In the contracting literature, this is known as the "hold up" problem.[61] The potential for hold-up has both ex ante and ex post effects. Ex ante, a potential investing party will rationally anticipate the possibility of hold-up and so decline to enter into contracts where that risk exists. Ex post, parties that do enter deals will dissipate resources on both hold-ups and resistance to hold-ups, resulting in intracontractual disputes and haggling that expend resources without commensurate social gain.[62]

In the constitutional context, we call these deficits of *will* and *trust* respectively. We address each in turn. Consider first deficits of will. Here the problem is that performance of the constitutional contract requires political capital. Setting up new institutions or passing legislation to fill in the constitutional contract requires the legislature to actually act. A new legislature, however, is burdened by its own bargaining challenges, which arise as a consequence of its own internal organization, in addition to those that linger from the drafting and ratification process. In the first period, it may not have developed the necessary apparatus of committees, agenda-setting rules, and deliberation frameworks necessary to resolve contested issues in a timely fashion.[63] It may as a result not implement the instructions given it by constitution-makers.

A similar dynamic can also happen at the administrative or regulatory level. Suppose a constitution institutes new rules of criminal procedure, but police commanders prefer the old ones and take no steps to train their officers. Or imagine an army that has been mired in civil war for decades, and is suddenly asked to pivot

---

[59] On the costs of such shading, see Oliver Hart and John Moore, "Contracts as Reference Points." *Quarterly Journal of Economics* 123 (1): 1–48 (2008).

[60] Benjamin Klein, Robert G. Crawford, and Armen A. Alchian, "Vertical Integration, Appropriable Rents, and the Competitive Contracting Process." *Journal of Law and Economics* 21 (2): 297–326 (1978).

[61] Benjamin Klein, "Why Holdups Occur: the Self-Enforcing Range of Contractual Relationships." *Economic Inquiry* 34 (3): 444–63 (1996).

[62] Ibid.; Christine Jolls, "Contracts as Bilateral Commitments: A New Perspective on Contract Modification." *Journal of Legal Studies* 26 (1): 203–37 (1997).

[63] Aziz Z. Huq, "The Constitutional Law of Agenda Control." *California Law Review* 104: 1401 (2016).

toward a wholly new peacetime role.[64] If officers or bureaucrats want to resist demands for institutional change, they have myriad ways of ensuring that the preservative rather than the transformative vector in constitution-making prevails. Constant monitoring of their dispersed and largely discretionary activities is prohibitively costly. Both legislative and bureaucratic agency problems are examples of the deficit of will.

The second deficit of implementation concerns trust. In a situation in which parties have concluded an agreement but don't trust each other, the one who must (as a matter of practicality) take the first steps may hesitate. Of course, sometimes parties can learn to trust each other over time, in what is called a course-of-dealing in contract theory. A famous constitutional example concerns the Spanish transition to democracy, embodied in the Constitution of 1978.[65] In the negotiations that led to the so-called Moncloa pact, the left accepted the monarchy, while the right agreed to allow the democratization of key political and social institutions. Some years later, in 1982, the Socialist Party won elections but it retained the monarchy during its long rule through 1996. In other words, Spain's left and right wings grew to trust each other in the course of dealing with each other over time.

If such trust is not forthcoming, either because of misinterpretation or because of genuine obstacles to performance, the constitutional contract can unravel in the first period. Suppose the Socialists, for example, had reneged on their promises when they won elections. It is conceivable that the Spanish right-wing would have sought to revisit its acquiescence to the deal; if sufficiently powerful it could have mobilized institutions to resist it. In an extreme case, reneging can tip into civil conflict.

Deficits of will and trust provide myriad possibilities for opportunists to ignore constitutional requirements and instead seek their own advantage. In anticipation, moreover, such deficits of implementation can prospectively shape the politics of bargaining and agreement. In this sense the two sets of deficits interact, and the phases of constitutional drafting and implementation are linked.

To see how these forces can interact, consider the path of constitutional review in Afghanistan under the 2004 Constitution. When the Constitution was being drafted, there had been agreement that there would be a constitutional court of some sort that would engage in judicial review. Constitutional courts were, at the time, a kind of standard feature of written constitutions, meant to oversee the separation of powers and protect human rights. There was, in this sense, no epistemic deficit in terms of what institution to adopt. But at the very last stage of constitution-making, with severe external time pressures on the process from the United States and NATO's International Security Force for Afghanistan, the Afghan President's office

---

[64] For a useful study of this problem in Afghanistan, see Mark Sedra, "Security Sector Reform in Afghanistan: The Slide towards Expediency." *International Peacekeeping* 13 (1): 94–110 (2006).

[65] Juan J. Linz and Alfred C. Stepan, "Toward Consolidated Democracies." *Journal of Democracy* 7 (2): 14–33 (1996).

decided unilaterally to remove the court from the draft. Some believe this was caused by fear that a constitutional court would turn into a theocratic power center, *a la* Iran. In this sense there was a genuine deficit of knowledge. The change upset other negotiators of the constitution, but faced with a take-it-or-leave it offer, the document was approved in early 2004.[66]

Even if one can say there was formal agreement on this change, the deficit of time meant that there were errors in the draft. The Supreme Court was given the power to review laws and treaties for compatibility with the constitution, but was not allowed the power of *constitutional* interpretation. In short, the Constitution did not explicitly give any institution the power to interpret it, though a generous reading would say that the Supreme Court should have the task. Three years later, parliament grew upset at the Supreme Court and exploited the constitution's poor drafting to set up a competitor. It relied on another vaguely specified institution, the Commission for Supervision of the Implementation of the Constitution, (ICSIC). ICSIC was intended, at one point, to be an institution to oversee the first period, by monitoring the setting up of institutions and passage of necessary legislation. But parliament transformed it into an institution that could bypass the Supreme Court on constitutional questions, setting off a conflict between the two institutions. In addition to creating political conflict, the lack of a clear interpreter exacerbated all kinds of constitutional issues bedeviling the troubled country.

The story exposes drafting deficits of time, knowledge, and agreement. Uncertainty over how a constitutional court would behave allowed the President to make a last-minute change. But time pressures meant that the change was poorly drafted. Once the constitution began to operate, a deficit of trust grew between President Karzai and the forces of the Northern Alliance, which were well-represented in the new parliament. This allowed opportunistic behavior – a deficit of will – in which parliament deviated from good faith understandings of the constitution to a self-serving interpretation. To be sure, the poor state of constitutional implementation in Afghanistan cannot be attributed to the story of this one institutional dysfunction alone. But it is emblematic of the broader forces that have beset that country since the optimistic moment of 2004.

Another illustration of the way these deficits interact comes from Nepal, which has been engaged in constitution-making for most of the past decade after a long civil war ended in 2006. In this instance, there was consensus on the need to eliminate the monarchy and produce a more inclusive constitution. But there were significant disagreements among parties as to how to design a new system. The traditional political parties, the Nepali Congress and the United Marxists-Leninists (yes, a conservative party!), sought to preserve their traditional dominance, and represented certain caste and geographical interests. The Maoists, and the Madhesi

---

[66] Tom Ginsburg and Aziz Huq, "What Can Constitutions Do? The Afghan Case." *Journal of Democracy* 25 (1): 116–30 (2014).

parties, who hail from the Southern part of the country, had been shut out of political power and so sought to reorganize the country along federal lines that would be more inclusive. The negotiations were supposed to be completed within two years of the election of a Constituent Assembly in 2008. But holdout problems hindered negotiations. Eventually, the 2008 deadline slipped and then slipped again, until the Supreme Court ruled that the Assembly had failed in its task and had to be disbanded. A new constituent assembly was elected, with a different political configuration. Holdout problems continued, however. Agreement on a federal structure was accompanied by an outbreak of severe disputes over the number and orientation of constituent states.

In the absence of consensus, the exogenous shock of the 2015 earthquake pushed the ruling parties to ram through a new constitution without the agreement of the Madhesi parties. While the other parties may have thought they had forged a stable coalition, the Madhesi grouping was upset that its territorial demands had not been met. Its members have since demanded renegotiation of the federal arrangements, and have several times led protests and border blockades to secure a reopening of constitutional bargaining. This was an instance of a deficit of agreement leading directly to deficits of implementation.

We might add finally to our list of problems in Nepal a deficit of knowledge. The "outsider" parties early on demanded federalism, even though it is not obvious that this sort of system would be viable in a relatively small country striated with 200 languages and many remote populations. More conventional decentralization schemes combined with proportional representation would probably suffice to produce representative and inclusive government in such a context. There were no prior boundaries on which to base the new states, nor prior administrative units that could become state governments. There are also mutually incompatible demands for previously underrepresented groups to be able to have their names associated with certain provinces. The bargaining focused on the numbers, names, and boundaries of territorial states, with central elites preferring fewer sub-units and traditionally marginalized areas preferring more.

This ambitious choice – to create a federal arrangement without any prior governmental structure – meant that Nepal was adopting a *costly* solution. The gap between prior arrangements and the proposed new ones was large, and expensive to bridge. Federalism in the Nepali context, moreover, was implicitly being relied on to resolve multiple problems simultaneously against a history of patchwork exclusions and stratification in a context of tremendous ethnic diversity. Nepal's highly asymmetrical and irregular geographic conditions only exacerbated problems. For the Madhesi population that lives in the lowlands that border India, territorial federalism made sense as a way of promoting self-governance. Yet, the constitution's delimitation of provinces did not satisfy them. This led to violent protests and a reopening of negotiations. Constitutional amendments to resolve the Madhesi challenge have not fully borne fruit at the time of this writing. Rather, an overly ambitious and unrealistic design choice led directly to failures in the first period of constitutional implementation.

At its core then, constitution-making is a highly fraught, politically charged, and time-sensitive negotiation in conditions of great epistemic uncertainty. This predisposes it to severe problems of implementation. Time deficits mean that mistakes will be made; knowledge deficits mean that, even if drafting is perfect, it will be based on un-anticipatable contingencies that will affect performance. And deficits of agreement will create yet another set of challenges, pushing parties toward abstraction in textual drafting, and subsequently perhaps also toward strategic withholding of consent. But once a constitution is adopted, implementation takes will and trust. Trust is often in short supply, and may have been damaged during the process of producing the constitutional agreement. Will is always in short supply, and is threatened by many of the strategic bargaining problems that threaten constitution-making itself. All of this means that we should expect many challenges in the first period of constitutional implementation.

1.3 THE PLAN OF THE BOOK

The balance of this book contains a set of case studies that illustrate the various ways in which the tensions inherent in a constitution's first period can be reconciled and managed. We briefly summarize the arguments of the subsequent chapters, and explain how they relate to the general themes of the book.

The first part of the book tackles the general theoretical problem in the context of several country experiences. The doyen of American constitutional politics, Sanford Levinson, begins by looking at the balance between transformation and adaptation in the early constitutional history of the United States. Taking us back to the perspective of the founders, he emphasizes the politics of constitutional formation, in which potential losers sought to torpedo the process, and its ultimate success depended on what the legal historian Michael Klarman has called a "coup" by the framers against more broadly inclusive democratic institutions. The final set of compromises extracted by the forces of preservation amounted to a "pact with the devil," and the first period of implementation witnessed a set of brutal battles over interpretation of the constitutional text, especially about issues of state sovereignty and the scope of national power. The preservation of the new country was hardly to be taken for granted, and this meant that those with transformationist aspirations had to of necessity temper their demands. Each step was brutally fought.

Where Levinson's account emphasizes the role of Chief Justice John Marshall, Rosalind Dixon and Theunis Roux emphasize the parallel function of South Africa's Constitutional Court in constitutional implementation. The 1996 Constitution of South Africa is justly recognized as demanding transformation from the apartheid order, but Dixon and Roux also identify preservationist, and certainly incrementalist, elements in the new constitutional dispensation. Transformation has been the mission of the country's dominant party, the African National Congress (ANC), but as time has gone on it has grown comfortable with its own power and has sought to preserve its own prerogatives. Identifying two distinct periods in the Court's relationship with the dominant party, Dixon and Roux observe that in the second, the Court has come to play a significant role in preserving the country's democratic pluralism by holding the ANC to account for illegal and ultra vires behavior. They argue, though, that this process would have been easier had the first period been managed differently. Helpfully, they identify a specific set of doctrinal moves that might have anticipated and mitigated the gradual erosion of South Africa's democracy.

Madhav Khosla's study of India's first period similarly focuses on the role of the court in balancing preservation and transformation in a context of sharply pressed demands for social and economic change. The Indian Constitution famously contains a set of "Directive Principles of State Policy," which cover topics that might be labelled rights in other contexts, but instead are explicitly unenforceable by the judiciary. This did not, however, eliminate the need to manage the relationship between rights and the Principles. Furthermore, the central issue of land reform was the topic of a series of constitutional dialogues between the Court and the Congress-led Parliament in the 1950s, leading to two important constitutional amendments. Like Dixon and Roux, Khosla pays close attention to the role of newly articulated doctrine in mediating between demands for transformation and preservation.

Next, Eric Alston tackles the case of Ecuador, whose 2008 Constitution is highly aspirational even by the standard of Bolivarians in Latin America. He argues that the extent of social and economic transformation demanded by the text will impact the discretion of those who implement it, perhaps leading to disappointment on the part of the citizens who demanded change in the first place. The scope for tradeoffs among the many goals of the Constitution required some adjustment, and Alston provides a compelling account of the politics of implementation, with its attendant compromises and necessary difficulties, through to the departure of President Rafael Correa. As Alston notes, Correa's decision to abide by term limits that required him to sit out one political cycle led to the reversal of some of his policies and so marks the end of the first period.

Part II contains two chapters that focus on the issue of gender. The existence of patriarchy in every society, combined with transformative international demands embodied in the Convention on the Elimination of Discrimination against Women (CEDAW), means that almost every moment of constitutional reform must often grapple with issues of gender equality. To be sure, many constitutions singularly fail to account for the endurance of gender hierarchies. The persistence and the pervasiveness of such failures only underscore the need to take seriously the problem of gender equity in constitutional creation.[67]

---

[67] Helen Irving, *Gender and the Constitution*. Cambridge University Press, 2008; Ruth Rubio-Marin and Helen Irving, eds. *Women as Constitution-Makers*. Cambridge University Press,

In her chapter on Zimbabwe, Claudia Flores examines the first period of Zimbabwe's 2013 Constitution. As she rightly observes, the simple fact that gender discrimination is deeply rooted and inevitably advantages one group over another pulls toward preservation. Constitutional reform is thus a necessary but not sufficient condition for advancing women's rights. The first period may end up being important for reformers in terms of setting goals and prioritizing strategies. Flores traces the role of reformers in producing a gender-responsive text, and then examines implementation in four areas: customary law and practices, gender quotas, violence against women, and reproductive rights. Her detailed account of the constitutional politics in each of these areas suggests that there is variation in practice and outcomes. Despite the deeply entrenched quality of malignant gender inequalities, constitutional reform can nonetheless create a measure of leverage for incremental gains. Notwithstanding the fact that true gender equality remains a major challenge, Flores's analysis suggests that constitutional change is a fruitful avenue of potential reform.

Whereas Flores compared multiple issues in a single process, Susan Williams takes a different strategy by looking at electoral gender quotas in post-Arab Spring Egypt, Tunisia, and Jordan. Contrasting bottom-up and top-down approaches, she notes that government leadership and legislative quality are critical variables for successful implementation.

Part III of the book turns to a focus on particular institutions and their roles in constitutional implementation. Diego Gonzalez, a scholar working at the Colombian Constitutional Court, examines that institution's great success in the first period of implementation of the 1991 Constitution. The Court's jurisprudence in socioeconomic rights and in the rights of internally displaced persons has gathered a good deal of attention in the field of comparative constitutional law. But Gonzalez considers a number of other factors that have allowed the Court to – somewhat surprisingly – assume a central role in Colombia's constitutional order.

James Thuo Gathii, writing on Kenya, uses elections and political parties as a lens to examine the implementation of the 2010 Constitution, with a special focus on the judiciary. That document, adopted with great fanfare, sought to deliver a responsive politics and social transformation to Kenyans through what he identifies as a Madisonian constitutional design. In the event, the first election was won by Uhuru Kenyatta and his running mate William Ruto, whose new Jubilee alliance (now the Jubilee Party) has used formal and informal mechanisms to consolidate power. Gathii illustrates how even the best institutional designs are not foolproof, particularly in a context in which informal linkages and forms of power remain intact and potent. He then shows judicial attempts to police the election rules have led to a

2019; Susan Williams, ed. *Constituting Equality: Gender Equality and Comparative Constitutional Law.* Cambridge University Press, 2011.

series of cases, with the nullification of the presidential election in 2017 marking the end of the first period.

The final section of the volume grapples with problems of authoritarian constitutions. Ginsburg uses the case of Chile to identify a new category that he labels the transformational authoritarian constitution. This is a document adopted by dictators that contemplates a return to democracy. In doing so, the transformative aspects are limited and channeled, with the preservation of a veto by the erstwhile authoritarian in the Chilean case. While the bargain may decay over time, as it did in Chile, there is still the preservation of the constitutional identity. In the next chapter, Melissa Crouch draws on this framework to examine the authoritarian transformation in Myanmar. The 2008 Constitution was produced by a military regime but has presided over a set of reforms that have introduced competitive elections and significant liberalization, even as the military retains a veto. She examines the role of the legislature and court in interpreting and modifying the formal provisions of the document, even as formal amendment has been stymied as of the time of her writing.

Finally, Daniel Abebe traces the history of the current Ethiopian Constitution and its distinctive ethnic federalism. An authoritarian regime sought to use ethnic federalism to help maintain its control, utilizing transformational institutional design to buy time and preserve power. Even as Ethiopia appears to be moving on toward a more liberal period, the legacy of the distinctive design analyzed by Abebe is likely to remain in place, with consequences into the "second period."

1.4 CONCLUSION

The examples developed in these chapters, to be sure, do not exhaust the field of possible ways in which a first-period problem can be navigated. We identify in concluding two alternative pathways that are not explored in detail in the chapters that follow. We hope these "untaken paths" will yield productive research agendas in the future.

To begin with, we have already noted that constitutional drafters might explore a possibility of partial or complete deferral in respect to some issues. We suspect that this is a common strategy, perhaps by default, insofar as the limited time and epistemic resources for constitutional drafting will often lead to issues being pushed down the road (albeit perhaps not as explicitly as the US Constitution's deferral on the international slave trade). The second possibility is, more simply, failure. As Figure 1.1 demonstrated, a substantial number of constitutions fail, and do so very early on in their lifetimes.[68]

---

[68] Most such events took place in the nineteenth and twentieth centuries, and are relatively rare after 1989.

Consider some recent examples of early constitutional failures. In Egypt, after President Mubarak was forced from power in 2011, the military issued a "Constitutional Declaration" to facilitate elections and lead to a permanent constitution. This was an interim constitution, designed to be superseded in short order by a more permanent dispensation. Subsequent elections were won by parties aligned with the Muslim Brotherhood, and in 2012, the constitution-making process began in earnest. But severe deficits of trust pervaded Egyptian society, handicapping that process. An initial constituent assembly was suspended by the courts, and a subsequent one was pervaded by charges that the Brotherhood was ignoring liberals. In late 2012, then-President Morsi gave himself the power to "protect" the constitutional adoption process from judicial scrutiny, and in December, rammed through a constitution with a distinctly Islamic tinge. The document was approved with the support of only about 20 percent of the electorate, as many voters stayed home. Within a few months this failure to bring in other groups led to massive street protests and Morsi's removal from office by the military. The Constitution was suspended, and the next year replaced. Deficits of drafting meant that implementation was imperiled from the outset.

Another recent case concerned the "Tulip Revolution," which overthrew Kyrgyz President Askar Akayev in 2005. In late 2006, voters approved amendments to the Constitution that shifted power to the parliament from the executive. However, these demands were undermined by pro-presidential lawmakers aligned with new president Kurmanbek Bakiev. The next year, the Constitutional Court annulled the amendments, restoring the 2003 version of the Constitution. The situation stabilized briefly, until new protests led to Bakiev's resignation in 2010, which were followed by new amendments moving again to a parliamentary system. The cycling among different institutional variants reflects a deficit of agreement, but also possibly a deficit of knowledge: No one could predict which arrangements would produce stable governance.

To summarize: All constitutions face a tradeoff between preservation and transformation, even if the rhetoric at the time tends to lean toward one or the other pole. These goals are in obvious tension. In navigating between them, the first period of implementation turns out to be crucial and can mark the difference between a constitutional order that survives, even if transformed in unpredictable ways, and one that fails or remains an empty vehicle.

PART I

The Problem of Transformation in Constitutional Design

2

Looking "Backward" or "Forward" to American Constitutional Development

Reflections on Constitutional "Endurance" and "Adaptation" in the "First Republic"

Sanford Levinson

It is really true what philosophy tells us, that life must be understood backwards. But with this, one forgets the second proposition, that it must be lived forwards. A proposition which, the more it is subjected to careful thought, the more it ends up concluding precisely that life at any given moment cannot really ever be fully understood; exactly because there is no single moment where time stops completely in order for me to take position [to do this]: going backwards.

Søren Kierkegaard[1]

What is true of understanding our own life in general is, of course, true also of understanding in real time the institutions under which we live, including constitutional orders. There is not only the stunning suggestion, usually attributed to Zhou en-Lai, that it is "too early to tell" what the consequences of the French Revolution have been, given that we are still living under its shadow and thus subject to whatever revised understandings the future will bring. But it is also the case that as historians – to whatever degree law professors choose to embrace that role – we should try to look at the world as much as possible as it likely appeared to the objects of our historical inquiries. We have the benefit of knowing, if not the completion of the story, at least what acts two, three, and even four might look like, whereas the would-be founders of any constitutional order are painstakingly trying to set down Act One, Scene One, with the hope that it will cohere enough (and, perhaps, receive enough support from the political equivalents of financial angels, editors, or whoever must be appeased) to move on to Scene Two and then, with inspiration and good fortune, to further acts.

One topic of this book is the degree to which constitutions can be successful in their presumed purposes. This presupposes, of course, that we can establish what the

---

[1] Søren Kierkegaard, *Journalen* JJ:167 (1843), *Søren Kierkegaards Skrifter*, Søren Kierkegaard Research Center, Copenhagen, 1997, volume 18, page 306, available at http://homepage .math.uiowa.edu/~jorgen/kierkegaardquotesource.html.

purposes are and then "grade" a given constitution against them. Indeed, my wife and I have recently published a book, directed primarily at a teenage audience, called *Fault Lines in the Constitution*, and we emphasize the value of looking closely at the Preamble to the United States Constitution in order to grasp its aspirations; then, at the end of the book, we grade the Constitution, as of 2017, with regard to achieving the goals set out. We give the Constitution a C+, which may in fact be generous! But, frankly, this presumes that the purpose of the Constitution was to be disruptive of at least some important aspects of the status quo, similar, perhaps, to the Indian Constitution, as notably described by Gary Jacobsohn in his book. Eliminating at least some aspects of the caste system was central to the aspirations, and therefore constitutional identity, of Indians who drafted that country's constitution in 1947.[2] One could devote an entire essay to examining the question of whether the 1787 Constitution is an example of what Stephen Gardbaum calls "revolutionary constitutionalism," i.e., the creation (almost *ex* nihilo) of a brand new constitution designed to instantiate the values and aims of a politically revolutionary movement.[3] It is almost necessarily true that any such constitutions are what Ginsburg and Huq in their introduction describe as "transformational" in their visions. The Preamble can certainly be read in such a fashion. The project of creating "more perfect Union" entails that the existing version may well have radical *imperfections* that should be overcome.

Yet it is obvious that one cannot understand the United States Constitution – or perhaps *any* constitution – without paying attention as well to what Ginsburg and Huq invite us to view as its *preservationist* aspects, unless, at least, the drafters are genuine utopians who believe that the past can be utterly eradicated and replaced with brand new transformational visions. For better or worse, the first example that comes to mind is the Khmer Rouge, who took over Cambodia in the aftermath of American defeat in the Vietnam War. There, of course, "transformation" meant the mass slaughter of those identified with the old order, and one might view even this one example as a decisive reason to temper all such impulses with a recognition that the past indeed has its claims. But it is also necessary to realize that these claims are not self-justifying unless one is almost literally a mindless traditionalist. This point is most strikingly illustrated, in the American context, by slavery. As noted by acerbic critics of the US Constitution, and, before that, of the American Revolution and the arguments presented in the Declaration of Independence, there is a potentially fatal contradiction between the aim of "establishing Justice" and entrenching slavery, even if that word was never actually used. And we continue to debate whether the drafters genuinely believed that slavery was a declining institution or, as argued by Charles Pinckney, among others, a thriving part of both the Southern ethos and

[2] Gary Jeffrey Jacobsohn, *Constitutional Identity*. Cambridge, MA: Harvard University Press, 2010.
[3] See Stephen Gardbaum, *Revolutionary Constitutionalism*, 15 I-CON 173 (2017).

economy. In any event, there were certainly many critics of slavery who nonetheless agreed that aspects of it must be preserved if one actually wished to achieve a workable constitution uniting the thirteen quite disparate states.

If, as I believe was the case, William Lloyd Garrison was basically correct in describing the Constitution as a "covenant with Death and an Agreement with Hell," then one might grade the Constitution by reference to the degree that it lived up to *that* agreement. From this perspective, cases like *Prigg* v. *Pennsylvania* and even *Dred Scott* are far from aberrational; instead, they represent entirely good-faith efforts to live up to the dreadful bargain struck in 1787. The Fugitive Slave Clause, for example, should not become a mere parchment barrier that would not in fact serve to protect the rights of slave-owners. The bargain entered into at Philadelphia and then ratified thereafter did not require disruption of the status quo in favor of radical visions of equal rights that were in fact nowhere spelled out in the Constitution, however important they might have been to the Declaration of Independence. Instead, one must emphasize the duty to maintain an uncertain and unsteady alliance among thirteen quite disparate colonies-become-states.

It is important, therefore, to try to imagine, to the degree we can, what were the central concerns of those framing the Constitution in 1787. Even if one shares Garrison's dour perspective, it seems entirely tendentious to deny that there were many Framers who had more admirable purposes in mind and, perhaps, believed that slavery was a declining institution that would naturally disappear in good time. It is also certainly thinkable that the central concern was simply whether the new Constitution was likely to survive any longer than America's "first constitution," the basically forgotten (or, in a Freudian sense, "repressed") Articles of Confederation. In a jurisprudential version of the Oedipal drama, perhaps, that first constitution was decisively slain by the Framers of 1787 because it was viewed, correctly or not, as having established an "imbecilic" form of government that would not in fact provide the basis for an enduring United States of America.[4]

As a culture we prefer not to dwell on this primal act of juridical violence, unlike, say, the more heroic and unambiguous violence attached to the secession of the colonies from the British Empire in 1776–83. But surely every single delegate in Philadelphia was aware that the Articles, drafted in 1777 and declared operative in 1781, with ratification by Maryland, were being eviscerated after a grand total of six years. Moreover, it is likely that at least the New England delegates were aware that the New Hampshire constitution of 1776 had been replaced in 1784, and one of the most interesting features of that constitution – which I confess I deeply wish had become part of the US Constitution – was the ability of the New Hampshire electorate at then-seven-year intervals to vote whether to have a new state constitutional convention. There was no good reason to believe that the 1784 constitution

---

[4]   See, e.g., *Federalist* 15. See generally Sanford Levinson, *An Argument Open to All: Reading the Federalist in the 21st Century*. New Haven, CT: Yale University Press, 2015.

would necessarily "stick."[5] And, no doubt, the Philadelphia delegates in 1787 were well aware of criticisms of the radical Pennsylvania constitution of 1776, which among other things was unicameral. They were surely not surprised that that constitution would in 1790 suffer the same ignoble fate as the Articles.

So if one imagines lives looking forward, there was no particular reason for members of the Framing generation to be particularly optimistic that their handiwork would survive even nineteen years, the time-span of the "typical" constitution established by the backward-looking analysis of Ginsburg, Elkins, and Melton.[6] One might, of course, cite the provision protecting the international slave trade for twenty years, until 1808, as evidence that they expected the Constitution to survive at least that long, though that might require a belief that the political cleavages necessitating the Clause in the first place would, for whatever reason, have dissipated by 1808.[7] Perhaps they would have been pleasantly surprised to be told that the 1787 Constitution would survive seventy-two years from its start-up date of 1789 until destroyed by the tensions surrounding slavery, the conflagration of war and the aptly named "Reconstruction Amendments." What they knew in 1787 (or, at least, believed), as Publius asserted in the first paragraph of *Federalist* 1, was that the existing government was "inefficacious" – by *Federalist* 15 he would describe it as "imbecilic" – and something had to be done, immediately, if the wobbling new nation was to survive. One could easily describe the mood of the time as one of "crisis," a term that, in its medical context, refers to a situation where a patient is literally in a life-or-death situation, with the outcome uncertain until, say, the fever breaks.[8] But when exactly had the American fever truly broken? And would historians give a different answer from that offered by those experiencing the crisis? As John Marshall wrote in his 1807 biography of George Washington, ratification of the Constitution had been a touch-and-go process, and "the old line of division was still as strongly marked as ever."[9] And Pauline Maier, in her magisterial book on the ratification process, suggests quite strongly that the delegates to the Virginia and New York ratification

---

[5] One of the more intriguing features of New Hampshire constitutional politics is that there have in fact been seventeen such conventions, which have successfully proposed many amendments to the constitution, but as a notional matter the state continues to operate under the 1784 constitution as amended. Constitutional metaphysicians might wish to address the question whether today's New Hampshire constitution is "really" that of 1784! Moreover, this raises important questions about the degree to which constitutions should be obdurate or relatively open to amendment. Full discussion of this point is well beyond the scope of this chapter.

[6] See Tom Ginsburg, Zachary Elkins, and James Melton, *The Endurance of National Constitutions*. New York: Cambridge University Press, 2009.

[7] See U.S. Const., art. I, section 9, cl. 1. I owe this point to Ronald Krotoszynski.

[8] See John Fiske, *The Critical Period of American History 1783–1789*. Boston and New York: Houghton Mifflin, 1888, for a classic, even if subsequently supplanted, presentation of the history of the period as a true crisis.

[9] John Marshall, 5 *The Life of George Washington* 299 (1807), quoted in Richard Primus, "Enumerated Powers and the Bank of the United States," 74 n. 279 (unpublished manuscript).

conventions were initially prone to reject the new Constitution.[10] Who knows what the final vote might have been had they not been the tenth and eleventh states, respectively, to hold their conventions. Would they have been more emboldened had they been, say, numbers five and six? And, in the case of New York in particular, it appears that at least some holdouts were won over by the assurances that a new post-ratification Article V Convention would be held that could tweak the Constitution with regard to some of its apparent defects (which for most critics went well beyond the absence of a Bill of Rights). Obviously, any such assurances came to naught.

Most historians today are probably impressed by the relative ease with which the new Constitution established its legitimacy. But that may simply exemplify the *ex post* nature of historical analysis with its opposition to counterfactual history and therefore a tendency at times to make whatever happened appear inevitable. Even if Marshall was in some sense "wrong," of course, the important point is whether he believed what he wrote and what consequences such a belief might have on the definition of the reality of the challenges facing the American constitutional order.

But even general agreement that something needed to be done did not establish necessary agreement on the particulars. Politics did not stop simply because of a shared sense of urgency. Any doubt on this score should be dispelled by reading Michael Klarman's magnificent reconstruction of the process of constitutional formation.[11] So one important aspect of the history of '87 is the compromises that were necessary to achieve the overarching goal, which was not to "establish Justice" but, rather, to get agreement of the thirteen states to establish at least some kind of new, far more "consolidated," government in lieu of the "imbecilic" status quo that appeared destined for failure. And such failure would likely result in the dissolution of the ostensible "perpetual Union" into two or three contentious new countries along the Atlantic coast, with attendant prospects of European-like endless warfare (not least because of the incentive of those European powers to seek alliances with one of the new countries, whether New England, Mid-Atlantica, or Dixie, against the others).[12]

And, of course, there was also justified worry about conflict with American Indian tribes, many of whom had understandably supported the British during the Revolutionary War. One cannot possibly understand *The Federalist*, especially its early essays, without acknowledging the beat of potential war drums in the background and the raw fear of what a disunited United States would portend. Publius expressed no confidence that the country would survive in the absence of accepting the

---

[10] Pauline Maier, *Ratification: The People Debate the Constitution, 1787–1788*. New York: Simon and Schuster, 2010.

[11] Michael Klarman, *The Framers' Coup: The Making of The United States Constitution*. New York: Oxford University Press, 2016.

[12] See David Hendrickson's important book, *Peace Pact: The Lost World of The American Founding*. Lawrence: The University Press of Kansas, 2003.

radically new constitutional order that had been designed in Philadelphia. The new Constitution would give us quite literally a fighting chance, but one could not feel truly secure about the long-term prospects for survival. After all, 1791 would see the absolutely disastrous defeat of American forces headed by General Arthur St. Clair in the Battle of Wabash River. Warriors from five different tribes – the Miami, Shawnee, Delaware (Lenape), Potawatomi, and the Saint Joseph Michigan – decisively defeated the roughly one thousand members of the US army, of which only twenty-four escaped unharmed. Not surprisingly, President Washington in effect fired St. Clair, and Congress conducted its investigation of the military.

It should be clear, then, that the Constitution was not in fact the result of a Rawlsian-like process of the disinterested "reflection and choice" valorized in *Federalist* 1. And this is not only because of the fears expressed over what we today call "national security." As Klarman demonstrates, various interests contended with one another in Philadelphia, each fully believing that they could figure out the consequences for their groups of various proposals presented to the Convention. John Roche famously referred to the Convention as a "reform caucus in action," with the kinds of sausage-like compromises necessary to achieve political goals.[13] If the reformers sometimes were able to move the Convention two steps forward, they also had to accede to backward moves as well in order to get the necessary support. I have several times quoted Roche, a notable political scientist of the mid-twentieth century, for what I am sure I heard him say at a gathering of the American Political Science Association: "Power corrupts, and the prospect of losing power corrupts absolutely." So, one must understand the Convention, and then constitutional politics thereafter, in terms of those most fearful of losing their power and the threats they could make against those who wanted to take it away. "Transformation" often involves such transfers, whether of resources or political power, and it is not surprising that those asked to pay the costs will resist in the name of preservation of their various privileges.

In Philadelphia itself, the chief mode of resistance was the threat simply to walk out and torpedo the project of constitutional reform. This was the technique especially used by Delaware. But Rhode Island may be even more relevant, inasmuch as that state simply refused to send any delegates at all. They correctly feared what we today would label a "runaway convention"; they were totally delusionary, however, in believing as well that they would necessarily be able to retain the veto power granted by Article XIII of the Articles that required unanimous consent of all state legislatures to any proposed changes in the Articles. Rhode Island finally ratified the Constitution on May 29, 1790, a full year after Washington's inauguration on April 30, 1789, by the less than inspiring vote of 34–32.

---

[13] John P. Roche, "The Founding Fathers: A Reform Caucus in Action." *American Political Science Review* 55: 799 (1961).

The chief compromises that made the Constitution possible concerned both slavery and the allocation of voting power in the Senate. The latter is often described as the "Great Compromise," though that title is rarely used with regard to protecting the international slave trade until 1808 or, even more, to the three-fifths rule that gave slave-owning states a significant bonus in the House of Representatives and, therefore, the electoral college and, because of presidential ability to name judges, the judiciary as well. But Madison detested the "Great Compromise," describing it in *Federalist* 62 only as a "lesser evil" than dissolution of the Union. Obviously, the same could be said of the compromises with slavery. The lesson is that one must sometimes make (preservationist?) pacts with the devil because the perceived alternative, at least for lives being lived forward and, therefore, being perceived only through a glass darkly, appears worse. From our vantage point, we can assess the validity of what was seen earlier and distinguish paranoid fears from reasonable worries. That is the advantage that those of us looking backward have, but we should, at the least, be charitable toward those who enjoyed no such possibilities.

We can, of course, adopt a Kantian posture and declare that it is simply illegitimate *ever* to make compromises that we know are, in at least some sense, "evil," but that is to reject the wisdom of Michael Walzer, Max Weber, and, perhaps, Machiavelli about the difference between living in a distinctly political world of "dirty hands" and a very different world where one can think only of ultimate values and ends. And one is most likely to dirty one's hands when one fears the adverse consequences of not doing so. After all, if one is not simply a sociopath, why would one ever consciously dirty one's hands if no perceived gains were viewed to follow? And these ends need not be merely the selfish maximizing of one's own interests. We can surely imagine that some persons would genuinely be committed to "the common good," whatever the difficulties involved in comprehending that notion, and feel the need to make sometimes anguishing choices as to what compromises one might have to make in order to move marginally closer to one's conception of that good. Perhaps the calculation will turn out to be a mistake, but at this point we get into the world of prophylactic decision-making and the precautionary principle, both of which are necessarily relevant to constitutional designers and others, such as judges, charged afterward with giving concrete meaning to the words on the page.

It may be worth noting, though, that raw compromises reached as the result of bargaining, in contrast to outcomes of a genuinely deliberative process in which a genuine consensus is reached as to what is desirable, are likely to be particularly unstable. After all, even if one has written down the terms of the compromise in, say, the Fugitive Slave Clause, what reason is there not to believe that it will indeed turn out to be simply a "parchment barrier" that states antagonistic to slavery will feel altogether free to ignore the moment the balance of practical power has shifted in their favor? One must have an almost perverse notion of the obligation to keep one's political promises if one views the original circumstances eliciting the promise as more akin to extortion than genuine agreement. This is why the 3/5 Clause is far more important than the Fugitive Slave Clause, because the former bakes into the Constitution additional representation for the slave-owners in need of protection, whereas the latter offers only abstract promises.

So if one begins by emphasizing the anxieties that were pervasive in 1787–88 about the very survival of the young nation, when is it plausible to believe that those anxieties came to an end, with attendant consequences for the enterprise of constitutional interpretation or, especially at the state level, significant constitutional amendment if not outright replacement by a new constitution? It is worth noting, incidentally, that the circumstances of constitutional formation were scarcely designed to assure success. The Philadelphia Convention was not only a gathering of barely representative elites chosen by state legislatures and not, in any sense, by "the people" themselves; perhaps more to the point, as Jon Elster has particularly emphasized, is that the Convention was completely opaque with regard to the American public. It is almost impossible for anyone today to appreciate the degree to which the members of the Convention adhered to their oath of secrecy, even if they disagreed quite radically with decisions made (and, as with two of the three New York delegates, walked out in protest). And, of course, the ratification process involved "representative democracy" and not the more "direct democracy" found, for example, in Massachusetts with regard to the 1780 constitution in that state.

Although there is significant contemporary debate about the relationship between processes of constitutional formation and the success afterward,[14] it is hard to believe that the process underlying the US Constitution of 1787 would be truly recommended, even if possible, today in a culture of social media and attendant publicity. Klarman offers an insightful, and quite devastating, summary:

> [I]n 1787-88, Federalist leaders – recognizing that the more participatory the ratifying process was, the lower their chances of success – sought to minimize direct popular influence on the decision over ratification. They favored state conventions over referenda or decisions by town meetings, opposed the instruction of delegates to ratifying conventions, resisted the adjournment of convention for the purpose of consulting constituents, and opposed efforts to alter the Constitution they had drafted by conditioning ratification upon prior amendments. Only a ratifying process that was less participatory than the governance norms employed in many states could have secured endorsement of a constitution that was less democratic in its substance than were all state constitutions of the era. In sum, what most Federalists wanted was not a genuine national debate on the merits of the Constitution but simply its ratification.[15]

They were obviously successful in gaining ratification (though by a margin of only three votes in New York, 30–27), but it would have been foolhardy to predict a very

---

[14] See, e.g., Tom Ginsburg, Zachary Elkins, and Jason Blount, "Does the Process of Constitution-Making Matter." *Annual Review of Law and Social Science* 5: 201 (2009).

[15] Klarman, at 618.

long life for the Constitution itself, especially after George Washington, with his peculiar charisma, departed from the scene, leaving in his wake a fractious and bitterly contentious party system.

Although much understudied and undertaught, the pre-Marshall period of American constitutionalism certainly manifests some of the relevant anxieties. The first great Supreme Court decision, after all, was *Chisholm v. Georgia*,[16] in which four of the five justices held, I believe altogether correctly, that Georgia had no immunity from being brought before a federal court to defend itself against a charge that it owed an estate a debt for services rendered during the Revolutionary War. Chief Justice Jay and Justice Wilson in particular both emphasized that the idea of "state sovereignty" was simply a chimera, that there was no sovereign in the United States other than "We the People." Although there is some dispute about the magnitude of the response to *Chisholm*, there can be no doubt that sufficient political resources were found to elicit the Eleventh Amendment in order to negate *Chisholm* and underscore the unhappiness of at least three-quarters of the states with what they obviously viewed as the heretical rejection of their sovereign status. And by 1798, with the Kentucky and Virginia Resolutions, one saw a more fully elaborated theory of state sovereignty via the "Compact Theory." The former Resolution, drafted by Jefferson, raised the specter of "nullification" as a particular threat to one form of the constitutional order. It also establishes the most dramatic illustration of the conflict between a "transformational" vision of a de-facto "consolidated" national government and a "preservationist" hope of retaining the functional preeminence of ostensibly "sovereign" states.

The Resolutions are vivid examples of "the Constitution outside the courts," but no less important for that. After all, their basic claim, beyond the Compact Argument, was that the Federalist Congress had treated the First Amendment as a mere parchment barrier in its zeal to criminalize the Jeffersonian opposition. This is, of course, most memorably instantiated in the fact that it was a criminal offense to call the President (John Adams) but not the Vice President (Thomas Jefferson) into disrepute. One might also mention in this context the Whiskey Rebellion that took place over 1791–94, very near the beginning of the new constitutional order. At the time, it forced George Washington quite literally to get back on his horse and to become a very concrete Commander-in-Chief of US forces putting down a traitorous rebellion. Perhaps no one really believed that it threatened the survival of the regime, but we'll never know what would have happened had the forces not been called out.

Interestingly enough, Washington illustrated both his magnanimity and political good sense in using his pardon power to erase the death sentences imposed on John Mitchell and Philip Wigle. The most interesting defense offered of the Pardon power by Publius in *Federalist* 72 was a *realpolitik* analysis of the wisdom of giving to

[16]   2 (2 Dall.) U.S. 419 (1793).

the President the power to pardon even acknowledged traitors or rebels in order to demonstrate mercy and reintegrate them and their followers back into the political order rather than create martyrs and sullen devotees of their memories who might become forces of continued instability. To put it mildly, the Whiskey Rebellion plays little role in the way legal academics, at least, teach American constitutional development, but that is precisely because we have the luxury of looking backward and being able, rightly or not, to dismiss any genuine light it might cast on the constitutional enterprise.

For most members of the legal academy, it is John Marshall and his cases, quite literally as well as figuratively, that frame the first great period American constitutional development. But what if we try to look at this period from a forward-looking perspective? In this context, I want to look at two great cases – or chestnuts – indelibly linked with Marshall Court, *Marbury* v. *Madison* and *McCulloch* v. *Maryland*. Although it will be necessary, at least at points, to refer to doctrines they may be thought to stand for, I am more interested in what they might tell us about constitutional decision-making when one is (or is not) worried about regime (or even institutional) survival. And, as already illustrated by reference to Kentucky and Virginia Resolutions and the Whiskey Rebellion, it is advisable to keep looking beyond the judiciary if we are to grapple with the full panoply of threats to the constitutional order and how, at least until 1861, they were surmounted.

Rightly or wrongly, I have developed a certain amount of notoriety for my failure to teach *Marbury* v. *Madison*.[17] In an article defending my practice, based primarily on the opportunity costs involved in taking the time to teach *Marbury* to students who are unlikely to have adequate grounding in the relevant American history, I explicitly noted that I taught the case at the Central European University in Budapest to a variety of representatives from what was then called "the region," which extended well into the former Soviet Union. More to the point, the reason that these individuals, some law students and some, as I recall, practicing judges, might well find the case interesting is not in the least the inherent interest of whether Congress has the authority to add to the original jurisdiction of the Supreme Court, an issue that almost no serious adult could really care about. Rather, the case can easily be interpreted in the context both of regime and institutional maintenance. Both are of obvious interest to anyone from Central Europe.

Indeed, at the time one of the front-page issues was the willingness of Serbs in the region of Republika Srbska, notionally within the country of Bosnia-Herzegovina, to obey decisions of the Bosnian Constitutional Court. Perhaps it is worth noting in this context that two of the tribunal's nine members are selected by the National

---

[17] See Sanford Levinson, "Why I Don't Teach Marbury (Except to Eastern Europeans) and Why You Shouldn't Either." *Wake Forest Law Review* 38: 553 (2003). See also Jack Balkin and Sanford Levinson, "What Are the Facts of Marbury?" *Constitutional Commentary* 20: 255 (2004).

Assembly of the Republika Srbska, while four are selected by the House of Representatives of the Federation of Bosnia and Herzegovina. The remaining three members are selected by the President of the European Court of Justice in consultation with the president of Bosnia-Herzegovina, but they cannot be citizens of the country of an adjoining state. Establishing and maintaining new national institutions is scarcely a topic of merely academic institutions to anyone in "the region," whereas it is a question of surprisingly little interest to most academic lawyers in the United States.

In any event, if one does take the time to teach *Marbury*, then students should be made aware that those living their lives in 1800 could not be completely confident that the United States would survive its first encounter with the patent deficiency and dysfunctionality of the electoral college as a means of selecting the President of the United States.[18] The stupidity of the Democratic-Republicans led them, unlike the Federalists, to ignore the necessity of making sure that their "genuine" champion, Thomas Jefferson, received at least one more electoral vote than his running mate, Aaron Burr. This created the tie vote, which required a majority of the states represented in the House of Representatives to break the tie, on a one-state/one-vote basis. This was finally done on the 36th ballot when Delaware's sole Federalist representative, James Bayard, agreed to forego voting for Burr, instead leaving his ballot blank. Perhaps he simply acquiesced to the fervent opposition against Burr by Alexander Hamilton. But it is possible as well that he was all too aware that the governors of both Pennsylvania and Virginia had threatened to call out their state militias and to march on the brand new national capital of Washington, DC, in order to assure Jefferson's selection.

We know, looking backward, that the United States would successfully weather the dispute. Students might even learn about the Twelfth Amendment, which was designed not only to make impossible a repetition of the particular kind of tie vote received in 1800 but also, and perhaps more importantly, implicitly to recognize the reality of political parties (and, therefore, of "tickets" running together for the separate offices of president and vice-president). Mark Graber has argued that from one perspective, this could be said to represent the conclusion of the constitutional order of 1787, based, however implausibly, on the hope to tame "faction" by the mechanisms of an "extended republic" and reliance on public-spirited and virtuous Publians.

At the very least, the Twelfth Amendment is not a merely "technical" tweak; it represents a fundamental shift in the way our constitutional order would be governed. Among other things, the reality, with some exceptions, is that almost no serious person in the future would regard vice-presidents as in fact the set of second-most-capable persons in the country to enter the White House. They would, with

---

[18] See Bruce Ackerman, *The Failure of the Founding Fathers: Jefferson, Marshall, and the Rise of Presidential Democracy*. Cambridge, MA: Harvard University Press, 2005.

rare exceptions, be picked to "balance" tickets and appeal to given constituencies. Actual capacity to serve as an effective president, should that become necessary, is only intermittently a criterion.

As it happened, Thomas Jefferson as President indeed presided over the doubling of the size of the new country with the Louisiana Purchase of 1803, which was far more significant in every conceivable way than *Marbury* (though I believe that the University of Texas Law School was unique in observing the bicentennial of the former instead of the latter in 2003). Jefferson firmly doubted that he had the constitutional authority to engage in it, not least because by any reckoning it fundamentally transformed every aspect of the United States as a social, economic, political, and constitutional order – and, ultimately, led quite directly to the dissolution of the Union in 1861.

Marshall in 1802–3 could scarcely have been confident of an entirely happy ending to the issues roiling America at the time, beginning with his own survival as Chief Justice against potential attempts at impeachment. And, of course, there was the little matter of the Jeffersonian purge of the entirety of the intermediate federal judiciary that was created as part of the 1801 Judiciary Act. The Act was a magnificent, though ill-fated, farewell gift by the Federalist lame-duck Congress to the repudiated John Adams, who promptly appointed sixteen Federalists to fill the newly created six circuits. Not surprisingly, at least to anyone with a political sensibility, the Act did not stand.

The Judiciary Act of 1802 retained "circuit courts," but there were no "circuit judges" as such. Instead, circuit courts would consist of a given Supreme Court justice "riding circuit" and district judges from the locality. This purge was upheld in a case decided a week after *Marbury, Stuart v. Laird*.[19] Except to the legal professoriate and their students, it is by almost any account more important than *Marbury* with regard to the central concerns of this book. One reason, perhaps, for the general ignorance of the case is that it is one of the relatively few constitutional cases that Marshall assigned to others, in this case Justice William Patterson, who wrote a perfunctory and near-opaque opinion explaining why the purge raised no constitutional problems. It appears that there may have been internal dissents within the Court and that at least one justice suggested the equivalent of a "strike" with regard to the onerous duties of circuit riding. None of this happened, of course, because prudence suggested that angry Jeffersonians would not be likely to accept such a challenge to their authority with equanimity.

There are surely interesting passages in *Marbury* about the difference between ministerial duty and discretionary authority, the status of written constitutions, and the role of the judiciary. But, as my mentor Robert McCloskey suggested long ago in his almost breathless encomium to Marshall in *The American Supreme Court*, what is most significant about the decision is the abject failure of Marshall in fact to issue

---

[19] 5 U.S. 299 (1803).

an order to James Madison (or Thomas Jefferson) that would quite likely be ignored. The Supreme Court, most definitely looking backward, might have exclaimed in the 1958 *Cooper v. Aaron*[20] that *Marbury* established "the basic principle that the Federal judiciary is supreme in the exposition of the law of the Constitution, and that principle has ever since been respected by the Court and the Country as a permanent and indispensable feature of our constitutional system." Yet it should be obvious that this is patently incorrect as a forward-looking statement in 1803 or, for that matter, through most of our history, not to mention its accuracy even as a paraphrase of what Marshall actually said in his opinion.

Perhaps one reason for the whistling-past-the-graveyard tone of *Cooper* is precisely that the Court in 1958 had at least some reason to wonder about establishing itself as the "supreme expositor of the Constitution." Although President Eisenhower's support, however reluctant, for *Brown v. Board of Education* was surely reassuring, there was also the reality of the so-called Southern Manifesto, signed by the overwhelming number of the Southern representatives and senators and presenting a linguistically temperate critique of the legitimacy of *Brown* as unwarranted judicial legislation.[21]

In any event, *Marbury* is, above all, exemplary of the "passive virtues," even if we amend that notion by adopting Mark Graber's description of Marshall as often exhibiting the "passive-aggressive" virtues making truculent statements, as in *Marbury* itself, while withdrawing from the genuine field of battle and acquiescing in what Marshall had suggested was executive misconduct. Gerald Gunther, no fan of Bickel's concept, denounced those virtues as the patent interjection of raw politics into the sacrosanct temple of legal reasoning. As he so memorably put it, Bickel was advocating that the Court be 100 percent principled, but only 20 percent of the time. Those who agree with Bickel would respond that it is simply impossible to be 100 percent principled all the time, which would entail never making compromises thought to be necessary to serve important ends, including, obviously, maintenance of a possibly fragile constitutional or political order.

But does our response to the jibe depend on our reading of the historical record and our own evaluation of the empirical circumstances facing the court – or anyone else claiming to be acting under the imprimatur of constitutional authority? Should conscientious constitutionalists, whether on the Court or in the White House (or anywhere else), be like captains of great vessels prepared to go down with their ships in the name of abstract constitutional principles, or should they be instead prepared to do whatever it takes to save the "ship of state," even if this necessarily includes disregarding some constitutional principles and treating them indeed as mere "parchment barriers"? And, incidentally, does the answer to this question depend on the substantive importance of the principles at stake? With regard to the relatively

---

[20] 358 U.S. 1, 18 (1958).
[21] See Justin Driver, "Supremacies and the Southern Manifest." *Texas Law Review* 92: 1053 (2014).

few parts of the Constitution that are explicitly devoted to "establishing justice," perhaps one might believe that they merit obedience even at high costs. We could transform the negative image of the Constitution as a "suicide pact" into one that requires, like other religious texts, the willingness of adherents to martyr themselves (and their communities) on behalf of basic principles. But why would anyone believe, for example, that adherence to baroque features of the separation of power – or even adherence to the principle of fixed elections in the midst of war – would constitute such a principle?

What we can say, looking backward, is that Marshall navigated the problems presented by 1800 and its aftermath with great skill (and, perhaps, some raw luck). But could this necessarily have been predicted in 1803? One thing we do know is that Marshall never directly confronted presidential authority, save in the very odd case of *Little* v. *Barreme*,[22] where the overreaching president in question was the now-retired (and defeated) John Adams. Perhaps Jefferson believed that he was the "real" target, but there is no case law to support this.

McCulloch v. *Maryland*, about which I endlessly obsess, is altogether different from *Marbury*. If the latter exemplifies the passive virtues, then *McCulloch* is almost strident in its invocation of both judicial and national power. One might analyze it entirely internally, with regard to its "fidelity," or lack of same, to the 1787 Constitution, but that is really beside the point. One might well agree, for example, with James Boyd White, who both described *McCulloch* as an "amendment" rather than a truly good-faith "interpretation" of the preexisting Constitution, and then went on to say that he doesn't mean that as a criticism.[23] Perhaps we should put this in the context of the famous mid-nineteenth-century diarist George Templeton Strong, who said of Abraham Lincoln that if he felt it necessary to violate the Constitution in order to maintain the Union, then all the better for Lincoln.[24]

I have come to agree with Felix Frankfurter that the most important single sentence in the canon is Marshall's statement never to forget "that it is a constitution we are expounding," but only if that is combined with a statement several paragraphs later that if one wishes the Constitution to "endure," then it "must be adapted to the various crises of human affairs." Constitutions that cannot be so adapted, or regimes who are led by persons too rigid to engage in necessary adaptation, will fail. So, inevitably, the metaquestion hanging over a book like ours is the success, or failure, of sufficient constitutional adaptation in given countries that has allowed (or will allow in the future) the overall maintenance of the constitutional order even if not

---

[22] 6 U.S. 170 (1804).

[23] James Boyd White, *When Words Lose Their Meaning*. University of Chicago Press, 1984.

[24] See Sanford Levinson, *Constitutional Faith*. Princeton, NJ: Princeton University Press, 2nd ed. 2011. "Should learned counsel prove by word-splitting," Strong wrote, that Lincoln "saved [the Union] unconstitutionally, I shall honor his memory even more reverently than I do now." One might read this as a valorization of "spirit" over "letter" of the law, though, of course, purposive spirit is no more self-evident in its meaning than is barebones text.

some particular version of "the Constitution" in all of its pristine glory. The late Walter Murphy distinguished between a commitment to *constitutionalism* and what might even be viewed as a fetishistic regard for a particular constitution, what might be denigrated as *constitutionism*. The former is clearly more important. Many given "constitutional orders" might be congruent with the overall project of "constitutionalism." Under what circumstances do we regard "adaptations" as signaling the conclusion of one constitutional order and the replacement by a new one? After all, as Ginsburg et al. freely admit, it is no easy matter to decide exactly how long a given constitution "endures" in the absence of certain formal criteria that may rarely be present. But why exactly should we care all that much if a particular constitution endures, so long as "constitutionalism" remains a constant in a given society?

So, what does *McCulloch* do, performatively? Consider only the truly remarkable first paragraph, which I always have my students read aloud, with frequent interruptions in order to try to understand Marshall's rhetorical strategies:

> In the case now to be determined, the defendant, *a sovereign State*, denies the obligation of a law enacted by the legislature of the Union, and the plaintiff, on his part, contests the validity of an act which has been passed by the legislature of that State. The Constitution of our country, in its most interesting and vital parts, is to be considered, the conflicting powers of the Government of the Union and of its members, as marked in that Constitution, are to be discussed, and an opinion given which may essentially influence the great operations of the Government. No tribunal can approach such a question without a deep sense of its importance, and of the awful responsibility involved in its decision. *But it must be decided peacefully, or remain a source of hostile legislation, perhaps, of hostility of a still more serious nature; and if it is to be so decided, by this tribunal alone can the decision be made. On the Supreme Court of the United States has the Constitution of our country devolved this important duty.*

> (emphasis added)

Surely one must ask what possessed Marshall to begin his opinion by referring to Maryland as a "sovereign state," a term, incidentally, nowhere used within the text of the Constitution itself. Perhaps the most standard meaning of "sovereignty" has to do with the notion of unrestrained power. This is not surprising if one accepts, for example, Carl Schmitt's notion that the modern "state" is simply a secularized version of an older divine order featuring a sometimes terrifyingly all-powerful God. I've already alluded to the first great constitutional opinion delivered by the Supreme Court, *Chisholm* v. *Georgia*, which thoroughly rejects the very possibility of Marshall's later description of Maryland.

Chisholm, of course, was written before one of the most important aspects of the Marshallian revolution, which was the displacement of the British custom of seriatim opinions with an "Opinion of the Court," preferably, at least for Marshall, without dissent (and written by himself). But consider only the words of Justice

James Wilson, by any account one of the most important figures at the Philadelphia
Convention and the Pennsylvania ratifying convention afterward and the author of
the first great American book on law in a democratic republic: "To the Constitution
of the United States," wrote Wilson,

> the term SOVEREIGN, is totally unknown ... They might have announced
> themselves "SOVEREIGN" people of the United States. But serenely conscious
> of the fact, they avoided the ostentatious declaration ... In one sense, the term
> "sovereign" has for its correlative "subject." In this sense, the term can receive no
> application, for it has no object in the Constitution of the United states. Under that
> Constitution, there are citizens, but no subjects ... As a citizen, I know the
> government of [Georgia] to be republican; and my short definition of such a
> government is one constructed on this principle – that the supreme power resides
> in the body of the people ... As to the purposes of the Union, therefore, Georgia is
> NOT a sovereign state ... [capitalization in original]

So, we might ask, why did Marshall choose to open the Pandora's box of "state
sovereignty" within an opinion that thoroughly rejects the notion, whether as a
theory of constitutional formation – see paragraphs 7–11, where he attempts to rebut
the Jefferson-Madison "compact theory" of constitutional ontology – or practical
interpretation, as in the second part of the opinion ruthlessly limiting the power of
Maryland to invoke its taxing power against the Bank of the United States? Is this a
tip of the Marshallian hat to a post-1793 constitutional culture that he recognizes
now includes the concept of "state sovereignty," whatever his own views of the
matter? Or is it a tacit recognition of the implications of the Treaty of Paris of
1783 that formally ended the secessionist struggle between the American colonies
and the British Empire? Article One of that Treaty reads as follows: "His Brittanic
Majesty acknowledges the said United States, viz., New Hampshire, Massachusetts
Bay, Rhode Island and Providence Plantations, Connecticut, New York, New Jersey,
Pennsylvania, Maryland, Virginia, North Carolina, South Carolina and Georgia, *to
be free sovereign and independent states*, that he treats with them as such ... "
Federalist 39 appears to accept the notion that the states even within the Articles of
Confederation maintained their "sovereignty."

There is a reason, after all, that the original United States was deemed a confederation; Pufendorf and Montesquieu indeed recognized that sovereign states could
agree to place limited aspects of their powers into, say, a military alliance. But the
point is that confederations were indeed "limited governments" with only very
narrow assigned powers, as was the notorious case with the Articles – and explained
the perception that the government created by them was "imbecilic." The Constitution did create a brand new, decidedly *non*-confederal form of government, as
Marshall both realized and celebrated. But that only underscores the oddity of his
beginning the opinion the way he does. Was Homer nodding, or was there some
ascertainable purpose to it? I frankly have no real idea.

But perhaps it is worth taking time to dwell on the beginning of the second emphasized portion of Marshall's opening paragraph, which alludes to the background conditions of the decision. Nothing, of course, is spelled out – yet another problem when teaching students who are basically ignorant about American history – but presumably we who are teaching the case are aware that 1819 is the year of the great debate over the admission of Missouri to the Union. What William Freehling has accurately denominated the "Midwest Purchase," insofar as Louisiana turned out to be a relatively trivial part of the vast new lands incorporated within the United States in 1803, was beginning to reveal its full complexities. As much as anything, of course, it was Jefferson's decision in 1803 to accept the remarkable deal offered by Napoleon, almost infinitely more far-reaching than the modest hopes of America's negotiators simply to procure New Orleans and a bit of surrounding territory, that sent us on our inexorable course to civil war. Putting one's views about the morality of slavery to one's side, it is easily possible to imagine a stable equilibrium with regard to the original territory of the United States even including the addition of Louisiana alone. The House Divided *would* stand, at least so long as the benefits of Union were recognizable and the political structures established by the Constitution of 1787 guaranteed the maintenance of what Graber has called bi-sectionality, i.e., the inability of either North or South to impose its wishes on the other. But 1803 in its actual domain changed everything, even if not immediately. By 1819, though, it was becoming obvious that the equilibrium of 1787 and the addition of both the "Northwest states" that we now call the American mid-West and the "Southwest states" carved out of Virginia, North Carolina, and Georgia was open to what Joseph Schumpeter might have called "disruption," whether or not "creative."

Marshall was necessarily living his life forward. In 1803, this counseled abject capitulation to the Jeffersonian critics of the Midnight judges in *Marbury* and *Stuart*. By 1819, perhaps he shared the backward-looking perception that he was living in an "Era of Good Feelings," but the first paragraph suggests a more complex reality. There was the possibility of "hostility" of a more … serious nature" than simple litigation and angry editorials in the partisan press. Was he being sensationalist or even paranoid? Looking backward, we answer yes at our peril. Within a half-century, 750,000 Americans (depending on how one classifies those who fought for the Confederacy) would die. Perhaps what is most amazing, even bizarre, is his claim, offered without the slightest substantiation by way of ordinary evidence, that "by this tribunal alone can the decision be made" and that "the Constitution of our country devolved this important duty" upon the Supreme Court. If one is maximally uncharitable, one might hear echoes of a later Donald Trump proclaiming that "I alone" can save the country from its presumptively dangerous situation.

But I most certainly do not mean to equate the republican statesman John Marshall with the unhinged and demagogic Donald Trump. One must assume that Marshall genuinely thought that the country was at risk of potential hostilities and even dissolution. The year 1819 was thirty years removed from Washington's inauguration; he didn't need to read Ginsburg et al. to know that constitutional endurance was a contingent and not a necessary reality. Things could easily have gone the other way in 1800–3. Perhaps the country *was* more stable in 1819; it had, after all, seemingly "won" the War of 1812 (which necessitated chartering a Second Bank of the United States in 1816) and established itself more certainly as a genuinely independent nation that could hold its own with the British hegemon. But one suspects that Marshall was aware of the Hartford Convention and the rumors that at least some of the New Englanders had muttered about secession, given that their attempts to "nullify" the Jeffersonian Embargo were unsuccessful. This also underscores the mistake we make if we identify "nullification" and "secessionism" only with slave-owners and the Slavocracy. So the cautionary note at the very beginning of the opinion warns us against taking our good fortune for granted. The Supreme Court, instead of acting passively as in *Marbury*, should step up and help "adapt" the Constitution to make national endurance more likely than it might otherwise be.

This required an open-ended reading of the Constitution, including, of course, the Necessary and Proper Clause, coupled with reining in the power of Maryland, the so-called sovereign state, to tax the Bank. Madison was appalled by the reasoning in the opinion; as Eric Lazaroff has shown, Madisonian support in 1816 for rechartering the Bank was based on its connection with Congress's assigned power over "coinage," an argument totally unrecognized by Marshall in 1819. But, as is usually the case, results were more important than reasoning, and most national elites accepted the desirability of the Bank by 1819.

However, Ohio, another would-be "sovereign state" did not go gently into the new Marshallian world. It, too, tried to cripple the Bank by seizing the assets of the branch located in Chillicothe, and it was not clear that Ohio would peacefully submit to the doctrine enunciated in *McCulloch*. Looking backward, we know what the answer was; *Osborne* v. *Bank of the United States* was a stinging defeat for Ohioans who hoped to generate a reconsideration – and reversal – of *McCulloch*. Still, Marshall had at least some reason to be anxious, even as he asserted the prerogatives of the Supreme Court. This doesn't really explain some of his rhetorical maneuvers. I am inclined to believe that he viewed the Union as sturdy enough in 1819, even given the drama surrounding Missouri, to believe that this was a good time to reinforce the joint notion of de-facto national plenary power that would be legitimized, as Charles Black argued decades ago, by a highly deferential Supreme Court that would, at the same time, give evidence of its increasing willingness to monitor overreaching by so-called sovereign states within the Union.

Can we say that the Ship of State was fully operating and a good bet to remain so into the indefinite future as of 1820? Andrew Jackson submitted with what in context is relatively good grace to the election of 1824, where he had clearly been the first-past-the-post winner, but failed to get a majority of the electoral vote and then lost in the House of Representatives. One suspects that Donald Trump, who professes to admire Jackson, would not have submitted in such fashion. But if living well is the best revenge, then Old Hickory's subsequent two terms in the White House must have been very satisfying indeed, as was his ability to wreck the Bank of the United States and, in his veto message, acerbically suggest that Supreme Court opinions were entitled only to so much deference "as the force of their reasoning may deserve." This makes hash of the notion of stare decisis, let alone judicial suprem- acy, both of which rest on claims of deference even when one believes that they are "in fact" mistaken in their readings of the law (whatever one believes the term "in fact" means jurisprudentially).

A key event in Jackson's presidency, of course, was South Carolina's attempt to nullify the 1828 tariff, and the potential threat of civil war that was forestalled by a combination of Jacksonian resolve and the de facto willingness to compromise over the precise terms of the tariff. More to the point, perhaps, was that the Nullification Crisis provoked former Vice President John C. Calhoun to write his Fort Hill Address that set out the theory not only of nullification but also, and more import- antly, the logic of secession that would prove telling some three decades later. One might think that most major constitutional controversies thereafter were considered against the background of this possibility. Could the constitutional order endure without yet more "adaptation," including that of the Supreme Court?

One might also put into this context the set of opinions written by Marshall concerning the rights – or lack of same – of American Indians. *Cherokee Nation v. Georgia*[25] could certainly be placed within the framework of a "passive virtues" decision inasmuch as Marshall refused to recognize the Cherokee Nation as a foreign state that could invoke the original jurisdiction of the Supreme Court in its suit against Georgia's clear overreaching. Charles Warren described the struggle as "the most serious crisis in the history of the Court."[26] Perhaps more to the point, in terms of the central focus of this essay, is John Quincy Adams's comment that "the Union is in the most imminent danger of dissolution."[27] Looking backward, we can dismiss this as hyperbole, but can we really dismiss Adams's concern as hyster- ical? What would, after all, have happened had the Marshall Court clearly taken on Georgia's claims to sovereign control of what it claimed to be its own territory, especially given the almost certain lack of presidential support for any strong effort by the Court to curb the renegade state? Perhaps *Worcester v. Georgia*[28] was an effort at least somewhat to redeem the Court's stature, but we know that it was certainly ineffective, whether or not Andrew Jackson actually stated that John Marshall had made his decision, so let him try to enforce it as well.

---

[25] 30 U.S. (5 Peters) 1 (1831).
[26] Charles Warren, *The Supreme Court in American History*, Vol. 1. Boston: Little, Brown, and Company, 1922, 189.
[27] G. Edward White, *The Marshall Court and Cultural Change*. Macmillan Publishing Com- pany, 1988, 71.
[28] 31 US 515 (1832).

So the final case worth considering in this context is the 1842 decision in *Prigg* v. *Pennsylvania*, which I have publicly declared to be a candidate as the worst decision in our history.[29] Doctrinally, it is even more of an "implied powers" interpretation of the Constitution than is *McCulloch*. Its invalidation of Pennsylvania's personal liberty law, which in modern terms can be viewed as analogous to a "sanctuary state" law designed to make sure that any ostensible fugitive slaves are really and truly such, rather than the mere object of self-serving allegations by professional slave-catchers, is at least as much a limit on state "sovereignty" as is Marshall's invalidation of the tax levied on the Bank of the United States. But that is not my primary interest today. Instead, we should ask, or speculate, why Joseph Story thought it necessary to write such an execrable opinion.

As Paul Finkelman argues in a recent book on Justices Marshall, Story, and Taney,[30] Story was notable among Supreme Court justices in having been a truly vigorous critic of slavery. Indeed, he appears to have been slightly chastised by Marshall, in the latter's opinion in *The Antelope*, for his passionate critique, which might have violated Marshall's distinction expressed in that case between the "jurist" and the "moralist." (In any such distinction, especially when proffered by a judge, one knows which will be treated as privileged.) So did Story, who was never an Abolitionist, develop a new perspective on the merits of slavery by 1842? The answer is clearly not. As Finkelman argues, what most likely happened is that Story became ever more nationalist and convinced that accommodations had to be made to the "slavocracy" if the Union were to endure. After all, that was the justification for the three-fifths compromise in 1787. If one is willing to endorse the Constitution in 1787 – and the compromises necessary to bring it into being – then why not accept the perceived "necessity" in 1842 to reassure ever-more-restive slave states that their interests would in fact be protected by the Supreme Court? Story emphasized that no general theory of constitutional interpretation underlay his analysis other than, one might say, the Marshallian emphasis that endurance required adaptation. And adaptation *Prigg* surely was.

We will never know, of course, what the consequences would have been of a contrary decision establishing the legitimacy of Pennsylvania as a de-facto "sanctuary state." Hovering over the issue of Pennsylvania's "sovereign" powers was the duty of that state (or, more to the point, Ohio) to offer peaceful "transit" through the state to slave-owners (or slave-dealers) bringing slaves from, say, Virginia to Missouri and passing through the purported "free state" of Ohio. In any event, by 1842, we are within two decades of the collapse of the Constitution of 1787 and its replacement,

---

[29] See Sanford Levinson, "Is *Dred Scott* Really the Worst Opinion of All Time? Why *Prigg* Is Worse Than *Dred Scott* (But Is Likely to Stay Out of the 'Anti-Canon')." *Harvard Law Review Forum* 125: 23–32 (2011), available at www.harvardlawreview.org/issues/125/december11/forum_768.php.

[30] Paul Finkelman, *Supreme Injustice: Slavery in the Nation's Highest Court*. Cambridge, MA: Harvard University Press, 2018.

after the conflagration of 1861–65, of a quite different Constitution of 1868, at least with regard to potential (and even actual) national power and further limitations on the rights of "sovereign" states. Once more, if we imagine Joseph Story "looking forward," as it were, unable to know exactly what the future would bring, *Prigg* might seem an acceptable price to pay for maintaining the Union. If we are critics of *Prigg*, as I am, is it because we disagree with the "empirics" of such an argument, which requires dismissing the Southern secessionists, at least as of 1842, as simply a hot-headed minority, of no more political significance than the Abolitionists who were proclaiming "No Union with Slaveholders"? Even if we defend "pacts with the devil," after all, it requires agreement that the circumstances are sufficiently dire to require such awful deals. Or, perhaps, we object to *Prigg* because it reveals, in many ways even more so than *Dred Scott*, the true horrors of chattel slavery inasmuch as Margaret Morgan and, without doubt, her children, were likely *not* fugitive slaves at all but were nonetheless "sent South" because of Story's holding that the Constitution required recognizing "self-help repossession" as part of the property right attached to owning other human beings.

Prigg, more than any other single case, forces us to look backwards and forward at the same instant. As already suggested, might Story be correct that acceptance of the Compromise of 1787 entails, both logically and politically, the willingness to continue appeasing slave-owners who can make credible threats to bring the entire system down should their interests not be recognized (and reinforced, as with the Fugitive Slave Act of 1850, described by Freehling as part of the "Armistice of 1850")? And, looking forward, does it at least call into question Abraham Lincoln's obdurate unwillingness to compromise over the near-theoretical issue of expanding slavery into the American territories bought in 1803 and then conquered in 1847. Where do we draw lines about permissible and impermissible "adaptations" of patches of parchment once we commit ourselves to the overarching goal of constitutional "endurance" even at the price of preserving undesirable – indeed, patently unjust – features of our older order?

My friend Mark Graber, in his indispensable book *Dred Scott and the Problem of Constitutional Evil*, makes the case that the preferable candidate in the 1860 presidential race was John Bell, the "centrist" who was willing to seek accommodation with Southern secessionists. The electoral college, however, made his election de facto impossible; indeed, only true specialists can now identify who he is. Lincoln, of course, was elected with 39.8 percent of the popular vote, though a majority of the electoral vote. If one celebrates that, in part because his election (far more than *Dred Scott*) triggered the Civil War (and 750,000 lost lives), then that obviously raises questions as to the desirability of the original 1787 compromise and other efforts to maintain the Union that required accommodation (or appeasement) of slave interests. Why *should* the United States Constitution have endured even to 1860, assuming one believes that there was in fact a singular constitution between 1789 and the time of Lincoln's election? But if one believes in the telos of endurance, then why isn't Graber correct in his near-lament of Lincoln's election? Would our answer be different, incidentally, if the Southerners, who also could only look through the glass darkly toward future possibilities, had accepted Lincoln's heartfelt offer for compensated emancipation that would in fact not be finalized until, say, 1900? In fact, especially looking backward, we might wonder if Southern secessionists in retrospect might have regretted their rejection of James Buchanan's argument in his final Message to Congress that they had relatively little to worry about in a Lincoln Administration inasmuch as they possessed enough power in Congress to prevent passage of the Republican program. They could thus outwait the minority president and retake the White House in 1864.

In summary, I suggest first of all that anyone seriously interested in "constitutional development," including the project of "constitutional maintenance," is well advised to adopt a "forward-looking" perspective that almost necessarily becomes consequentialist inasmuch as we ask what "adaptations" must be made in order to assure survival. But this also takes us to a second notion identified with Kierkegaard, "the teleological suspension of the ethical." That is, we are not in fact Kantians or deontologists who ask only if some act accords, at least in its intentions, with our values. We instead in effect "suspend" our ethical commitments in light of the ends actually produced, the *telos*, by our actions (including constitutional interpretations). As a practical matter, this may necessarily test the depth of our "transformational" impulses when faced with the costs of overcoming "preservationist" forces who continue to adhere to the very values that we believe to be in need of transformation.

3

Marking Constitutional Transitions

The Law and Politics of Constitutional Implementation in South Africa

Rosalind Dixon and Theunis Roux

3.1 INTRODUCTION

South Africa is often seen as one of the most successful recent instances of constitutional implementation: After decades of authoritarian, racially discriminatory rule under apartheid, its 1996 Constitution[1] established a system of multi-party democracy and rights-based constitutionalism. In the first ten years of democracy, the African National Congress (ANC) government passed a range of transformational statutes that re-moralized the legal system and began to address the consequences of past economic exploitation and discrimination. From a new, more worker-friendly industrial relations regime,[2] to land reform,[3] and administrative justice,[4] the Constitution's vision for a just legal and political order was given concrete legislative form. To be sure, in the second decade of democracy, from around 2008, the ANC's reputation as the driver of social and economic transformation began to decline, and the wheels have come off the South African democratic miracle to a certain extent. But the Constitution has not been substantially amended during this period, and it remains at the center of public discussion about how to restore the democratic system to health.

This chapter suggests that one important explanation for this experience lies in the degree to which key actors – such as the South African Constitutional Court – have implemented constitutional transformation imperatives in ways that are sensitive to the broader political context, particularly the context of political (non-) competition or dominant-party democracy. Initially, the chapter argues, the Court adopted a restrained role that avoided direct confrontations with the ANC

---

[1] Constitution of the Republic of South Africa 1996.
[2] The Labour Relations Act 66 of 1995.
[3] See, for example, Restitution of Land Rights Act 22 of 1994 and the Extension of Security of Tenure Act 62 of 1997.
[4] The Promotion of Administrative Justice Act 3 of 2000.

government, and sought to encourage legislative and executive responsibility for constitutional implementation (the first constitutional period). Over time, as the ANC became less committed to the constitutional project, the Court gradually assumed a more active role in encouraging political pluralism and accountability, both within the ANC and more broadly (the second constitutional period).

Despite these efforts, the project of constitutional implementation in South Africa clearly remains incomplete. As a recent collection we edited documents,[5] South Africa continues to grapple with problems of endemic corruption, the nondelivery of key services, and sexual and other violence. The ANC's ongoing electoral dominance means that it is in many ways part of the problem rather than the solution. Entrenched in power for more than twenty years, the ANC has been able to take control of nominally independent state institutions and turn them to its not always benign purposes. Worse than this, overwhelming evidence is now emerging that the previously dominant faction within the ANC, with former President Jacob Zuma at its head, was involved in a systematically corrupt relationship with powerful business interests. This disabled state organs from properly implementing constitutionally mandated programs.

In light of these developments, several scholars have criticized the Constitutional Court for being too slow to fashion robust constitutional doctrines to arrest the slide into corruption, clientelism, and nepotism. While the Court's switch from 2008 to a more circumspect attitude toward the ANC was a move in the right direction, this argument goes, the Court might have done more sooner to combat the pathologies that have emerged. In particular, taking its cue from the Colombian Constitutional Court and the Indian Supreme Court, the Court should have engaged in substantive constitutional policy analysis of the problems facing South Africa's democracy, and developed the doctrines required to combat them.

This chapter agrees with these critiques up to a point, but stresses the need for the Court to respect culturally specific understandings of the law/politics boundary, and to work from within traditionally accepted modes of legal reasoning to develop the required doctrines. In particular, South Africa's relatively formalist legal culture means that substantive constitutional policy analysis was more or less off the table as a legitimate doctrinal strategy. Rather, any successful transition by the Court from the first to the second constitutional period required the Court to find either clear textual authority or previously developed precedents for its interventions.

Using that understanding as the appropriate measure, the Court, in the first constitutional period, arguably failed to create the necessary doctrinal markers – or forms of second-order "doctrinal deferral"[6] – that might have better supported its

---

[5]   Rosalind Dixon and Theunis Roux (eds.), *Constitutional Triumphs, Constitutional Disappointments: A Critical Assessment of the 1996 South African Constitution's Local and International Influence*. New York: Cambridge University Press, 2018.

[6]   This term is explained later.

role in the second period and encouraged the kind of litigation that would have seen it intervening sooner and more robustly. While the Court did much to elaborate its role, a close analysis of its case law reveals that several opportunities were missed for the Court to have laid the groundwork for later interventions.

The comparative insight emerging from this analysis is that successful constitutional implementation, by a court and other key institutions, will depend on a mix of sensitivity to the immediate political context, and the degree to which it may change over time, and a legal-doctrinal response that is not only flexible enough to accommodate such a change but supports the litigation and doctrinal developments capable of underpinning the court's changing role.

The remainder of the chapter is divided into four sections. Section 3.2 sets out the background to the 1996 South African Constitution, and its substantive commitments, and the complex nature of any analysis focused on notions of forward-looking constitutional implementation. Section 3.3 explores the first and second periods of constitutional implementation in South Africa: the first, during which the Court tried to enlist the ANC as a partner in constitutional implementation, and the second, in which the Court has shifted to a more active role in constraining the ANC as the dominant political party while building pluralism. Section 3.4 explores criticisms of the government's record of constitutional implementation and the Court's tardiness in responding to these failures. Section 3.5 suggests that for the transition from the first to the second constitutional period to have occurred more effectively, doctrinal markers for this transition were required, and that in many cases, markers of this kind were notably absent in cases in the first period. Section 3.6 offers a brief conclusion about the complex relationship between constitutional politics and legal legitimacy in processes of constitutional implementation, and the role of courts as strategic actors attentive to notions of both political and legal legitimacy.

3.2 THE 1996 CONSTITUTION'S BALANCE BETWEEN CHANGE AND CONTINUITY

In an early commentary, Cass Sunstein described the 1996 South African Constitution as "the world's leading example of a transformative constitution."[7] Much of the literature on post-apartheid constitutionalism has been devoted to developing this idea, with Karl Klare's 1998 paper on "transformative constitutionalism" achieving something close to canonical status.[8] In fact, however, the 1996 South

---

[7] Cass R. Sunstein, "Social and Economic Rights? Lesson from South Africa." *Constitutional Forum* 11 (4): 125 (2000/2001).

[8] Karl E. Klare, "Legal Culture and Transformative Constitutionalism." *South African Journal on Human Rights* 14 (1): 146–88 (1998). (arguing that the success of the transformative South African constitutional project depended on a prior transformation of South African legal culture to embrace a more politicized conception of constitutional adjudication). *See also*

African Constitution is arguably more accurately described as containing both transformative and preservative elements. Its transformative aspect consists in its commitment to an imagined post-apartheid future free of racial and gender discrimination in which the rule of law has been extended to the country's entire population.[9] But the 1996 Constitution is also preservative in the sense that it was the end-product of a negotiated settlement in which the old-order political regime sought to safeguard its constituents' key interests.[10] This feature is most clearly represented by the thirty-four Constitutional Principles, to which the 1996 Constitution had to conform and which to that extent give it a more backward-looking character.[11] But there is an element of preservationism, too, in the general philosophy of social and economic transformation that underpins the 1996 Constitution. Even as it sets out its programmatic vision for social and economic justice, the 1996 Constitution clearly commits itself to gradualist, rights-based reform rather than the revolutionary overthrow of the old order.

With hindsight, it is possible to see that constitution-makers in South Africa were faced with two distinct risks that they had to mitigate. The first was the risk that social and economic transformation would be too radical – that the advent of democracy would be followed by a rush to change all existing institutions and that in the process much that was potentially beneficial about South Africa's colonial legacy – its legal tradition, strong banking and tertiary education sectors, reasonably sound fiscal policies, and the like – would be sacrificed, with no real gains in economic development or poverty reduction. The second risk was just the opposite – that in pursuing gradualist, rights-based social and economic reform, the pace of transformation would be too slow, giving rise to a reactive populism that eventually destroyed the constitutional project.

Of those two possible risks, South Africa's constitution-makers chose to mitigate the first, and hope for the best about the second. Attractive as the 1996 Constitution's vision is, its insistence on gradualist, rights-based social and economic change puts it clearly at the reformist end of the continuum. If change was to occur, it had to occur through law, clear regulatory frameworks and processes that respected existing rights as far as possible and pursued careful balances between those rights and the rights of the new majority.

Etienne Mureinik, "A Bridge to Where? Introducing the Interim Bill of Rights." *South African Journal on Human Rights* 10 (1): 31–48 (1994) (describing the point of South Africa's commitment to rights-based constitutionalism as being to develop a new 'culture of justification').

[9] Jens Meierhenrich, *The Legacies of Law: Long-Run Consequences of Legal Development in South Africa, 1652–2000.* Cambridge University Press, 2008.

[10] On the idea of rights-based constitutions as tools of preservationism, see Ran Hirschl, *Towards Juristocracy: The Origins and Consequences of the New Constitutionalism.* Cambridge, MA: Harvard University Press, 2007.

[11] Schedule IV of the Constitution of the Republic of South Africa 1993 (interim Constitution).

In choosing to go this route, constitution-makers in South Africa tied the fate of liberal-democratic constitutionalism to the success of the gradualist reform model. Wittingly or unwittingly, but now with hindsight quite clearly, the choice of this model meant that popular support for liberal-democratic constitutionalism would be vulnerable to facts on the ground about the actual extent of the reduction of inequality and racial and gender discrimination. More than this, the fate of liberal-democratic constitutionalism as measured by those indicators would not be entirely in the hands of its proponents. To the extent that factors beyond their control – global economic forces, say, or corrupt and nepotistic local politicians – frustrated the achievement of the Constitution's transformative vision, the South African public would not necessarily discriminate between those parts of the failed constitutional project that were attributable to the Constitution's chosen model of reform and those that were not. Liberal-democratic constitutionalism would shoulder the blame either way.

We may ponder now from a distance of a little more than twenty years whether this larger risk was foreseen and, if it was, whether it was taken on with eyes wide open. Almost certainly, the choice in favor of liberal-democratic constitutionalism was not unconstrained. Both South Africa's institutionalized legal tradition and the political dynamics of the constitutional negotiations process itself clearly structured this choice. The option of a more radical approach to social and economic transformation was more or less put off the table as soon as the two major political groupings – the National Party (NP) and the African National Congress (ANC) – decided, for their different reasons, to go the negotiated-settlement route.[12] Once pragmatic, pro-negotiations factions on both sides won out, the gradualist, rights-based model was the only real game in town.

With the 1996 Constitution taking that form, custodianship of the constitutional project was to a large extent handed over to the judiciary. A range of other constitutional institutions – including Parliament and the so-called Chapter 9 integrity institutions – clearly had an important role to play in the process of constitutional implementation. But the dominance of the ANC within many of those institutions, combined with the emphasis on the part of both the ANC and NP on a legally mediated transition, put the newly established Constitutional Court at the center of the constitutional enterprise. While it would clearly be able to draw on the support of civil society organizations – of public impact litigation firms like the Legal Resources Centre and social movements like the Treatment Action Campaign[13] – in the end it was the Constitutional Court that was handed the primary

---

[12] See Mark Gevisser, *Thabo Mbeki: The Dream Deferred*. Johannesburg: Jonathan Ball Publishers, 2007, 526–54 (explaining how Thabo Mbeki's pragmatic vision for negotiated democratic transition triumphed over Chris Hani's more radical, revolutionary vision).

[13] Charles Epp, *The Rights Revolution: Lawyers, Activists, and Supreme Courts in Comparative Perspective*. Chicago: University of Chicago Press, 1998 (on the "support structures" required for a successful rights revolution).

responsibility for making the gradualist, rights-based approach to social and economic transformation work. It is to the Court's performance in that respect that the next section turns.

3.3 TWO PERIODS

If the literature on constitutional courts in new democracies teaches us anything, it is that such courts need to build a constituency.[14] Over and above the particular doctrinal choices that they make, constitutional courts in new democracies face an overarching choice about the general posture they wish to adopt toward major political actors and other potential partners in the constitutional project, whether those be dominant political parties, civil society organizations, business organizations, or the public more generally. That choice of posture must be made on the basis of an analysis of the political context – of the balance of forces favoring the success of the constitutional project, to which the Court's own success as an institution is ultimately tied.

This overarching posture is not something that the Court typically articulates in its judgments. It is not even something that is necessarily consciously discussed among the judges at judicial conferences. But it is nevertheless real and may be discerned in what the Court does and the doctrines it develops.

In South Africa's case, we suggest, there have been two such basic postures since 1994. The first, which spanned roughly the period from 1995–2007, was a posture in which the Court enlisted the ANC as its major ally in the implementation of the constitutional project. The second, spanning the period since then, has been one in which the Court has more or less given up on the ANC as a credible partner, and has sought instead a more diverse set of partners, apparently sensing that South Africa's dominant-party democracy is the major threat to the consolidation of liberal-democratic constitutionalism.

In many of the Court's early cases we thus see the Court paying respectful homage to the ANC as the driving force behind the establishment of democracy and as integral to the success of the constitutional project.[15] The most obvious

[14] See, for example, James L. Gibson, Gregory A. Caldeira, and Vanessa A. Baird, "On the Legitimacy of National High Courts." *American Political Science Review* 92 (2): 343–58 (1998); Lee Epstein, Jack Knight, and Olga Shvetsova, "The Role of Constitutional Courts in the Establishment and Maintenance of Democratic Systems of Government." *Law & Society Review* 35: 117 (2001).

[15] Full a longer version of this argument, see Theunis Roux, *The Politics of Principle: The First South African Constitutional Court, 1995–2005*. Cambridge University Press, 2013 (arguing that the key to the South African Constitutional Court's early success was its ability to enlist the ANC as a partner in the constitutional project). In response to Roux's argument, James Gibson has acknowledged that the ANC's role in mediating the Court's popular support requires an adjustment to his legitimacy theory of judicial review. See James L. Gibson, "Reassessing the Institutional Legitimacy of the South African Constitutional Court: New Evidence, Revised Theory." *Politikon* 43: 53 (2016). For a further penetrating analysis of the Constitutional Court's approach to its mandate, which differs from Roux's account in certain respects, see James

example here is the *Grootboom* decision,[16] in which the Court resisted the invitation to adopt a minimum-core approach and instead opted for reasonableness review – an approach that explicitly opened up a cooperative dialogue with the ANC about how to implement the Constitution's vision for social and economic transformation.[17] The review standard was a deferential one, but deliberately so, leaving space for the ANC to "own" the constitutional project and take charge of it. Other examples include the Court's approach to affirmative action, its use of remedies such as suspended declarations of invalidity, and emphasis on the rejection of apartheid as a constitutional imperative.

As to the first of these additional mechanisms, the Court in early cases was asked to consider a variety of measures designed to address race-based inequalities. The Court consistently upheld these measures, applying a highly deferential standard of review. In *Van Heerden*, for example, the Court upheld a pension plan that distinguished between old (and predominantly white) and new (predominantly black) members of the National Assembly, holding that – provided such a plan sought to benefit a historically disadvantaged racial group – it was almost entirely for Parliament to determine the appropriate scope of such measures.[18] Similarly, in *Bato Star*, in hearing a procedural challenge to the allocation of fishing quotas to various commercial operators, including black empowerment businesses, the Court declined to engage in any form of substantive reasonableness review of the government's actions, suggesting that "the broad goals of transformation can be achieved in a myriad of ways," and that it was for the executive and not the Court to determine the precise means used to promote this goal.[19]

The Court also consistently relied on suspended declarations of invalidity as a tool for enlisting the support of the National Assembly, and thus the ANC, in implementing the constitutional project. For instance, in *Volks NO v. Robinson*, in finding that constitutional commitments to equality required *de facto* as well as legal partners to benefit from spousal support, on the death of a partner, the Court read language into the relevant statute to achieve this, but then suspended the declaration of invalidity for a period of two years.[20] Similarly, in *Fourie*, in finding that the nonrecognition of same-sex marriage was unconstitutional, the Court suspended the relevant declaration of invalidity for a period of twelve months to

---

Fowkes, *Building the Constitution: The Practice of Constitutional Interpretation in Post-Apartheid South Africa.* Cambridge University Press, 2016.

[16] *Government of the Republic of South Africa v. Grootboom* 2000 (11) BCLR 1169 (CC).

[17] See Rosalind Dixon, "Creating Dialogue about Socioeconomic Rights: Strong- v. Weak-Form Judicial Review Revisited." *International Journal of Constitutional Law* 5: 391 (2007).

[18] *Minister of Finance v. Van Heerden* 2004 (6) SA 121.

[19] *Bato Star Fishing (Pty) Ltd v. Minister of Environmental Affairs and Tourism* 2004 (4) SA 490 pars 35–41.

[20] *Volks NO v. Robinson* 2005 (5) BCLR 446.

give the National Assembly a chance to remedy the defect.[21] Remedies of this kind not only delay the legal effect of a finding of constitutional invalidity. They require legislators to take active steps to redress constitutional violations, thereby effectively enlisting them as partners in the constitutional project.[22]

Finally, in the first decade of the Constitution's operation, the Court repeatedly invoked the idea of apartheid as a form of constitutional "never again." In *Makwanyane*, the first case ever heard by the Court, the Court emphasized the link between the constitutional commitment to human dignity and the break from apartheid, reasoning that "apartheid was a denial of common humanity. Black people were refused respect and dignity and thereby the dignity of all South Africans was diminished."[23] In *Phillips* v. *Director of Public Prosecutions*, the Court connected commitments to freedom of expression to the repudiation of apartheid, by characterizing apartheid-era norms and practices as a "restrictive past where expression, especially political and artistic expression, was extensively circumscribed."[24] In *Bernstein* v. *Bester*, the Court characterized a broad commitment to privacy as a response to apartheid-era practices of restricting liberty, suggesting that "the government's frequent violation of individual freedom in the years of apartheid" was a reason to favor a broad view of the right to privacy under the 1996 Constitution.[25] In *Ferreira* v. *Levin*, the Court connected commitments to individual freedom to the repudiation of apartheid.[26] In *Lawyers for Human Rights* v. *Minister for Home Affairs*, the Court emphasized the importance of protections against arbitrary detention "in light of [South Africa's apartheid-era] history during which illegitimate detentions without trial of many effective opponents of the pre-1994 government policy of apartheid abounded."[27] In *S* v. *Lawrence*, the Court linked a commitment to religious pluralism, or the avoidance of giving preference to Christianity, as a response to the history of religious discrimination under apartheid.[28] In the *Gauteng School Bill Case*, the Court linked the scope of education rights under s 32 of the 1993 Interim Constitution to the apartheid-era system of Bantu education, which

---

[21] *Minister of Home Affairs* v. *Fourie* 2006 (1) SA 524. In the course of its judgment, the Court stated that "[i]t needs to be remembered that not only the courts are responsible for vindicating the rights enshrined in the Bill of Rights. The legislature is in the frontline in this respect." Ibid. para 138.
[22] Compare Rosalind Dixon and Samuel Issacharoff, "Living to Fight Another Day: Judicial Deferral in Defense of Democracy." *Wisconsin Law Review* 583 (2016). See also Kent Roach, "Remedial Consensus and Dialogue under the Charter: General Declarations and Delayed Declarations of Invalidity." *University of British Columbia Law Review* 35: 211 (2001); Po Jen Yap, *Constitutional Dialogue in Common Law Asia*. Oxford: Oxford University Press, 2015.
[23] 1995 (3) SA 391 par 51.
[24] 2003 (3) SA 345 par 23.
[25] 1996 (2) SA 751 par 144.
[26] 1996 (1) SA 984 par 51.
[27] 2017 (5) SA 480 par 37 (further emphasizing that "we must never again allow a situation in which that is countenanced").
[28] 1997 (4) SA 1176 pars 148–52.

created a racially segregated public education and prohibition on private schools (including multi-racial schools).[29] In *Bhe* v. *Khayelitsha*, in holding that customary law should be developed in light of the Constitution, the Court linked this project to the repudiation of apartheid-era practices of marginalizing and fossilizing customary law.[30] In taking this approach, the Court also effectively connected the entire South African constitutional project to the ANC's political agenda – of creating a transition to true multi-racial democracy, or black-majority rule.

The adoption of the Court's second basic posture began around 2008 and corres-ponded to the deposing of Thabo Mbeki as President and the rise of Jacob Zuma.[31] From this time, the Court progressively lost confidence in the ANC as a central partner in the constitutional project. Instead, it sought to enlist a wider range of partners in an apparent effort to contribute to the building of a more diffuse, pluralist democracy. The main shifts in its jurisprudence that signal this underlying change in posture are: (1) the emergence of "meaningful engagement" as the preferred approach to the resolution of social and economic rights claims (thus changing the Court's partners from national-level policy makers to local-level municipalities responsible for implementation);[32] (2) a growing concern for the quality of the ANC's *internal* democratic processes as a way of stimulating pluralism within South Africa's dominant political party;[33] and (3) the more direct targeting of pathologies of nepotism and corruption (for example, by insisting on proper

---

[29] *Gauteng Provincial Legislature In re: Gauteng School Education Bill of 1995* 1996 (3) SA 165 par 8. See also par 46 per Sachs J.

[30] 2005 (1) SA 580 par 43. Compare also Penelope Andrews, "Women and Rights," in *The Post-Apartheid Constitution: Perspectives on South Africa's Basic Law*, ed. P. Andrews and S. Ellman. Athens: Ohio University Press, 2001, 347–48; Dennis Davis, "Deconstructing and Reconstructing the Argument for a Bill of Rights within the Context of South African Nationalism," in *The Post-Apartheid Constitution: Perspectives on South Africa's Basic Law*, ed. P. Andrews and S. Ellman. Athens: Ohio University Press, 2001, 207, 228.

[31] Mbeki was deposed as President of the ANC at the 52nd ANC National Conference in Polokwane in December 2007. Mbeki resigned as President of South Africa in September 2008. See Jeremy Gordin, *Zuma: A Biography*. Johannesburg: Jonathan Ball, 2008; William Mervyn Gumede, *Thabo Mbeki and the Battle for the Soul of the ANC*. Cape Town: Zebra Press, 2007.

[32] See, for example, *Occupiers of 51 Olivia Road, Berea Township and 197 Main Street Johannes-burg* v. *City of Johannesburg and Others* 2008 (5) BCLR 475 (CC); *Residents of Joe Slovo Community, Western Cape* v. *Thebelisha Homes and Others* 2011 (7) BCLR 651 (CC). The Court's "meaningful engagement" jurisprudence is discussed in Brian Ray, *Engaging with Social Rights: Procedure, Participation, and Democracy in South Africa's Second Wave*. Cam-bridge University Press, 2016, 105–29.

[33] See, for example *Ramakatsa* v. *Magashule* 2013 (2) BCLR 202 (CC) (enforcing ANC's procedural rules governing the selection of delegates to a provincial party conference, discussed in Theunis Roux, "Constitutional Courts as Democratic Consolidators: Insights from South Africa after Twenty Years." *Journal of Southern African Studies* 42: 5, 16 (2016).

qualifications for senior appointees and challenging the ANC's policy of cadre deployment to that extent).[34]

The case that perhaps best exemplifies this second period is the so-called *Nkandla Case*, which involved a challenge to the non-implementation of certain recommendations made by the Public Protector.[35] Previously lacking in independence, the Public Protector had been emboldened by the courageous leadership of its then head, Thuli Madonsela, to produce a damning report on unauthorized state expenditure on former President's Zuma's rural homestead. When the National Assembly purported to absolve the President of the need to act on the report's recommendations, two opposition political parties applied to the Constitutional Court for a declaration that the President and the Speaker of the National Assembly had breached their constitutional obligations. In a highly critical judgment, the Court ruled that there had indeed been a violation of the Constitution and ordered the President personally to pay for that portion of the state expenditure that could not be justified.[36]

The significance of the *Nkandla Case* is that it (a) signaled a clear shift toward enlisting the 'Chapter 9 institutions' (institutions supporting constitutional democracy) as partners in the enforcement of the Constitution and (b) showed that the Court was prepared to directly criticize a senior national leader and identify his behavior as a threat to constitutional democracy. This much may be inferred from the fact that the Court's decision, while legally plausible, was not doctrinally compelled. Section 181(5) of the 1996 Constitution provides that the Public Protector is "accountable to the National Assembly," seemingly suggesting that the lower house of Parliament has the power to decide whether to act on the Public Protector's recommendations. Against this, the Constitutional Court needed to do a fair bit of legal work to justify its holding that recommendations made by the Public Protector could not be overridden by the National Assembly. Its preparedness to do that work is indicative of its post-2007 posture of broadening the pool of partners responsible for the implementation of the constitutional project.

At the same time, the *Nkandla Case* arguably had the indirect effect of contributing to political diffusion by damaging the ANC's reputation among voters. In the

---

[34] See *Justice Alliance of South Africa* v. *President of Republic of South Africa* 2011 (5) SA 388 (CC) (overturning parliamentary delegation of power to President to extend Chief Justice's term of office); *Democratic Alliance* v. *President of the Republic of South Africa* 2013 (1) SA 248 (CC) (rescinding the appointment of a new National Director of Public Prosecutions on the basis that the constitutional specifications for the position had not been fulfilled and the fact that adverse findings had been made by a commission of inquiry about the appointee's reliability as a witness).

[35] *Economic Freedom Fighters* v. *Speaker of the National Assembly and Others; Democratic Alliance* v. *Speaker of the National Assembly and Others* (2016) 3 SA 580 (CC). See Heinz Klug, "Corruption, the Rule of Law & the Role of Independent Institutions," in Rosalind Dixon and Theunis Roux, n. 5.

[36] *Economic Freedom Fighters*, n. 35.

2016 South African municipal elections held on August 3, four months after the *Nkandla Case*, the ANC's overall share of the vote declined to 53.9 percent,[37] a shocking result for a party previously assured of a near two-thirds majority. While the *Nkandla Case*'s contribution to this result cannot, of course, be determined with any certainty, it is fair to assume that it played at least some role, along with other factors discussed in the next section.

3.4 CRITICISM OF THE ANC'S RECORD AND OF THE COURT'S RESPONSE

The shine has long ago come off South Africa's democratic transition "miracle."[38] As numerous studies over the last ten years attest, significant problems of neo-patrimonialism, clientelism, and corruption have emerged. Mocking the Constitution's grand promises, economic inequality has in fact deepened since 1993, with the Gini co-efficient (expenditure per capita excluding taxes) sliding from 0.59 in that year to 0.67 in 2006.[39] Health and other quality of life indicators are also down. In KwaZulu-Natal, there are only two oncologists left in the public-sector hospital system, with none in the capital city of Durban able to train new doctors.[40] The secondary education system has long been in crisis, with textbooks regularly undelivered in Limpopo and Eastern Cape Provinces.[41] The university student fees crisis dominated the news in 2016, with most major tertiary education institutions forced to close down for several months and exams missed.[42] Imprudent economic management decisions are regular occurrences, including the politically inspired ousting of trusted Finance Minister Pravin Gordhan on March 30, 2017, which led to the downgrading of South Africa's credit rating to junk status.[43] Earlier, in October 2016,

---

[37] Available at www.elections.org.za/content/Elections/Municipal-elections-results/.

[38] The use of the term "miracle" to describe South Africa's democratic transition is ubiquitous in journalistic accounts. See for example, Patti Waldmeir, *Anatomy of a Miracle: The End of Apartheid and the Birth of the New South Africa*. London: Viking, 1997; Allister Sparks, *Beyond the Miracle: Inside the New South Africa*. University of Chicago Press, 2003.

[39] The World Bank, *World Development Indicators: Distribution of Income or Consumption* (2013).

[40] Katharine Child, "Too Few Oncologists Left in KZN to Train New Cancer Specialists," Times Live (NZ), June 25, 2017, www.timeslive.co.za/news/2017-06-25-too-few-oncologists-left-in-kzn-to-train-new-cancer-specialists/. Since 2006, South Africa's Gini-coefficient has improved slightly, to 0.65 in 2011 (Statistics South Africa, *Poverty Trends in South Africa: An Examination of Absolute Poverty between 2006 and 2011* [2014] 14).

[41] See Bongani Nkosi, "South Africa's Hidden Textbook Crisis," *Mail and Guardian* (NZ), August 23, 2013, https://mg.co.za/article/2013-08-23-00-south-africas-hidden-textbook-crisis.

[42] See Janet Cherry, "The Successes and Failures of South Africa's Student Movement," *Waging Non-Violence*, June 29, 2017, https://wagingnonviolence.org/feature/south-africa-fees-must-fall/.

[43] S&P Global rating of April 3, 2017.

South Africa had slipped down the rankings in the Mo Ibrahim Foundation's report on "a decade of African democracy."[44]

Most significant of all these problems, perhaps, has been the rise and seeming entrenchment of corruption and nepotism. The second edition of R. W. Johnson's classic *How Long Will South Africa Survive?* documents in excruciating detail how public tenders and other processes have been manipulated.[45] Even before the ousting of former President Jacob Zuma in early 2018, evidence began emerging of how South Africa had been captured by a "power elite" that exploited the "symbiotic relationship" between the "constitutional state" and a "shadow state."[46] Following a report by the Public Protector,[47] the so-called Zondo Commission on State Capture was established in 2019 to hear testimony on how the Gupta brothers, who came to South Africa from India in 1993, managed to influence the dismissal and appointment of senior managers of State-Owned Enterprises.[48]

South Africa's descent into economic mismanagement and corruption has had the predictable result of stimulating the growth of populist parties, with the Economic Freedom Fighters (EFF) chief among them. The EFF's policy platform calls for radical land reform and nationalization of the mining and banking sectors.[49] It garnered 8.2 percent of the vote at the August 2016 municipal elections,[50] giving it the balance of power in several large municipalities evenly divided between the ANC and the main opposition party, the Democratic Alliance. The ANC, in response, has itself become more populist, with leading spokesmen talking about the second stage of national democratic revolution in which economic liberation, through radical land reform and other measures, will follow political liberation.[51]

It is clear to most informed observers that the ANC's talk of radical social and economic transformation is largely rhetoric, and that it has no viable plan to implement such a program. Under former President Zuma, this talk was simply an ideological smokescreen for the real project of state capture.[52] Now, under

---

[44] Mo Ibrahim Foundation, *A Decade of African Governance 2006–2015* (October 2016) (as cited in Tom Daly, "Diagnosing Democratic Decay," paper presented at Comparative Constitutional Law Roundtable, Gilbert & Tobin Centre of Public Law, UNSW, Sydney, August 7, 2017).

[45] R. W. Johnson, *How Long Will South Africa Survive? The Looming Crisis*. Johannesburg: Jonathan Ball Publishers, 2015. See also Andrew Feinstein, *After the Party: A Personal and Political Journey inside the ANC*. Johannesburg: Jonathan Ball Publishers, 2007 (detailing the corruption surrounding the Arms Deal).

[46] Haroon Bhorat et al, *Betrayal of the Promise: How South Africa Is Being Stolen*. State Capacity Research Project, May 2017.

[47] Public Protector, *State of Capture*, Report 6 of 2016/17 (October 14, 2016).

[48] www.sastatecapture.org.za/.

[49] See www.effonline.org/policy.

[50] See www.elections.org.za/content/Elections/Municipal-elections-results/.

[51] See ANC "Is the National Democratic Revolution in Danger?" NGC 2015 Discussion Documents available at www.anc.org.za/docs/discus/2015/balancer.pdf.

[52] Bhorat et al., n 48.

President Cyril Ramaphosa, policy proposals such as the amendment of the 1996 Constitution's property clause are being driven by the need to combat the EFF's populist agenda. Nevertheless, at this rhetorical level, the path of radical reform that South Africa chose to avoid in 1994 is seemingly back on the agenda, and with that, a reinvigorated critique of the failings of the gradualist reform model associated with liberal-democratic constitutionalism. After a lull of some years, the 1996 Constitution is once again openly being spoken about as a white-minority compromise constitution that needs to be comprehensively overhauled if the national democratic revolution is to succeed.

It is not all doom and gloom. The Constitutional Court has had remarkable successes – chief among them the *Nkandla Case*. It is significant here that the EFF was a party to that case, as the Congress of South African Trade Unions (COSATU) had earlier been party to the *Treatment Action Campaign Case*.[53] But the EFF's respect for constitutionalism is clearly opportunistic – it exploits popular disaffection with the Constitution as a barrier to radical reform one day, and uses the opportunities it provides for challenging the ANC and exposing its flaws the next.

For many, the Constitutional Court has been too slow in reacting to this changed political context. In a 2009 paper, for example, Sujit Choudhry called for the Court to develop a series of "anti-domination," "anti-capture," "non-usurpation," "anti-seizure," and "anti-centralization" doctrines to counter the pathological effects of the ANC's political dominance.[54] Samuel Issacharoff, too, in various publications, has called for the Court to adopt a more robust and creative approach to its mandate, on the model of the Indian Supreme Court and the Colombian Constitutional Court.[55] One of the main targets of his and Choudhry's critique in this respect has been the *UDM* case,[56] in which the Court dismissed a claim that the removal of a constitutional ban on floor-crossing undermined South Africa's democracy. In Choudhry and Issacharoff's view, the Court should have renounced formalism and engaged in substantive constitutional policy analysis of the problems facing the country, and the pathologies of South Africa's dominant-party democracy in particular.

---

[53] *Minister of Health* v. *Treatment Action Campaign* 2002 (5) SA 721.

[54] Sujit Choudhry, "'He Had a Mandate': The South African Constitutional Court and the African National Congress in a Dominant Party Democracy." *Constitutional Court Review* 2: 1, 6 (2009).

[55] Samuel Issacharoff, "Constitutional Courts and Democratic Hedging." *Georgetown Law Journal* 99: 961 (2011); Samuel Issacharoff, "The Democratic Risk to Democratic Transitions." *Constitutional Court Review* 5: 1 (2014).

[56] *United Democratic Movement* v. *President of the Republic of South Africa and Others* (*African Christian Democratic Party and Others Intervening; Institute for Democracy and Another as Amici Curiae*) (*No 1*) 2003 (1) SA 488 (CC), 2002 (11) BCLR 1179 (CC).

Earlier, the Court's reasonableness review standard had been vigorously critiqued as too deferential – as not recognizing the urgency of the poor's needs.[57] Others have accused the Court of "proceduralizing" social and economic rights, to the point where they have largely been blunted as tools for driving meaningful change.[58] The next section turns to assess the merits of these claims and to inquire whether the Court might have done more to anticipate the shift to the second constitutional period sketched in Section 3.3.

3.5 DOCTRINAL MARKERS

Could the Constitutional Court have done more to anticipate and prepare for the decline in the quality of South Africa's democracy and the problems of constitutional implementation this has brought with it? Our answer to this question is mixed. While sympathetic to Choudhry and Issacharoff's analysis that the Court should have responded more creatively and robustly to the ANC's dominant position, we take a slightly different approach to the institutional context in which it was operating. Given the constraints of South Africa's legal tradition, we argue, the Court could not, and should not, have engaged in the sort of substantive constitutional policy analysis in which the Indian Supreme Court and Colombian Constitutional Court have engaged. Nevertheless, the Court might have begun earlier to lay down doctrinal markers that would have smoothed the transition to the new political context it faced after 2007.[59]

Choudhry's suggestions about anti-domination doctrines, in particular, seem to us to downplay the constitutional-cultural constraints that the Court was under – the constraints, that is, not so much of doctrine but of legal tradition.[60] Any developed legal tradition, this line of thinking goes, maintains an understanding of the appropriate relationship between law and politics – of the judiciary's legitimate sphere of authority as defined by past decisions, its remedial powers and legitimate forms of legal reasoning.[61] With the adoption of judicial review, traditional understandings of the boundary between law and politics become in many ways more important to respect, even as the introduction of judicial review provides a justification for

---

[57] David Bilchitz, *Poverty and Fundamental Rights: The Justification and Enforcement of Socio-Economic Rights.* Oxford University Press, 2007.

[58] Danie Brand, "The Proceduralisation of South African Socio-Economic Rights Jurisprudence or 'What Are Socio-economic Rights for?'" in *Rights and Democracy in a Transformative Constitution*, ed. Henk Botha, Andre van der Walt, and Johan van der Walt. Stellenbosch: Sun Press, 2003, 33.

[59] See Dixon and Issacharoff, n. 22. This section also draws on the related concept of "adjudicative strategy" developed in Roux, n. 15, 99–101.

[60] The idea of law's constraining role here derives from Karl N. Llewellyn, *The Common Law Tradition: Deciding Appeals.* Boston, MA: Little Brown, 1960.

[61] See also Theunis Roux, "The South African Constitutional Court's Democratic Rights Jurisprudence: A Response to Samuel Issacharoff." *Constitutional Court Review* 5: 33 (2014).

reimagining them. Precisely because it threatens to politicize their role, courts with the power of judicial review need to work hard to maintain an impression of themselves as legal actors. The requirement that they remain within the culturally defined bounds of permissible judicial conduct exerts a moderately constraining influence on their capacity to respond to a changing political context. If new constitutional doctrines are required to combat emerging democratic pathologies, judges in formalist legal traditions,[62] for example, may have to work toward those doctrines more systematically than judges in substantive traditions, where doctrines may be derived through constitutional policy analysis of the threat posed to democracy by the political actors the Court is trying to rein in.

This law/politics boundary as defined by past decisions, remedial powers, and legitimate forms of legal reasoning is not static or uncontested, of course. Precedents and the scope of the court's remedial powers will be open to interpretation and development, particularly in a new constitutional democracy where judicial review has been introduced for the first time. Different forms of legal reasoning – more formalist and more substantive styles, for example – will also be present in a single legal tradition, and it may be internally contested within that tradition which best serves the rule of law or best justifies the court's powers. Nevertheless, beneath these differences, there may be a dominant conception of the appropriate role of the court in developing new doctrines and asserting new powers that exerts a moderately constraining influence on what a court may do. In the South African case, the "cautious traditions of analysis," to which Karl Klare referred in his article on "transformative constitutionalism,"[63] arguably constrained the sort of response Choudhry recommended – of developing anti-domination doctrines on the back of an explicitly substantive constitutional policy analysis of the problems facing the country. Rather, the Court had to work more systematically to build an adequate legal justification for its changing role. If it was to address the problem of the ANC's political dominance, there had to be clear textual basis or other authority for its interventions, and the required doctrines had to be developed on the basis of that authority, however formalistically.

A good example of the operation of these moderate constraints is *Glenister II*,[64] in which a narrow majority of the Court turned to international law rather than substantive constitutional policy analysis to hold that the disbanding of the Directorate of Special Operations (aka the Scorpions), an effective corruption-fighting unit within the National Prosecuting Authority, and the transfer of its functions to the Directorate of Priority Crime Investigation (aka the Hawks), under the control of the

---

[62] See Patrick S. Atiyah and Robert S. Summers, *Form and Substance in Anglo-American Law: A Comparative Study of Legal Reasoning, Legal Theory, and Legal Institutions*. Oxford: Clarendon Press, 1987.

[63] Klare, n 8.

[64] *Glenister v. President of the Republic of South Africa and Others* 2011 (3) SA 347 (CC); 2011 (7) BCLR 651 (CC).

South African Police Service, was unconstitutional. Rather than confronting head-on the politically explosive allegation that the disbanding of the Scorpions had been motivated by a corrupt desire to incapacitate it, the majority reached for a strained deduction from general international-law norms to develop specific constitutional duties.[65] In South Africa's legal tradition, this kind of reasoning, which may seem highly formalistic to an American observer, is seen to be more authentically legal, and thus carries greater authority, than substantive constitutional policy analysis.

Within these moderate constraints of background legal tradition and constitutional culture, of course, courts do have some capacity for agency. Even in very formalist legal traditions, judges may work toward new doctrines by progressively building authority for them. Elsewhere, in joint work with Samuel Issacharoff, one of us called this the strategy of second-order – or *Marbury* v. *Madison*-style – judicial "deferral."[66] In essence, this strategy involves the court laying down doctrinal markers that anticipate future problems and provide a basis for it later to move into areas that may currently be regarded as off-limits. Specifically, we suggest that courts can use deferral as a tool for anticipating future threats to democracy – or marking the potential for future judicial doctrines limiting the actions of democratic elites. From a democratic "hedging" perspective, the key function of doctrinal markers of this kind is to (a) articulate the institutional "minimum core" necessary for a system of true, multi-party democracy and (b) anticipate the potential long-term, as well as short-term, threats to this democratic minimum core.[67] Doctrinal markers of this kind serve a number of important functions: They suggest to lawyers or advocates potential lines of argument to which members of the court might be receptive.[68] This also has both direct and indirect effects on constitutional litigation. It encourages lawyers to make certain arguments, or bring cases, that allow the court to develop its jurisprudence in a particular direction. And it indicates to lower courts the direction the court might be willing to take in later cases, so that those courts are more willing to develop new lines of reasoning and argument, and parties have a higher chance of success at first instance, or at a lower court level, in ways that substantially reduce the costs of – and thus encourage – new and creative forms of constitutional litigation. One of the defining features of courts, compared to other

---

[65] See the discussion in Samuel Issacharoff, "The Democratic Risk to Democratic Transitions." *Constitutional Court Review* 5: 1, 27–29 (2014).

[66] Dixon and Issacharoff, n. 22. See also Roux, n. 15, 99–101 (referring to this kind of strategy and as an "adjudicative strategy" and distinguishing it from the purely political strategies – such as those contemplated in "tolerance-interval theory" – recommended by political-science accounts of institutional-legitimacy building).

[67] In this way they are similar to, but also distinct from, other forms of dicta found in dissenting or concurring opinions.

[68] Compare the function of dissenting and concurring opinions generally as discussed in Richard B. Stephens, "The Function of Concurring and Dissenting Opinions in Courts of Last Resort." *University of Florida Law Review* 5: 394 (1952); William J. Brennan Jr, "In Defence of Dissents." *Hastings Law Journal* 37: 427 (1987); Ruth Bader Ginsburg, "Remarks on Writing Separately." *Washington Law Review* 65: 133 (1990).

institutions, is that they have control over their docket only in one direction: they can decline to hear particular cases, but they cannot add cases to their agenda without parties first bringing a case to court.

Doctrinal markers of this kind can also gradually shift the broader perception of lawyers, and legal scholars, as to the bounds of legitimate constitutional argument. By setting out certain arguments in dictum, reasoning of this kind can create a body of reasoning that, over time, re-shapes the attitudes of lawyers of what counts as an argument that is internal to the legal system.[69] In countries where lawyers are also important political players, this can also shape broader perceptions of the legitimacy of certain forms of judicial review.[70] This is also extremely important in cases in which a court ultimately attempts to confront powerful political actors: For doctrinal markers to be part of a strategy of "deferral," rather than persistent avoidance, courts must at some point be willing to enforce the constraints they have foreshadowed, if and when the relevant threats to democracy arise.[71] But judicial review of this kind also poses clear risks for a court: it can provoke a severe political backlash that undermines the court's independence, jurisdiction, and budget, and thus its capacity to perform its most constitutional functions.[72] It will thus be critical for a court to have as many allies as possible – including lawyers, and the legal profession, as an important part of the support structure for courts.[73] This understanding of the South African Constitutional Court's capacity for agency, we suggest, is the appropriate measure of whether it did enough to ensure the successful implementation of the gradualist, rights-based constitutional project it was asked to oversee. Did it exploit the opportunities that it had to invite litigation and prepare the doctrinal way for the time when it could no longer rely on the ANC as a constitutional partner? Did it

---

[69] Compare Dixon and Issacharoff, n. 22.

[70] See, e.g., Steven A. Boutcher, "Lawyering for Social Change: Pro Bono Publico, Cause Lawyering, and the Social Movement Society." *Mobilization* 18 (2013); Sandra R. Levitsky, "To Lead with Law: Reassessing the Influence of Legal Advocacy Organizations in Social Movements," in *Cause Lawyers and Social Movements*, ed. A. Sarat and S. A. Scheingold. Stanford, CA: Stanford University Press, 145.

[71] See ibid. Compare Erin F. Delaney, "Analyzing Avoidance: Judicial Strategy in Comparative Perspective." *Duke Law Journal* 66: 1 (2016) (distinguishing avoidance as a distinct strategy). *Courts that promise deferral, but then consistently avoid confronting an issue, may also rapidly lose legitimacy and authority because of such actions.*

[72] See Stephen Gardbaum, "Are Strong Constitutional Courts Always a Good Thing for New Democracies?" *Columbia Journal of Transnational Law* 53: 285 (2015) (Gardbaum argues against judicial review of this kind in part for this reason). See also Tom Gerald Daly, "The Alchemists: Courts as Democracy-Builders in Contemporary Thought." *Global Constitutionalism* 6: 101 (2017) (for a critical review of judicial review of this kind).

[73] Compare Siri Gloppen, *Social Rights Litigation as Transformation: South African Perspectives*. Chr Micelsen Institute, 2005 (on a somewhat different notion of the support structure for social rights litigation provided by civil society). Compare also Michael McCann, "Law and Social Movements: Contemporary Perspectives." *Annual Review of Law and Social Science* 2: 17 (2006); Charles R. Epp, *The Rights Revolution: Lawyers, Activists, and Supreme Courts in Comparative Perspective*. University of Chicago Press, 1998.

move quickly enough to realize that the ANC was not going to be the partner it expected, and begin to lay down doctrinal markers for the second period, the period when the success of the constitutional project depended on its contributing to greater political pluralism?

The answer to these questions depends in part, of course, on the knowledge of members of the Constitutional Court about the potential future threats to constitutional democracy in South Africa, or how foreseeable those risks were to the justices at various times: It is, of course, possible that it is only with the benefit of hindsight that we now see the importance of doctrinal markers of this kind.[74] But we also believe that there were factors making the risk at least somewhat foreseeable to the justices: first, comparative experience in Africa and globally clearly points to the dangers for a new democracy, as it confronts the transition from the first- to the second-generation of political leadership. Many of the justices would also have been aware of that experience, from years spent working and studying while in exile, or for their broader professional experience. Second, several of the justices had first-hand experience working with President Mandela,[75] and so would have known how exceptional Mandela was in his commitment to the Court and the constitutional project, and thus that this level of commitment would inevitably decline within the ANC, over time. Third, the Court itself showed some real awareness of these future risks in its judgment in the *First Certification Case*.[76] The Court, for instance, stressed the need for heightened entrenchment of the Bill of Rights, and more onerous procedures for constitutional amendment generally, thereby implicitly anticipating the ANC's likely future dominance in the National Assembly.[77] It stressed the independence of the judiciary as a key constitutional principle, and suggested that this principle would be compromised if judicial appointments could be made by the President and National Assembly alone, without the involvement of the judiciary and profession.[78] And it held that the independence of various Chapter 9 institutions, such as the public protector, was "vital to ensuring effective, accountable and responsible government."[79] This again also seemed implicitly to acknowledge the potential future risk to democracy if the ANC were to continue to control both the executive and legislative branches of government. The decision thus confirms that the Court was a high-capacity court, with an appreciation of its legal and political role, capable of crafting a constitutional jurisprudence containing valuable democratic markers. We thus suggest two possible important doctrinal markers available to the Court in the first period, in addition to those it laid down

---

[74] We are indebted to Richard Joseph for pressing us on this point.

[75] See Rosalind Dixon, "Constitutional Design Two Ways: Constitutional Drafters as Judges." *Virginia Journal of International Law* 51: 1 (2017).

[76] *Certification of the Constitution of the Republic of South Africa* 1996 (4) SA 744.

[77] Ibid. pars 156, 159.

[78] Ibid. par 124.

[79] Ibid. par 163.

in the *First Certification Case*, which could arguably have helped lay the groundwork for a more rapid and effective transition to the second period: first, a greater
emphasis on transparency and good process in cases that gave the Court broad
substantive freedom to define the scope of relevant government programs; and
second, an emphasis on some form of "democratic minimum core," not capable
of being altered by either legislation or constitutional amendment.

In *Van Heerden*,[80] for instance, in upholding the broad scope of legislators and
executive officials to determine the scope of measures to benefit a historically
disadvantaged racial groups, the Court could readily have adopted a notion of
political *transparency* as a prerequisite for reliance on section 9(3): It could have
required that before this special constitutional gate-way can be engaged, the Assembly must announce a decision to rely on a power of this kind, and thus take political
accountability for such a decision. Similarly, in *Bato Star*,[81] the Court could have
endorsed a highly deferential standard of substantive view of economic transformation decisions but announced a more demanding set of procedural constraints on
decisions of this kind *in dictum*.

Traces of an approach of this kind may in fact be found in the Court's earlier
decision in *Walker* addressing the constitutionality of a Pretoria City Council water
policy with racially disparate impacts.[82] The substantive disparate impact, the Court
held, was substantively justified under section 9 of the Constitution, as a means of
promoting a culture of payment in historically under-serviced black neighborhoods.
But the Court also imposed a high procedural standard for the Council – in terms of
the need for an official process of debate over such a policy, and transparency and
consistency in approach. This was also all by way of dictum: The Court found that
the policy was unlawful for failure to follow such procedures and requirements of
proper legal authorization under section 33 of the Interim Constitution, but refused
to grant Mr. Walker any concrete remedy – on the basis that he did not have a right
to refuse to pay his water rates, only a claim that others should pay more in certain
circumstances.

Similarly, in early cases concerning the democratic process, the Court focused
largely on rights-based violations, without taking the opportunity to lay down
markers for a more *structural* approach to the defense of democracy.[83] For instance,
in *August* v. *Electoral Commission*,[84] the Court emphasized the foundational nature
of the right to vote, as "a badge of dignity and of personhood,"[85] and that prisoners
could not be denied the right to vote without proper legislative authorization. But it

---

[80] *Minister of Finance* v. *Van Heerden* 2004 (6) SA 121 (CC).

[81] *Bato Star Fishing (Pty) Ltd* v. *Minister of Environmental Affairs and Tourism* 2004 (4) SA 490.

[82] *City of Pretoria* v. *Walker* 1998 (2) SA 363.

[83] Compare Samuel Issacharoff, Pamela S. Karlan, and Richard H. Pildes, *The Law of Democracy: Legal Structure of the Political Process*. Foundation Press, 2002.

[84] 1999 (3) SA 1 (CC).

[85] Ibid. par 17.

did relatively little to spell out the idea that the right to vote "is one of the foundational values of our entire constitutional order,"[86] or that legislative or executive action that threatened the democratic constitutional order could itself be subject to judicial review. In *NICRO*, in considering the new form of limitation on prisoner voting imposed by the National Assembly, the Court likewise emphasized the importance of the relevant right,[87] and the need for transparent legislative deliberation about any decision to limit the right,[88] without any real emphasis on the degree to which decisions of this kind could affect the competitiveness of democracy, or accountability of key government institutions.

Similarly, in early cases concerning the law of defamation, and its relation to constitutional commitments to freedom of expression, privacy, and dignity, the Court largely focused on the individual rights-based dimension to these questions – and failed to draw out the importance of a free media, public criticism of government officials, and *robust political competition* for the health of democracy in South Africa. In *Khumalo*, the Court emphasized the balance struck by the Supreme Court in *Bogoshi* "between freedom of expression and the values of human dignity,"[89] without pausing to emphasize the importance – to competitive democracy – of freedom to criticize leaders of the *dominant political party* – i.e. Khumalo, as a leading ANC politician,[90] alleged to have been involved in a gang of bank robbers, and to be under police investigation.

In cases such as *UDM* v. *Speaker of the National Assembly*,[91] this also made it more difficult for the Court to identify any formal doctrinal basis on which to limit the partisan consolidation of power by the ANC. The petitioners in the *UDM* case argued that the Speaker of the Assembly was wrong to refuse to authorize a secret ballot for motions of no confidence in the President. The Court responded with a ruling that fit with the relatively restrained conception of its role, which predominated in the first period: It made it clear that it was open to the Speaker to adopt a process of this kind, and that the Speaker had a constitutional duty to uphold the values of the Constitution – including openness – in this context, but that it was ultimately for the Speaker and not the Court to stipulate the relevant voting procedure. One possible contributing factor to this decision could also clearly have been the fact that, in the first period, the Court laid down few doctrinal markers to support the idea that the intensity of judicial review should be calibrated to the seriousness of the threat posed to South Africa's democracy.[92]

---

[86] Ibid.

[87] *Minister of Home Affairs* v. *National Institute for Crime Prevention and the Re-integration of Offenders* 2005 (3) SA 280. See also at par 113 per Madala J (dissenting).

[88] Ibid. pars 66–67.

[89] *Khumalo* v. *Holomisa* 2002 (5) SA 401 par 43.

[90] Vincent Khumalo, *Gauteng Provincial Legislature*, www.pa.org.za/person/khumalo-sakhiwe/.

[91] *United Democratic Movement* v. *Speaker of the National Assembly* 2017 (8) BCLR 1061 (CC).

[92] The only exception was the *Certification Case*. See e.g. discussion of the case in *United Democratic Movement* v. *Speaker of the National Assembly* 2017 (8) BCLR 1061 par 77.

Doctrinal markers of this kind would clearly have required a certain degree of delicacy or diplomacy on the part of the Court: Too strong or blunt an emphasis on future threats to democracy could readily have undermined the Court's attempt, in the first period, to engage the ANC as a partner in the process of constitutional implementation. But courts also have a variety of tools with which to anticipate future dangers, while still maintaining (at least rhetorically) a belief in the good faith of current decision-makers: they can choose to place certain markers in footnotes, or phrase them in relatively abstract terms, or emphasize the dangers to democracy from potential actors, while emphasizing the good faith of current actors. Lower courts can also play a valuable role in instructing markers of this kind – by laying down relatively low-profile markers, which an appellate court can then simply affirm in passing.

Further, not all judges will be equally motivated to adopt markers of this kind: Some judges clearly have a stronger focus on long-term doctrinal change, and/or their own long-term reputation, than others. Doctrinal markers of this kind require courts to adopt a relatively long-term focus. And not all judges will have the same interest in long-term doctrinal change, and/or their own long-term reputation. But doctrinal markers can often be effective even if they appear in a single judgment. Providing they do not attract the express disapproval of other judges, the reasons of a single judge in dissent, or concurrence, can often have an important impact on the development of the law.[93]

3.6 CONCLUSION

The South African constitutional experience over the last two decades has been of enormous interest to constitutional scholars worldwide: It is a leading democracy on a continent with a limited history of democratic rule, a significant economic player, and a country that has attempted to achieve major social, political, and economic transformation through constitutional means. The South African experience therefore offers a useful test-case for the question that animates this volume – i.e. how constitutions fare at the implementation stage, or when "parchment becomes practice."

We have suggested that, at least in the first decade, South African constitutionalism fared quite well at the level of implementation: The Constitutional Court handed down a number of important decisions giving effect to core constitutional guarantees, and the political branches consistently complied with those decisions, despite the dominance of the ANC across all branches. An important factor that contributed to this "successful" implementation in the first constitutional period was the skillful way in which the Court accommodated itself to the fact of ANC

---

[93] See n. 69.

dominance – by adopting a relatively deferential, "weak" approach to judicial review, which effectively remanded a range of questions to the National Assembly and the government, and attempted to make the ANC a true partner in the process of constitutional implementation.[94]

In the second period of the Constitution and the Court's operation, in contrast, many scholars suggest that the South African record is distinctly less positive: There has been a steady erosion of norms of openness and transparency within the ANC and the government, and consolidation in the power of certain ANC elites, at the expense of the political opposition both within and outside the ANC. Despite opportunities to do otherwise, until recently, when it directly confronted former President Zuma in the *Nkandla Case*, the Court has also largely failed to impose substantive breaks on this trend.[95] This has also legitimately been called a failure of democratic constitutional implementation – or "hedging" – by critics.[96]

We argue, however, that for a more substantive form of democratic hedging of this kind to have occurred in South Africa in the second period, a critical legal precondition was required – a set of legal doctrines, laid down by the court in earlier, less controversial cases, which were capable of encouraging and legitimating the development of the kind of doctrinal limits required to support judicial hedging of this kind.

In fact, we suggest, this may ultimately be a quite general requirement for successful democratic "hedging" by any constitutional court: Successful constitutional implementation will almost always be a function of background political and legal preconditions. While some of these preconditions may be outside the control of courts, others will be shaped by the court's own jurisprudence: A court or other constitutional decision-maker that fails to take politics seriously will inevitably fail to translate constitutional parchment into practice. But so too will a court that fails to take law and legal culture seriously: Courts can only ever succeed in implementing a constitution through arguments that the domestic legal culture accepts as legally plausible or legitimate. To succeed in implementing a democratic constitution,[97] courts must therefore always be sensitive to evolving political conditions and the

---

[94] On weak-form judicial review, see Mark Tushnet, *Weak Courts, Strong Rights: Judicial Review and Social Welfare Rights in Comparative Constitutional Law.* Princeton, NJ: Princeton University Press, 2008; Rosalind Dixon, "The Forms, Functions, and Varieties of Weak(ened) Judicial Review." *International Journal of Constitutional Law* 17: 904 (2019).

[95] Choudhry, n. 54.

[96] Ibid.; Issacharoff, n. 55.

[97] This argument assumes, of course, that the judges are motivated to establish constitutional democracy. That may not always be the case. See Bjoern Dressel, Raul Sanchez-Urribarri, and Alexander Stroh, "The Informal Dimension of Judicial Politics: A Relational Perspective."*Annual Review of Law and Social Science* 13 (2017) (arguing that in non-Western contexts, the assumption that judges are friends of liberty motivated to restrain political actors who undermine democratic constitutionalism may not always hold).

need to develop the legal doctrines capable, at a later point, of supporting the legitimacy of the interventions they might need to make.

This, we suggest, may ultimately be the most important lesson to be gained from the implementation of the South African Constitution: If the South African Court may be criticized, it is in respect of its failure to do more, during the first period, to lay down doctrinal markers of this kind.

4

India's First Period

Constitutional Doctrine and Constitutional Stability

Madhav Khosla[*]

4.1 INTRODUCTION

In the introduction to this volume, the editors offer an account of the tensions that constitutions face during their early years. The most basic tension that they rightly identify is one between competing goals, which often arise if some goals are radical and transformative whereas others are more preservative in nature. The concern here is partly one of constitutional efficacy – how might a new constitutional order fulfill its objectives when those objectives do not perfectly cohere or require the balancing of different stakeholders? The related concern is one of constitutional stability. A constitutional order that does not manage extant tensions will collapse. This fear is hardly an unreal one; recent work has established the rarity and difficulty of constitutional endurance.[1] The editors identify two primary sources of constitutional failure during the initial period of a new constitutional order. The first relate to drafting deficits, for instance the presence of incomplete or ambiguous clauses. The second involve deficits of implementation – institutions may struggle to get established, law-applying officials may reluctantly embrace new rules, different stakeholders and interest groups may divest from the constitutional project, and so forth.

It is, simply put, far from easy to stabilize a new constitutional order. There are, of course, numerous extra-legal historical and social forces that are part of any process of stabilization. Rather than turn to them, however, this chapter attempts to explore what relationship, if any, might exist between constitutional doctrine and constitutional stability. I consider this relationship by studying the first period in Indian constitutional development. The survival of India's constitutional project is a

[*] I am grateful to the editors for invaluable comments, and to Pratap Bhanu Mehta and Ananth Padmanabhan for helpful conversations.
[1] See Zachary Elkins, Tom Ginsburg, and James Melton, *The Endurance of National Constitutions*. New York: Cambridge University Press, 2009.

startling fact of twentieth-century constitutionalism, not least when one sees the fate experienced by other postcolonial constitutional projects that were undertaken in Asia and Africa in the 1950s and 1960s. The fact that Indian democracy has managed to persist is a fact that has invited considerable attention within comparative politics.[2] Yet, surprisingly little has been said about the related endurance of the nation's constitutional project.

Studies of Indian constitutional development, such as Granville Austin's *Working a Democratic Constitution*, often present the early years in India as a period involving a variety of tensions.[3] The initial part of Austin's definitive work covered the first sixteen years of Indian constitutionalism (1950–66). According to Austin, constitutional tensions during this period took one of the following forms: conflicts between the President and the Council of Ministers; conflicts within the Council of Ministers; conflicts between Parliament and the Council of Ministers; conflicts between the executive and judiciary; conflicts between the Central and State governments; and conflicts between the government and the ruling political party, the Indian National Congress. The second kind of description that Austin offered related to specific themes. The early years of Indian constitutionalism, he noted, witnessed fierce contestation over free speech, preventive detention, and the right to property. For Austin, this was a period involving both the formation of constitutional practices and conventions and the presence of certain intense clashes between the judiciary and other branches of government.

Comparative constitutional scholars have seen the early years of Indian constitutionalism in terms that are not altogether different. Consider Theunis Roux's notable study *The Politico-Legal Dynamics of Judicial Review*.[4] For Roux, the period from 1950–67 was marked by a traditional separation of power between the judiciary and representative institutions. The courts engaged in conventional forms of judicial reasoning, paying careful attention to the text, and Parliament was considered supreme. Even though the judiciary and legislature were often in conflict, both were nonetheless respected – the former was permitted to interpret legal instruments and limit state action, and the latter was permitted to respond by way of constitutional amendments. Neither institution was challenged in performing this role, and, as a result, the place of both the Supreme Court and Parliament was affirmed

---

[2] See Arend Lijphart, "The Puzzle of Indian Democracy: A Consociational Interpretation." *American Political Science Review* 90: 258 (1996); Ashutosh Varshney, "Why Democracy Survives." *Journal of Democracy* 9: 36 (1998); Devesh Kapur, "Explaining Democratic Durability and Economic Performance," in *Public Institutions in India*, ed. Devesh Kapur and Pratap Bhanu Mehta. New Delhi: Oxford University Press, 2005, 28; Ashutosh Varshney, *Battles Half Won: India's Improbable Democracy*. New Delhi: Penguin, 2013, 11–15.

[3] Granville Austin, *Working a Democratic Constitution: A History of the Indian Experience*. New Delhi: Oxford University Press, 1999, chapters 1–6.

[4] Theunis Roux, *The Politico-Legal Dynamics of Judicial Review: A Comparative Analysis*. Cambridge University Press, 2018, 149–55.

and established during these early years. The period was one where law and politics were separated, and a certain constitutional framework was set in place.

Similarly, Bruce Ackerman's recent wide-ranging project, *Revolutionary Constitutions*, has noted that India's initial years were marked by a serious confrontation over land reform between Parliament and the Supreme Court, a confrontation that resulted in a careful demarcation of roles between Parliament and the Supreme Court. Ackerman rightly observes that the confrontation did not destroy the constitutional order. Though Jawaharlal Nehru's government reacted strongly to the judicial invalidation of land reform measures, "the Justices refused to challenge [the] blatant effort to consign them to a subordinate role."[5] He notes that both Parliament and the Supreme Court respected and furthered constitutional principles in important ways – Nehru chose to amend rather than bypass the constitutional text; the judges spoke with authority on a number of issues and articulated a clear and limited conception of the judicial role in a constitutional democracy.

These studies capture episodes of both constitutional drama as well as constitutional consolidation. But they are noticeably silent on the role that doctrine played in the process of cementing constitutionalism on Indian soil. The Supreme Court is seen through an external lens and light is shed on its relationship with other institutional actors. Yet, rather little is observed about the specific doctrinal approaches and forms of judicial reasoning that characterized the early years of India's apex judicial body. This chapter will attempt to fill some of this scholarly void by turning to two areas of constitutional doctrine during India's first period: the place of the Directive Principles in India's constitutional schema, and the confrontation between the judiciary and the legislature over land reform. Through a study of the Supreme Court's approach in these areas, I hope to show that constitutional doctrine can assist in the achievement of constitutional stability. In the first instance, I explore how constitutional tensions might sometimes be managed by, quite simply, being avoided. In the second case, I suggest that what might seem to be tense contests are in hindsight better seen as efforts at establishing constitutional norms. In other words, the first case demonstrates how tensions that could have been serious were sidestepped, whereas the second case is an example of widely regarded conflicts that, on closer inspection, were less dramatic than we have been led to understand. In each case, the judiciary played a role in preserving the constitutional order, whether by denying tensions or by carefully tailoring its disagreement. There are many helpers on the path from parchment to practice, but a certain role will have to be performed by courts and served by constitutional doctrine. This chapter gestures at some ways for this to occur.

---

[5] Bruce Ackerman, *Revolutionary Constitutions: Charismatic Leadership and the Rule of Law*. Cambridge, MA: Harvard University Press, 2019, 64.

4.2 DIRECTIVE PRINCIPLES AND THE DENIAL OF TENSION

Among the most curious and striking features of the Indian Constitution are the Directive Principles of State Policy contained in Part IV of the text. Although the idea of Directive Principles is slowly beginning to invite the interests of comparative scholars, they have generally been subject to less study than one might anticipate.[6] The provisions in Part IV outline a range of social and economic goals, but they are judicially unenforceable. Article 37 of the Constitution states that "The provisions contained in this Part shall not be enforceable by any court, but the principles therein laid down are nevertheless fundamental in the governance of the country and it shall be the duty of the State to apply these principles in making laws."[7] The historical reasons for the inclusion of the Directive Principles are varied, and do not need rehearsing for present purposes.[8] The relationship between the Directive Principles and the Fundamental Rights – a set of guarantees that are enforceable by courts – has been the source of considerable tension within Indian constitutionalism. For years, Indian constitutionalism has wrestled with how best to understand the power and meaning of the Directive Principles. Can they trump the Fundamental Rights? Are they simply pointless and of no *legal* value? Do they have any role at all in understanding the constitutional text?

These are serious and important questions, but, interestingly enough, the conflict over the Directive Principles remained relatively dormant during India's first period. The clash between these prescriptions and other constitutional commands was the subject of legal and political drama in later years, but it did not blow up during the initial period of Indian constitutionalism. How was this conflict contained, and what might this teach us about constitutional consolidation during the first period? Of course, the tension between the Directive Principles and Fundamental Rights is not a distinctively first period problem. The tension could have manifested in later years, and it could have been avoided during the first period for a host of ordinary reasons – for example, the period could have witnessed legislation that did not relate to the potential conflict between both sets of provisions. Yet, this is not the reason why the tension between the Directive Principles and Fundamental Rights was avoided during India's first period. While the fact that laws were enacted that had the potential for a major constitutional breakdown was of course a contingent matter, the Supreme Court's response to this reality, its approach to both the structural nature of the Indian Constitution and to the substance of the conflicts at hand, seems to hold some broader lessons.

---

[6] For a recent effort, see Lael K. Weis, "Constitutional Directive Principles." *Oxford Journal of Legal Studies* 37: 916 (2017).

[7] Article 37, Constitution of India, 1950.

[8] See Niraja Gopal Jayal, *Citizenship and Its Discontents: An Indian History*. Cambridge, MA: Harvard University Press, 2013, 136–62; Madhav Khosla, *India's Founding Moment: The Constitution of a Most Surprising Democracy*. Cambridge, MA: Harvard University Press, 2020, 44–55.

An early case in which the role of the Directive Principles arose was *Champakam Dorairajan*.[9] The case dealt with the admissions policy of colleges in the State of Madras, and the way in which a fixed number of seats had been reserved for select communities. By determining admissions based on the caste of the candidate, the Supreme Court observed, the State of Madras had violated Article 29(2) of the Constitution. This provision prohibited discrimination into a state-funded educational institution on, *inter alia*, the criterion of caste. The right guaranteed by this provision was, the Court observed, "a right which an individual citizen has as a citizen and not as a member of any community or class of citizens."[10] An applicant could, of course, be denied admission on academic grounds. If, however, the Court noted, "he has the academic qualifications but is refused admission only on grounds of religion, race, caste, language or any of them, then there is a clear breach of his Fundamental Right."[11] The State of Madras's defense of the impugned scheme rested partly on a consideration of the other provisions in the Constitution. It placed reliance, in particular, on Article 46 in the Directive Principles chapter, a provision that calls on the state to work toward promoting the interests of disadvantaged sections in society and explicitly mentions the Scheduled Castes and Scheduled Tribes. The State of Madras did not merely rely on Article 46 – it went so far as to argue that Article 46 took precedence over Article 29(2), and thus any conflict between a Directive Principle and a Fundamental Right was to be decided in favor of the former.

The Court rejected this argument. It declared that the Fundamental Rights occupied a distinct place under the Constitution: They were enforceable in a court of law, and could therefore be infringed by neither legislative nor executive action. It is important to take note of this exact argument. The Court did not engage in a serious analysis of why the Fundamental Rights took precedence over the Directive Principles. Rather, it suggested that there was no conflict that could in principle arise between both sets of provisions. That is to say, the Court posited that there was simply no possibility of any conflict because both sets of provisions were fundamentally different. The Court escaped any attempt at resolving a constitutional tension by merely asserting, in an almost matter of fact manner, that the way in which the Directive Principles would have to be implemented would be no different from how any law would have to be implemented. All laws would have to meet the standard set out by the Fundamental Rights.[12]

Champakam Dorairajan characterized the Supreme Court's dominant approach during the 1950s, but there were cases where a slightly different orientation was

---

[9] *State of Madras* v. *Champakam Dorairajan*, AIR 1951 SC 226.

[10] *Champakam Dorairajan*, para 9.

[11] *Champakam Dorairajan*, para 9.

[12] The Court also made other observations, such as the fact that the Constitution had made a specific exception for reservations in public employment in Article 16(4) but had no such exception regarding education.

visible. A good example is *F. N. Balsara*.[13] Here, the Court was faced with a challenge to the Bombay Prohibition Act, 1949. A major issue before the lower court had been the statute's definition of the word "liquor." The definition that existed, the lower court had held, was far too wide and fell beyond the competence of the concerned legislature. Other matters of legislative competence were also implicated in the case, and the primary issue before the Court was whether the impugned law fell within the powers of Bombay legislature or whether, instead, it fell within the competence of the federal government. Legislative competence under the Indian Constitution is outlined in Schedule VII to the document. This Schedule contains three lists: List I populates matters that fall within the exclusive power of the federal government; List II details items that fall within the exclusive power of the state governments; and List III contains items where both the federal and state governments have concurrent jurisdiction. In addition, the Court was asked to consider whether the Bombay Prohibition Act interfered with the constitutional provisions dealing with the right to interstate trade and commerce; and whether, in case certain provisions were invalid, the statute could be severed, as the lower court had suggested, or whether it must instead fall entirely.

For our purposes, what is noteworthy is that the Directive Principles did play *some* role in the Supreme Court's determination. As noted, one of the major issues regarding the impugned law was the meaning of "liquor." Section 2(24) of the Bombay Prohibition Act had provided a rather wide definition, resulting in the High Court holding that even though the legislature was empowered to "prevent the consumption of non-intoxicating beverages and also prevent the use as drinks of alcoholic liquids which are not normally consumed as drinks, it cannot prevent the legitimate use of alcoholic preparations which are not beverages nor the use of medicinal and toilet preparations containing alcohol."[14] The Supreme Court surveyed several domestic and comparative sources to assess the meaning of "liquor." Both foreign and domestic sources led the Court to hold that "the word 'liquor' covers not only those alcoholic liquids which are generally used for beverage purposes and produce intoxication, but also all liquids containing alcohol."[15]

Interestingly, the Court suggested that independently of arriving at this conclusion through studying the sources that it did, one could also reach the same conclusion by way of a careful reading of the constitutional text. The relevant entry relating to legislative competence was not only Entry 31 of List II, but also Entry 14 of the same list, which was an entry relating to public health. Article 47 in the Directive Principles chapter, the Court observed, directed the state to attend to standards of nutrition and living and noted that the advancement of public health was to be one of its chief objectives. In fact, the Court pointed out that the provision specifically

---

[13] *State of Bombay* v. *F. N. Balsara*, AIR 1951 SC 318.
[14] *F. N. Balsara*, para 27.
[15] *F. N. Balsara*, para 32.

mandated that "the State shall endeavour to bring about prohibition of the consumption, except for medicinal purposes, of intoxicating drinks and of drugs which are injurious to health."[16] The upshot of this was that the Constitution drew a clear link between prohibition and public health, and that the question of legislative competence could not be judged by merely turning to Entry 31. The Court thus concluded that the lower court had erred in finding fault with the definition of the word "liquor."

The Court considered other grounds of challenge to the Bombay Prohibition Act, such as ones based on equality and on excessive delegation. Our focus here, however, should be on a different challenge that is worth exploring in some detail, namely one based on the right to property guaranteed by Article 19(1)(g), as it then existed in the Indian Constitution. The provision granted citizens the right to "acquire, hold and dispose of property," and the suggestion was that the prohibition on the possession, sale etc. of "liquor" infringed this guarantee.[17] The question was whether the impugned law could fall under the exception to Article 19(1)(g), which was listed in Article 19(5) and provided that "reasonable restrictions" could be imposed on the right to property in, *inter alia*, "the interests of the general public."[18] In answer to this question, the Court again relied on Article 47 in the Directive Principles chapter. "In judging the reasonableness of the restrictions imposed by the Act," it observed, "one has to bear in mind the Directive Principles of State Policy set forth in Article 47 of the Constitution."[19] There was no debate, it noted, on the fact that the general restrictions on wine, beer etc. that the law had imposed were, when seen in light of Article 47, "quite reasonable."[20] The question was whether it might be reasonable to extend the restrictions, as the law did, to "toilet and medicinal preparations containing alcohol."[21] The High Court, which the Supreme Court relied on at some length, had noted that the legitimate use of substances that contain alcohol but are not drunk (say, eau-de-cologne) was in no way harmful to the public interest, and thus it was not proper to prevent their use merely because abuses may occur. When it came to the other substances – ones that were consumed – the case was different. In reiterating this, the Court again made use of the Directive Principles:

> There can be no doubt whatever that the earlier categories of liquor, namely, spirits of wine, methylated spirit, wine, beer, toddy are distinctly separable items which are easily severable from the last category, namely, all liquids consisting of or containing alcohol. These items being thus treated separately by the legislature itself and being severable, and it not being contended, in view of the Directive Principles of

[16] Article 47, Constitution of India, 1950.
[17] Article 19(1)(g), Constitution of India, 1950.
[18] Article 19(1)(5), Constitution of India, 1950.
[19] *F. N. Balsara*, para 46.
[20] *F. N. Balsara*, para 46.
[21] *F. N. Balsara*, para 46.

State Policy regarding prohibition, that the restrictions imposed upon the right to possess or sell or buy or consume or use those categories of properties are unreasonable, the impugned sections must be held valid so far as these categories are concerned.[22]

The Court proceeded to conclude that the impugned law was severable. A separation of a similar kind between medicinal and other uses had been done in other countries, it observed, such as in the United States statute, the National Prohibition Act, 1919. Moreover, the Court noted that the text of Article 47 also confirmed the possibility of severability, because it specifically exempted medicinal preparations when it came to prohibition.

F. N. Balsara is an interesting case and seems to be an exception to the Supreme Court's general approach, as outlined in *Champakam Dorairajan*, that shaped the early years of Indian constitutional doctrine. In *F. N. Balsara*, the Directive Principles did play some interpretive role. But what precise role did they play? First, the Court did not offer any account or theory for the place of the Directive Principles within India's constitutional framework. The silence is telling – there seems to be a conscious attempt to avoid making too much of the matter. Second, even though *Champakam Dorairajan* was decided only a month before *F. N. Balsara* and the case had addressed the question of the Directive Principles in a clear and deliberate fashion, *F. N. Balsara* does not even mention *Champakam Dorairajan*, let alone engage with the latter's seemingly contrasting approach to the role of the Directive Principles. Third, let us revisit the exact reliance on the Directive Principles in *F. N. Balsara*. In the first instance, the Directive Principles were referenced while interpreting the competence of the legislature. Here, as noted, the Court surveyed several sources to make the same point. Thus, as per this logic, the Directive Principles were not providing anything new or reflecting any kind of tension with what the other sources or provisions indicated – they were confirming what had already been somewhat determined. In the second instance, the use to which the Directive Principles was put was more significant, and potentially more controversial. Here, the suggestion was that the scope of a Fundamental Right (the right to property in Article 19(1)(g)) is to be ascertained by considering Article 47 in the Directive Principles chapter.

The strong version of such a suggestion would be that the Fundamental Rights must *conform* to the Directive Principles, which would signify a radical departure from *Champakam Dorairajan*. But the Supreme Court did not appear to offer this strong version of the argument. Instead, it used the Directive Principles in an illustrative fashion. The question before the Court was whether a certain kind of regulatory law – a law pertaining to prohibition – was a reasonable infringement on the right to property. The issue was an application of the law (Article 19(1)(g)) to a specific factual scenario (prohibition). The Directive Principle (Article 47) was

[22] F N Balsara, para 47.

useful because it showed that the Constitution had envisaged the kind of state regulation at issue, and it had considered such regulation to be permissible. Thus, Article 47 was an example that came to be useful in better understanding the application of the law in the context of the right to property. But there was no suggestion in *F. N. Balsara* that the Fundamental Rights must be interpreted in light of the Directive Principles, or even that this might be a desirable if optional interpretive practice. Moreover, by avoiding any strong thesis of this sort, the Court was able to continue the trend in *Champakam Dorairajan* in one important respect – it was able to continue to suggest that there was no constitutional tension to be worked out.

As I mentioned, the approach in *Champakam Dorairajan* marked the trend adopted by the Supreme Court throughout the 1950s. In *Hanif Quareshi's* case, which arose at the very end of the decade, we see some important similarities.[23] In this case, a number of statutes that banned the slaughter of cows came up for challenge before the Supreme Court. The state contended that the impugned laws were valid in part because they had been based on the Directive Principles. It went so far as to argue that because the Directive Principles imposed obligations on the state, they should take precedence over the Fundamental Rights. The Court rejected this argument. As the Constitution specifically declared that no law could violate the Fundamental Rights, there was no space for an exception for laws that furthered the Directive Principles. The state, the Court noted, "should certainly implement the Directive Principles but it must do so in such a way that its laws do not take away or abridge the Fundamental Rights."[24] In making this observation, the Court cited and affirmed *Champakam Dorairajan*, declaring that the Directive Principles would have to be operationalized within the limits prescribed by the Fundamental Rights.

The statutes under challenge had different features. One involved a ban on the slaughter of bovine cattle; in another, the ban was on the slaughter of cows and their progeny, including bulls, calves etc.; and the final law declared a ban on the slaughter of cows, their progeny, and provided for the regulation of the slaughter of buffaloes. Interestingly, despite confirming the view expressed in *Champakam Dorairajan*, the Court began its study of the impugned laws by observing that it was necessary to consider the constitutional provisions that had motivated the laws. The first place that it turned to was Article 48 in the Directive Principles chapter that called on the state to "endeavor to organize agriculture and animal husbandry on modern and scientific lines [and to] take steps for preserving and improving the breeds, and prohibiting the slaughter, of cows and calves and other milch and draught cattle."[25] Of further interest is the fact that when the Court arrived at its

---

[23] *Hanif Quareshi v. State of Bihar*, AIR 1958 SC 731.
[24] *Hanif Quareshi*, para 12.
[25] Article 48, Constitution of India, 1950.

conclusion, which by and large involved an upholding of the measures under challenge, it noted that the measures were "in consonance with the Directive Principles laid down in Article 48."[26]

In *Hanif Quareshi*, we see shades of what was visible in *F. N. Balsara*: some interpretive place accorded to the Directive Principles without any gesture that this opened up a constitutional tension or controversy or conflict. It is only in the case of *In Re The Kerala Education Bill, 1957*, that a genuine shift in the Supreme Court's approach can be discerned. This case, which arose very soon after *Hanif Quareshi*, involved a presidential reference to the Supreme Court under Article 143 of the Constitution.[27] The Bill in question had been passed by the Legislative Assembly of the State of Kerala and forwarded to the President for his assent. Having concerns as to its constitutionality, the President referred the matter to the Court. The details of the Bill can be avoided for present purposes. Suffice it to note that it dealt with educational institutions in the State of Kerala and gave the government considerable powers relating to the regulation and management of schools.

A major question before the Supreme Court was the reconciliation of two principles that seemed to be at odds with one another. The first was Article 30(1) in the Fundamental Rights chapter that gave minorities the power to establish and administer educational institutions. The other was Article 45 in the Directive Principles chapter, which obliged the state to work toward free and compulsory education. Notice how the Court's framing in *In Re The Kerala Education Bill* – its very suggestion that there was a textual conflict to be resolved – marked a radical departure from the approach adopted in the aforementioned cases. The Court proceeded to note that the Directive Principles could not take precedence over the Fundamental Rights. Instead, there must be an effort to harmonize both features of the Constitution. The aim should be, the Court declared, to "reconcile between these two conflicting interests and to give effect to both if that is possible and bring about a synthesis between the two."[28] It concluded that the right to administer did not preclude all forms of regulation. The point here is not which specific regulations were judged to be permissible, but rather that the Court sought hard to strike some sort of balance between autonomy and regulation – that is, between the Directive Principles and Fundamental Rights.

The early approach of the Supreme Court invited criticism from a number of commentators. A major scholar of Indian law, P. K. Tripathi, wondered why the standard approach toward constitutional interpretation, where different provisions are read in light of one another and where there is an attempt to give effect to the document as a complete text, could not be applied to interpreting the Directive Principles and Fundamental Rights. He argued that

---

[26] *Hanif Quareshi*, para 45.
[27] *In Re The Kerala Education Bill, 1957*, AIR 1958 SC 956.
[28] *In Re The Kerala Education Bill, 1957*, para 31.

in the case of an apparent conflict between the scope of a fundamental right of the individual on the one hand and a Directive Principle of State Policy on the other, it should be presumed that the conflict is apparent and resoluble when the two conflicting rules are properly interpreted, and, in the process of interpretation it would be proper and appropriate to remember that the Directive Principles of State Policy embody a set of social principles that come into existence to check the wild extravagance of the fundamental rights of the individual and to eliminate the clogs in the functioning of the modern welfare state which were the by-products of the orthodox view regarding the scope of the fundamental rights.[29]

For scholars like Tripathi, there were major stakes in the doctrinal approach toward the Directive Principles. If constitutional interpretation did not sufficiently involve the Principles, it was feared that the state's power would be curbed, and it would lack the legal force to undertake numerous radical progressive measures. Whether the Principles could have been used in this way is debatable, but it is unquestionable that many felt that their role had been unduly suppressed – and that the consequence was a reduction in the state's regulatory power. The contemporary scholarship adopts a similar view to Tripathi's. In an important recent essay, for example, the Supreme Court's early approach toward the Directive Principles is termed as "judicial minimalism," and an argument is posited for why the Directive Principles should inform, even control, our understanding of the Fundamental Rights.[30]

Regardless of the merits of the Court's early approach, it did not last long. For some years now, the Court has openly accepted that the effort must be to harmonize and strike a balance between the Directive Principles and Fundamental Rights. This effort has been the source of much constitutional argument. Some relationship between the Directive Principles and Fundamental Rights has been forged, and while that relationship has not always been clear and settled, the endeavor to create and manage such a relationship signifies a notable shift from the Court's initial years.[31] Both scholars and the judiciary have come to regard the approach embraced in the early period as a mistaken one – Directive Principles were, the argument runs, ignored and put aside, even though they were (and remain) a vital part of the constitutional text. I do not want to explore whether the Court's early interpretive attitude was worthy and deserves more credit than it has come to receive. But what is worth noticing – and what seems to have been unnoticed in the commentary on this

---

[29] P. K. Tripathi, *Spotlights on Constitutional Interpretation.* Bombay: N. M. Tripathi, 1972, 293.

[30] Gautam Bhatia, "Directive Principles of State Policy," in *Oxford Handbook of the Indian Constitution*, ed. Sujit Choudhry, Madhav Khosla, and Pratap Bhanu Mehta. Oxford University Press, 2016, 644. Bhatia is quite right to note, as a doctrinal matter, that *In Re The Kerala Education Bill* is the case that signals a shift in the Supreme Court's approach.

[31] On the relationship between the Directive Principles and Fundamental Rights, see P. P. Craig and S. L. Deshpande, "Rights, Autonomy and Process: Public Interest Litigation in India." *Oxford Journal of Legal Studies* 9: 356 (1989); Madhav Khosla, "Making Social Rights Conditional: Lessons from India." *International Journal of Constitutional Law* 8: 739 (2010); Gautam Bhatia, "Directive Principles of State Policy."

early period – is how the Court's approach avoided a doctrinal minefield and prevented the escalation of tensions over potentially conflicting aspects of the constitutional text. A lesson that we may perhaps draw from the Court's engagement with the Directive Principles during India's first period is that one simple technique by which judges can and do bypass and manage tensions in a constitutional text is by denying that such tensions exist.

4.3 LAND REFORM AND CONSTITUTIONAL CONSOLIDATION

Among the measures most likely to provoke tensions between the transformative and preservative elements in a constitutional order are those involving the redistribution of wealth. In the Indian case, tensions of this sort arose early with land reform measures. The right to property was among the most debated provisions in the drafting of India's Constitution.[32] The final document secured the right by way of two provisions, Articles 19(1)(f) and 31. These provisions guaranteed citizens the right to hold and transfer property, and declared that property could only be acquired by legislation, for a public purpose, and with the payment of compensation, respectively. These provisions were a product of a legal compromise of sorts – compensation was to be awarded for land acquisition, but the Constituent Assembly broadly felt that the quantum of compensation would fall outside the purview of judicial review.[33] Controversy over the validity of land acquisition arose nearly immediately after the enactment of the Constitution. The constitutional history on this point is familiar: High Court decisions were delivered, some of which struck down land reform legislation; Parliament reacted by amending the Constitution in 1951; the amendment power itself was then challenged; and, eventually, the Supreme Court delivered its verdict on the appeals that followed the High Court decisions. The story does not end here, of course. There was a subsequent amendment relating to the right to property in 1955, a total of ten constitutional amendments have taken place in relation to this right, and the question of land acquisition continues to see developments till this date.[34]

This is not the place for an exhaustive study of the right to property in India, but the initial years of this history are worth examining. In this section, I want to consider the earliest segment of this history; that is, the period extending from the initial challenges to land reform that came up in India's High Courts to the enactment of the First Amendment to the Constitution only a year after the document came into force to the Fourth Amendment a few years later. A careful reading of this period,

---

[32] See Granville Austin, *The Indian Constitution: Cornerstone of a Nation.* New Delhi: Oxford University Press, 1966.

[33] See H. C. L. Merillat, *Land and the Constitution of India.* New York: Columbia University Press, 1970, 52–78.

[34] See Namita Wahi, "Property," in *Oxford Handbook of the Indian Constitution,* ed. Sujit Choudhry, Madhav Khosla, and Pratap Bhanu Mehta. Oxford University Press, 2016, 943.

I shall show, is crucial to forming a picture of constitutional consolidation during these initial years. This history has typically been understood as a fierce clash between the legislature and the judiciary. The legislature enacts land reform measures, the judiciary strikes them down, the legislature responds to undo judicial action, the judiciary in turn replies, and so forth. The familiar story told is one of conflicting ideologies and institutional tension, of judicial pushbacks against legislative action and strong legislative retaliation.[35]

This is not an unreasonable narrative, but it misses something important. If our interest lies in constitutional consolidation, we might instead see this period as one of noticeable judicial discipline and institutional fidelity and one that marked a serious constitutional conversation between the judiciary and legislature. In each instance that the judiciary pushed against a legislature measure, neither did it challenge the legislature power to enact the measure nor did it challenge the measure itself. Instead, it located independent grounds, which fell outside the contours of the measure itself, for why the measure might fail. As such, it displayed a remarkable degree of respect toward the legislature. This was not, in other words, a clash between conservative and radical forces – one committed to land redistribution, the other to private property – but rather an attempt at clarifying the principles that govern lawmaking. The kind of judicial engagement that I hope to capture might reveal one way by which new constitutional systems might successfully confront the problem of radical change as they travel from parchment to practice.

To fully understand the constitutional consolidation during the early years of the Indian republic, we cannot merely consider the actions and reactions between Parliament and the Supreme Court. We must further scrutinize the kind of judicial reasoning at work and the nature of constitutional doctrine that evolved. The Constitution's original text tried to make secure the earliest attempts at land reform by including provisions in Article 31 that protected measures that were already in motion when the Constitution became operationalized. But not all laws managed to meet the conditions specified by the savings clause. This fact, coupled with grounds that were found to challenge land reform measures that fell outside the savings provision, meant that land reform measures were challenged across different High Courts in India. Perhaps the most significant case in this regard was the Patna High Court decision in *Kameshwar Singh*.[36] The case involved a challenge to the Bihar Land Reforms Act, 1950. The impugned statute either took away or modified the rights of certain proprietors and tenure-holders. In sum, the statute attempted to change the system of land holding such that the new system would vest power in the individuals who were actually cultivating the land.

---

[35] See Granville Austin, *Working a Democratic Constitution*.
[36] *Kameshwar Singh v. State of Bihar*, 30 Indian Law Reports 454 (1951) (Patna High Court).

In *Kameshwar Singh*, the Patna High Court struck down the impugned measure. The decision proved controversial and led to a strong legislative reaction. In response to the verdict, Parliament enacted the First Amendment to the Constitution. The changes introduced by the Amendment were radical. A new provision was introduced in the text – Article 31A – that declared that "no law providing for the acquisition by the State of any estate or of any rights therein ... shall be deemed to be void on the ground" that it violated the Fundamental Rights chapter in the Constitution.[37] The First Amendment also introduced a further change in the Constitution. It created a constitutional black hole, the Ninth Schedule to the document. As per a new provision, Article 31B, all laws placed in this Schedule would be similarly immune from any judicial challenge that was based on such laws being in violation of the Fundamental Rights chapter.

This piece of Indian constitutional history is relatively well-known but more deserves to be said about the reasoning in *Kameshwar Singh*. A striking feature of the Patna High Court's decision was its clear and candid acknowledgment that Articles 31(4)–(6) protected the impugned law on the question of compensation. The Court observed that "if clauses 4 to 6 had not been inserted in Article 31, [the petitioners] could have appealed to the courts on challenging the validity of the law on, among other grounds, that the compensation provided represented less than the market value of their property."[38] The reason for such savings clauses, the Court noted, was obvious enough. Assessing compensation was a hard matter, payment of such compensation in full may well have been impossible, and the absence of such clauses would have enabled ceaseless litigation. The Court also dismissed the claim that the acquisition in question was not for a public purpose. Given the text of the Constitution, the Court found that it was "stopped from saying that the acquisition of estates and tenures is not an acquisition for [a public purpose]."[39]

The Patna High Court, thus, fully resisted any kind of review relating to the adequacy of compensation. It did, to be sure, find the impugned state action vulnerable, but on a different if related ground. The impugned action was found vulnerable under the Constitution's equal protection guarantee (Article 14). This was because the way in which the compensation scheme was arranged involved a classification that was discriminatory:

> The impugned Act ... discriminates between individuals falling with the class which it affected. In fact, it divides the class into a large number of sub-classes, and to these sub-classes, differential treatment is meted out. It is quite impossible to say that this subdivision is based on any rational grounds. On what principle, for instance, ought a proprietor or tenure-holder, whose net income is Rs. 20,000, to be

[37] Article 31A, Constitution of India, 1950.
[38] *Kameshwar Singh*, 465.
[39] Ibid., 476.

given eight years' purchase, while a proprietor or tenure-holder, whose net income is Rs. 20,001 is given only six years' purchase?[40]

Thus, even though the petitioners could not challenge the Bihar Land Reforms Act on the ground that the compensation awarded was inadequate, they could still assert that "the impugned Act specifies different principles of compensation for different categories of persons affected by the Act, the subdivision of such persons into categories being wholly artificial or irrational one."[41] In developing this line of reasoning, the Court put forth an important point regarding lawmaking and the respective institutional role of the judiciary and the legislature: Taking the subject of compensation outside the domain of judicial review did not empower the legislature to award compensation in any way that it deemed fit – the awarding of compensation needed to satisfy an internal logic and meet the Constitution's equal protection guarantee.

Parliament, as we have observed, responded by amending the Constitution. This amendment itself became the subject of challenge in *Sankari Prasad*.[42] India's basic structure doctrine and the limitations placed on the substantive power of constitutional amendment are familiar features of its jurisprudence, and they have been at the heart of a global and emerging conversation on constitutional amendment powers.[43] Yet, it is rarely observed that even though the doctrine itself was only developed in the 1970s, the question that it grappled with arose with the very first amendment to the Constitution. Given the jurisprudence that was to develop on the matter of constitutional amendment, and given the comparative trends we now see, it is interesting to notice the ease with which that the Supreme Court upheld the Constitution (First Amendment) Act, 1951. After all, the amendment precluded judicial review on legislation that was inserted into the Constitution's Ninth Schedule – such laws could openly violate the Fundamental Rights chapter in the Constitution and the judiciary could do nothing.

Sankari Prasad hardly endorsed the virtue of such a constitutional practice, but it remained committed to the idea that this was not a matter for courts to adjudicate. The challenge to the Constitution (First Amendment) Act partly dealt with procedural questions, such as the power of India's transitional Parliament. We can leave aside these questions for present purposes and focus instead on the Supreme Court's response to the question of whether any substantive limitations exist on the amendment power. As the amendment effectively infringed the rights protected by Part III of the Constitution, it was argued that the measure could not stand. The Fundamental Rights, it was contended, were immune not merely from legislation but also

---

[40] Ibid., 477.
[41] Ibid., 491.
[42] *Sankari Prasad* v. *Union of India*, AIR 1951 SC 458.
[43] On the Indian position, see Madhav Khosla, "Constitutional Amendment," in *Oxford Handbook of the Indian Constitution*, ed. Sujit Choudhry, Madhav Khosla, and Pratap Bhanu Mehta. Oxford University Press, 2016, 232.

from constitutional amendments. Without this, the argument ran, the protection they offered would not amount to very much. The Court rejected this argument, appealing to a distinction between ordinary law and constitutional law. The latter, it observed, was an exercise of sovereign constituent power. As such, there could be no review of such action. The Constitution had, with specific requirements and safeguards, vested that power with Parliament, and thus Parliament had the power to amendment the Constitution "without any exception whatsoever."[44] The Supreme Court in *Sankari Prasad*, thus, clearly set the terms for constitutional change – the judiciary could review the procedural requirements for an amendment, but it had no role to play when it came to substantive limitations on the amendment power.

This case was followed by a Supreme Court challenge to various High Court decisions dealing with land reform, including the Patna High Court's decision in *Kameshwar Singh*.[45] The facts remained the same, but the First Amendment meant that by the time the matter had reached the Supreme Court, the legal reality had changed. The new provisions in the Constitution, namely Articles 31A and 31B, had been inserted with retrospective effect. As the Court noted, this meant that "the impugned Acts [could] no longer be attacked on the ground of alleged infringement of any of the rights conferred by the provisions of Part III."[46] The Court openly conceded that it could no longer test the impugned legislation against the equality guarantee in Article 14. The rationale that the Patna High Court had offered, that is, could no longer be of any use.

What the Supreme Court did observe, however, is that Articles 31A and 31B only saved land reform measures from potential rights-based violations. They did not protect the measures from other grounds of challenge. In particular, the new provisions did not preclude challenges based on the ground of legislative competence. The argument from legislative competence was an interesting one. The relevant legislative entries allowed state legislatures to enact legislation to acquire property, and to specify the principles determining the payment of compensation and the meaning of a public purpose. These entries therefore implied, the argument ran, that two conditions were necessary for a valid law enabling property acquisition: The law must provide for the payment of compensation, and it must require that acquisition be for a public purpose. If such conditions were not required, then it would have made no sense to have a legislative entry specifying that the law must establish the principles relating to the payment of compensation and the meaning of a public purpose. But if a valid law must provide for compensation, then might one argue that it must also provide for compensation to be of a certain amount? If the compensation provided was illusory, would that mean that the law was invalid on

[44] *Sankari Prasad*, para 13.
[45] *State of Bihar* v. *Kameshwar Singh*, 1952 SCR 889 (Supreme Court (SC)).
[46] *Kameshwar Singh* (SC), para 2.

grounds of legislative competence? Similarly, if laws were created that were merely reorganizing a landholding pattern, say substituting previous landlords for the government, rather than distributing land, could such laws be challenged as not being for a public purpose?

Chief Justice M. Patanjali Sastri answered these questions in the negative. He found such arguments to be "devoid of substance and force."[47] The two grounds of challenge – namely, the payment of compensation and the acquisition for a public purpose – were, he felt, already precluded by Articles 31A and 31B, and to locate a new challenge under the ground of legislative competence rather than the Fundamental Rights was merely a strategy to circumvent these Articles. "The fact is," Justice Sastri observed, "that Article 31(4) was designed to bar the jurisdiction of courts to entertain objections to the validity of a certain class of enactments on the two-fold ground [discussed], and its whole purpose would stand defeated if the *zamindars'* contention were to prevail."[48] Justice Mehr Chand Mahajan felt similarly to Justice Sastri. He sharply observed that the impugned measure was not, in fact, one involving land reform. It was simply concerned with transferring the ownership of estates to the state. But, in and of itself, this was hardly problematic. This was constitutional. Yet it did clarify the nature of the measure. "There is no scheme of land reform within the framework of the statute," Justice Mahajan observed, "except that a pious hope is expressed that the commission may produce one."[49] The state was certainly empowered to acquire property compulsorily, but the payment of compensation was a vital part of the eminent domain doctrine. The core question before the Court, Justice Mahajan felt, was where one might locate the right to compensation under India's constitutional framework. It would be a mistake, he felt, to locate this right within the idea of legislative competence:

> I agree with the learned Attorney General that the concept of acquisition and that of compensation are two different notions having their origins in different sources. One is founded on the sovereign power of the state to take, the other is based on the natural right of the person who is deprived of property to be compensated for his loss. One is the power to take, the other is the condition for the exercise of that power. Power to take was mentioned in Entry 36, while the condition for the exercise of that power was embodied in Article 31(2) and there was no duty to pay compensation implicit in the content of the entry itself.[50]

Like Justice Sastri, Justice Mahajan observed that the entire purpose of Article 31(4) was to disallow judicial review on the question of compensation. He did find the nature of compensation troubling but expressed an inability to intervene on the

---

[47] Ibid., para 10.
[48] Ibid., para 12.
[49] Ibid., para 38.
[50] Ibid., para 44.

matter. The matter had, quite simply, been taken outside the purview of the judiciary.

Justice Mahajan did, however, observe that the matter was different when it came to the question of what might be regarded as a public purpose. The clause did not prevent courts from looking into the purpose for which property had been acquired. The power to acquire property for a public purpose was essential to the nature of the law itself – there was simply no legislative power to enact legislation to acquire property for the purposes of a transfer to private individuals. "The exercise of the power to acquire compulsorily," he noted, "is not an express provision of Article 31 (2) but exists *aliunde* in the content of the power itself and that in fact is the assumption upon which this clause of the Article proceeds."[51] At the heart of the public purpose challenge was the claim that the law did not offer any reason for the acquisition. It merely transferred rents and lands to the State, but it did not demonstrate how this money would benefit anyone and what, if any, redistribution might take place. This was, the claim went, a kind of nationalization, but no clear public purpose was served. Even though Justice Mahajan felt that courts could look into this matter, he rejected the claim. It was not necessary, he observed, for a statute to lay down the precise purpose for which property might be acquired. The "whole tenor and intendment" of the measure, he felt, made it clear that the purpose was public in nature.[52]

Two provisions of the impugned law, though, were declared unconstitutional by Justice Mahajan. The first was a provision pertaining to the acquisition of arrears of rent. Half the rent that was to be paid to a landlord had been vested with the state. This payment simply increased state revenues to eventually allow the state to pay for the acquisition of land. A key principle pertaining to acquisition, it was observed, is that it cannot be used for the sole purpose of increasing the state's revenue. Thus, there was no public purpose at work here. The second unconstitutional clause was one that effectively permitted the nonpayment of compensation by artificially creating deductions that had no factual basis. This, Justice Mahajan declared, was a clear case of confiscation, which was beyond the competence of the legislature. No power of legislation existed for such a provision.

Justice Mahajan's opinion was the majority stance. Justice Bijan Kumar Mukherjea and Justice N. Chandrasekhara Aiyar similarly upheld the Bihar Land Reforms Act but struck down the two aforementioned provisions. "If the principles [for compensation] are so formulated as to result in non-payment altogether," Justice Aiyar observed, "then the legislature would be evading the law not only covertly but flagrantly."[53] To not pay any compensation would be to violate the terms of the legislative entry under which the law was sought to be created. The core

---

[51] Ibid., para 48.
[52] Ibid., para 54.
[53] Ibid., para 123.

disagreement between the majority and minority opinions, then, was the question of whether the concerns relating to public purpose and compensation, which dealt with the two clauses that had been declared unconstitutional, were to be answered with reference to the Fundamental Rights chapter or not. For the majority, they were based on independent grounds outside of the Fundamental Rights, grounds such as legislative competence, and were therefore unaffected by the savings clauses that had been inserted. In offering such reasoning, the Supreme Court underlined the kinds of constitutional challenges that could impact legislation outside of rights-based challenges.

It is important to underscore the narrowness of the Supreme Court's opinion in this case– only two provisions of the impugned legislation were struck down – and there was complete restraint on all rights-based matters. Moreover, in other cases decided at the same time, the Supreme Court upheld similar land reform legislation.[54] The Supreme Court's reliance on the text of the lists outlining the powers of legislation in Schedule Seven to the Constitution would later be followed by a constitutional amendment that altered the text of the specific legislative entry in question (Entry 42, List III). In the interim, there were further tussles between the judiciary and the legislature in the area of land reform. The meaning and nature of "compensation" became a major point of contention, along with what constitutes the difference between the acquisition and regulation of property in the absence of a transfer for title. Several important judicial decisions were handed down on the matter; and Parliament eventually enacted the Fourth Amendment to the Constitution in 1955 – a change that drastically altered the power of courts to review legislation relating to all kinds of property interests.[55]

The apparent conflict on land reform between the legislature and the judiciary has, as I have noted, been the familiar narrative of the early years of Indian constitutionalism. The Supreme Court's attitude, Granville Austin once observed, placed "the social revolution" that the Constitution had envisaged in trouble.[56] Even a recent study observed that the Ninth Schedule and savings clauses including Articles 31A and 31B "should be seen as a legislative reaction to judicial overreach reflected in an overzealous protection of the erstwhile fundamental right to property against legislation aimed at socioeconomic justice."[57] But the reading of the initial cases that I have held up for consideration presents us with a different picture. Constitutions are at least in part cemented by a culture of constitutional argument. The constitutional battles over land reform during India's first period should not be

---

[54] See *Surajpal Singh v. State of Uttar Pradesh*, AIR 1952 SC 52; *Visheshwar Rao v. State of Madhya Pradesh*, 1952 SCR 1020.

[55] See H. C. L. Merillat, *Land and the Constitution of India*, 140–49.

[56] Granville Austin, *Working a Democratic Constitution*, 80.

[57] Surya Deva, "Savings Clauses: The Ninth Schedules and Articles 31A-C," in *Oxford Handbook of the Indian Constitution*, ed. Sujit Choudhry, Madhav Khosla, and Pratap Bhanu Mehta. Oxford University Press, 2016, 627 at 627.

seen as an intense clash of principle or ideology between Parliament and the judiciary. Instead, the period was one of constitutional consolidation. It was a period where judiciary review was exercised on narrow and technical grounds, and where the principles that were to determine the making and the application of laws were carefully worked out between the legislature and the judiciary. This working out can never be forged in theory. It is always determined in practice, and the early contests over land reform in India are an excellent example of the careful, dialogic way in which that practice can be performed, a culture of constitutional argument and engagement can exist, and constitutionalism can be consolidated.

4.4 CONCLUSION

In this chapter, I have tried to explore certain areas of constitutional tension in India's first period and suggested how they might have paved the way toward constitutional stability. It is worth saying a little more about the connection between the doctrinal development in the two areas that I have identified and the larger account of the institutional and political success of India's Constitution. While the story that I have offered has elements of an inter-branch dialogue of the kind that is well-known to comparative constitutional scholars, there is a deeper relationship between the doctrinal account presented and the achievement of stability that the constitutional text came to acquire. One way to think about the relationship of the doctrinal arc to the more materialist criterion of constitutional consolidation is to explore how the approach that the Supreme Court adopted in India's first period generated norms and conventions that had a long-term stabilizing effect.

In the case of land reform, this can be seen by acknowledging that the Court's careful engagement established constitutional practices, including the practice of constitutional amendments to undo judicial decisions. Whatever we might make of the amendments in question, they revealed a commitment to settling a controversial sociopolitical matter constitutionally, and thereby helped in the task of constitutional consolidation. The Court's doctrinal response to the amendments was, in turn, equally deferential to the enterprise of constitutionalism. Contrary to most writing on this period, the Court's approach was not an example of an ideological clash with Parliament, but rather an effort to resist such an ideological clash to ensure that the contest was performed in the least ideological way. Indeed, seen in this way, it is hardly fortuitous that the institutional crises faced in Indian political life from the 1970s onward, including a crisis in the judiciary, went alongside the collapse of numerous established norms relating to legal reasoning and judicial law-making.[58] In the case of the Directive Principles and the Fundamental Rights, on

---

[58] Although such collapse was often seen as a mark of doctrinal inventiveness and ambition, most notably in the case of public interest litigation, legal scholars are now beginning to see the period in more critical terms. See, for example, Anuj Bhuwania, *Courting the People: Public*

the other hand, the Court's approach was to avoid rather than engage – it was to contain a potential conflict that could have had extralegal consequences and spillover effects. Here, constitutional doctrine was used to see that tensions do not hijack the constitutional project before it acquires some degree of stability.

The two case studies that I have presented also reveal that the approach toward constitutional questions during the first period often does not resolve matters; it merely shapes the future. In the Indian case, both the areas that I have considered were neither settled nor stabilized by the Supreme Court's initial approach. The relationship between the Directive Principles and the Fundamental Rights is still a matter of both confusion and contestation. The Supreme Court's approach in *Champakam Dorairajan* – which did not involve a serious explication of how and why the Directive Principles do and do not matter – merely postponed the issue, and it left the constitutional relationship between the Directive Principles and Fundamental Rights to be worked out in the future. On land reform, a different story presents itself. Here, as I have argued, the Court was neither evasive nor confrontational – it engaged in careful judicial reasoning. But the Court's watchful engagement only led to further technical debates (say, on the meaning of compensation), more amendments, and a battle that is ongoing until today. The fact that the first period is not a period that settles questions, that it is not a period where permanent answers emerge, is not necessarily a cause for worry or a marker of failure. It may, in fact, be an important sign of success, for one indicator of a working constitutional system is that it allows for unending constitutional conversations and that it allows for conversations to occur within constitutional limits.

One might conclude by making an observation of a somewhat different kind. While the aforementioned study has tried to understand the relationship between constitutional doctrine and constitutional stability as a rather general matter, it is true that sometimes constitutional tensions can take very specific forms that may not be usefully generalizable. In the postcolonial context, particularly, one such tension might be the tension between the colonial legal order and the new independently created legal order. This is not a tension that I have explored in this chapter, but it is one that was visible during India's first period.

Prominent examples in this regard are the cases relating to the freedom of speech and expression. In May 1950, only a few months after the Constitution of India came into force, the Supreme Court delivered two verdicts on free speech and public order. Both contributed to the enactment of the First Amendment to the Constitution, which inserted a new restriction on free speech in Article 19 as well as a fresh

Interest Litigation in Post-Emergency India. Cambridge University Press, 2017. For meditations on the decline of the rule of law in India, see Pratap Bhanu Mehta, "The Rise of Judicial Sovereignty," *Journal of Democracy* 18: 70 (2007); Pratap Bhanu Mehta, "The Indian Supreme Court and the Art of Democratic Positioning," in *Unstable Constitutionalism: Law and Politics in South Asia,* ed. Mark Tushnet and Madhav Khosla. New York: Cambridge University Press, 2015, 233.

requirement that the restrictions be reasonable in nature.[59] The first of these cases, *Romesh Thappar*, involved a ban on the entry, sale, and circulation of a weekly journal, *Cross Roads*, in the State of Madras.[60] The ban was challenged as being in violation of the free speech guarantee in Article 19 of the Constitution, the specific ground being that the reason for the ban – the maintenance of public order – did not fall under the enumerated limitations to free speech that were listed in Article 19(2). The Supreme Court upheld this challenge. Justice Patanjali Sastri, who spoke for the majority, found that only instances that undermined the security of the state or were targeted at its overthrow could fall under the permissible restriction on free speech. A general attempt at preserving public order fell outside the scope of allowable exceptions. The second case, *Brij Bhushan*, was similar in nature.[61] The petition was filed by the publisher and editor of an English weekly, *The Organizer*. They challenged an order requiring them to submit all material that related to Pakistan prior to its publication on grounds of maintaining public order. The majority struck down the order by way of a brief verdict: It affirmed the decision in *Romesh Thappar* and the reasons that were offered therein.

Notably, both cases dealt with colonial-era statutes. The impugned measures in *Romesh Thappar* and *Brij Bhushan* were issued under the Madras Maintenance of Public Order Act, 1949, and the East Punjab Public Safety Act, 1949. Both statutes had been passed under the Government of India Act, 1935, a matter of history that is important. When we imagine that a new constitutional order has been created and a prior legal tradition has been replaced, we might conceive of a conflict in a socio-political sense – that is, a conflict between a formal legal order and informal social norms and practices. But, here, the conflict was one between valid legal measures, and it captures how conflicts can arise when the assumed validity of prior measures gets called into question. The point I hope to make is that we not only need further work on the approach toward constitutional tensions during the first period but also work on the kinds of tensions that might exist; some tensions might be less obvious and more unique than we expect. And courts, in managing these and other tensions and in stabilizing the constitutional order, may be more creative in formulating doctrine than current studies recognize.

---

[59] On the first amendment to the Indian Constitution, see Abhinav Chandrachud, *Republic of Rhetoric: Free Speech and the Constitution of India*. Haryana: Penguin Random House, 2017, 72–97.

[60] *Romesh Thappar* v. *State of Madras*, AIR 1950 SC 124.

[61] *Brij Bhushan* v. *State of Delhi*, AIR 1950 SC 129.

5

Two Steps "Forward," One Step "Back"?

Transformation and Correction in the Implementation of Ecuador's 2008 Constitution

Eric Alston

5.1 INTRODUCTION

Ecuador's 2008 Constitution serves as a valuable case study for understanding the implementation dynamic created by a highly transformative constitution. The implementation of such a constitution demands a good deal from the implementing government but also affords the government considerable discretion as to how it should prioritize the realization of the new constitution's myriad requirements. Ecuador's experience since the enactment of the 2008 Constitution demonstrates how this weighty blend of implementation costs and discretion over priorities can result in a need for constitutional corrections, after missteps in implementation have become clear. These corrections may take the form of political action, popular protests, and ultimately, revision of the constitution itself.

In the following sections, I develop an analytical framework by which to understand constitutions as a function of the extent of social, political, and economic transformation their implementation requires. I argue that the greater the extent of change a constitution demands, the wider is the implementation path it provides to the incoming government, and the greater the set of implementation tradeoffs this requires. The greater scope and likelihood of tradeoffs increases the potential for variance from the ideal implementation path as envisioned by the set of interests who demanded the new constitution. As an implementing government increasingly trades off among competing implementation priorities, the likelihood that it oversteps the "right" constitutional balance increases, posing a need for corrections to the implementation path.

The implementation of Ecuador's highly transformative 2008 Constitution provides a rich context in which to examine how tradeoffs in implementation led to a variety of these corrections, during the administration of the government that shepherded the creation of the constitution but also in the following years as the next administration tapped into popular dissatisfaction with the implementation path to that point. In particular, these corrections can be categorized by whether they address substantive problems in constitutional implementation, or problems associated with the process by which the implementing government sought to satisfy constitutional obligations. Ecuador's modern constitutional experience is also notable because it is a case where a political movement's success under an existing set of democratic arrangements led to the movement altering these arrangements in profound ways. Maintaining the support of the coalition that brought the movement to power has proven to be challenging as implementing the new constitution in line with the diverse demands contained therein has necessarily involved the government prioritizing some constitutional objectives over others. This suggests that actual satisfaction of the social contract forged in a moment of demand for fundamental institutional change may be more costly than reaching the terms of the contract itself. Put more simply, agreeing on the need for change may be easier than agreeing on exactly how that change should occur.

Section 5.2 considers how the extent to which a constitution makes transformative demands has direct implications for the way implementation will proceed. Greater scope for tradeoffs similarly increases the likelihood for implementation outside the ideal bounds of those expected by core constituents, which in turn increases the need for downstream corrections to the implementation path. Section 5.3 describes how the recent historical context that gave rise to Ecuador's 2008 Constitution and different transformative demands in drafting necessarily resulted in implementation tradeoffs for the government under President Correa. Section 5.4 describes the outcomes of the constitutional drafting process, examining the extent to which different demands in the drafting process were realized in the final document. Section 5.5 highlights two substantive constitutional corrections that implementation under Correa and Alianza País ultimately entailed, while Section 5.6 treats two areas where the Correa government strained constitutional boundaries in the means by which it sought to simultaneously ensure constitutional and political objectives.

5.2 IMPLEMENTING A TRANSFORMATIVE CONSTITUTION IN THEORY

Most new constitutions arise as a result of demand for fundamental change in society and government. Regardless of the antecedents, a new constitution typically represents a major break in the governance institutions of a given nation, and so can be considered transformative by definition. However, one way in which constitutions vary is in the extent of transformation, or change, the new constitution implies compared to the reality that exists at the time of constitutional enactment, a reality greatly defined by the prior constitutional regime, for better or worse. From a cost-based perspective of constitutional implementation, the magnitude of change a given constitution implies closely tracks the net cost of implementation.

Relatedly, the extent of transformation a new constitution requires compared to the status quo directly creates a broad canvas for the implementing government. Put differently, the implementing government under a transformative constitution has a wide range of tasks of both high priority and high cost from which to choose. An increase in the scope of constitutional priorities the initial implementing government faces suggests an increased risk in terms of the government's ability to satisfy the range of transformative demands that have been formalized into the new constitution. As an implementing government increasingly trades off between costly implementation priorities, the costs of these tradeoffs create the need for "constitutional implementation corrections" at the legislative, executive, and constitutional level.

Cost here is used quite broadly to characterize all government resources, including the time and consideration of the different branches of government. The legislature can only consider so many topics during its annual sessions, and the courts can only hear so many cases brought before them.[1] Similarly, the executive branch can only spend so many resources on a set number of implementation priorities. This cost includes actual financial expenditure, or the more general constraint of the amount of government programs and priorities a new government can achieve at one time. State capacity clearly plays a large role in determining the upper bound of government output in a given period. Nonetheless, the change each constitutional provision implies, both singularly and in conjunction with other provisions, can require significant time to be carried out in full. The greater the change in society and government contemplated by a new constitution, the more transformative that constitution is.[2] At some theoretical point, it is likely that the marginal costs of additional change demanded by the constitution outweigh the marginal benefits this change implies. This suggests a number of consequences for the transformative potential of a given constitution.

One immediate consequence of increasing the transformative nature of a constitution is that it facilitates governmental discretion in terms of which rights and policies to prioritize. This is due to inherent structural and economic limitations on the extent to which any government can identify and execute on its agenda in a given time period. Trading off among implementation priorities is a task that faces every regime formed under a new constitution,[3] due simply to the rigidities of constitutional rights structures in particular[4] but also constitutional provisions more

---

[1]   See Michael P. Van Alstine, "The Costs of Legal Change." *UCLA Law Review* 49: 789 (2001); and Francesco Parisi, Vincy Fon, and Nita Ghei, "The Value of Waiting in Lawmaking." *European Journal of Law and Economics* 18 (2): 135 (2004).

[2]   Eric Alston, "Ecuador's 2008 Constitution: The Political Economy of Securing an Aspirational Social Contract." *Constitutional Studies* 3 (1): (2018).

[3]   Connor Gearty, "Do Human Rights Help or Hinder Environmental Protection?" *Journal of Human Rights and the Environment* 1 (1): 7–22 (2010).

[4]   See, e.g., Eric A. Posner, "Human Welfare, Not Human Rights." *Columbia Law Review* 108 (7): 1760 (2009); Louis Henkin, Sarah Cleveland, Laurence Helfer, Gerald Neuman, and Diane Orentlicher, *Human Rights* 2nd ed. Foundation Press, 2009, 107–9; and Klaus Bosselmann,

generally due to the fact that constitutionalizing a given government objective by definition removes that goal from the process of ordinary political exchange. Nonetheless, as the degree of transformation contemplated by the constitutional document increases, the extent of discretion afforded to the implementing government as to which rights to prioritize also increases. If the range of rights a government is intended to both protect and provide is sufficiently broad, then the implementing government must prioritize the implementation of some rights, both from a legislative and judicial standpoint.[5]

In a context where the magnitude of change implied by the constitution dwarfs the ability of the government to immediately implement its promises, which aspects of implementation are likely to receive priority by the first governments under the new constitution? One possibility is that governments are likely to prioritize those policies that are most likely to result in their reelection, are most popular with the public at large, or with the groups whose wealth or votes are needed to secure reelection.[6] In newly counterhegemonic regimes, the coalition of interests that gave rise to the process is often composed of those who were most disenfranchised under the previous regime.[7] In order to legitimize itself to such groups, the implementing government needs to provide tangible signs of progress.

As pertains to wholesale revision of the constitution itself, provided a given regime keeps the expected likelihood of present and future demand for constitutional rupture below a critical level, the regime's implementation of a given constitution can be characterized as sustainable. This means that the tradeoff any implementing government faces involves catering to the unique set of preservative and transformative demands to a level where the costs of collective action to demand constitutional corrections outweigh the benefits. Such a view of implementation in light of citizens' transformative demands obviously hinges on the underlying distribution of preferences. This perspective involves a role for citizens both as rights claims are made before the courts but also as the ultimate stopgap, for citizens ultimately demand constitutional change in the event the government, or a particular branch (including the judiciary), is failing in its constitutional obligations to where fundamental systemic change is needed. Even though ordinary citizens themselves may not prove to be the forcing mechanism by which such change is wrought, their demand for a fundamental break is often the critical trigger for a response by more powerful actors.[8]

"Global Environmental Constitutionalism: Mapping the Terrain." *Widener Law Review* 21: 177 (2015).

[5] Alston, n. 2.

[6] Ibid.

[7] Phoebe King, "Neo-Bolivarian Constitutional Design: Comparing the 1999 Venezuelan, 2008 Ecuadorian, and 2009 Bolivian Constitutions," in *Social and Political Foundations of Constitutions*, ed. Denis J. Galligan and Mila Versteeg. Cambridge University Press, 366–97, 2013.

[8] The events of the Arab Spring that led to constitutional turnover in a number of autocratic regimes emphasize this point clearly.

Nonetheless, in the immediate periods of implementing a constitution a clear alternative to citizen disillusionment and wholesale constitutional overhaul exists. To the extent that citizens have an input to the political process, their dissatisfaction with the observed level of transformation, as compared to the anticipated level of transformation created by the constitution's enactment, creates an opportunity for political correction to the transformative path. This suggests that the unpopular implementation of a transformative constitution can be self-correcting to the extent politicians capitalize on popular dissatisfaction. In some instances, adjustment of legislative and executive agendas may be sufficient to correct the course of a given transformative constitution's implementation. In other instances, constitutional amendment may be required to correct deficiencies that a given government's implementation of the constitution has revealed. Importantly, both these solutions avoid the much larger costs of constitutional redrafting entirely. The case of consti-tutional amendment to avoid constitutional overhaul is one way to view the creation of the Bill of Rights in the United States Constitution.

If constitutional drafters themselves are uncertain as to which aspects of a consti-tution will bind with more force than others,[9] comparative constitutional scholars face a difficult question when it comes to assessing the transformative demands formalized in a given constitution. Case studies of constitutional implementation can provide generalizable insights when considered with the logic of transformative constitutions developed in this book. In a constitutional moment, a variety of competing interests all want to transform the governance institutions of society, but their demands for transformation may be quite divergent from one another. One way to resolve competing demands at drafting has been labeled the "Christmas tree" approach, where every interest group gets an ornament.[10] This approach to consti-tutional design essentially punts much of the transformative question to the imple-menting government, which decides which ornaments to prioritize in implementation. However, this example of strategic behavior, among a variety of other strategic models of constitutional drafting,[11] suggests that assessing the extent to which a constitution is actually transformative requires an examination of that constitution's implementation.

In more granularly considering a given country's constitutional process from drafting through implementation, there are three periods where transformative and preservative demands are most salient: (i) during the drafting process, in terms of the specific demands each interest or group represented has for change; (ii) on

[9] These uncertainties are among the strategic pressures operating on constitutional drafters discussed in the introduction to this book.
[10] Lee J. Alston, Marcus André Melo, Bernardo Mueller, and Carlos Pereira, *Brazil in Transition: Beliefs, Leadership, and Institutional Change.* Princeton, NJ: Princeton University Press, 2016.
[11] The introduction to this book surveys a variety of strategic behavior in drafting processes that make inferring the actual extent and scope of transformative demands from the constitutional text a problematic exercise.

constitutional enactment, in terms of the extent to which each interest or group represented in the process was successful in obtaining its demands for change; and (iii) during implementation, in which we can assess the extent to which actual change contemplated by the constitution maps to the expectation (and ongoing demand) for change from enactment. The significance of the initial phases of implementation derives from the "first period problem" defined in the introduction to this book. In order to adequately understand the lessons from implementation of a transformative constitution within a given country, consideration of each stage of the process is necessary with regards to any given issue area subject to transformation under the new constitutional regime.

Many of the most salient constitutions to emerge under modern drafting processes tend to display considerable transformation to a given society's fundamental institutions of governance, as a response to the preceding regime's perceived shortcomings or abuses.[12] This suggests that highly transformative examples are ripe with lessons for constitutional scholars and practitioners. In this chapter, I consider the implementation of Ecuador's 2008 Constitution, a document that was highly transformative compared to the institutions of governance that existed previously. In particular, two broad areas of implementation, surrounding (i) substantive tensions within the constitutional document itself and (ii) the extent to which the implementing government tested constitutional boundaries, provide a means to assess how transformative constitutional demands are realized through a process that may as much involve correction as it does progress toward these transformative demands in the initial phases of implementation.

5.3 ECUADOR'S 2008 CONSTITUTIONAL ANTECEDENTS

In nations that have been governed by more than one constitution, a given constitution's origins are often greatly defined by the failures of the preceding constitutional regime. In Ecuador, the 1998 Constitution was demarcated by three elements: (i) neoliberal reforms; (ii) political crisis; and (iii) the rise of new indigenous and citizens' movements. While driven by a desire for more participatory democracy, the new constitution of 1998 did not avoid the eventual political demand for change that resulted in the 2008 Constitution. Although decentralization begun under the 1998 Constitution resulted in a favorable environment for participatory democracy on the local and provincial level (and accordingly favorable development policy), it did not result in the possibility for reform of the central government. This meant that the policies that operated largely to the benefit of elites at the national level were outside the reach of indigenous and citizen's movements

---

[12] The constitutional processes of South Africa and Kenya are both notable as to the extent to which their constitutions emerged as the result of demand for fundamental change to the institutions of governance.

at the subnational level, movements nevertheless empowered by the changes in governance that the 1998 Constitution did contemplate.[13] The considerable political liberalization on the subnational level created by the 1998 Constitution led to the emergence of numerous citizens' movements whose demands frequently included enhanced environmental protections, autonomy for indigenous groups, or both.

Ecuador is like many countries where the conceptually distinct areas of environmental and indigenous rights are tightly interwoven in practice. The identities of Ecuadorean indigenous communities are closely tied to concepts of environmental well-being and biodiversity. Two indigenous concepts that ultimately received constitutional treatment in 2008 emphasize this link clearly. Pacha Mama is an indigenous term that refers to "Mother Earth" in a way that emphasizes the fundamental dependence of human existence on the environment, with all the connotations of nurturing and support that motherhood entails.[14] A related term, Sumak Kawsay, loosely translates as the "good life," but the meaning of "good" that animates the term is one suffused with environmental ideals.[15] According to indigenous Ecuadorean understanding of the term, an individual's well-being is inextricable from the well-being of the environment in which they reside.

Ecuador is a country of immense natural resource abundance, a characteristic that has created economic reliance on natural resource extraction. The link between economic development and natural resources means the practice of mining has had political salience within the country during its entire modern period. But Ecuador's experience with the industry has not been a clearly positive one, for a number of foreign mining companies' practices resulted in well-documented environmental degradation. Perhaps the most famous example of these practices occurred with Texaco in the Oriente region of Ecuador, part of the Amazonian highlands and among the most biodiverse regions in the country. Texaco's disposal of petroleum byproducts in the Lago Agria region polluted waterways, and left visible dead zones in places.[16] These outcomes received considerable publicity in the nation and resulted in protests from indigenous groups but also among the general population more broadly. Persistent levels of poverty and inequality within the country exacerbated the situation by adding the perception that the environmental abuses were not resulting in economic benefits that were enjoyed by most of the population.[17]

The perception of widespread abuses by mining companies proved to be a source of considerable political support for the Alianza País party, headed by Rafael Correa.

---

[13] Santiago Ortiz Crespo, "Participación ciudadana: la Constitución de 1998 y el nuevo proyecto constitucional." *Revista de Ciencias Sociales* 32: 14 (2008).

[14] Pascal Lupien, "The Incorporation of Indigenous Concepts of Plurinationality into the New Constitutions of Ecuador and Bolivia." *Democratization* 18 (3): 780 (2011).

[15] Ibid.

[16] Nicole Fourtané, "Las poblaciones indígenas y campesinas de la Amazonía frente a la petrolera Chevron-Texaco: un juicio histórico." *Revista AFESE* 59 (59) (2017).

[17] Murat Arsel, "Between 'Marx and Markets'? The State, the 'Left Turn' and Nature in Ecuador." *Tijdschrift voor Economische en Sociale Geografie* 103 (2): 151 (2012).

The economic disenfranchisement of much of the country was instrumental in bringing Correa to power in 2006. Correa's political movement counted indigenous and environmental interest groups among its prominent supporters, and regularly affirmed its commitment to the objectives of these groups.[18] Correa's argument that the country needed wholesale overhaul in its fundamental institutions met with widespread popular support, especially among environmental and indigenous interest groups. Nonetheless, the level of economic and political disenfranchisement that many segments of the population had experienced during the preceding periods of corruption and instability meant that Correa's coalition encompassed a broad swath of interests beyond the environmental and indigenous interest groups. Thus, while environmental and indigenous rights protections were a major plank of the Alianza País platform, they were only a subset of the transformative aims that were debated in the Constituent Assembly that Correa was instrumental in organizing following his rise to power in 2006. The interests represented, from broad social movements among Ecuador's poorer classes, to a range of indigenous groups and subnational communities, to groups championing the cause of environmental issues more generally, influenced the definition of the 2008 Constitution, which ultimately guaranteed rights governing most, if not all, of the principal aims of the groups, including an extensive suite of environmental rights whose implementation has proven less transformative than many groups hoped. The open canvas of a new constitution can provide ample room for a diverse group of interests to each achieve formalization of their transformative demands, but realizing all of these demands in the initial phases of implementation is another question entirely.

The initial electoral results for Correa display how effectively he and his party tapped into widespread levels of dissatisfaction with the preceding periods of instability and corruption. By prevailing so soundly over his opponent, Correa had the mandate he needed to formalize the popular demand for fundamental transformation to the nation's governance institutions. The referendum to elect a Constituent Assembly resoundingly echoed this mandate, with 82 percent of respondents approving the need for a new constitution.[19] Although the referendum to approve the new constitution passed by a wide margin, with a 64 percent approval of voters,[20] the comparative decrease suggests tensions as to the extent to which the document reflected all the demands of the diverse coalition of interests that gave rise to Correa. The divergence in support between the referendum for a new constitution, and the referendum that ultimately approved the new constitution, displays how the realization of transformative demands in a new constitutional process may fall short of the

---

[18] Marc Becker, "Correa, Indigenous Movements, and the Writing of a New Constitution in Ecuador." *Latin American Perspectives* 38 (1): 47–62 (2011).

[19] Simón Pachano, "Ecuador: New Political System into Operation." *Revista de Ciencia Política* 30 (2): 297–317 (2010).

[20] Eduardo Gudynas, "The Political Ecology of the Biocentric Turn in Ecuador's New Constitution." *Revista de Estudios Sociales* 32. 38 (2009).

expectations of those who most hope for change to result from the process. Whether these outcomes were the result of transformative demands that were directly competitive with each other or if they reflected the more fundamental tension between transformative and preservative demands considered in the introduction to this book is beyond the scope of this analysis, but presents an additional dimension by which to consider the outcomes of a particular constitutional drafting process. It is the outcomes of this stage of Ecuador's modern constitutional history with which the next section of this chapter is concerned.

5.4 THE CONSTITUTIONALIZATION OF TRANSFORMATIVE DEMANDS

Given the preceding set of transformative demands, it is no surprise that the 2008 Constitution was widely recognized as marking a wholesale change in the nation's fundamental institutions. Progressive legal scholars both domestically and abroad lauded the extent to which the constitution secured traditional leftist aims generally but also how groundbreaking the environmental protections were.[21] Rights to a clean and healthy environment,[22] rights of organisms themselves to life and preservation of habitat,[23] and rights to environmental restoration[24] are among the most noteworthy of the sweeping suite of environmental rights seen in the 2008 Constitution. The formal recognition of indigenous languages,[25] the plurinational nature of the nation,[26] the consistent emphasis on the indigenous concepts of Sumak Kawsay and Pacha Mama,[27] and the right to consultation with affected communities[28] stand among the suite of benefits indigenous groups fought for, and obtained, in the drafting process. Finally, the more traditional social rights such as health care,[29] education,[30] social security,[31] and decent standard of living[32] are also outlined in clear detail throughout. In comparison to the preceding periods of

---

[21] See, e.g., Paul Dosh and Nicole Kligerman, "Correa vs. Social Movements: Showdown in Ecuador." NACLA *Report on the Americas* 42 (5): 22 (2009); Gudynas, n. 20; Pachano, n. 19; and Becker, n. 18.

[22] 2008 Constitution of the Republic of Ecuador, Art. 14; Art. 66.27.

[23] Ibid. Art. 71.

[24] Ibid. Art. 72.

[25] Ibid. Art. 2.

[26] Ibid. Art. 1.

[27] References to Pacha Mama appear in the 2008 Constitution of the Republic of Ecuador in the Preamble and Art. 71. References to Sumak Kawsay appear in the 2008 Constitution of the Republic of Ecuador in the Preamble; and Arts. 14, 250, 275, and 387.

[28] 2008 Constitution of the Republic of Ecuador, Art. 57.7; 57.17.

[29] Ibid. Art. 32.

[30] Ibid. Arts. 26–29.

[31] Ibid. Art. 34.

[32] Ibid. Art. 30; 66.2.

high inequality, perceived corruption, and political instability, the 2008 Constitution lay out a progressive vision of Ecuador that was profoundly transformative.

Drafters were also sensitive to questions of the accessibility of rights claims. On its face, Article 86 provides for "jurisdictional guarantees," an expansive procedure for resolution of citizens' claims of unconstitutional government behavior, seemingly apart from traditional legal remedies, as well as more extraordinary constitutional remedies like habeas corpus, habeas data, and amparo,[33] each of which also appears in the 2008 Constitution.[34] As an example of the expansiveness of the jurisdictional guarantees, Article 86.1 provides that any "person, group of persons, community, people or nation will be able to propose actions envisaged in the Constitution," and in 86.2.c, provides that support of an attorney in order to file an action is not a requirement. As importantly, claimants are not required to articulate which constitutional norm or rule has been violated, and the burden of proof, once a claim of unconstitutionality has been raised, lies with the government.[35] These provisions highlight the extent to which drafters wanted the transformation the constitution suggested to be accessible to ordinary individuals across society.

Similarly, Ecuador's protection of the environment does not limit itself to the enumeration of rights to a clean environment but also imposes duties on citizens to adopt measures necessary to avoid negative environmental impacts from their actions.[36] Further, environmental restoration in the case of degradation by extractive industries is an obligation required by the Constitution in Article 72, specified as a right granted to nature apart from the compensation required of the state or private entities in the case of affected communities or individuals. Again, the distinction between an individual right and a collective right or one granted to nature is notable.

One way the Constituent Assembly sought to resolve this tension was to focus on negative public health outcomes associated with environmental degradation, and to guarantee in Article 14 the right to a "healthy environment" immediately following the rights to water and food that appear in Articles 12 and 13, the first rights enumerated in the Title II Rights section. Such a focus on public health is also likely a function of the outcomes surrounding governance of natural resource extraction under previous regimes. Further, alongside the right to housing seen in Article 30, the 2008 Constitution guarantees the right to a healthy habitat. To the

---

[33] The right to amparo in Latin America guarantees ordinary citizens the right to prompt judicial redress of rights infringements in the case of unconstitutional laws or government actions or omissions. See, e.g., Allan R. Brewer-Carias, *Constitutional Protection of Human Rights in Latin America: A Comparative Study of Amparo Proceedings.* Cambridge University Press, 2009, 77. The similarity of this right with a lengthy tradition in Latin American jurisprudence to the jurisdictional guarantees in Article 86 is worth noting, because it displays part of the structural tensions that led to the practice of neoconstitutionalism discussed in the next section.

[34] 2008 Constitution of the Republic of Ecuador, Arts. 89–90; 92; 95.

[35] Ibid. Art. 86.3.

[36] Ibid. Art. 83.

extent that environmental degradation impacts the health of individuals, they likely have an actionable claim under these provisions, which fits cleanly with the broad-based conception of Sumak Kawsay that was central to the rejection of the policies of previous governments. Nonetheless, the extent that such a broad definition provided immediately actionable rights to the groups with whom the term originated is another question entirely, as seen by the difficulties in getting a judgment against Chevron in a jurisdiction in which the company would have to pay.[37]

Despite the conflicts indigenous groups had with the constitutional provisions on language, and the tension between the provisions on natural resources and recognition of Pachamama and Sumak Kawsay, "the indigenous movements decided to take what they could get rather than losing everything with a more principled stance."[38] In other words, indigenous groups saw the limits of their bargaining power in the diverse coalition represented within Correa's movement, and prioritized the aims of increased political recognition and definition of environmental rights over the full suite of transformative outcomes they desired. As will be discussed subsequently, the extent to which a transformative guarantee is realized in practice by definition influences citizens' demand for corrections to the implementation path of a given constitution.

5.5 SUBSTANTIVE CORRECTIONS: IMPLEMENTATION REVEALS TENSIONS WITHIN THE CONSTITUTION

Some underlying constitutional issues only become clear through implementation. The need for continued judicial oversight of the legal system and the power of judicial review itself indicate the overarching need for maintenance of the constitutional order to continue to define the boundaries of constitutional jurisprudence and legislation. Similarly, no constitutional right is unlimited in scope, whether it be the right to freedom of speech, to property, or to life; each exists in a constellation of rights whose importance from time to time must impose constraints on the exercise of other rights. These tensions among rights may only become apparent as cases that test the boundaries of rights guarantees slowly emerge from the complexities of human behavior. Ecuador's 2008 Constitution provides two examples of how substantive tensions in constitutional rights guarantees emerged during the immediate phases of implementation. In the first case of the tension created by continued

---

[37] The changes in the petroleum industry wrought by Alianza País meant a 2013 Ecuadorian court award of $9.5 billion against Chevron went unpaid because the company no longer had any assets within the country to which to attach the judgment. *See* Simon Romero and Clifford Krauss, "Ecuador Judge Orders Chevron to Pay $9 Billion." *New York Times.* February 14, 2011. Following this outcome, the Ecuadorean government supported a lawsuit that indigenous groups brought against Chevron in United States courts, but the indigenous plaintiffs ultimately lost the case due to findings of misconduct on the part of their attorney.

[38] Becker, n. 18 at 59.

natural resource extraction and the rights of nature, the Correa administration's initial implementing legislation was sufficiently controversial that the correction took the form of a constitutional amendment by popular referendum. In the second case regarding the practice of neoconstitutionalism created by expansive procedure in the case of claims of unconstitutional government behavior, the correction came via simple adjustment to the implementing legislation itself.

5.5.1 *Environmental Rights Tradeoffs*

In the context of Ecuador, these competing transformative demands, as realized in the 2008 Constitution, created conflicting implementation priorities. A large component of Alianza País' platform during its rise to power and constitutional drafting was a rejection of neoliberal economic policies, tapping into the widespread perception of Western financial and economic hegemony in the region, which was linked in political rhetoric to the high levels of poverty and inequality in the country.[39] This led to the enhanced guarantees to health care, education, and well-being that ultimately appeared in the 2008 Constitution. In light of these implementation priorities, the first years under the new constitution involved economic restructuring including the repudiation of debt and the development of new sources of government revenue, such as accepting a loan from China in exchange for petroleum in the future. Following an initial period of economic contraction, Ecuador's economy grew significantly during most of the Correa presidency, thanks in large part to a commodities price boom. In line with the transformative expectations, much of this economic growth translated into improved standards of living in the country, especially in regards to poverty measures.[40]

However, the relationship between commodities prices and economic growth in Ecuador is a testament to the nation's dependence on natural resource extraction. Between 30 to 40 percent of government revenues in a given year were from the oil sector alone, which comprised 50–60 percent of total export earnings in the same year.[41] In such an economic context, squaring continued economic dependence on natural resource development with transformative demands for environmental and indigenous rights improvements posed an immediate conflict for the implementing

[39] See, e.g., Dosh and Kligerman, n. 21; Gudynas, n. 20; Pachano, n. 19, and Becker, n. 18.
[40] For example, Ecuador's poverty headcount ratio at national poverty lines went from 64.4 percent in 2000 to 22.9 percent in 2016. Similarly, Ecuador's Gini index decreased from 53.2 to 46.5 from 2006 to 2015. See "GINI index (World Bank estimate)" and "Poverty headcount ratio at national poverty lines (% of population)." World Bank Development Indicators. https://data.worldbank.org/country/ecuador. It should be noted significant poverty reductions occurred in the years preceding Correa, but his administration clearly facilitated continued reductions in poverty levels, leveraging commodities price changes that were similarly instrumental to previous improvements.
[41] June S. Beittel, "Ecuador: Political and Economic Conditions and U.S. Relations." *Current Politics and Economics of South and Central America* 6 (2): 243–54 (2013)

government.[42] As opposed to an inclusive political process, some scholars character-ized the immediate post-constitutional period as one of authoritarianism and pater-nalism, in which Alianza País formed alliances with evangelist indigenous movements, and launched media campaigns that questioned the motives of groups opposed to the government's immediate policy objectives. Such actions were justi-fied in official rhetoric by stressing that indigenous, poor, and leftist groups had representatives in the political process, and that extra-political means of resistance were illegitimate attacks on this process.[43] As will be discussed in the next section, the problems in maintaining such a broad-based coalition of support for the choices made during initial phases of implementation would persist throughout the Correa administration.

Reactions to the implementation of the indigenous and environmental rights were initially mixed, in which some indigenous groups saw the inclusion of the concept of Sumak Kawsay in the goals of every ministry as a "major conquest," whereas others saw such inclusion as paying lip service to constitutional require-ments, without creating fundamental changes in the policy space that Sumak Kawsay should imply.[44] The implementation priorities as articulated by the Correa regime were alleviation of poverty, improving the quality of education, the con-tinued development of social security, and a broad conception of health. Such priorities closely coincide with the broader conception of Sumak Kawsay that has come to the fore in party rhetoric, although the necessary relationship to a clean and healthy environment is conspicuously absent from such implementation priorities. At a minimum, plurinationalism's recognition in the 2008 Constitution highlights the heterogeneity of the citizenry,[45] and provides a basis by which the indigenous communities have received more governance powers than in regimes past. These communities have been less pleased in regards to the enforcement of the rights of nature tied up with the recognition of Pacha Mama, though. Notably, both concep-tions of Sumak Kawsay enjoy considerable support within the country,[46] a testament to how the term's constitutional inclusion gave the precise definition of the term considerable political implications.

One such perspective within the country considers it the priority of the state to ensure that individuals as well as groups have their rights guaranteed. However, this characterization of the development plan leaves the rights of nature to the sidelines,

---

[42] One way to view the Yasuní-ITT project discussed later in this subsection is that it was a means by which the Correa administration proposed to sell petroleum extraction rights to the West not to drill, an attempt which was ultimately unsuccessful.

[43] Pachano, n. 19 at 308.

[44] Sarah A. Radcliffe, "Development for a Postneoliberal Era? Sumak Kawsay, Living Well and the Limits to Decolonisation in Ecuador." *Geoforum* 43: 246 (2012).

[45] Ibid. at 244.

[46] Jorge Guardiola and Fernando Garcia-Quero, "Buen Vivir (Living Well) in Ecuador: Com-munity and Environmental Satisfaction without Household Material Prosperity?" *Ecological Economics* 107: 177–82 (2014).

focusing on the redistributive aspects of national development. This is not to argue that environmental sustainability is always at odds with resource extraction, but that beyond some low threshold, these guarantees are in tension. This tension emphasizes the constraint that economic dependence on certain industries can place on institutional change itself: The need to finance increases in government outlays could only have come from resource extraction that past a certain level conflicts with constitutional guarantees to environmental well-being. Thus, the transformative demands that receive constitutional treatment can themselves be subject to extra-constitutional constraints as to the extent to which they can be realized in practice.

In order to facilitate the ongoing natural resource extraction that would underwrite the costly implementation priorities created by the 2008 Constitution, one of the first controversial actions of the Correa administration was to pass a Mining Law in 2009. The law granted expansive abilities to private companies to prospect on public lands for natural resources, and a process by which such resources could then be developed. The passage of the law was met with immediate protests. These reflected both the fact that natural resource extraction had been a persistent point of contention under the preceding regimes, and also the hopes for major change that the rise of Alianza País and the 2008 Constitution had created. The law defined mining as a public activity and greatly nationalized control of mines and oil fields but also allowed private companies to "liberally prospect for mineral substances."[47]

Ultimately, the law was subject to challenge before the Constitutional Court, due to the argument that the ability to prospect for and develop mineral resources was at odds with environmental and indigenous protections found in the constitution. Notably, some of the same groups that had been counted among Correa's early supporters were among those who challenged the 2009 Mining Law. The basis of these groups' claims surrounded how the law was in conflict with rights to access to clean drinking water and the rights to a healthy environment. In addition to the conflict that development priorities created with constitutional requirements on their face, the fact that a set of nationally influential interests were opposing the regime was remarkable in its own right.[48]

This rationale remained putative because the Constitutional Court decided in favor of the Mining Law, noting environmental protections in the law that made it more likely that future natural resource extraction would be conducted in a sustainable fashion. The ruling in favor of the Mining Law was itself a victory for the Correa administration, but the Court went further by granting "the State the authority to make exceptions to constitutional restrictions on mining in environmentally sensitive areas when the government declares this to be in the national

[47] Dosh and Kligerman, n. 21, at 22.
[48] Ibid. at 23.

interest."⁴⁹ An overt reference to the national interest being in tension with environ-mental protections, in the interpretation of the 2008 Constitution itself, is indicative of how some substantive tensions in the constitutional text may only become apparent after implementation. It should also be noted that the Court's interpret-ation ceded the power to determine whether a given natural resource extraction project was in the national interest to the government itself. This cession is consist-ent with ongoing scholarly criticism of the judiciary's lack of independence from the executive branch.⁵⁰

Since the Constitutional Court's ruling in favor of the 2009 Mining Law, Ecua-dorian courts have considered the rights of nature in a variety of different contexts. By 2016, thirteen claims under the rights of nature had been treated by the judiciary.⁵¹ Although ten out of these thirteen claims prevailed, seven of these prevailing cases were brought by a government official or ministry, with the Ministry of the Environment bringing the largest portion of victorious claims. These claims were victorious against three kinds of respondents: (i) private individuals; (ii) private companies; and (iii) local governments. In sum, early rights of nature claims that were most likely to prevail in Ecuador were brought by the national government against private actors or subnational authorities.⁵² Given the extent to which the Constitutional Court gave the government license to exempt itself from the most stringent environmental protections, it is unsurprising that claims against the Correa administration are absent from those cases where the rights of nature were impli-cated to date.

Beyond case outcomes under the rights of nature themselves, one specific example of proposed petroleum development displays the fundamental underlying

---

⁴⁹ Craig Kauffman and Pam Martin, "Can Rights of Nature Make Development More Sustain-able? Why Some Ecuadorian Lawsuits Succeed and Others Fail." *World Development* 92: 130–42 (2017).
⁵⁰ See, e.g., Santiago Basabe-Serrano, "Presidential Power and the Judicialization of Politics as Determinants of Institutional Change in the Judiciary: The Supreme Court of Ecuador (1979–2009)." *Politics & Policy* 40 (2): 2012, 339–61. See also Santiago Basabe-Serrano and John Polga-Hecimovich, "Legislative Coalitions and Judicial Turnover under Political Uncer-tainty: The Case of Ecuador." *Political Research Quarterly* 66 (1): 2013, 154–66.
⁵¹ Ibid.
⁵² Those successful claims not brought by the government came from two groups of local citizens and one couple, Nora Huddle and Fredrick Wheeler. The facts underlying Huddle and Wheeler's case are the type that would prevail in many nations under ordinary torts surround-ing damages to property. In expanding a local road, a provincial government disposed of gravel and rocks into a river, which caused it to flood the property of Wheeler and Huddle. Despite the fact that the provincial court cited the rights of nature, it is not clear whether it was damage to the environment or appreciable damage to the property that led to the claimants bringing suit. *Richard Frederick Wheeler y Eleanor Geer Huddle c/ Gobierno Provincial de Loja*, juicio 11121-2011-0010 (March 30, 2011). By one estimate, the costs of property restoration exceeded $43,000, an amount far greater than the per capita income in Ecuador. See Natalia Greene, "The First Successful Case of the Rights of Nature Implementation in Ecuador." Global Alliance for the Rights of Nature. http://therightsofnature.org/first-ron-case-ecuador/.

tension created by specific transformative demands of sharing in the nation's natural resource wealth while guaranteeing improvements in environmental protections.[53] One of Correa's most well-documented and ambitious environmental projects surrounded the discovery of massive oil reserves within the Ishpingo-Tambococha-Tiputini ("ITT") region of the Yasuní National Park, which is recognized as one of the world's most biodiverse regions.[54] The oil discovery totaled nearly 20 percent of the country's known reserves at that time. The Yasuní-ITT project was unusual in that its guarantees to preserve lands of high environmental value were contingent on large financial contributions from other nations. If a sufficient amount of foreign donations were secured in comparison to the value of the reserves at 2007 price levels, which was $7.2 billion, then the Ecuadorean government would agree to forego development of the petroleum.[55] The Alianza País administration premised international involvement on the fact that the world should value biodiversity and reduction in carbon emissions, and is part and parcel of the global demand for commodities that led to the controversy in the first place.

Nonetheless, by August 2013, the Correa administration announced that it was abandoning the project after only raising $13 million of the $3.6 billion the project proposal required at 2007 commodities price levels.[56] While the project was undeniably popular within the country, drilling in the region began by late 2016.[57] However, the extent to which the region will ever be fully developed has more recently been brought into question after a referendum explicitly restricted oil development in the area along several dimensions.[58] It should be noted that petroleum extraction within the Yasuní-ITT region was among a total of only seven items given specific treatment in the referendum held on February 4, 2018 under President Lenín Moreno, Correa's successor with the Alianza País party. (I will describe Moreno's relationship with Correa further later.) The referendum also

---

[53] Nathalie Rühs and Aled Jones, "The Implementation of Earth Jurisprudence through Substantive Constitutional Rights of Nature." *Sustainability* 8: 174–93 (2016).

[54] Arsel, n. 17 at 157–59.

[55] Arsel, n. 17 at 150–63; Murat Arsel and Natalia Avila Angel. "'Stating' Nature's Role in Ecuadorian Development Civil Society and the Yasuní-ITT Initiative," *Journal of Developing Societies* 28 (2): 203–27 (2012); Matt Finer, Remi Moncel, and Clinton N. Jenkins, "Leaving the Oil under the Amazon: Ecuador's Yasuní-ITT Initiative." *Biotropica* 42 (1): 63–66 (2010); Carlos Larrea and Lavinia Warnars, "Ecuador's Yasuní-ITT Initiative: Avoiding Emissions by Keeping Petroleum Underground." *Energy for Sustainable Development* 13 (3): 219–23 (2009); Laura Rival, "Ecuador's Yasuní-ITT Initiative: The Old and New Values of Petroleum." *Ecological Economics* 70 (2): 358–65 (2010).

[56] Kevin Koenig, "Ecuador Breaks Its Amazon Deal." *New York Times*. June 11, 2014. www.nytimes.com/2014/06/12/opinion/ecuador-breaks-its-amazon-deal.html.

[57] John Vidal. "Oil Drilling Underway beneath Ecuador's Yasuní National Park," *The Guardian*. October 26, 2016. www.theguardian.com/environment/2016/oct/26/oil-drilling-underway-beneath-ecuadors-Yasuní-national-park.

[58] "Ecuador le dice no al petróleo en el Amazonas," *El Espectador*. February 5, 2018. Available at www.elespectador.com/noticias/medio-ambiente/ecuador-le-dice-no-al-petroleo-en-el-amazonas-articulo-/3/35//.

contained a more general constitutional amendment that prevented all mineral development in parks, natural areas, and urban areas, alongside other issues that will be treated in the next section.[59]

While the restriction on further mining in the Yasuní-ITT region did not itself require an amendment to the constitution, the more general restriction directly changed the constitutional text pertaining to mining. The question as posed on the referendum was unambiguous in asking whether to prohibit without exception metallic mining in all its phases in natural and protected areas and urban centers. Like the other ballot issues, the questions treating a constitutional amendment restricting mining and a new restriction on oil extraction in the Yasuní-ITT region passed resoundingly in early February 2018.[60] It is unclear whether the constitutional corrections orchestrated by Moreno were based primarily in political opportunism in catering to popular dissatisfaction with implementation decisions made under Correa, or if the referendum also displayed political leadership on the part of Moreno in correcting the constitutional implementation path for its own sake. What is clear is that absent the levels of popular dissatisfaction with constitutional implementation experienced thus far, Moreno would likely have been unable to engage in the extent of constitutional correction that has occurred since he took office.

Thus, Lenín Moreno has publicly addressed the perceived excesses of the Correa regime, and these corrections, both through constitutional amendment and public consultation, directly display the implementation dynamic created by a transformative constitution as creating a need for adjustments to the implementation path in subsequent periods. Nonetheless, recent events suggest the persistent need for constitutional resolution that Ecuador's indigenous and environmental rights have created. Mineral development proceeds at larger proposed scales than ever before, which has resulted in a variety of claims before the constitutional court surrounding the rights to consultation. In the most recent cases, governing the rights of affected communities to consultation, the mining interests have prevailed, including in a case surrounding "one of Ecuador's biggest mining projects to date."[61] These cases also surrounded a demand from affected regions that large-scale mining projects require a public referendum in order to proceed, but the Constitutional Court similarly rebuffed these arguments, allowing the government to proceed under the 2009 Mining Law.[62] Thus, while mining has been restricted in parks and near cities

[59] Consejo Nacional Electoral, "Referendum y Consulta Popular 2018." February 4, 2018.
[60] Simeon Tegel, "A Referendum in Ecuador Is Another Defeat for South America's Left-Wing Populists." *Washington Post.* February 5, 2018. www.washingtonpost.com/news/worldviews/wp/2018/02/05/a-referendum-in-ecuador-is-another-defeat-for-south-americas-left-wing-populists/.
[61] "Ecuador Constitutional Court Backs Copper Miner SolGold." *Reuters.* September 19, 2019. Available at: www.reuters.com/article/solgold-ecuador-court/ecuador-constitutional-court-backs-copper-miner-solgold-idUSL5N26A1P6.
[62] "Mineral-Rich Ecuadorean Province Requests Popular Referendum on Mining." Reuters. July 30, 2019. Available at www.reuters.com/article/us-ecuador-mining/mineral-rich-ecuadorean-province-requests-popular-referendum-on-mining-idUSKCN1UP2CN; "Ecuador Court Denies

thanks to the constitutional referendum discussed previously, the larger question of the extent to which environmental rights govern mineral activities is likely to persist well past Moreno's administration. Unlike the persistent structural tension surrounding environmental and indigenous rights and natural resource extraction, the issue of "neo-constitutionalism" (neoconstitucionalismo) treated in the following subsection did not require constitutional amendment to address the distortions its inclusion in the constitutional text created.

5.5.2 *"Neo-constitutionalism"*

In addition to the implementation tradeoff between social and environmental rights, one particular article treating jurisdictional guarantees has led to conflicting legal decisions in Ecuador since the Constitution was enacted, to the point that resolving the issues it created was an express priority for the Alianza País administration under Correa. This was the previously mentioned Article 86, which creates an unusual procedural recourse for claims of unconstitutional government actions or omissions.

Where the article created problems in implementation was in granting original jurisdiction to courts to consider claims in "the place where the deed or omission originated or where its impacts were exerted."[63] The ability to rule on constitutional issues at all levels of jurisdiction is by no means an innovation, but Article 86 lays out an unusual procedure by which claims of unconstitutional government behavior will proceed. In addition to defining general objectives for the proceedings like simplicity, speed, and efficiency; the Article requires that the proceedings shall be verbal, and the person or group making the claim is not required to identify the specific constitutional rule they think has been violated as a result of government action or inaction. Furthermore, on reaching a ruling in the public proceedings, Article 86.3 requires the deciding judge at courts of first instance to enunciate which rights have been infringed in a given course of action. Finally, and perhaps most importantly, the "claim alleged by the person filing the complaint shall be presumed to be true as long as that public institution that is called on does not prove contrary or does not provide information."[64] In short, Article 86 places the burden of proof on the government, once someone has made a claim of unconstitutionality, to prove the constitutionality of their act or omission.

Article 86 was noted as one of the most significant changes in the constitution in terms of how claims of unconstitutionality could be brought against the

---

Requests for Popular Approval of Mining Projects." Reuters. September 18, 2019. Available at www.reuters.com/article/ecuador-mining/ecuador-court-denies-requests-for-popular-approval-of-mining-projects-idUSL2N2690V8.
[63] 2008 Constitution of the Republic of Ecuador, Art. 86.2.
[64] Ibid. Art. 86.3.

government,[65] and stands among the areas where Ecuador's 2008 Constitution outstripped that of Bolivia in terms of changes to procedure designed to ensure constitutional rights provisions.[66] That another neo-Bolivarian constitution in the region does not go so far in terms of procedural guarantees is telling, given the ideological similarities underlying the groundswell of popular support that brought the regimes to power in both countries. For example, the right to amparo is present in both the Ecuadorean and Bolivian constitutions, a fact that one scholar notes places the additional procedure defined in Article 86 in strange tension with existing legal procedures.[67] For extraordinary violations of rights, the rights to habeas corpus, habeas data, and amparo all have well-established procedures governing how and when such claims can proceed. As to all other legal claims, these also have a constitutional base in the fundaments of the legal system, such that allowing another avenue of rights claims to proceed at any court of first instance with the burden of proof on the respondent provides another avenue for constitutional relief whose relationship with existing procedural safeguards was unclear.[68]

By 2010, the role of judges as "enforcers" of constitutional rights guarantees created an identifiable controversy among legal scholars in the country, as was the role of the executive in trying to resolve the issue.[69] Furthermore, analysis of existing claims brought under the enhanced jurisdictional guarantees suggested that even the procedural guarantees, requiring verbal proceedings that are simple, quick, and effective, were not being adhered to in practice. In particular, the requirement that such claims proceed through oral arguments was recognized as a goal that might only be achievable after a wholesale change in the legal culture and training of the country.[70] A competing perspective held that the jurisdictional guarantees were necessary to realize the extent of change that the constitution envisioned for the access of ordinary citizens to remedies when the government did not live up to its constitutional obligations. One proponent of this perspective argued that many of the existing procedural requirements under the law would have to be done away with in order to achieve the speedy and effective resolution of claims that Article 86 contemplates.[71] This view was not without constitutional foundation, for Article

---

[65] Illares Lupercio and Luis Alberto, "El neoconstitucialismo y las garantías jurisdiccionales en la actual constitución." University of Cuenca Bachelor's thesis. 2010 at 3.

[66] Claudia Storini, "Las garantías de los derechos en las constituciones de Bolivia y Ecuador." *Foro Revista de Derecho* 14: 104–5 (2017).

[67] Ibid. at 120.

[68] For an extensive discussion of the interpretive challenges created by the expansive jurisdictional guarantees found in the 2008 Constitution, see David Cordero Heredia and Nathaly Yépez Pulles, "Manual (crítico) de Garantías Jurisdiccionales Constitucionales." Fundación Regional de Asesoría en Derechos Humanos. INREDH. 2015.

[69] Agustín Grijalva. "Independencia judicial y derechos en Ecuador." *Ecuador Debate* 83: 35–42 (2011).

[70] Marco Washington Avila Solano, *Garantías jurisdiccionales en la Constitución de la República del Ecuador.* University of Cuenca Bachelor's thesis, 2010.

[71] Ibid. at 12.

86.2.e notes that "those procedural standards which tend to slow the speedy disposition will not be applicable." However, the extent to which these procedural standards, equivalent to notions of due process in the United States legal system, did not provide valuable protections to either claimants or respondents in these cases is not clear, such that their removal would not be without its own constitutional implications.

President Correa's Legal Secretary, Dr. Alexis Mera, characterized this issue as a policy priority of chief importance in the years of Correa's final term because of the pattern of conflicting lower court decisions regarding constitutional rights that had emerged as a result of the jurisdictional guarantees seen in Article 86.[72] This problem was exacerbated under such a transformative constitution. The increased scope and substance of the constitution has been linked to amplifying the interpretive challenges associated with adjudicating claims brought under new constitutional provisions.[73] The change was not perceived negatively by all legal commentators in the country, with one scholar noting how judges are no longer "the mute mouth of the law" but have instead been converted into the "protagonist of State action."[74] Debates over the appropriate interpretive and lawmaking stance of judicial consideration of claims brought before the courts are not specific to Ecuador, but the extent to which lower court judges should feel empowered to articulate the application of constitutional rules to cases brought to them by claimants who cannot themselves identify a constitutional violation is a specific extension of judicial activism that unsurprisingly created costs for reconciling conflicting applications of constitutional rules to different fact patterns in different jurisdictions.

By 2015, the Correa administration had succeeded in its aim of correcting this implementation challenge. The refinement to implementing legislation supporting the guarantees found in Article 86 was clearly designed to address the problems the expansive procedural characteristics afforded claimants of unconstitutional government behavior. Such a correction, by design, restricted the means by which judges could articulate new interpretations of constitutional rules based on the fact patterns presented to them. This legislative correction to legislation implementing constitutional rights has been characterized as "undoubtedly restricting constitutional rights."[75] By rendering the process more stringent by which claims of unconstitutional government action or omission can proceed, the change narrows the scope of claims that could have otherwise proceeded. Nonetheless, some members of the constitutional drafting assembly have supported a narrower interpretation of the

[72] Alexis Mera. Interview by author. Personal Interview. Quito, May 16, 2013.

[73] Israel Patrício Celi Toldo and Pablo José Castillo Álvarez, "La interpretación constitucional en relación con el constitucionalismo ecuatoriano." *Âmbito Jurídico*, XIX (147): (2016).

[74] Patricio Pazmino Freire, "Garantias Jurisdiccionales." Derecho Ecuador (2013). www.derechoecuador.com/garantias-jurisdiccionales.

[75] Ana Isabel Abril Olivo, "La Acción Extraordinaria de Protección en la Constitución 2008 del Ecuador." Doctoral Thesis. Universidad Andina Simon Bolivar Sede Ecuador 2014 85

procedural guarantees, noting the problems that a more expansive approach to the disposition of the jurisdictional guarantees would create for legal finality.[76]

In sum, Article 86 as enacted created a tension with other legal remedies such as amparo, as well as the increased likelihood of legal conflict at a constitutional level because of the ability of courts of first instance to identify and rule on constitutional claims in proceedings where the burden of proof lay with the respondent. The Alianza País administration's response to the problem shows how a drafting choice intended to facilitate the access of ordinary citizens to judicial recourse in light of unconstitutional government behavior resulted in clear implementation tensions alongside other procedures for remedying rights deficiencies. In this case, however, legislative and executive action was all that was required to correct the substantive tensions that came to be known as neo-constitutionalism within the country. In addition to these tensions in constitutional substance that become apparent through implementation, the case of Ecuador further displays how the means by which the implementing government exercises its constitutional mandate can also result in the need for constitutional corrections, a question discussed in the following section.

5.6 PROCEDURAL CORRECTIONS: CONSTITUTIONAL PROCESS MATTERS TOO

The Correa administration enjoyed high levels of popular support in the phases leading up to the enactment of the 2008 Constitution. In subsequent years, the administration's popularity waxed and waned as the country underwent economic restructuring and was subsequently subject to commodities price fluctuations. As the Correa government engaged in its implementation agenda over this period, a successful one if measured by aggregate poverty reductions, the administration's broad support wavered in a number of areas. This was due in part to the perception that the Correa regime only paid lip service to constitutional obligations in terms of consultations of affected communities, and was able to adjust the boundaries of constitutional constraints in consequential ways, as initial outcomes in the Constitutional Court with the 2009 Mining Law suggested. The aggressive pursuit of party priorities under a unified government with a strong executive led to several clear examples where the Correa administration tested the limits of constitutional boundaries with respect to term limits and the rights of freedom of association and freedom of the press. The first such example is the case of a 2015 constitutional amendment to the term limit provisions in the 2008 Constitution, a change that was ultimately undone by an amendment via popular referendum under Correa's successor in February 2018. The second surrounds the Correa administration's fraught relationship with dissenting voices in the country, including public sector workers such as the police and school teachers. In this latter case, the corrective response under

---

[76] Ibid. at 93.

Lenín Moreno involved a revocation of controversial executive decrees under Correa but also a constitutional amendment to create an independent council tasked with oversight of civil society organizations within the country. The fact that Moreno still leads Correa's former party means these constitutional corrections are simultaneously adjustments to the political party that gave rise to the new constitution, in terms of the party's implementation priorities and the constitutional boundaries within which any public actor in the country must remain.

5.6.1 *Term Limits*

From 2015 onward, there were news reports of continued efforts by President Correa and Alianza País to extend term limits. Initial reports highlighted the administration's intent to amend constitutional term limit restrictions via referendum, a proposal that was immediately met with skepticism given its implications for the strength of constitutionalism.[77] President Correa argued that extending term limits was needed to preserve the progress that had been made during his first two terms under the 2008 Constitution, and the concomitant risk that Alianza País would be running if they put up a weaker candidate in the presidential contest. Despite the talk of a referendum, term limits were ultimately extended through a legislative amendment on December 5, 2015. Notably, however, the law prohibited currently elected officials from contesting in the subsequent election, which effectively prevented Correa from running for a third term.[78] Prior to the 2017 presidential contest, Alianza País supporters submitted a petition to the Constitutional Court to permit Correa to run for a third term, maintaining that unbroken leadership was essential to the continued implementation of the 2008 Constitution under Alianza País' rule. Nonetheless, the choice to proceed with constitutional amendment via legislative means as opposed to popular referendum suggests that the Correa administration was not confident in its ability to prevail in a popular contest, as Correa's popularity had been flagging during his final years in office. The fall in popularity is both linked to diminished economic performance due to commodities price decreases, as well as the tensions in implementation that emerged surrounding natural resource extraction and treatment of dissenting voices.

As of late 2017, Correa stated he had no intention of returning to the executive office in Ecuador, unless the security of his revolution were at risk,[79] a qualification

---

[77] Mercedes Alvaro, "Ecuador's National Assembly to Vote on Term Limits." *Wall Street Journal*, November 1, 2014. www.wsj.com/articles/ecuadors-national-assembly-to-vote-on-term-limits-1414791747.

[78] "Ecuador's Current President Will Not Be Its Next," *Stratfor*, December 8, 2015. www.stratfor.com/analysis/ecuadors-current-president-will-not-be-its-next. (Accessed January 20, 2017.)

[79] "Ecuador President: Term Limit Needed to Restore Constitution," *ABC News*. November 29, 2017. Available at http://abcnews.go.com/amp/International/wireStory/ecuador-president-referendum-needed-restore-constitution-51467262.

which would swiftly prove to be a necessary one. One of Correa's former vice presidents, Lenín Moreno, won the close presidential election against a conservative opponent,[80] which emphasizes the extent of disillusionment with the Alianza País party compared to the periods in which Correa rose to power and oversaw the creation of a new transformative charter for the nation. The close electoral contest and the popular and political pressure to amend the Constitution to allow Correa to run again signal the fact Alianza País' political dominance in Ecuador is not assured, which explains how Moreno subsequently turned away from his predecessor, both in terms of rhetoric, but ultimately in correcting a variety of Correa's most unpopular actions in the 2008 Constitution's initial implementation phases. Subsequent to being elected, President Moreno voiced his opposition to the way the term limit extension was passed, and stated his intention to put the question to referendum on February 4, 2018.[81] As noted previously, the referendum contained specific and general restrictions on natural resource extraction within the country. In addition to the definition of a national council that is discussed in the following subsection, and enhanced penalties for child sex criminals and politicians found guilty of corruption, the referendum directly asked whether respondents would like to undo the amendment to term limits, and return to the original constitutional text.

Moreno was initially seen by political commentators as likely to keep the seat warm for Correa who would return to office after having satisfied the bar to consecutive terms, and whose approval ratings were expected to improve as oil prices rebounded. Instead, Moreno adopted a moderate position compared to the dominant role of the executive that had come to define the implementation period under Correa. Notwithstanding Correa's comments about not returning to the presidency, he created a new party following a public dispute with Moreno after the announcement of the public referendum. It is notable that Correa split from the party that he had founded as a citizens' response to the instability and corruption of preceding regimes. Ultimately, the public resoundingly approved the referendum, barring any president from serving more than two terms, and as noted previously, restricting natural resource extraction generally, as well as within the Yasuní region specifically.[82] The popular referendum indicates how unpopular decisions made during initial implementation periods are subject to popular and political correction, in some instances all the way to the constitutional level. While initial implementation decisions are crucial in defining the boundaries of the constitution within a given political system, the example of Ecuador also emphasizes that such decisions

---

[80] "Ecuador Recount Confirms Lenín Moreno Won Presidential Poll," *BBC News*. April 19, 2017. Available at www.bbc.com/news/world-latin-america-39640144.

[81] "Ecuador Names New Vice President; Correa Begins Campaign against Referendum to Limit Re-election," *MercoPress*. January 7, 2018. Available at http://en.mercopress.com/2018/01/07/ecuador-names-new-vice-president-correa-begins-campaign-against-referendum-to-limit-re-election.

[82] Simeon Tegel, n. 60. Available at www.washingtonpost.com/news/worldviews/wp/2018/02/05/a-referendum-in-ecuador-is-another-defeat-for-south-americas-left-wing-populists/.

are not necessarily irreversible, and are subject to the extent to which they map to citizens' expectations for transformation under the new constitutional regime.

5.6.2 *Associational and Press Freedoms*

Among the tensions that emerged in the immediate years of constitutional implementation was the pay and work conditions of government employees. An early example of alienation in terms of implementation outcomes was a dispute with the national teacher's union (UNE) regarding the detailed educational provisions in the Constitution,[83] and what these implied for the duties and compensation of existing teachers. From a broad perspective, ensuring continued increases in the standards of living of ordinary citizens can create demands on the part of public servants for similar improvements in their treatment under the new constitutional order. As will be discussed subsequently, the dispute with the teacher's union continued throughout the period of Correa's regime, and bears similarities to another dispute that emerged between the Alianza País administration and the police. The case of the police brought to the forefront concerns over the administration's treatment of press outlets, in a similar way to how the ongoing dispute with the UNE raised the question as to the extent to which associational freedoms under the 2008 Constitution[84] were guaranteed as against the dominant executive regime of Alianza País.

In 2010, the police in Quito participated in a well-publicized walkout over pay and working conditions that ultimately led to President Correa needing to be rescued from the Presidential Palace in what the administration labeled as an attempted coup.[85] The Correa administration was opposed to the strike, and the ensuing protests led to the deaths of five police officers. One newspaper's editorial criticism of the way the Correa administration handled the protest led to them facing a government lawsuit brought under a controversial bill passed in 2013, the Organic Communication Law. The newspaper lost the lawsuit, with ensuing penalties that were quite severe: The author of the editorial received a three-year jail sentence alongside three of the newspaper's executives, while the newspaper itself was fined $40 million. After the sanctions provoked an outcry, everyone involved received presidential pardons.[86] Nonetheless, it would be difficult to argue that such an outcome was not without its downstream chilling effects, for Ecuadorean news sources subsequently had to question where the boundaries of appropriate criticism lay, and if they exceeded the boundaries, ran the risk of massive penalties in the event President Correa did not choose to exercise his pardon power in future cases. Subsequently, the body tasked with oversight of the press, the

---

[83] 2008 Constitution of the Republic of Ecuador, Arts. 26–29.

[84] Ibid. Art. 66.13.

[85] See, e.g., "Ecuador Declares State of Emergency Amid 'Coup Attempt'," *BBC News*. October 1, 2010. www.bbc.com/news/world-latin-america-11447519.

[86] Beittel, n. 41 at 245.

Communications Superintendence, was criticized for being insufficiently independent of the executive branch. Moreover, the communications law itself grants a set of rights to the government, authorizing action in order to "protect the honor and reputation of public officials" as well as the right to correct and respond to criticisms made by the press. Regardless of the exact balance of journalistic and political motivations underlying press critiques of the regime, Alianza País has responded quite strongly in terms of its limitations on the continued ability of the press to level criticisms without fear of reprisal.[87]

As further evidence of the response to the police protests not being an isolated event, human rights oversight commissions from a number of international organizations highlighted a pattern of reprimands and warnings to press outlets from an authority empowered by the OCA in 2013. Explicit condemnations of the state of press freedoms in the country came subsequently from the United Nations Special Rapporteur and the Inter-American Commission on Human Rights.[88] This pattern apparently continued until the final days of the Correa administration, for in January 2017, the government moved to dissolve an environmental organization within the country after a set of violent protests erupted in response to the development of a Chinese copper mine.[89] As a sign that the administration may have overreached in its final phases, the Ministry of the Environment subsequently revoked the order dissolving the environmental group.[90]

Efforts to dissolve dissenting organizations were not limited to the environmental realm. As noted previously, the Correa administration's relationship with the UNE was one of contention from the early phases of constitutional implementation onward. Following a period of continued protests over working conditions and improvements the union felt were guaranteed under the 2008 Constitution, the Correa administration issued two decrees that were ultimately influential in dissolving the UNE entirely. Decree 16 in 2013 and Decree 739 in 2015 both numerically emphasize Correa's heavy use of the Decree power in later phases of his administration, but their specifics also expanded the power of the government to unilaterally

---

[87] The Correa regime's position regarding the press argued that every press outlet in the country is owned by wealthy opposition supporters who fell from power following the rise of Alianza País. See Antonio Checa-Godoy, "The Banking Sector and Media Ownership: The Case of Ecuador." *Revista Latina de Comunicación Social* 67: 125–47 (2012).

[88] OAS IACHR, "UN and IACHR Rapporteurs warn of arbitrary application of the Organic Communications Act," Organization of American States IACHR Joint Press Release R163/16. November 3, 2016. www.oas.org/en/iachr/expression/showarticle.asp?artID=1045&lID=1.

[89] David Hill, "Ecuador's Leading Environmental Group Fights to Stop Forced Closure." *The Guardian.* January 7, 2017. www.theguardian.com/environment/andes-to-the-amazon/2017/jan/07/ecuadors-leading-environmental-group-fights-forced-closure.

[90] Daniela Aguilar, "Court Dismisses Ecuadorian Government Bid to Shut Down Environmental NGO." *Mongabay.* January 26, 2017. https://news.mongabay.com/2017/01/court-dismisses-ecuadorian-govt-bid-to-shut-down-environmental-ngo/.

dissolve civil society organizations within the country,[91] along the lines of the Correa administration's move to dissolve the dissenting environmental rights group in early 2017. One prominent activist organization was dismissed under the terms of Correa's executive decrees because of its continued treatment of political issues in public communications, something that ran afoul of the stringent provisions found in the decrees.[92] This highlights the tight link between the freedoms of press, speech, and association under a regime that is unwilling to tolerate dissenting voices.

Such a fraught position for civil society organizations made the ongoing state of associational freedoms another area where Moreno immediately faced corrective pressures on assuming office. The corrective response in this case displays constitutional remedies as well as those emanating from ordinary executive authority. Moreno revoked Decrees 16 and 739 during his first year in office,[93] and in keeping with his slate of corrections via referendum, one of the issues treated on the ballot defined a new council with constitutional authority to oversee citizen participation and civil society organizations within the country. The new Council of Citizen Participation and Social Control is currently being formed as of this writing, but existing requirements for members include clear separation from the political process,[94] an institutional choice designed to insulate the Council from the political pressures that greatly defined the Correa administration's relationship with the press and NGOs during his time in office. Once again, corrective pressures that emerged as the Correa administration engaged in the implementation of its constitutional mandate eventually demanded formal resolution, in this case taking the form of both executive action and constitutional amendment.

5.7 CONCLUSION

Ecuador's 2008 constitutional redefinition of the fundamental institutions of governance was a radical departure from the preceding periods. The drafting process displays the competing transformative demands that led to the rise of President Correa and his former party, Alianza País. The transformative demands that were formalized into the 2008 Constitution included a broad range of progressive guarantees to health care and standard of living, a suite of environmental protections that became known as the rights of nature, and an unusual set of procedural guarantees designed to facilitate rights claims by ordinary citizens. These demands were the

[91] Catherine Conaghan, "Legal Norms and Civil Society Organizations." *LASA Forum* Xlvii: 2 (2016).

[92] Ibid.

[93] "Lenín Moreno derogó los decretos 16 y 739 y establece seis causales de disolución de ONG," *El Comercio.* October 23, 2017. www.elcomercio.com/actualidad/Lenínmoreno-deroga-decreto16-organizacionessociales-rafaelcorrea.html.

[94] "Aprobado informe para elegir al nuevo Consejo de Participación Ciudadana." March 7, 2018. *El Universo.* www.eluniverso.com/noticias/2018/03/07/nota/6655000/aprobado-informe-elegir-nuevo-consejo.

fruit of a political movement whose success within an existing set of democratic arrangements led to changes in these arrangements, all of which could not be realized simultaneously. Political agreement over the need for fundamental change may thus be less costly than political agreement over the set of immediate changes that receive prioritization over others.

This suggests that the extent to which the change contemplated by a constitution is actually realized poses a fundamental task for the government during initial phases of implementation. As the magnitude of change in a new constitution increases, so does the cost to the implementing government. Fixed constraints on the amount a given government can legislate or expend create the necessity for implementation tradeoffs. The need for these tradeoffs coupled with fixed upper limits on the government's output in a given period means the amount or scope of these tradeoffs increases with the extent of transformation a given constitution contemplates. A higher likelihood or scope of implementation tradeoffs increases the possibility for missteps in implementation that fall short of the transformation expected by core constituencies in society. Accordingly, the choices made by the implementing government can result in a demand for constitutional corrections. The need for these corrections can become apparent as substantive tensions within the constitution are revealed through implementation. However, the means by which the government implements the transformation demanded by the constitution can also create the need for these constitutional corrections.

The case of Ecuador displays two salient examples of structural tensions within the constitution that were only revealed through the initial course of implementation. First, the provisions guaranteeing improvements in health care, education, and standard of living all required significant increases in government expenditure. Given Ecuador's fundamental reliance on natural resource extraction for government revenues, this meant that securing these progressive guarantees required a level of resource extraction that created tensions with the sweeping constitutional protections granted to the environment. Despite the experience with foreign natural resource companies that led to the demand for increased environmental protections, the Correa administration prioritized natural resource extraction under a controversial mining law that was interpreted to permit the national government to exempt mining projects from the full set of environmental protections found in the Constitution. Continued outcomes surrounding natural resource extraction, including moving forward with petroleum extraction in the biodiverse Yasuní-ITT region, led to popular dissatisfaction with the Correa regime. Under Correa's successor, Lenín Moreno, enhanced restrictions on mining were imposed at the constitutional level, and the amount of the Yasuní-ITT region open to petroleum extraction was reduced. Although both these corrections occurred via referendum, the general restriction on mining ended up amending the constitution directly.

Another substantive tension that became apparent during implementation surrounded "neo-constitutionalism," a pattern of conflicting lower court judgments interpreting constitutional rights claims. The expansive procedural guarantees found in the constitution included not only the rights to habeas corpus, habeas data, and amparo but also set up a new procedure by which citizens could make claims of unconstitutional government actions or omissions. Importantly, the procedure did not require claimants to identify which rights had been violated, and placed the burden of proof on the government once a claim had been raised. The practice was identified as problematic by both legal scholars and government officials, and was eventually restricted through changes to the implementing legislation. In contrast to the tension created by environmental rights guarantees and natural resource extraction, this substantive correction proceeded through ordinary legislation.

In addition to the substantive tensions created by constitutional drafting choices, the means by which the government implements the constitution can also create the need for corrections. In the case of the Correa administration, two national controversies involved the extension of term limits that would have allowed Correa to run again in future elections, and the treatment of dissenting voices in the press and civil society organizations. The constitutional amendment to term limits proceeded through the legislature after Correa could not secure enough popular support to hold a referendum on the issue, an additionally unpopular choice amid the other problems in implementation already discussed. The Correa administration also had a fraught relationship with the press and NGOs within the country, taking public steps to silence dissent such as fining newspapers critical of his administration, and using executive decrees to expand the ability of the government to dissolve civil society organizations. Ultimately, the Correa government dissolved a teacher's union that persistently protested the implementation of constitutional provisions treating education, and moved to dissolve an environmental activist group in the regime's final months of power. The extension of term limits and treatment of dissenting voices were issues that led to demands for correction under President Moreno. Moreno quickly reversed Correa's executive decrees but also made the term limits and treatment of civil society organizations elements of the February 2018 referendum, both of which prevailed along with the other issues presented. This meant the Constitution was amended to reinstate the term limits originally enshrined by drafters, and an existing government council was significantly redefined to provide greater citizen input to how and why the government regulates independent organizations in society.

Through a given constitutional drafting process, transformative demands are formalized in a context where different interests vie for the extent and type of transformation that is realized in the final document. Thus, a constitution can be characterized as more or less transformative compared to the previous institutions that governed a particular society. This variance in transformation contemplated by a constitution suggests that the immediate phases of implementation are essential to understanding the extent to which the expected transformation is actually realized. The process of implementation to secure transformative demands can result in the need for corrections as structural tensions within the constitution itself become apparent, or as the government strains constitutional boundaries in pursuit of its implementation and political objectives. The extent to which Ecuador's 2008 Constitution was transformative makes the country a valuable case study in which to consider these outcomes.

PART II

The Issue of Gender

6

The Long Road Ahead

The First Period of a Gender-Responsive Constitution in Zimbabwe

Claudia Flores

6.1 INTRODUCTION

In the last decade alone, more than forty countries have amended and rewritten their constitutions to incorporate provisions advancing women's rights.[1] Most constitutions today contain some commitment to eradicating status discrimination based on gender or sex.[2] Increasingly, constitutions are revised to incorporate the progressive notion of gender equality captured in the Convention on All Forms of Discrimination against Women (CEDAW).[3] Parties to CEDAW, which include nearly all UN member states, agree to pursue actual equality between women and men.[4] Constitutions in eighty-five countries contemplate or require affirmative measures to remedy and address barriers to gender equality.[5] Increasingly, constitutions regulate private conduct that advances harmful stereotypes and unequal treatment of women

---

[1] Ecuador, Costa Rica, Dominican Republic, Bolivia, Angola, Burundi, Kenya, Guinea, Madagascar, Mozambique, South Sudan, Swaziland, Morocco, Niger, Tunisia, Montenegro, Rwanda, Zimbabwe, Qatar, Iraq, Kyrgyz Republic, Turkmenistan, Armenia, Azerbaijan, Laos, Myanmar, Thailand, Vietnam, Hungary, Kosovo, Montenegro, Fiji, Samoa, Nepal, Bhutan, Afghanistan, Sierra Leone, Egypt, Namibia, Libya, Columbia, and Maldives.

[2] WORLD Policy Analysis Center, *Does the Constitution Take at Least one Approach to Gender Equality*, available at https://worldpolicycenter.org/data-tables/policy/does-the-constitution-take-at-least-one-approach-to-gender-equality [accessed October 1, 2017].

[3] UN General Assembly, Convention on the Elimination of All Forms of Discrimination against Women (CEDAW), December 18, 1979, United Nations, Treaty Series, vol. 1249: 13. Available at www.refworld.org/docid/3ae6b3970.html [accessed May 2, 2018]. All states have ratified CEDAW, with the exception of United States, Palau, Iran, Somalia, Sudan, and Tonga.

[4] CEDAW Committee. "General Recommendation No. 25" (2004); para 6–10. Available at www.un.org/womenwatch/daw/cedaw/recommendations/recomm.htm [accessed September 11, 2018].

[5] UN Women, "Affirmative Action (Broadly)," *Global Gender Equality Constitutional Database*. Available at http://constitutions.unwomen.org/en/search?provisioncategory=d91f71586bb546 10baa13236037086c1 [accessed May 2, 2018]. Countries include Namibia, Ghana, Burundi, Italy, Turkey, Germany, Egypt, Viet Nam, South Sudan, Slovenia, Malta, Switzerland, Nepal, Sweden, Ethiopia, Uganda, Somalia, Swaziland, Luxembourg, Zambia, Sudan, Senegal, Malawi, Paraguay,

in areas such as employer–employee relationships (e.g. equal pay for equal work), parent–child relationships (e.g. parenting rights and responsibilities), and adult family relationships (e.g. partner and family violence).[6]

More and more, these overarching constitutional commitments are supplemented by language targeting women's equality in specific areas. In Kenya, women are provided sexual and reproductive rights: in Bolivia, access to healthcare without discrimination; in Armenia, paid maternity leave; in South Sudan, freedom from discrimination in the context of marriage; in Niger, protections from domestic violence; in Rwanda, equal pay and equal employment benefits; and in Somalia, prohibitions against sex and labor trafficking.[7]

These developments have been celebrated by the international human rights community, governments, and global and domestic women's movements. The inclusion of gender equality mandates in new constitutions has been interpreted as signaling positive change in the global struggle against women's inequality and as evidence of domestication of women's human rights. With many constitutions now guaranteeing equal rights and access to women, attention has now turned toward implementation of these promises and the question of how to maximize constitutional protections and properly assess state performance.

This book concerns itself with the first period of constitutional implementation. The first period of a new constitution, as we have defined it, is the bridge between the past and future, when a society may seek to preserve elements of its past while commencing pursuit of the changes that motivated reform.[8] While a new constitution may adopt an amended social and political vision, it is also subject to the same social and cultural dynamics and distribution of resources that existed prior to its installation. Understandably, these and other factors will pull toward preservation,

---

Belgium, India, Saint Lucia, Ecuador, Serbia, Portugal, Canada, Madagascar, Nicaragua, France, St. Vincent and the Grenadines, Argentina, Guyana, Cabo Verde, Sri Lanka, Peru, Zimbabwe, Niger, Cuba, Romania, Austria, Timor-Leste, Finland, Vanuatu, Fiji, Bolivia, Papua New Guinea, Rwanda, Samoa, Morocco, Algeria, Pakistan, Gambia, Tunisia, Equatorial Guinea, Congo, Grenada, Lesotho, Mauritius, South Africa, D.R. Congo, Mauritania, CAR, Bangladesh, China, Syrian Arab Republic, Antigua & Barbuda, New Zealand, Haiti, Belize, Montenegro, Kyrgyzstan, Solomon Islands, St. Kitts & Nevis, Dominica, Dominican Republic, Greece, Kenya, Sierra Leone, Colombia, and Tanzania.

[6] The Constitution of Romania of 1991(with amendments through 2003): Art. 41(4) ("women receive the same pay as men for equal work") (English translation quoted from www.constitu teproject.org/); The Constitution of the Republic of Uganda of 1995 (with amendments through 2017): Art. 31(equal rights in marriage and parenting responsibilities); The Constitution of Ecuador (2008): Art. 81 (protection from domestic violence).

[7] The Constitution of Kenya (2010): Arts. 26, 43; Constitution of the Plurinational State of Bolivia of 2009 (with amendments through 2005): Art. 45(v); The Constitution of the Republic of Armenia of 1995: Art. 35; The Transitional Constitution of South Sudan, 2011 (Rev. 2013): Arts. 15, 16; Constitution of the Republic of Niger of 2010: Art. 22; Constitution of the Republic of Rwanda of 2003: Art. 37 (with amendments through 2010); and Provisional Constitution of the Federal Republic of Somalia of 2012: Art. 14.

[8] [Introduction: 1].

while the desire to set new priorities, relationships, and expectations will motivate transformation.[9]

This chapter seeks to contribute to the book's exploration of the first period of constitutional reform by considering this inquiry in the context of a particular goal of reform – gender equality and women's rights. A constitution that aims to be gender-responsive, which I will define as a constitution with a substantive vision of gender equality as reflected in CEDAW, faces significant challenges. True social transform-ation of gendered power dynamics requires uprooting deeply entrenched inequities and hierarchies that will pull forcefully toward preservation. Thus, most consti-tutional mandates seeking reform of gender inequalities will struggle to accomplish their stated goals. The failures and achievements of a gender-responsive constitution must be viewed through a lens that appreciates the Herculean task such consti-tutions face. And so, as I will suggest in this chapter, while constitutionalization of gender equality may be properly understood as an important first step to women's advancement, it is only one step on a long road ahead.

In the meantime, advocates, commentators, and policymakers need better tools to assess the progress made by gender-responsive constitutions and to determine how to capitalize on the opportunities reforms provide. The first period can be critical to maximizing the benefits of reform, as this window has some potential to re-shift social dynamics or at least generate conversations and dialogue around reticent women's equality issues before such issues are once again almost inevitably sidelined and the *status quo* becomes re-entrenched. But the first period will not be equally beneficial or even necessarily beneficial for all the tasks of a gender-responsive constitution.

Using Zimbabwe as an illustrative case study, I will attempt to model the kind of review and analysis most informative in making sense of gender-responsive language and its first-period journey. Zimbabwe provides a useful case study for this task for a number of reasons. Zimbabwe's most recent reform in 2013 was preceded by a reform nearly a decade earlier, providing comparative processes that can highlight changes in textual priorities and paths to inclusion. Zimbabwe's 2013 reform process was instigated by a moment of social reorganization, a moment which was useful in addressing social inequalities, such as those based on gender. Finally, Zimbabwe approved one of the most gender-responsive constitutions globally that has emerged from any reform conducted in the last twenty years.

I will follow some of the dynamics generated during the initial implementation of the Zimbabwean reform process to provide a more nuanced representation of how the constitution might be understood as responsive to gender.[10] By viewing relevant

---

[9] [Introduction: 3].

[10] Some interviews and documentation cited in this chapter are sourced from research conducted for - Flores, Claudia and Patricia A. Made, *The Politics of Engagement: Women's Participation and Influence in Constitution-Making Processes*, UN Women (2016): 11. Available at www.onu .cl/es/wp-content/uploads/2016/06/Politics of-Engagement pdf [accessed August 15, 2018].

elements of the constitution within this context, we can begin to set expectations, identify priorities and develop strategies to ultimately maximize the work of the many individuals and institutions that have endeavored to realize women's equality through constitutional protections.

6.2 SETTING EXPECTATIONS

The diverse tasks of a constitutional reform process vary in difficulty and attainability. Among the social ills a constitution may seek to remedy, gender inequality is among the more reticent. Gender inequality is a global reality consistent across economies and political systems, pervasive and entrenched in law, institutions, customs, and practices.[11] Women experience lower levels of economic, social, and political capital than men by all measures even in the most progressive societies.[12] According to the World Economic Forum's 2017 Global Gender Gap Index, which ranks 144 countries, a gap exists between men and women in most countries on all four measured index components (relative educational attainment, participation in political leadership, health and survival, and economic opportunity) and in all countries on at least one.[13] Within the family, regardless of women's race, ethnicity, and class, women still play subordinate roles.[14]

Despite some progress, gendered social norms continue to hinder the development of women and girls in their public and professional lives. Female political leaders occupy less than a quarter of the seats in legislative bodies globally, face significant barriers to entry, and those who do seek office are subjected to gender-based discrimination and violence.[15] Women's labor remains globally undervalued. Women, on average, earn 60 to 75 percent of the wages of their male

---

[11] United Nations Development Programme (UNDP), *Table 5: Gender Inequality Index, Human Development Report 2016*. Available at http://hdr.undp.org/en/composite/GII [accessed October 1, 2017]; Simmons, Beth A., *Mobilizing for Human Rights: International Law in Domestic Politics*. Cambridge University Press, 2009, 203–4.

[12] UNDP, *Table 5: Gender Inequality Index*; World Economic Forum, *The Global Gender Gap Report 2017*. Available at www3.weforum.org/docs/WEF_GGGR_2017.pdf [accessed May 2, 2018].

[13] World Economic Forum, *The Global Gender Gap Report 2017*.

[14] I-Ching Lee, Felicia Pratto, and Blair T. Johnson, "Intergroup Consensus/Disagreement in Support of Group-Based Hierarchy: An Examination of Socio-Structural and Psycho-Cultural Factors." *Psychological Bulletin* 137 (6): 1029–64 (2011) Available at www.ncbi.nlm.nih.gov/pmc/articles/PMC3205474/ [accessed March 11, 2018].

[15] The World Bank, Proportion of Seats Held by Women in National Parliaments (%), data from Inter-parliamentary Union. Available at https://data.worldbank.org/indicator/sg.gen.parl.zs [accessed April 8, 2019].; See Inter-Parliamentary Union, "Sexism, Harassment and Violence against Women Parliamentarians." *Issues Brief*. October 2016. Available at www.ipu.org/resources/publications/reports/2016-10/sexism-harassment-and-violence-against-women-parliamentarians [accessed September 24, 2018].

counterparts.[16] With very few exceptions, girls' access to education is significantly more limited than that of boys.[17] In struggling economies, relative to men, women are deprived of basic resources such as access to healthcare and nutrition with life-changing and ending consequences.[18] This experience of inequality is magnified for women from marginalized or disadvantaged groups, due to ethnicity, race, or other status, who often occupy the very bottom rung of the economic, social, cultural, and political ladder.[19]

Violence against women persists in both public and private spaces. The sexual harassment of women is a prominent feature of many workplaces yet has received insufficient and uneven attention within legal and policy frameworks.[20] In their personal lives, nearly 30 percent of women experience physical and/or sexual violence by their partner or spouse.[21] Protections against sexual violence remain irregular – over thirty countries uphold laws exempting perpetrators of rape from prosecution when they are married to the victim.[22]

6.2.1 *The Gender-Responsive Constitution*

Women's inequality is so entrenched that a truly gender-responsive constitution requires mechanisms to address both women's subordination and transformation of the social, cultural, and economic conditions that cause it. The mandate for substantive equality contained in the Convention on All Forms of Discrimination against Women (CEDAW), the globally adopted standard for the overwhelming majority of UN member states, arguably represents the best effort to affect that

[16] The World Bank, "Removing Restrictions to Enhance Gender Equality," *Women, Business and Law* (2014). Available at http://documents.worldbank.org/curated/en/893551468147874555/pdf/922710PUB0v20W00B0x385355B00PUBLIC0.pdf [accessed August 14, 2018].

[17] UNESCO, *UNESCO eAtlas of Gender Inequality in Education: How Many Girls Are Excluded from Education?* Available at https://tellmaps.com/uis/gender/#!/tellmap/78041830 [accessed May 7, 2018].

[18] See Amartya Sen, "More than 100 Million Women Are Missing." *New York* (1990): 61–66.

[19] UNDP, n. 11.

[20] Int'l Labor Org. (ILO), *Ending Violence and Harassment against Women and Men in the World of Work, Report* V(1), ILC. 107/V/1, 1–31, 45–59, 77–83 (May 12, 2017), www.ilo.org/wcmsp5/groups/public/—ed_norm/—relconf/documents/meetingdocument/wcms_553577.pdf [https://perma.cc/BW68-KCRF].

[21] World Health Organization, Department of Reproductive Health and Research, London School of Hygiene and Tropical Medicine, South African Medical Research Council, "Global and Regional Estimates of Violence against Women: Prevalence and Health Effects of Intimate Partner Violence and Non-partner Sexual Violence" (2013): 2. Available at www.unwomen.org/en/what-we-do/ending-violence-against-women/facts-and-figures [accessed August 14, 2018].

[22] The World Bank, "Getting to Equal," *Women, Business and the Law 2016*. World Bank Group, 2016. Available at http://documents.worldbank.org/curated/en/455971467992805787/pdf/99454-PUB-Box393200B-PUBLIC-disclosed-9-9-15-PUBDATE-9-9-15-DOI-10-1596-978-1-4648-0677-3-EPI-210677.pdf [accessed August 14, 2018].

transformation.[23] CEDAW commits states to the pursuit of *de jure* and *de facto* equality between women and men.[24] This has been interpreted to mean that state parties to CEDAW must not only refrain from discriminating on the basis of gender in their laws, policies, and programs but also must affirmatively address and remedy existing discrimination against women in both the public and private spheres.[25] CEDAW's substantive equality mandate creates three primary state duties: ensuring that laws do not engage in direct or indirect discrimination; improving the *de facto* position of women through policies and programs in all spheres; and addressing gender relations and stereotypes in the private sphere.[26]

Article 2(a) of CEDAW requires that state parties "embody the principle of the equality of men and women in their national constitutions" or other appropriate legislation to ensure realization of substantive equality.[27] Thus, for a state party to CEDAW, a gender-responsive constitution should seek to implement and domesticate the goal of substantive equality. This includes ensuring services provided by the state, such as healthcare and education, are available equally to women and men.[28] It also includes making efforts to address social discrimination and stereotyping that adversely impact women's lives, such as women's roles in the family, duties in reproduction, and attributed physical and mental strengths and weaknesses.[29] A truly gender-responsive constitution also requires the state to transform how its institutions and administration receive and accommodate women.[30] The state must go beyond inclusion of women in governance and adapt its institutions to provide services like maternity leave and childcare that facilitate women's participation in governance.[31]

6.2.2 *Gender Equality and the Realities of Reform*

Constitutions that emerge from reform processes represent and express diverse interests, perspectives, and priorities. In practice, the language contained in a final text may be embraced for a number of reasons and often has a variety of origins; language is borrowed from neighboring countries, international treaties, existing legislation, cultural norms, or former constitutions. The commitments in a

[23] For a discussion of CEDAW's vision of status equality, see Samuel Moyn, *Not Enough: Human Rights in an Unequal World*. Cambridge, MA: Harvard University Press (2018): 202–7.
[24] CEDAW Committee, "General Recommendation No. 25, para 6–10," n. 4.
[25] Ibid.
[26] Ibid.
[27] UN General Assembly, n. 3: Art. 2(A).
[28] See United Nations Economic and Social Council, *General Comment No. 20: Non-discrimination in economic, social and cultural rights*, E/C.12/GC/20 (2009).
[29] Anna Diedzic, "From Paper to Lived Reality: Gender-Responsive Constitutional Implementation," *Discussion Paper* 20. International Institute for Democracy and Electoral Assistance, 2016, 12.
[30] Ibid. 11.
[31] Ibid.

constitution may be specific and proscriptive or vague to allow meaning to evolve over time or express a longer-term aspiration.[32] Thus, depending on the circumstances, there can be a narrow gap or a vast gulf between the ideals expressed and impact on the targeted rights-bearers and beneficiaries.

Sanford Levinson's framework that conceives of constitutional provisions as either settling or inviting a conversation about an issue is useful to understanding gender-responsive language in constitutions, which often seeks to alter deep-seeded social and cultural norms.[33] Under this framework, language is understood as engaging in an ongoing dialogue with pre-existing norms and either prompting further conversation or declaring consensus.[34] Thus, progress or backsliding occurs within the context of these conversations. For example, inclusion of a provision on reproductive rights may settle a long-running dialogue, while a provision on the right to education may merely initiate a conversation on girls' equal access to primary school.

From this vantage point, constitutional language that invites a new conversation around a particular issue in the first period of constitutional implementation is likely to follow a different path from language that reflects a social consensus or, in some other way, borrows from already existing principles, standards, or laws. This is likely true as well for language that serves only to prevent backsliding on a principle that has been challenged, language that memorializes the contours of a right or duty, or language that signals a desire to further develop a commitment. In each scenario, the language at issue will vary in social significance and implementation.

Thus, while the first period may be critical to setting the tone for some conversations prompted, continued, or settled by reform, its immediate relevance will depend on many factors, including the history of the language, how stakeholders understand and use the language, and how decision-makers receive it. For instance, while the first period following the reform process may generate the social energy necessary to engage with and act on conversations prompted or reignited by reform, gender-responsive language could also significantly impact women's reality in the short term. The energy generated by the reform may be sufficient to push reticent dynamics that maintain gender inequalities toward transformation and instill a heightened willingness to address difficult and controversial issues. However, for other issues, including longstanding symptoms of women's inequality (such as the lack of women in high level positions in the private sector), or issues just beginning to enjoy legal recognition (such as domestic violence), the first period may only reflect limited practical advancements but will still be significant for achieving constitutional recognition.

[32] Michael Dorf, "The Aspirational Constitution." *George Washington Law Review* 77: 1631 (2009).

[33] Sanford Levinson, "Do Constitutions Have a Point? Reflections on 'Parchment Barriers' and Preambles." *Social Philosophy and Policy* 28 (1): 150–78 (2011).

[34] Ibid.

This is true for all constitutional language added in reforms. However, women's inequality is so ingrained in the social fabric of most societies that reformed constitutions enter their first period with a particularly strong pull toward preservation in this area. The pull toward preservation on women's equality issues is evident in the dynamics of recent reform processes – e.g. Kenya, Somalia, Colombia, Zimbabwe, and Tunisia, among many others – where, nearly uniformly, women's issues were sidelined, minimized, or, at best, leveraged against more important matters.[35] Even accounts that document the involvement of civil society and women's movements acknowledge the uphill battle in focusing attention on these issues.[36] The majority of constitution-making bodies have dedicated little debate or attention to most gender-equality related issues. This is the case even in reform processes that resulted in highly gender-responsive texts, like in Zimbabwe. In Tunisia, an example of a process that resulted in many textual gains for women, women leaders recount being told "this is not the time to talk about women's rights – we have to talk about freedom of speech, etc. That is more important."[37]

The lack of prioritization of women's issues is reflected in the composition and functioning of the constitution-making bodies themselves. Though women's representation on these bodies has increased in post-conflict constitutional processes over time, even in recent processes in Tunisia, Philippines and Nepal, women's presence only constituted approximately 25 percent of the overall constitutional body membership.[38] Even when women are present, a number of challenges make it difficult

---

[35] For examples of the role of women in reform processes, see Nanako Tamaru and Marie O'Reilly. *How Women Influence Constitution Making after Conflict and Unrest*, Inclusive Security (January 2018). Available at www.inclusivesecurity.org/wp-content/uploads/2018/02/How-Women-Influence-Constitution-Making.pdf [Accessed March 8, 2018]; for account of Kenya, Somalia, and Colombia's processes and the resistance faced by women, see Pilar Domingo, Aoife McCullough, Florence Simbiri, and Bernadette Wanjala, *Women and Power: Shaping the Development of Kenya's 2010 Constitution*. Overseas Development Institute, 2016; Martha Morgan and Monica Maria Alzate Buitrago, "Constitution-Making in a Time of Cholera: Women and the 1991 Colombian Constitution." *Yale JL & Feminism* 4 (1991); and Aili Mari Tripp, "Women's Movements and Constitution Making after Civil Unrest and Conflict in Africa: The Cases of Kenya and Somalia." *Politics and Gender* 12 (2016) 78–106.

[36] Tamaru and O'Reilly, n. 35 at 10–15. For various accounts on how women have impacted constitutional reforms processes as well as the challenges faced by advocates see Tripp, n. 35: 82 (Kenya and Somalia); Dia Anagnostou, "*Gender Constitutional Reform and Feminist Mobilization in Greece and the EU: From Formal to Substantive Equality*." *Canadian Journal of Law & Society* 2: 133 (2013); Amy Lind, "'Revolution with a Woman's Face'? Family Norms, Constitutional Reform, and the Politics of Redistribution in Post-Neoliberal Ecuador." *Rethinking Marxism* 24 (4) : 536–55 (2012); Nancy Ruth, "Work Women Did to Make Constitutional Rights Work for Women." *Atlantis: Critical Studies in Gender, Culture & Social Justice* 37 (2): 126–31 (2016); Grace Maingi, "*The Kenyan Constitutional Reform Process: A Case Study on the Work of FIDA Kenya in Securing Women's Rights*." *Feminist Africa Legal Voice: Special Issue* 15: 63–82 (2011); and Stéphanie Rousseau, n. 42: 5–28.

[37] Tamaru and O'Reilly: 42 (quoting from Interview with Sana Ben Achour in Tunis, Tunisia, October 3, 2016).

[38] Ibid. 4 (figure 1).

for them to be influential. While in some contexts women's interests have been advanced by a few key, well-placed leaders,[39] more commonly, female political leaders lack independence from political parties and are limited by paltry financial resources and inadequate political allies.[40] The absence of women with influence only adds to already existing cultural norms of gender inequality to create conditions in which women's issues are sidelined.

As a consequence, women have had to rely on other strategies to benefit from moments of constitutional change, such as leveraging existing political dynamics. Again, in Tunisia, women's rights were invoked as a "useful wedge issue – one that could deflect attention from hastily constructed economic programs and isolate electoral opponents as either 'too secular' or 'too Islamist' to please the population at large."[41] In other cases, women's equality language has ridden on a wave of a broader human rights agenda. In Bolivia, for example, women's issues were able to gain traction through affiliations with a larger indigenous rights agenda central to the reform process.[42] The language in many of these processes appears not to have been generated by political will, debate, and social consensus-building but was instead entered into the text despite a lack of interest, attention, and resistance by the dominant parties.

In light of all this, what can we expect from implementation in the first period and how can we maximize its impact on the lives of women? As noted above, Zimbabwe's 2013 constitutional reform process provides an interesting case study; not only did the 2013 reform yield a highly gender-responsive constitution; it was preceded by a well-documented reform attempt a decade earlier. These reforms provide a useful point of comparison for assessing the evolution of various social conversations that occurred between the two events. While the gender-responsive components of the constitution were many, I will look specifically at the language on gender equality and customary practices, legislative quotas, domestic violence, and reproductive rights to illustrate the path followed by this language from conception to implementation in the first period.

---

[39] See Tamaru and O'Reilly, n. 35: 14–16 (discussing the importance of leveraging relationships between women in the reform process and those in civil society).
[40] Marginalized Groups and Constitutional Building (a roundtable report), International IDEA, (October 2013): 18–20. Available at www.idea.int/sites/default/files/publications/marginalized-groups-and-constitution-building.pdf [accessed September 23, 2018]; See Drude Dahlerup et al., "Atlas of Electoral Gender Quotas," International Institute for Democracy and Electoral Assistance (2013), 1–40.
[41] Silvia Suteu, "Women and Participatory Constitution-Making," *Constitutions and Gender*. Elgar Publishing: 2017, 19.
[42] Stéphanie Rousseau, "Indigenous and Feminist Movements at the Constituent Assembly in Bolivia: Locating the Representation of Indigenous Women." *Latin American Research Review* 46 (2). 5–28 (2011).

6.3 ZIMBABWEAN CASE STUDY

6.3.1 *Background*

Zimbabwe's first constitution, the Lancaster House Constitution, was in place from 1979, the year of its independence, to 2013. Aside from a brief attempt to replace it in 1990, the only full-fledged (though ultimately failed) prior reform attempt was in 1999. The 1999 process was initiated by the National Constitutional Assembly (NCA), a coalition of civil society organizations, academics, and unions that had emerged in political and social resistance to the Zimbabwe African National Union-Patriotic Front (ZANU PF), the party in power controlled by the late Robert Mugabe. The NCA sought to engage the public in civic discussion by initiating a process to replace the Lancaster House constitution, which the party considered outdated and a relic of Zimbabwe's colonial past. However, in the midst of the NCA-coordinated reform process, ZANU PF sought to derail NCA's mobilization. As the governing party, it was able to coopt the process and incorporate it into its platform. The NCA and its allies, including those in the women's movement, responded by organizing in opposition to the process. These efforts proved to be successful. When the draft was finally submitted for a referendum vote, it was rejected.

For women in Zimbabwe, this meant another decade without constitutional protections from gender discrimination. While the Lancaster House Constitution had been amended in 1996 to add sex and gender as prohibited grounds of discrimination, this change had made little difference to women's lives. The constitution exempted all matters of customary and personal law from nondiscrimination protections – an exemption commonly known as the "claw-back clause." The claw-back clause left women unprotected from discrimination in the context of marriage, divorce, adoption, custody, inheritance, and land acquisition – areas central to women's inequality.[43]

The draft rejected by the 1999 process was a significant advancement on issues of gender equality compared to the Lancaster House Constitution. The 1999 draft included a nondiscrimination provision without the claw-back clause and permitted the use of affirmative measures to remedy gender inequality. It recognized gender-based violence as a form of torture and identified gender balance in the country's leadership as a fundamental constitutional principle. The pronouns used in the draft were also inclusive of women.[44]

Yet, despite this progressive language, documentation and accounts from the process indicate limited discussion of gender equality or women's rights issues.

---

[43] Lancaster House Constitution of Zimbabwe of 1979 (replaced in 2013): Sec. 22 (3).
[44] National Constitutional Assembly, *Proposed Draft Constitution for Zimbabwe* (2000). Available at http://archive.kubatana.net/docs/demgg/ncaconsto201.pdf [accessed August 15, 2018].

Committee debates that included gender issues did not move beyond basic concepts such as definitional conversations about the meaning of "sex" and "gender."[45] Few women were included in the bodies responsible for the constitution-making process. Of the 400-member constitutional commission, only 13 percent were women. Three of the fifteen members of the legal drafting review committee were women.[46] Moreover, the women who were appointed to the commission struggled to advocate for discussion on gender issues. They reported that these issues were regularly sidelined and dismissed.[47]

There were, however, several factors that likely motivated the inclusion of gender equality language despite its lack of prominence in the reform process overall. First, the 1999 process was self-identified as a movement for social reform with a human rights platform. At the time, global and regional human rights systems were active in promoting gender equality and Zimbabwe's women's movements were participating in those discussions and processes. A few years earlier, the Fourth World Conference on Women had taken place in Beijing and had consolidated global movements to advocate for women's equality. The region was also in the midst of developing the Protocol to the African Union Charter on Human and People's Rights on the Rights of Women in Africa (Maputo Protocol), which committed states to the pursuit of women's equality.[48] This process generated a great deal of attention and led to the appointment of the first Special Rapporteur on the Rights of Women in Africa. In this overall context, there was an expectation that women's rights would be incorporated into a larger human rights agenda of social reform.

Second, the claw-back clause and its adverse impact on women had gained some international prominence. The CEDAW Committee[49] had admonished Zimbabwe for failing to address the personal and customary law exclusions to nondiscrimination protections in the constitution in Zimbabwe's prior two reports.[50] Making

---

[45] Claudia Flores and Patricia A. Made, *The Politics of Engagement: Women's Participation and Influence in Constitution-Making Processes*, UN Women (2016): 11. Available at www.onu.cl/es/wp-content/uploads/2016/06/Politics-of-Engagement.pdf [accessed August 15, 2018] (referring to Zimbabwe Report of National Commission of Inquiry into the Establishment of a New Constitution (1999–2000)).

[46] Ibid. 12.

[47] Ibid. 11.

[48] Protocol to the African Union Charter on Human and People's Rights on the Rights of Women in Africa (Maputo Protocol) (adopted in 2003). Available at www.sadc.int/issues/gender/ [accessed August 20, 2018].

[49] *Ratification Status for Zimbabwe*, U.N. Human Rights, Office of the High Commissioner. Available at http://tbinternet.ohchr.org/_layouts/TreatyBodyExternal/Treaty.aspx [accessed August 15, 2018].

[50] *Combined Report of the Republic of Zimbabwe in Terms of CEDAW* (2009). Available at www1.uneca.org/Portals/ngm/Documents/ProfileNGMs/Zimbabwe%20CEDAW%20Combined%20Report.pdf [accessed August 15, 2018]; *Zimbabwe Civil Society's Shadow Report to the CEDAW Committee* (2012). Available at https://tbinternet.ohchr.org/Treaties/CEDAW/Shared%20Documents/ZWE/INT_CEDAW_NGO_ZWE_51_10382_E.pdf [accessed August 15, 2018].

matters worse, the year of the reform, the Supreme Court ruled that a customary rule that denied women the right to inherit family property was constitutional under the claw-back clause.[51] The court reasoned that women were prohibited from inheriting family land because their roles in African society required they focus on caring for their husband's families once married. This ruling increased external and internal pressure on the commission to address the customary and personal law exclusions.

Regardless, the process ultimately failed with the blessing of the majority of the women's movement which felt compelled to join their allies in opposing the draft despite the benefits it would have provided. In fact, the NCA listed the draft's shortcomings on gender equality as one of the reasons for rejection (though it did not specify what the shortcomings were).[52] However, for years following the reform process, leaders in the women's movement bemoaned the difficult choice they had made and vowed to be ready for the next opportunity for reform.[53] In anticipation, they formed the Women's Coalition, a network of organizations that prepared to act in concert to advance women's rights in future reforms and other prospects for change.

The next opportunity came in the 2013 reform process which was commenced by the Global Political Agreement (GPA), a peacekeeping agreement between Zimbabwe's dominant political parties. The GPA was mediated by the Southern Africa Development Community (SADC) in an effort to stem the instability caused in the region by its internal politics.[54] Among other things, it required that the three political parties engage in a collaborative constitution-making process. One of the stated primary goals of the process was "the enhancement of full citizenship and equality for women."[55]

Women were again underrepresented in the constitution-making bodies. The COPAC Constitution Select Committee, the committee responsible for day to day implementation of the reform, had seven women out of its twenty-five members. The COPAC Management Committee, which directed the process and resolved disputes, was composed of nine men and one woman. The COPAC Drafting Committee, which took direction from the two other committees on content, was composed of one woman and two men.[56]

---

[51] *Magaya* v. *Magaya*, 1999 (1) ZLR (2000).
[52] National Constitutional Assembly, *Proposed Draft Constitution for Zimbabwe* (2000), n. 44: 5.
[53] Flores and Made, n. 45: 14.
[54] Global Political Agreement (GPA), (September 15, 2008) "Agreements between the Zimbabwe African National Union-Patriotic Front (ZANU-PF), and the two Movements for Democratic Change (MDC) formations, on resolving the challenges facing Zimbabwe": Arts. 6 and 7.1. Available at www.constitutionnet.org/sites/default/files/global_political_agreements_2008.pdf. [accessed August 17, 2018].
[55] Ibid.
[56] Flores and Made, n. 45: 12.

The public consultation process organized by COPAC involved limited female participation as well, initially only approximately 10 percent of participants were women. In response, the Women's Coalition organized their own consultations and petitioned COPAC to increase women's participation. Female participation in COPAC's local consultations was ultimately increased to between 34–45 percent, varying by locality.[57] Neither of the two national public consultations held in Harare involved significant female participation.[58]

The Women's Coalition held strategy meetings at the outset of the process and defined its role as coordinating civil society and academia, and serving as the chair of the Group of 20 Women Leaders (Group of 20). The Group of 20 was formed to bring together key women in politics, academia, and the civil service with the ability to influence the reform process.[59] The Minister of Women's Affairs, Gender and Community Development, a member of the Group of 20, also named the development of a gender-responsive constitution as the priority goal of her term as minister.[60] The Group of 20 worked in close coordination, conducted gender audits, negotiated behind-the-scenes, and made public commentary on circulated drafts.[61]

Despite their evident organization this time around, again, women involved in the process reported that their issues were "trivialized"[62] and treated as if they must be "gotten 'out of the way' so the committee could talk about the real issues."[63] As the process went forward, advocates embraced strategies that adapted to the marginalization of women's issues. They focused on influencing the process from the "sidelines"[64] by forming "shadow groups" to track progress and relying on "women at the very top echelon of political parties" to communicate their requests.[65] They also pushed for language that they anticipated would benefit women in the future. According to Coalition leadership, it was "[m]uch easier to get them [women's issues] pushed in because men's eyes were on what they assumed were the bigger

---

[57] Ibid. 13 (citing interviews with Netsai Mushonga, director of Women's Coalition, and Beatrice Nyamupinga, parliamentarian); Report of the Constitutional Select Committee to Parliament (February 7, 2013): 15. Available at www.google.com/url?sa=t&rct=j&q=&esrc=s&source=web&cd=1&ved=2ahUKEwitn5e8wtfdAhXEyoMKHSyrC78QFjAAegQICRAC&url=http%3A%2F%2Fwww.veritaszim.net%2Fsites%2Fveritas_d%2Ffiles%2FCOPAC%2527s%2520Final%2520Narrative%2520Report%2520to%2520Parliament%2520-%2520%2520Feb%25202013.doc&usg=AOvVawowlXjdI8SmaYXtTX_5fyEt [accessed September 20, 2018].
[58] Flores and Made, n. 45:14.
[59] Ibid. 18
[60] Ibid. 17
[61] Ibid. 19.
[62] Ibid. 16 (quoting Emilia Muchawa, former director of the Zimbabwe Women's Lawyers Association).
[63] Ibid. 20 (quoting Hon. Priscilla Misihairambwi-Mushonga, female member of COPAC management committee).
[64] Ibid. (quoting Hon. Priscilla Misihairambwi-Mushonga).
[65] Ibid. (quoting Choice Damiso, legal advisor to Group of 20).

fights."[66] Thus, for most issues, the focus was on minimizing any resistance to textual changes rather than garnering affirmative support.[67]

The final text approved by referendum contained a comprehensive set of provisions guaranteeing gender equality and advancing women's rights. The new constitution listed "gender equality" as a founding principle of the state and committed the state to promoting "the full participation of women in all spheres of Zimbabwean society on the basis of equality with men."[68] Constitutional prohibitions on discrimination included various grounds related to women including sex, gender, pregnancy, and marital status and mandated affirmative measures to remedy discrimination or inequality.[69] The text stated explicitly that "all laws, customs, traditions and cultural practices that infringe the rights of women conferred by this Constitution are void to the extent of the infringement."[70] The text also mandated affirmative measures to achieve gender equality and created a Gender Commission to monitor compliance.[71] A multitude of specific provisions promised fully paid maternity leave, equal pay for equal work, reproductive healthcare, equal access to education for girls, child care programs, freedom from public and private violence, a state mandate to prevent domestic violence, and legislative gender quotas.[72]

6.3.2 *Customary Law and Practices*

The Process

Perhaps the most predictable change in the 2013 constitution was the inclusion of customary practices and personal law in its nondiscrimination protections. However, there were some other changes in the 2013 draft on the issue of nondiscrimination. In the 1999 process, committee members debated the exact meaning of nondiscrimination and whether affirmative measures were appropriate to remedy past-discrimination.[73] In 2013, nondiscrimination protections, an overt gender equality mandate, and language on affirmative measures were all listed as "agreed upon" principles at the outset of the process.[74] In fact, the language on affirmative measures was converted from "the government *may* take affirmative measures" in

---

[66] Ibid. (quoting Hon. Priscilla Misihairambwi-Mushonga).

[67] Ibid. 43 (quoting Hon. Priscilla Misihairambwi-Mushonga).

[68] The Constitution of Zimbabwe of 2013 (revisions through 2017): Secs. 3 and 17(1)(a).

[69] Ibid. Sec. 56.

[70] Ibid. Sec. 80(3).

[71] Ibid. Secs. 80, 245 and 246.

[72] Ibid. Sec. 65(7) (maternity leave), sec. 76(1) (reproductive healthcare), sec. 19(2)(d)(equal education for girls), 24(2)(d)(child care), sec, 52(a)(violence), sec. 25(b)(domestic violence) & sec. 124(1)(b)(political quotas).

[73] Flores and Made, n. 45: 24.

[74] COPAC Drafting Instruments, Second All-Stakeholders Conference 2012: 11-15. Available at http://archive.kubatana.net/docs/legisl/copac_drafting_instruments_121022.pdf [accessed September 20, 2018].

the 1999 draft to the "government *must* take such measures" in the 2013 constitution.[75]

The 2013 nondiscrimination provision contained similar grounds as the 1999 draft with a few notable differences. The 2013 version added whether a person was "born out of wedlock" to the grounds of prohibited discrimination and eliminated "natural difference or condition," which had been included in the 1999 draft.[76] Accounts indicate that the latter was viewed as potentially providing protections from discrimination on the basis of sexual identity. This was seen as contrary to dominant cultural norms.[77]

The records from the 2013 process indicate a consensus that the nondiscrimination exception for customary practices and personal law would be eliminated in the new draft.[78] In contrast, in the 1999 process, the question of whether customary practices should be excluded from nondiscrimination prohibitions and, more generally, how women's rights should be understood within customary law was presented as open to debate. Questions posed in the 1999 local consultations included "[s]hould the constitution permit discrimination on the grounds of gender on any issues at all? [s]hould the constitution recognize the legal age of marriage? ... and [s]hould the new constitution require affirmative action for women and youth with regard to traditional leadership positions, customary allocation of resources such as land and adjudication by traditional authorities?"[79] The 1999 Fundamental Rights Committee of the constitutional commission concluded that, despite agreement in public consultations that customary law be subject to the bill of rights, a "moderated" approach should accommodate customary practices by allowing customary law to prevail over the bill of rights except in areas of inheritance, right to land, consent to marriage, and equality between men and women.[80]

This reluctance to regulate the customary system was nearly absent in 2013. There are a number of developments that took place between the two processes that may help to explain this. First, after the 1999 process, civil society made deliberate efforts to engage with traditional leaders through programming and dialogue with the intention of establishing a more collaborative approach between the leaders and women's rights advocates.[81] Second, criticism from the CEDAW committee as well as accession to a number of regional protocols on gender and customary practices had compelled Zimbabwe into a more tangible commitment to address these

---

[75] Flores and Made, n. 45: 26.
[76] The Constitution of Zimbabwe of 2013: Sec. 56(3); Proposed Draft Constitution for Zimbabwe (2000) n. 45: Art. 43.
[77] Flores and Made, n. 45: 25.
[78] The Constitution of Zimbabwe of 2013: Sec. 56(3).
[79] Flores and Made, n. 45: 24.
[80] Ibid.
[81] Ibid. 25.

practices as they harmed or disadvantaged women.[82] By 2013, there was no meaningful opposition by customary leaders to being subject to the constitutional bill of
rights.[83] The general agreement among advocates was that past debates, external
pressure, advocacy, and high profile examples of how these exclusions harmed
women had moved the social conversation to a point of consensus. At least in the
formal sense, by 2013, it was simply no longer viable to continue to claim that
traditional practices negatively impacting women should be exempt from nondiscrimination provisions.

This did not mean the 2013 process remedied women's inequality within the
customary system. In fact, despite significant gains on women's political leadership
(described later in the chapter), no progress was made on female leadership within
the customary system. Under most customary systems, women were not allowed to
become chiefs and were rarely in positions of any leadership, significantly limiting
their influence on rules and practices. In the 1999 process, committees discussed the
possibility of mandating that women be allowed to become chiefs but ultimately
decided that this determination would be made by each community.[84] The 2013 process concluded the same, referring the issue to legislation.[85] The 2013 constitution
contains no mandate for gender equality in customary leadership apart from a
general mandate to abolish cultural practices that infringe on women's equality.[86]

In contrast, customary leaders were successful in advocating for a permanent
position on the Gender Commission, which was tasked with interpreting and
supervising implementation of gender equality mandates in the constitution.[87]
Some advocates were concerned that their presence on the Commission would
dilute or minimize the Commission's role in ensuring accountability, but others saw
it as a positive development that indicated investment of traditional leadership in
advancing women's equality.

The First Period

The application of nondiscrimination protections to customary and personal law
was relatively settled in the 2013 process. Yet, the first period has suggested an
ongoing tension between the transformative potential of this shift and the preservative forces that maintain traditional views in customary systems. Like many such

---

[82] Concluding Observations of the Committee on the Elimination of Discrimination against
   Women, Zimbabwe, CEDAW/C/ZWE/CO/2-5 (51st Session, February 13 to March 2, 2012);
   para. 13. Available at www2.ohchr.org/english/bodies/cedaw/docs/co/cedaw-c-zwe-co-2-5.pdf
   [accessed September 20, 2018].
[83] Flores and Made, n. 45: 25 (quoting Choice Damiso).
[84] Ibid.: 27.
[85] COPAC National Statistical Report Version 1 – Second All Stakeholders Conference October
   2012, 117–131: 120, Available at http://archive.kubatana.net/docs/legisl/copac_national_statis
   tical_report_v1_121022.pdf [accessed September 1, 2018].
[86] The Constitution of Zimbabwe of 2013: Sec. 80(3).
[87] Ibid. Sec. 245(1)b(ii).

tensions, an inconsistency has developed (or been maintained) between formal legal rules and local practice.

Two years after the reform process, the Supreme Court of Zimbabwe held, in *Loveness Mudzuru, and Ruvimbo Tsopodzi* v. *the Minister of Justice, Legal and Parliamentary Affairs and others*, that child marriages were unconstitutional under the new constitution.[88] The ruling relied both on the customary law exclusion and the constitutional prohibition on child marriage.[89] Following this decision, a bill was introduced outlawing child marriages and bride pricing (lobola). In an overall slow alignment process, the bill remains pending in 2018.

Yet, five years after the passage of the new constitution, resistance to transformation remains evident in the traditional system. Customary systems have continued to propagate practices that cause violence against women at worst and discriminate against and limit them at best.[90] Research on practices like forced virginity testing, female genital mutilation, pledging of young women or girls for the purpose of appeasing spirits, forced marriage, forced wife inheritance, and sexual intercourse between newly married women and fathers has documented continuation of such practices. Studies credit their continued practice to barriers such as limited access to legal recourse and lack of local training for law enforcement and judicial personnel on constitutional requirements.[91] Similarly, women's leadership in the customary system has remained limited following the reform process. After the 2013 elections, only 5 of more than 286 chiefs elected in Zimbabwe were women.[92]

Regardless, the consensus achieved (or reflected) in the reform process generated some first-period implementation in the form of judicial interpretation and legislative alignment. At minimum, the constitution served to memorialize the commitment to hold customary practices accountable for their treatment of women. The implementation changes at the customary level understandably require longer term investment and engagement. These sorts of cultural changes present the greatest complications for first-period implementation and are most dependent on real

[88] *Loveness Mudzuru, and Ruvimbo Tsopodzi* v. *the Minister of Justice, Legal and Parliamentary Affairs and others judgment*, CCZ12/ 2015; Cowen Dziva and Delis Mazambani, "The Constitutional Court Ruling against Child Marriages in Zimbabwe: A Landmark Decision for Advancing the Rights of the Girl Child." *Eastern Africa Social Science Research Review* 33 (1): 73–87 (2017).
[89] The Constitution of Zimbabwe of 2013: Sec. 26(b).
[90] See Obediah Dodo. "Traditional Leadership Systems and Gender Recognition: Zimbabwe." *International Journal of Gender and Women's Studies* 1 (1): 29–44 (2013).
[91] Sylvia Chirawu-Mugomba. "A Reflection on the Domestic Violence Act [chapter 5:16] and Harmful Cultural Practices in Zimbabwe," *The Zimbabwe Electronic Journal, Commentary on Contemporary Legal Issue*, 2016. Available at https://zimlii.org/system/files/journals/A%20Reflection%20on%20the%20Domestic%20Violence%20Act%20%5BChapter%205-16%5D.pdf (accessed September 20, 2018].
[92] Veneranda Langa, "Government Urged to Install Female Chiefs, Newsday, August 21, 2018. Available at www.newsday.co.zw/2018/08/govts-urged-to-install-female-chiefs/ [accessed September 10, 2018].

sociocultural shifts. Even the formal legal change that did take place related to an issue that was unambiguous in the constitution. Child marriage was made unconstitutional both through general mandates for equality (Secs. 17 and 56) and a specific provision outlawing child marriage (Sec. 26).[93] It remains to be seen whether issues that necessitate greater levels of judicial interpretation will fare as well.

6.3.3 *Legislative Gender Quotas*

Process

The establishment of a constitutionally mandated gender quota in Zimbabwe's parliament was easily the most publicly discussed gender equality issue in the 2013 process. It received extensive coverage in the media and was the cornerstone of the Women's Coalition advocacy campaign. It was also the greatest disappointment for the women's movement.

Prior to the 2013 elections, women made up 14 percent of the national assembly, 24 percent of the senate, 19 percent of the municipal government, and 20 percent of government cabinet ministers.[94] Female candidates faced a number of obstacles including insufficient resources, lack of support by their parties, death threats, and sexual impropriety and prostitution accusations.[95] Violence against female candidates was a major deterrent to women running for office.

Regionally, women's political leadership and gender quotas were much discussed. Regional protocols signed by Zimbabwe prioritized women's equal political representation as a national goal. The SADC Protocol, in particular, set a 2015 target of equal representation between genders in national parliaments.[96] A few years before the reform in Zimbabwe, the dominant political party in South Africa, which occupied two-thirds of the national legislature, had adopted a 50 percent quota for its female representatives.[97] At the time, as well, the 2010 Kenyan Constitution, which called for a one-third legislative gender quota, was in its final draft form.[98] Rwanda had also received acclaim for the high proportion of women in its legislature (64 percent in 2013), which had reached and surpassed the 30 percent constitutional benchmark.[99] The success of the Rwandan mechanism was highly influential in Zimbabwe. Women political leaders went on study visits to

---

[93] The Constitution of Zimbabwe of 2013: Secs. 17, 26(b) & 56.
[94] Flores and Made, n. 45: 28.
[95] Panashe Chigumadzi. *In Zimbabwe, the Enduring Fear of Single Women*, Opinion, July 2, 2018. Available at www.nytimes.com/2018/07/02/opinion/zimbabwe-elections-mugabe-fear-women.html.
[96] SADC Protocol on Gender and Development (2008): Art. 12(1).
[97] IDEA Gender Quotas Database – South Africa. Available at www.idea.int/data-tools/data/gender-quotas/country-view/310/35 [accessed September 10, 2018]. ANC holds 264 seats in the National Assembly, a little less than a two-thirds majority.
[98] The Constitution of Kenya of 2010: Art. 27 (8).
[99] See Constitution of the Republic of Rwanda of 2003 (with amendments until 2015): Art. 76.

Rwanda[100] and were energized by the possibility of a 50 percent mandated representation in the national legislature.

The issue of female political representation had been completely absent in the 1999 process, but in 2013, it was initially identified as a priority issue for reform. The Group of 20, heavily influenced by key female political leaders, identified women's political leadership as their primary advocacy platform in 2013. The Group coordinated public campaigns encouraging women to vote and to demand higher levels of political representation. According to results of the consultations, 58.62 percent of the population agreed that women should have equal representation in parliament.[101] The Minister of Women's Affairs, Gender and Community Development drafted and submitted a discussion paper to COPAC on the various options for electoral quotas that would ensure women's equality.[102]

However, as the process unfolded, support began to wane, "on the ground, the people said: 'we have no problems with gender equality, but we want no special treatment for women.' Then, of course, in these discussions you would say, how do women catch up if there are no special provisions?"[103] Powerful, predominantly male, political leaders also began to push back through informal negotiations as they began to see the implications of a gender quota and the threat to their positions. Priscilla Misihairabwi-Mushonga, a female parliamentarian and the only female member of the COPAC Management Committee, recalled being told, "as long as it doesn't challenge my present hold on a particular seat, I can freely give it to you. But at this time, if you put it initially on the table as something that dislocates where I am and my position, then you are assured you are not going to win."[104]

As the reform process went forward, it became evident that a 50 percent quota would encounter significant resistance. Women began considering a 30 percent quota as an alternative, which was commensurate with quota mechanisms in neighboring countries. However, at that point, the negotiations had advanced on the 50 percent quota and, in something close to the final hour, a third alternative was incorporated into the draft. The constitutional language submitted and approved by referendum mandated a 50 percent quota in the senate, but required only a temporary quota of 30 percent for women in the National Assembly achieved by adding sixty additional seats reserved for women for the two election cycles that followed approval of the constitution.[105]

[100] Flores and Made, n. 45: 29.
[101] COPAC National Statistical Report. Vsn. 1, n. 85: http://archive.kubatana.net/docs/legisl/copac_national_statistical_report_v1_121022.pdf.
[102] Flores and Made, n. 45: 30.
[103] Ibid. 31 (quoting Dr. Olivia Muchena).
[104] Ibid. (quoting Priscilla Misihairambwi-Mushonga).
[105] Ibid. 30.

First Period

Various factors are likely relevant to the astonishing momentum gained by the legislative gender quota in the 2013 process. The prominence that politics has in Zimbabwean society, the self-interest of powerful female politicians, regional pressure from neighboring countries, and relevant commitments in regional human rights agreements and targets all aligned to propel a serious conversation on gender quotas that resulted in significant gains for women. Still, internal forces – the male-dominated political environment, the traditional exclusion of women from governance and the desire to preserve power in an unstable environment – all served to curtail the change achieved in the final hour.

The resulting language was met with mixed reactions from advocates who saw the adverse implications for first-period implementation of the temporary allocated seats. The temporary seats were allocated to the National Assembly, the more powerful house of parliament, which left open the possibility that the quota may eventually be eliminated or reduced. It thus minimizes the overall impact women will have on lawmaking, as most female representatives in the more powerful house of parliament are likely to have less influence and be viewed as transient. The addition of temporary seats – many have argued – was a disingenuous move to give the appearance of a quota without actually instituting one.[106] According to Beatrice Nyamupinga, a lead parliamentarian and member of the Group of 20 Women Leaders, women had "shot [themselves] in the foot" and should not be "hood-winked" into thinking they had achieved a real quota.[107]

Thus, like the elimination of the claw-back clause, the gender quota was limited in its challenge to existing power structures around political leadership. Still, prominent female advocates have continued to vocalize their disappointment in the final compromise. Interestingly, the quota mechanism was one of the few gender equality measures implemented immediately following reform and the only one that benefitted from legislative alignment.[108] The high profile public battle, the clear and tangible time-sensitive mandate, and the prominence of politics in

---

[106] Mandlenkosi Maphosa, Nevel Tshuma, and Gracsious Maviza, "Participation of Women in Zimbabwean Politics and the Mirage of Gender Equity." *Ubuntu: Journal of Conflict Transformation* 4 (2): 127–59: 130 (2015).

[107] Agora, "Zimbabwe's Female MP's Demand More Parliamentary Seats," Portal for Parliamentary Development, June 26, 2017. Available at www.agora-parl.org/interact/blog/zimbabwe-female-mps-demand-more-parliamentary-seats [accessed September 20, 2018].

[108] In fact, two rounds of amendments to the Electoral Act have both included language that relates to gender equality. The Electoral Amendment Act of 2014 instituted the quotas. The Electoral Amendment Act of 2018 requires gender mainstreaming throughout the electoral process. The Electoral Amendment Act of 2014, Act 6-2014. Available at www.veritaszim.net/node/1086 [accessed September 20, 2018]; The Electoral Amendment Act of 2018, GNA 307A/2018, in force May 28, 2018. Available at www.veritaszim.net/sites/veritas_d/files/Electoral%20Amendment%20Act%2C%202018r.pdf [accessed September 20, 2018].

Zimbabwe were likely factors in the efficacy of implementation, in addition to the influence of the few women with political clout who put their weight behind the measure. In the elections that followed the reform, 35 percent of MPs were women overall. In the National Assembly, women's presence increased from 14 percent in the 2008 elections to 31.4 percent in 2013. In addition to the 60 reserved seats, women won 25 constituency seats, becoming 85 of 270 members. In the Senate, women's presence increased from 24.2 percent in the 2008 elections, or 24 of 99 members, to 47.5 percent, or 38 of 80 members.[109]

Following the realization of the gender quota, female representatives faced various challenges from their colleagues and the public. New female parliamentarians were undermined by male colleagues, who publically described them as inadequate and incompetent. Male parliamentarians argued that the female representatives added no value: "[t]hey just come here to warm the benches, not different from the women we have left in our rural areas."[110] Female parliamentarians reported being "heckled" and silenced: "[t]here is a lot of patriarchy, and if a mistake is done by a male MP, there is no heckling, but there is a lot of heckling if it is a woman."[111]

Moreover, the legislative quotas did not appear to reflect a general openness to female leadership and may have even led to some backlash. Initially, there was actually a decrease in female representation in non-parliamentary government leadership positions. Of President Mugabe's Cabinet appointments, three of the twenty-six were women, bringing female representation down from 20 percent to 11.5 percent.[112] Among the twenty-four deputy ministers President Mugabe appointed, only five were women and they were relegated to ministerial appointments associated with "women's roles" such as tourism, environment, and women's affairs. These appointments were interpreted as communicating a lack of value for women's leadership and were consistent with public comments President Mugabe made questioning women's capacity to govern.[113] Little changed when President Mugabe

---

[109] Zimbabwe Government Country Report Beijing +20 2013. Available at https://sustainabledevelopment.un.org/content/documents/13229Zimbabwe_review_Beijing20.pdf [accessed August 15, 2018].

[110] Butaumocho, Ruth, "50 pc or Nothing for Zim Women as 2018 Beckons," *Gender Forum – Newsday*, June 28, 2017. Available at www.herald.co.zw/50pc-or-nothing-for-zim-women-as-2018-beckons/ [accessed September 20, 2018].

[111] Goromonzi, West. "Nyamupinga Fears for Her Life," *Newsday*, March 20, 2018. Available at www.newsday.co.zw/2018/03/nyamupinga-fears-for-her-life/ [accessed September 20, 2018].

[112] Zimbabwe Government Country Report Beijing +20 2013. Available at https://sustainabledevelopment.un.org/content/documents/13229Zimbabwe_review_Beijing20.pdf [accessed August 15, 2018].

[113] MacDonald Dzirutwe, "Zimbabwe's Mugabe Says Deputy Planned to Unseat Him: State Media," *Reuters*, December 3, 2014. Available at https://af.reuters.com/article/topNews/idAFKCN0JH0HO20141203 [accessed September 2, 2018].

was replaced by Emmerson Mnangagwa, who appointed only three women to twenty-two ministerial positions.[114]

Again, first-period implementation of the legislative gender quota evidenced both transformative and preservative tendencies. While the 50 percent quota in the senate is a permanent requirement, the temporary quota for the National Assembly could follow various paths. Much of the stereotyping and discrimination evident in the treatment of female politicians occupying those positions is likely to be employed to justify elimination of those positions.[115] Advocates for women's political leadership have advocated for a permanent gain; most recently they have proposed an amendment to the constitution to make permanent the temporary additional seats[116] and they have launched a 50/50 gender parity advocacy campaign.[117] If the amendment goes through, the quota will be instituted in stages, allowing current leaders to adjust to the development. There is some evidence that the quota has emboldened women to seek political office; following the resignation of Mugabe, an unprecedented four women ran for the presidency.[118] Still, resistance to women's leadership is evident at all levels. Female political representation was clearly a conversation in its early stages, which was catapulted into existence by the reform. The vulnerability of the quota so soon after its establishment may lead to some regressive movement.

6.3.4 *Violence against Women*

The Process

Prior to the 2013 reform, it was evident that violence against women was a serious problem in Zimbabwe. According to national statistics from 2015, 35 percent of women had experienced physical or sexual violence from an intimate partner at some point in their lifetime and 20 percent had experienced intimate partner violence in the last twelve months.[119] Since matters of personal and customary law

---

[114] Mandipa Ndlovu, "Reining Men: Where Are All the Women in This New Zimbabwe," *Africa Arguments*, May 6, 2018. Available at http://africanarguments.org/2018/05/16/reigning-men-where-are-all-the-women-in-this-new-zimbabwe-women/ [Accessed September 20, 2018].

[115] See Jason Burke, "Battling Tokenism: Zimbabwe's Female Politicians Pin Hopes on polls." *The Guardian*, June20, 2018. Available at www.theguardian.com/global-development/2018/jun/20/zimbabwe-female-politicians-pin-hopes-on-polls-july [accessed June 20, 2018].

[116] Ruth Butaumocho, "Women Seek to Amend Constitution." *The Herald*, March 28, 2018. Available at www.herald.co.zw/women-seek-to-amend-constitution/ [accessed August 20, 2018].

[117] Veneranda Langa, "Women Parliamentarians Caucus Promises Man Tight Battle at Polls." *Newsday*, March 7, 2018. Available at www.newsday.co.zw/2018/03/women-parliamentarians-caucus-promises-man-tight-battle-at-polls/ [Accessed August 3, 2018].

[118] Colleen Morna and Tapiwa Zvaraya, "Women the Biggest Losers in Zim Election." *Mail and Guardian*, Jul 6, 2018 00:00. Available at https://mg.co.za/article/2018-07-06-00-women-the-biggest-losers-in-zim-election [Accessed September 3, 2018].

[119] Zimbabwe National Statistics Agency and ICF International, *Zimbabwe Demographic and Health Survey 2015: Final Report* (2016): 315–24. Available at https://dhsprogram.com/pubs/pdf/FR322/FR322.pdf [accessed September 4, 2018].

were excluded from nondiscrimination provisions, protections against domestic violence were not constitutionally mandated by the Lancaster House Constitution. By 2013, however, legislation on domestic violence had been in place for nearly a decade. Over time, there has been an increase in reported cases of domestic violence.[120]

Domestic violence was discussed in the 1999 process. The constitutional commission initially declined to include language in the constitution to address it, but noted that the state needed to consider more effective responses to the issue of "so called domestic violence."[121] However, two prominent feminist legal scholars appointed to the commission successfully advocated for the inclusion of both domestic violence and gender-based violence in the text. The draft submitted for public consultation contained language that mandated protection for individuals from public and private violence, identified gender-based violence as cruel, inhuman, and degrading treatment, and required the state to develop programs to prevent domestic violence.[122]

In the 2013 process, a committee tasked with this issue again questioned whether domestic violence was appropriate to include in the constitution, but ultimately both gender-based violence and domestic violence were identified as appropriately falling under the constitutional right to personal security.[123] The language included in the approved draft was similar to the 1999 language that required the state to take steps to prevent domestic violence and recognized the right to be free from public and private violence. It did not, however, identify gender-based violence as constituting cruel, inhuman, and degrading treatment as did the 1999 draft. Some advocates saw this as a narrower approach to violence that failed to recognize its severity.

The First Period

There is little evidence that the language on domestic violence prompted any first period implementation. A National Gender-Based Violence Strategy was adopted for the period of 2012–15 in 2013.[124] But no new legislative changes have occurred and the same barriers to services have persisted, including harmful cultural norms

---

[120] Canada: Immigration and Refugee Board of Canada, *Zimbabwe: Domestic violence, including legislation; state protection and support services available to victims (June 2012–May 2015)*, June 3, 2015, ZWE105170.E. Available at www.refworld.org/docid/5587b7144.html [accessed September 20, 2018].

[121] Flores and Made, n. 45: 33.

[122] Ibid. 35.

[123] Ibid. 34.

[124] *National Gender Based Violence Strategy 2012–2015*, Ministry of Women Affairs, Gender and Community Development (2012). Available at www.veritaszim.net/sites/veritas_d/files/Zimbabwe%20National%20Gender%20Based%20Violence%20Strategy%202012%20-%202015.pdf [accessed August 15, 2018].

and lack of access to representation and legal protection.[125] The one area of violence
against women that may have benefitted from the reform is political violence, which
has enjoyed some focus in the context of legislative quotas as it is considered a major
deterrent to women's participation in politics. According to a recent report, over
60 percent of abusive and violent online discourse around political actors from
2013 to 2018 was directed at women in politics, although women only constitute a
third of parliament.[126]

   Domestic violence is a challenging issue for many countries. In the context of
Zimbabwe, it is likely that the language in the 2013 constitution will mainly serve as
an acknowledgment of the issue. Its inclusion arguably elevates it from its position as
a once unrecognized social harm. The legislation in place had already benefited
from international movements and external pressures.[127] The language of the
2013 constitution did not include additional mandates or make any attempt to
change the approach to violence. In contrast, for example, Ecuador's constitution
contains three separate provisions that created a right, mandated positive action, and
spelled out specific proscriptions for accountability, including the appointment of
special prosecutors.[128] Similarly, the constitution of the Dominican Republic contains specific mandates for the government that "[i]nter-family and gender violence
in all its forms is condemned. The State shall guarantee through the law the
adoption of the necessary measures to prevent, sanction and eradicate violence
against women."[129] Zimbabwe's general provision is more likely to preserve in the
social conscience the seriousness of violence against women, leaving open the
potential for a renewed social commitment in the future.

6.3.5 *Reproductive Rights*

Like domestic violence, the absence of competent and accessible reproductive
healthcare was another well-known difficulty for women in Zimbabwe, especially
as it impacted maternal mortality. In 2009, the maternal mortality rate in Zimbabwe
stood at 960 deaths for 100,000 live births, among the highest in Africa, along with
Sierra Leone. At the time, Zimbabwe was one of only forty countries worldwide with

[125] Excellent Chireshe, "Barriers to the Utilisation of Provisions of the Zimbabwean Domestic
Violence Act among Abused Christian Women in Zimbabwe." *Journal of International
Women's Studies* 16 (2) (January 2015).
[126] Violence against Women in Elections in Zimbabwe: An IFES Assessment (2018), International
Foundation for Electoral Systems. Available at www.ifes.org/sites/default/files/vawie_in_zim
babwe_july_2018.pdf [accessed September 20, 2018].
[127] Sylvia Chirawu-Mugomba, "A Reflection on the Domestic Violence Act." n. 91: 4.
[128] The Constitution of Zimbabwe of 2013: Sec. 66(3) and Sec. 81.
[129] The Political Constitution of the Dominican Republic of 2010, Art. 56(2) (English translation
quoted from www.constituteproject.org/).

a maternal mortality rate above 900.[130] Since the 1990s, Zimbabwe's maternal mortality rate had steadily worsened, increasing by a total of 30 percent, due to inadequate access to medical care and the prevalence of traditional practices.[131] Legal prohibitions against abortion were also among the most extreme worldwide.[132]

Despite all this, reproductive rights and healthcare were barely discussed in either constitution-making process. Abortion, on the other hand, was a topic of significant focus. In fact, in the 1999 process, reproductive healthcare and rights were only discussed in the context of abortion.[133] Consultation results reflected that an overwhelming majority of Zimbabweans were against abortion entirely or only approved of abortion in the case of threats to life or death of the mother.[134] Committee documents clarified that abortion would not be protected by privacy considerations as it was in other countries.[135] One committee proposed adding constitutional language that specified that abortion would not be protected by privacy, a suggestion that was ultimately rejected as interfering excessively with the process of judicial interpretation. Ultimately, after extensive discussions, the 1999 draft contained no reference either to reproductive rights or abortion.[136]

In the 2013 process, advocates had dual goals of constitutionalizing reproductive rights while ensuring language was not added that would memorialize the criminalization of abortion. They knew that finding this balance would be a challenge. Early in the reform process, general reproductive rights, family planning, and protection from HIV were identified as appropriate issues to be exported to legislation.[137] However, in the final constitution, provisions on reproductive rights and healthcare were included along with language prohibiting abortion, except in limited circumstances.[138] Article 76(1) of the Constitution provides that "[e]very citizen and permanent resident of Zimbabwe has the right to have access to basic health-care services, including reproductive health-care services."[139] Article 29(1) requires the State to "take all practical measures to ensure the provision of basic, accessible and adequate health services throughout Zimbabwe."[140] Article (48)(3) states that an

[130] Gift Phiri, "Zimbabwe's Maternal Mortality Crisis." *Al Jazeera*, February 9, 2014. Available at www.aljazeera.com/indepth/features/2014/02/zimbabwe-maternal-mortality-crisis-2014256173919 8301.html [accessed September 20, 2018].
[131] World Health Organization, "WHO Perspectives on Maternal Mortality in Zimbabwe: A Reflection of the Year 2014." Available at https://afro.who.int/news/who-perspectives-maternal-mortality-zimbabwe-reflection-year-2014 [accessed September 22, 2018].
[132] Termination of Pregnancy Act, Acts 29/1977, 6/2000, 8/2001, 22/2001, chapter 15:10, section 4(a–c).
[133] Flores and Made, n. 45: 34.
[134] Ibid. 36.
[135] Ibid.
[136] Ibid.
[137] Ibid.
[138] The Constitution of Zimbabwe of 2013: Secs. 48 and 76.
[139] Ibid. Sec. 76(1).
[140] Ibid. Sec. 29(1).

"Act of Parliament must protect the lives of unborn children, and that Act must provide that pregnancy may be terminated only in accordance with the law."[141]

The First Period
In contrast to domestic violence, access to reproductive healthcare dramatically improved in the first period following the passage of the 2013 constitution. By 2014, Zimbabwe's maternal mortality rate had dropped by approximately 36 percent from its 2009 rate.[142] The 2013–17 National Gender Policy[143] along with partnerships with UN Population Fund and the World Health Organization to expand the provision of health services through Zimbabwe have been directly credited with the drop in maternal mortality.

Legislative revision and adjustment of national policies on reproductive health-care, as in other areas, has been sluggish. The National Family Planning Council Act and the Termination of Pregnancy Acts have yet to be realigned with the new Constitution. Alignments needed include the discrepancy between the age of consent for sexual intercourse (sixteen) and the age of consent for marriage (eighteen), the latter having recently been established by the Constitutional Court of Zimbabwe. This discrepancy often means that sexually active girls ages sixteen and seventeen have decreased access to contraceptives. This is made worse by cultural norms against premarital sex.

The reproductive healthcare provision, like the domestic violence provision, was not an area of focus during the 2013 reform. There was, however, an important distinction in the context of the two provisions that may have prompted a very different first period. Under the Millennium Development Goals, there was a fair amount of pressure on Zimbabwe and its partners to improve its maternal mortality rate in the short term. Zimbabwe's target for 2015 was to reduce maternal mortality to 71 deaths per 100,000 live births.[144] The passage of the constitution may have merely coincided with the final period in which Zimbabwe and its supporting partners made a push to meet these goals. It is likely, however, that the provision also provided an important platform for advocates and donors to engage the government in reproductive healthcare in the short term. Whether it will influence government priorities in the longer term is another matter. Moreover, because customary practices have been identified as one of the key barriers to improving maternal

[141] Ibid. Sec. 48(3).
[142] United Nations in Zimbabwe, Issue Paper Series, "Maternal Mortality in Zimbabwe, Evidence Costs and Implications," (2013). Available at www.zw.one.un.org/sites/default/files/UN-ZW_IssuePaperSeries-1_MMR_June2013.pdf [accessed September 20, 2018].
[143] Ministry of Women's Affairs, Gender and Community Development, Zimbabwe National Gender Policy 2013–17: 16. Available at www.zw.undp.org/content/zimbabwe/en/home/library/democratic_governance/national-gender-policy.html [accessed September 15].
[144] World Health Organization, "WHO Perspectives on Maternal Mortality in Zimbabwe: A Reflection of the Year 2014." Available at https://afro.who.int/news/who-perspectives-maternal-mortality-zimbabwe-reflection-year-2014 [accessed September 22, 2018].

mortality, long term success will also depend on the realization of constitutional protections that restrict such practices.

6.4 REFLECTIONS ON THE FIRST PERIOD

These examples from Zimbabwe illustrate a few basic points – first, gender-responsive constitutions contend with the strong pull of preservation and thus first-period implementation is a challenge overall. Even when a reform process benefits from circumstances that support the development of a gender-responsive constitution, implementation will contend with the many barriers firmly put in place by history and culture, and by institutions that are accustomed to and rely on women's inequality. As a result, advocates are often compelled to adopt strategies – such as invoking outside pressure or catering to and appeasing resistance. These strategies may, in turn, create disadvantages in engaging the transformative powers of reform and the debate, and the reflection and (re)commitment it can prompt. Accounts from various countries provide a fairly consistent portrayal of gender-equality advocacy that takes place in the context of indifference and opposition by those in positions of power. Countries with such reforms, moreover, do not generally evidence marked improvement in women's circumstances immediately following reform.[145]

Second, however, language that results from reforms taking place in the context of indifference or resistance can result in significant gains for women. Legislative quotas in Zimbabwe resulted in relatively quick implementation. This may have been because they were publically debated and scrutinized or simply because of the general importance of politics in Zimbabwe. A new legislative quota, for example, may have also been viewed as a vehicle for political gains by parties in the election that followed.

Third, the gains to be had may take the form of confirmation of a consolidation of views, a gain difficult to measure in the first period. The elimination of customary law exclusions, which was subjected to little discussion during reform and quickly accepted as a constitutional given, was a significant gain for women in Zimbabwe. The exclusion had been publically debated prior to reform and in the earlier process. The swift acceptance in the 2013 process likely reflected at least a basic common understanding of the general meaning and mandate of the provision that had emerged in the intervening years between the first and second reform process. This may not serve to eliminate noncompliance (harmful customary practices are still ongoing) or disagreements as to the extent of required reform in the future but at

---

[145] See, for example, the Gender Inequality Indices for countries listed in ftnt. 1 following their respective reforms. "Table 5: Gender Inequality Index" United Nations Development Programme, *Human Development Report 2016*. Available at http://hdr.undp.org/en/composite/GII [accessed October 1, 2017].

least stakeholders (including courts) have been compelled in the first period to commit to the same broad ideological principle – that customary practices are subject to prohibitions on nondiscrimination as well as other gender equality mandates. The involvement of customary leaders in the Gender Commission along with civil society engagement with customary practices are likely to support the impact of this language.

The reproductive health language, also little discussed and general in form, provides an example of a provision that generated first period implementation without extensive debate. Unlike the customary exclusion language, it did not appear to be a prominent issue in public debate prior to the 2013 reform process. Here, circumstances external to the reform process – the Millennium Development Goals and agreements with international partners – were likely influential in motivating the inclusion of the language as well as the first-period implementation. The provision provided a platform for international agencies to provide support to the government to combat maternal mortality. Women clearly benefited in the first period of implementation of this provision but it remains to be seen if the first-period implementation reflects a longer-term commitment of the state and whether it also sets a new normal for reductions in maternal mortality.

Finally, the language on domestic violence provides a scenario in which constitutional language may codify a prior commitment reflected elsewhere (legislation) but does not meaningfully advance or entrench that commitment in the first period. With discussion and a rather general provision, the language has generated little first-period action. This may be because there is a general complacency with existing, though ineffective, legislation, just general indifference to domestic violence or unresolvable barriers between the formal legal system and the customary system that resolves many domestic violence cases. Yet, the inclusion of domestic violence language in any constitution is not without significance – historically and globally women have battled for the recognition that domestic violence is a sociocultural phenomenon rather than a private matter. A constitutional commitment to protection from domestic violence would have been inconceivable in any country twenty years ago. Its recognition in a country's highest law has been recent and undoubtedly elevates its status as a social concern. Efforts to improve on existing legislation may still benefit from the constitutional provision added in 2013.

6.5 MAXIMIZING THE BENEFITS OF REFORM

For most women, advocacy for equal rights takes place in the context of social and political environments that have neither the commitment nor the capacity to truly engage in the kind of social transformation gender equality would require. Constitutional reform is no different. While the international human rights system, global and domestic women's movements, and some amount of general social progress have combined to produce an impressive number of gender-responsive constitutions, the impact these provisions could have on women's lives is difficult to determine in these early days without close and individualized analysis.

To maximize the benefits of reform, however, it is important to move beyond the focus on the inclusion of gender-responsive constitutional language to assess the factors and circumstances that lead to their efficacy. Attention must be paid to the circumstances of drafting and constitution-making, and the background of the process and the social context of the particular gender issue. These will impact implementation in the first period following its enactment and beyond. The issues that are settled on during reform have the potential for quicker implementation whereas others will necessitate further work to realize in the long term. As described earlier in the chapter, language may advance gender equality by initiating, re-charging, or resolving conversations that address equality issues or at least expose existing cultural and social barriers. This exposure, and the dialogue that ensues, can also impact women's equality in the longer-term.

There are some lessons for women and their supporters in maximizing the benefits of a reform process. One lesson is to tread carefully when organizing for language-inclusion rather than consensus-building. Where language is added by adopting international standards or neighboring templates without an engaged process, first-period implementation may be absent or minimal (depending on the influence of the international institutions or surrounding states) and even longer-term implementation may not meaningfully occur. The same is true for reliance on key female political figures, which may result in a shaky foundation for future advocacy. Ultimately, where language is obtained through means that do not engage the directive forces and conversational elements of reform, implementation may not occur in the first period unless other forces that motivate action are at work. For most reform processes unfocused on women's equality, immediate first period results are unlikely to be the norm.

More generally, constitutions can have relatively weak institutional influence over rights and benefits in practice, especially in countries with fragile rule of law. Where this is the case, the process itself may be more suited to prompting a cultural shift rather than a legal or policy-oriented one. Here again, focusing only on textual advances runs the risk of producing gender-responsive language that remains in print but never in fact. Thus, it may be worthwhile to refocus advocacy energy on maximizing the benefits of the process even where that may mean fewer textual advances. For example, it may be worthwhile to insist on a process that requires extensive opportunity for debates on gender-related issues even if those debates lead to disappointing results. Those provisions that are added through an engaged process may experience better first-period implementation and longer term commitment.

Finally, assessment of the impact of gender-responsive language that does make its way into the final draft should be holistic. Assessments should take into account how language can advance social conversations, avoid future harm, or create basic standards. Comparative approaches struggle to capture this kind of qualitative social transformation. While such approaches may offer some insight into the significance of gender-responsive language obtained in reform processes via indicators, they can also mask and obscure actual dynamics that ultimately provide more useful reflections on when a constitutional change matters, particularly in the first period. Equally problematic are accounts that identify the inclusion of gender-responsive language as an achievement in and of itself and take for granted implementation in the first period. More careful analysis will allow for a nuanced assessment that better directs allocations of resources, ensures targeted interventions, sets reasonable expectations, and properly identifies barriers to political will (some of which may need to be addressed immediately after reform and others with longer term strategies). Ultimately, a more careful review will ensure gender-responsive reform has the potential to realize the ultimate goal – a positive difference in the lives of women.

7

Constitutional Reform and Women's Political Participation

Electoral Gender Quotas in Post-Arab Spring Egypt, Tunisia, and Jordan

Susan H. Williams[*]

Women's political participation is, in many ways, the new frontier in gender equality globally.[1] While many of the familiar, old issues of inequality persist – violence against women, female poverty, unequal access to education and employment – there has been a growing focus on assuring that women have a voice in the policy and lawmaking bodies that address social problems like these. Globally, there has been a trend toward the adoption of electoral gender quotas as a "fast-track" to increase women's political representation.[2] And, because the self-interest of office-holders can make change in basic political institutions difficult within normal politics, the moment of constitutional reform may present a special opportunity for adopting quotas.[3] There is a large literature addressing the forces – both domestic and international – that may help to bring about the adoption of quotas.[4] The question raised by this book is what happens after that moment: How does the

---

[*] I would like to thank Yah Dolo-Barbu and Mary Christie for their research help on this chapter. And special thanks to Abeer Dababneh, of the Women's Studies Center at the University of Jordan, for sharing her expertise about the subject.

[1] This is one of the striking facts illustrated by the Global Gender Gap Report. The average across all nations is relatively high on both educational equality and health equality. The average is substantially lower on economic equality. But the dimension on which women are least equal globally is political equality. See Global Gender Gap Report 2016. Available at http://reports.weforum.org/global-gender-gap-report-2016/results-and-analysis/?doing_wp_cron=15 19746106.4378359317779541015625.

[2] See Drude Dahlerup, Preface in *The Impact of Gender Quotas* at vii, ed. Susan Franceschet, Mona Lena Krook, and Jennifer M. Picopo. Oxford University Press, 2012.

[3] In addition to the greater political fluidity in such moments of transition, there is also often a greater desire to confer international legitimacy on the new regime that can be leveraged to create quotas. See Drude Dahlerup, "Electoral Gender Quotas: Between Equality of Opportunity and Equality of Result." *Journal of Republican Democracy* 43: 73 (2007).

[4] For a review of this literature, see Mona Lena Krook, *Quotas for Women in Politics: Gender and Candidate Selection Reform Worldwide*, at 19–36. Oxford University Press, 2009.

process of implementation affect the outcome of quotas adopted as part of constitutional reforms?

This chapter will explore this issue through an analysis of the changes in women's political representation in three Arab Spring countries: Egypt, Jordan, and Tunisia. These countries were chosen because they share the following characteristics: none are oil-dependent economies; none are currently involved in a civil war; and all experienced significant change in terms of patterns of politics in the post-Arab Spring period. These characteristics distinguish them from most of the other countries in the region and allow a closer focus on the interaction of political and legal issues in women's representation.[5] Section 7.1 will briefly tell the story of the state of women's political representation before, during, and after the processes of constitutional reform in each country. Section 7.2 will use Mona Lena Krook's tripartite framework for assessing quota efficacy – focused on how the quota fits within systems, practices, and norms – to suggest some general insights that can be drawn from these stories. And Section 7.3 will situate these insights within a broader theoretical understanding of the purposes of gender quotas. The conclusion will suggest that quota effectiveness can only be assessed from the perspective of a particular understanding of the purposes behind increasing women's representation. In other words, the question must be: effective to what end? And in making this assessment, one crucial variable often ignored is the extent to which the political institution in which the women are participating is itself dysfunctional.

7.1 A TALE OF THREE COUNTRIES

7.1.1 *Egypt*

The story of women's political participation in Egypt over the course of recent years is a story of loss followed by some limited recoupment. The current situation in Egypt may suggest that there has been a loss of democratic opportunity in all forms, but the irony is that women seem to be doing better as the al-Sisi regime strengthens its grip on power. Indeed, it was during the period when more democracy seemed to be possible that there was a dramatic decline in women's participation in political institutions. Thus, Egypt stands as a reminder that a move from dictatorship toward

---

[5]   There are a few other countries that would also fit these requirements, most notably, Morocco. I chose Jordan rather than Morocco for three reasons: (1). It is more central to the MENA region; (2) it is generally less studied; and (3) I am currently working in Jordan, which provides access to more detailed information. For a discussion of the changes in women's political representation in post-Arab spring Morocco, see Hanane Darhour and Drude Dahlerup, "Sustainable Representation of Women through Gender Quotas: A Decade's Experience in Morocco," *Women's Studies International Forum* (2013). Available at www.peaceisloud.org/wp-content/uploads/2017/04/Sustainable-Representation-of-Women-Through-Gender-Quotas-A-Decade%E2%80%99s-Experience-in-Morocco.pdf.

democracy does not automatically carry with it an improvement in women's political representation.[6]

Under the Mubarak regime, there was, for a time, a 20 percent quota for women in Parliament.[7] Because of the electoral system, however, almost all of these seats were held by women within the ruling party.[8] There was also a significant women's policy machinery allied with the state, in the form of the National Council for Women, headed by the First Lady.[9] Indeed, the regime made gender equality and women's rights a centerpiece of its public image, particularly for Western consumption. And this attention to gender issues resulted in some significant policy initiatives, including raising the age of marriage, criminalizing Female Genital Mutilation (FGM), making divorce more accessible for women, abolishing the marriage defense in rape cases, allowing women to pass their nationality to their children, and allowing women to become judges.[10]

This impressive list of policy achievements is not, however, an accurate measure of the strength and effectiveness of women's organizations or of the public commitment to feminist ideas during the Mubarak regime. The women's movement was crippled politically by its dependence on the government. The members of women's organizations were able to acquire policy experience, but the groups engaged in little constituency-building, since their success depended not on the support of the public, but on the support of the regime.[11] Public attitudes toward gender equality in Egypt have consistently been conservative and not supportive of women's rights.[12] And many of the policy advances – and the quota in particular – were seen by the people as associated with the discredited regime, and with Suzanne Mubarak in particular.[13]

[6] See Valentine Moghadam, "Democratization and Women's Political Leadership in North Africa." *Journal of International Affairs* 68: 59, 60 (2014).
[7] Mariz Tadros, "The Politics of Mobilising for Gender Justice in Egypt from Mubarak to Morsi and Beyond," IDS Working Paper 442, p. 10 (April 2014). This quota was abandoned and revised in later laws, but still stood at sixty-four reserved seats in the last election before the revolution, in 2010.
[8] Ibid.
[9] See Sara Abel Rahim and Erin Fracolli, "Egypt's National Council for Women: A Substitute for Civil Society?" The Tahir Institute for Middle East Policy. Available at https://timep.org/commentary/egypts-national-council-for-women-a-substitute-for-civil-society/.
[10] Tadros, n. 7, at 8. The marriage defense in rape cases – a common provision in the region – allows a rapist to escape prosecution if he marries his victim after the crime was committed. The parallel provision has been the subject of recent activism in Jordan. *See* Zena Tahhan, "Historic Day as Jordanian Parliament Repeals Rape Law," *Al Jazeera.* August 1, 2017. Available at www.aljazeera.com/indepth/features/2017/08/day-jordanian-parliament-repeals-rape-law-170801103929836.html.
[11] See Tadros, n. 7 at 11.
[12] See Valentine M. Moghadam, "Women and Democracy after the Arab Spring: Theory, Practice, and Prospects," in *Empowering Women after the Arab Spring*, ed. Marwa Shalaby and Valentine M. Mogahadam. Palgrave, 2016, 193 at 206.
[13] See Tadros, n. 7 at 12.

Women were instrumental in the public uprising that brought down the Mubarak regime. They participated directly in the Tahrir Square protests and were crucial in the behind-the-scenes organization of food and medical help.[14] Indeed, women were among the public faces of the revolution internationally: It was a female blogger, Asma Mahfouz, who sparked the Egyptian Arab Spring by appealing on Facebook in early 2011 for protests.[15] As Mariz Tadros comments: "The assumption was that the conspicuous role and activism of women in the revolution would be rewarded with recognition. Yet this did not happen."[16] In the immediate aftermath of the revolution, the percentage of women in Parliament dropped from 13 percent in the 2010 election to 2 percent in the 2011 election, despite the fact that the number of women running for seats had doubled.[17] This drop is explained by the fact that in the 2010 election, there had been a quota of sixty-four reserved seats, while in the 2011 election, there was no meaningful quota. Each party was required to nominate at least one woman on its list in each district in which seats were allocated by proportional representation.[18] These seats accounted for two-thirds of the total number of seats in the house, but since the number of women was so low and there was no requirement for placing the women in winnable positions on the lists, almost none of them won. In fact, only eight women were elected in this way. When the SCAF (the Supreme Council of the Armed Forces) appointed two more, the legislature ended up with a total of 10 women out of 508.[19] This legislature was dominated by Islamist parties: The Muslim Brotherhood-associated Freedom and Justice Party and the Salafist Nour party together held over 70 percent of the seats.[20] Shortly afterward, Muhammad Morsi, the leader of the Freedom and Justice Party, was elected President.

As the constitution-writing process got underway, women were, again, largely excluded from representation. No women at all were present on the first Commission tasked with reforming the Constitution, and the first Constituent Assembly had only six women members out of a total of 100 and was dominated by the Islamist parties from the Parliament.[21] Despite constitutional challenges to the validity of the

[14] See "Women Have Emerged as Key Players in the Arab Spring," *The Guardian*. April 22, 2011. Available at www.theguardian.com/world/2011/apr/22/women-arab-spring.
[15] See Martina Sabra, "Women's Rights and the Arab Spring: The Female Face of the Revolution," *Quantara* http://en.qantara.de/content/womens-rights-and-the-arab-spring-the-female-face-of-the-revolution.
[16] Ibid. 16.
[17] Ibid.
[18] The PR districts each had between four and twelve representatives. See David M. Faris, "Constituting Institutions: The Electoral System in Egypt," Middle East Policy Council, Vol. XIX, No. 1 (spring). Available at www.mepc.org/constituting-institutions-electoral-system-egypt.
[19] See IDEA Quota Project, Country Data: Egypt. Available at www.idea.int/data-tools/data/gender-quotas/country-view/100/35.
[20] See "Egypt Court Suspends Constitutional Assembly," *BBC News*, April 10, 2012. Available at www.bbc.com/news/world-middle-east-17665048.
[21] See Tadros, n. 7 at 14.

Constituent Assembly,[22] that assembly (with President Morsi's support) pushed through a draft constitution, which was approved in a public referendum in December of 2012.[23]

Public protests erupted again later that year and the SCAF gave the Morsi administration a deadline for reaching a compromise with opposition forces. When no agreement was reached, the military again took control, ousting Morsi and his government. In the aftermath of the military coup, SCAF installed Adly Mansour, the Chief Justice of the Supreme Constitutional Court, as interim President. President Mansour then appointed a second constitution drafting body in 2013, charged with revising the suspended 2012 Constitution produced by the Morsi government.[24] This committee had five female members out of a total of fifty, and those women had experience as advocates for women's rights and had some allies on the committee (from which Islamists were excluded). As a result, they were able to include some important language in the Constitution on women's political representation. This Constitution was approved in 2014 and is the current Constitution of Egypt.

The 2014 Constitution includes general language endorsing political representation for women, but no explicit quota at the national level. Article 11 states: "The state commits to taking the necessary measures to ensure appropriate representation of women in the houses of parliament, in the manner specified by law."[25] The Constitution also affirms women's right to serve in high government positions, including in the judiciary, again, with no specific enforcement mechanism.[26] There is an explicit quota at the local level in Article 180: "Every local unit elects a local council by direct, secret ballot for a term of four years … The law regulates other conditions for candidacy and procedures of election, provided that one quarter of the seats are allocated to youth under 35 years old, one quarter is allocated to women …."[27] Law No. 46 of 2014 implements Article 11 of the Constitution by creating a quota for the first election of Parliament under the new Constitution. Art. 5 of that law requires that, for the single house of the national legislature, party lists in each PR district with fifteen seats had to include seven women. In districts with forty-five seats, the party lists had to include twenty-one women. These multi-member districts accounted for 120 out of 568 total seats in the legislature. The party

---

[22] See BBC report, n. 20.

[23] See USIP Peacebrief, January 25, 2013. Available at www.usip.org/sites/default/files/PB139-Egypt%E2%80%99s%202012%20Constitution.pdf.

[24] See Rainer Grote, "Constitutional Developments in Egypt: the New 2014 Egyptian Constitution," *Oxford Constitutional Law*. Available at http://oxcon.ouplaw.com/page/egyptian-constitution.

[25] See Egypt's Constitution of 2014, Art. 11, *ConstituteProject*. Available at www.constituteproject .org/constitution/Egypt_2014.pdf.

[26] See ibid. ("grants women the right to hold public posts and high management posts in the state, and to appointment in judicial bodies and entities without discrimination.")

[27] See ibid. Art. 180.

lists were not, however, required to place women in winnable positions on the list, so many were placed toward the bottom. As a result, only parties that took a high percentage of the seats in a given district would be likely to reach the women on their lists. Of the other seats, 420 were single-member districts filled by plurality voting, for which no quota applied. An additional twenty-eight were to be appointed by the President.

In the 2015 elections under this law there was a meaningful increase in the number of women MPs, mostly as a result of the proportional representation seats. Given the lack of a quota for the 420 single member district seats, very few parties ran women for those seats. As a result, a total of only 17 of the 420 seats were won by women. There were also fifty-six seats won through the quota in party lists.[28] Elected women thus represented about 13 percent of the legislature. President al-Sisi appointed another fourteen women to the seats he controls (half of those seats), bringing the total percentage to 15 percent.[29] This level of representation is an enormous improvement over the 2 percent in the 2011 election immediately after the revolution, highlighting the irony that, as Egypt has become less democratic since 2011, women's political representation has increased. The future is, however, uncertain. Since the quota was explicitly limited to this first election after the adoption of the new Constitution, it is very unclear whether the results will be repeated in future elections. In addition, since only five political parties won more than 5 percent of the seats in the legislature (and, as explained previously, only a party that won a substantial number of seats in a district would reach the women on its list), it is not clear whether the women in the parliament represent a real cross-section of Egyptian politics or are limited to the members of a few big parties.

At the time of writing, elections for the local councils under the new Constitution have not yet been held. The National Council for Women has been actively working to educate women about the opportunities in local government and encourage them to run.[30] There is some question, however, whether these local councils will have any significant power over policy or will simply be a sideshow to the authority of appointed local administrators.[31]

President al-Sisi has made women's rights a focus of his administration, calling 2017 "The Year of Women" in Egypt. There have been some significant legislative achievements in the past couple of years, including laws against sexual harassment

---

[28] See Marwa Shalaby, "Women's Political Representation and Authoritarianism in the Arab World," Paper Project on Middle East Political Science (March 2016). Available at http:// pomeps.org/2016/04/14/womens-political-representation-and-authoritarianism-in-the-arab-world/#_ftn2.

[29] See "Egyptian Women in 2015 Parliamentary Elections," Egyptian Center for Women's Rights, February 17, 2016. Available at http://ecwronline.org/?p=6788.

[30] See Angy Essam, "Women in Egypt Part IV," *Egypt Today*. Available at www.egypttoday.com/Article/6/38561/Women-in-Egypt-Part-4.

[31] See "Participatory Local Democracy," The Hunger Project. Available at https://localdemocracy.net/countries/africa-north/egypt/.

and guaranteeing women's inheritance rights. The President has also revived the National Council for Women and appointed experienced and committed activists to it.[32] And he has appointed a number of female ministers, recently reaching a high point of eight, including to important posts in areas such as the Ministry for Investment and International Cooperation and the Ministry of Planning.[33] At the same time, Egypt continues to rank very low on the Gender Gap Report by the World Economic Forum, placing 132nd out of 144 countries. This poor ranking rests on the significant gender gap between men and women in economic participation and opportunity and in political participation in Egypt. And it represents a meaningful drop from the status of the country ten years ago on these issues.[34] In addition, there is an epidemic of sexual violence against women in Egypt now, which has drawn the attention of both national and international policymakers but has not, as yet, been effectively addressed.[35] Egypt, then, appears to be a story about how the more things change, the more they stay the same. After dramatic upheaval and great uncertainty, the situation in Egypt now seems to be remarkably similar to the situation under the Mubarak regime, both in terms of the restrictions on democratic freedoms and the superficial attention to women's political representation while little really changes about women's lives.

7.1.2 *Tunisia*

While it is the cradle of the Arab Spring, Tunisia is distinct from most other countries in the MENA region in many ways. Most notably, the changes in women's status, in terms of economic participation and educational attainment, were earlier and more profound than in most other places in the region. These changes were the result of the same sort of state feminism under an authoritarian regime as in Egypt. But the striking difference is that a much broader and deeper social consensus seems

[32] See Miwa Kato, "Women of Egypt," *The Cairo Review of Global Affairs.* Available at www .thecairoreview.com/essays/women-of-egypt/.

[33] "For the First Time, 8 Female Ministers in Egypt's Cabinet," *Egypt Today,* Available at www .egypttoday.com/Article/2/52152/For-the-first-time-8-female-ministers-in-Egypt-s.

[34] See "Country Profile: Egypt," Gender Gap Report, World Economic Forum. Available at http://reports.weforum.org/global-gender-gap-report-2016/economies/#economy=EGY. However, it is worth noting that the actual scores on every dimension measured – economics, education, health, and politics – have improved over that period. The drop in rank comes from the fact that the rate of improvement in Egypt has not kept pace with the rate of improvement in other countries.

[35] See Mariz Tadros, n. 7 at 23–24 (April 2014) (describing the gender-based violence and responses by government and civil society.) There is political mobilization around the issue, and there have been some legislative and policy responses, but many are underfunded, understaffed, and ineffective. For a description of some of the changes and one of the responses to their ineffectiveness (The 16 Days of Activism against the Gender-Based Violence (GBV) Campaign in the fall of 2017), See Lowla Reda, "Violence against Women: Egyptian Laws, Policies in Place," *Egypt Today.* Friday, December 1, 2017. Available at www.egypttoday.com/ Article/2/34864/Violence-Against-Women-Egyptian-laws-policies-in-place.

to have been generated around the idea of women's equality in Tunisia. This consensus led to a very different approach to gender quotas and to substantial levels of women's political participation over the course of the recent constitutional transition.

President Zine El-Abidine Ben Ali, like Habib Bourguiba – the President he deposed – had made women's equality rights a central part of his political platform. This served his interests both internationally, by coopting Western governments that might otherwise object to his authoritarian policies, and domestically, by positioning him as the defender of women's rights against the threat posed by Islamist opponents of his government. While independent women's movements were squelched, there was a significant women's policy machinery within government. And Tunisia had some of the most progressive laws relating to women's issues in the region, far earlier than many other countries.[36] By the time of the Arab Spring, the women of Tunisia had for many years been more likely to be employed than their sisters in Egypt or Jordan.[37] For example, women had made substantial progress in the legal profession. The first woman judge was appointed in 1968, and, in 2010, 34 percent of judges and 31 percent of lawyers were women.[38] In terms of electoral political representation, the changes in Tunisia were more recent and came only shortly before the Arab Spring. In 1995, women made up 6.7 percent of the Tunisian parliament, as compared to 1.3 percent in Jordan and 2.2 percent in Egypt.[39] But by 2011, thanks to a gender quota adopted by the Ben Ali regime, women made up 26.3 percent of the Tunisian parliament.[40] Indeed, in 2011, Tunisia scored top of the MENA region on every category of women's rights under the Freedom House country ratings for women's equality.[41] And these concrete differences in women's status seem to have

[36] For example, the Personal Status Code was significantly reformed in 1956. See Sangeeta Sinha, "Women's Rights: Tunisian Women in the Workplace." *Journal of International Women's Studies* 12: 185, 186 (2011).

[37] For example, compare the country profiles for the three countries in the Gender Gap Report for 2006. The index numbers for women's economic opportunities were: Egypt 0.416; Jordan 0.442; Tunisia 0.480. See Gender Gap Report 2016, n. 34.

[38] See Rim Belhaj, "Gender Follow-Up in Tunisia," World Bank (2010). Available at http://siteresources.worldbank.org/INTGENDER/Resources/336003-1289616249857/tunisia_gender_rim.pdf.

[39] See "Women in Parliaments 1945–1995," Interparliamentary Union, at 113 (Egypt), 152 (Jordan), 247 (Tunisia). Available at http://archive.ipu.org/PDF/publications/women45–95_en.pdf.

[40] See "Women in Parliament in 2011," IPU at 2. Available at http://archive.ipu.org/pdf/publications/wmnpersp11-e.pdf. Compared to 20 percent in Egypt (before the change in regime, as described above) and a little over 10 percent in the lower house in Jordan. See "Jordan's Female Parliament Representation," KVINFO. Available at http://kvinfo.org/mena/jordans-female-parliament-representation (this was due to a quota of one reserved seat in each of twelve governorates, plus one woman who won a seat outside the quota – for a total of thirteen women out of 120 seats).

[41] See Sanja Kelly and Julia Breslin, ed., *Women's Rights in the Middle East and North Africa*. New York: Freedom House; Lanham, MD: Rowman & Littlefield, 2010. Available at www.freedomhouse.org.

been accompanied by different attitudes to gender issues. On the World Values Survey in 2013, for example, Tunisians exhibited more liberal attitudes on a range of gender issues than other people in the region, including 45 percent disagreeing with the statement that men make better political leaders.[42] These different starting places – in terms of (1) women's presence in government, the professions, and the workplace; (2) the early recognition for their rights in a variety of settings; and (3) shifting attitudes on gender – contributed to a different path during the constitutional transition. As one female party leader put it: "After years of playing a prominent role in society, women's empowerment is deeply engrained in our culture."[43] In light of this history, it appears that the guarantees for women's political representation in the new Constitution were not a radical transformation, but rather an extension of the hard-fought gains from the earlier era.

As in Egypt, women of all ages and classes were active participants in the protests that led to the regime change.[44] Unlike in Egypt, from the beginning of the transition, women were involved in the process of building the new system in significant numbers. Shortly after the fall of the Ben Ali government, the major political parties reached an agreement about a process for creating an interim government and a new constitution. They formed a High Commission for the Realization of Revolutionary Goals, Political Reforms, and Democratic Transition that included representatives of twelve parties and fourteen CSOs and national organizations.[45] This body included six women out of eighteen on its Expert Commission; 36 women out of 155 in its Committee of Representatives, and one woman Vice President.[46] The interim government included two women ministers.[47] The constitution would be drafted by a National Constituent Assembly (NCA); the Higher Independent Electoral Commission, which was charged with the task of overseeing the election of the NCA, adopted a parity rule for the election of the Assembly.[48] This rule required all parties to nominate equal numbers of men

---

[42] See Valentine Moghadam, "Democratization and Women's Political Leadership in North Africa." *Journal of International Affairs* 68: 59, 66 (2014). For comparison: the mean for the region on this question was 75 percent agreement. See Bozena C. Welborne, "No Agency Without Grassroots Autonomy: A Framework for Evaluating Women's Political Inclusion in Jordan, Bahrain, and Morocco 65," in *Empowering Women after the Arab Spring*, n. 12 at 80.

[43] See Moghadam, n. 12 at 204 (Quoting Ommezine Khelifa of the Ettakol Party.)

[44] See ibid. at 199; Marwa Shalaby, "Challenges Facing Women's Political Participation Post-Arab Spring: The Cases of Egypt and Tunisia," In *Empowering Women after the Arab Spring*, n. 12 at 171.

[45] See Khedija Arfaoui and Jane Tchaicha, "Governance, Women and the New Tunisia." *Politics and Religion* 8: 135, 144 (2014).

[46] See Moghadam, n. 12 at 203.

[47] See ibid.

[48] This commission had two women members, see Arfaoui and Tchaicha, n. 45 at 145, but the parity rule was supported by a clear majority.

and women and to alternate male and female names on their party lists. The penalty for failure to meet this rule was to have the list rejected by the Commission.[49]

One hundred and eleven parties registered for the NCA election. While women headed only 7 percent of the party lists, the quota was effective in generating a body with 49 women out of the total of 217 members, roughly 22.5 percent.[50] There was some dissatisfaction with this result, not only because it was substantially below the 50 percent quota for the lists but also because of the distribution of the seats. Because the district magnitude was small, many parties got only one seat. And since most of them had men at the top of their lists, the women came overwhelmingly from the single party able to win multiple seats in many districts: the moderate Islamist Ennahda Party.[51] Forty-two of the forty-nine women elected belonged to this party, leading many people to see this as inadequate representation for women's concerns in the Assembly.

The period of the interim government and the constitution-drafting was far from peaceful. Despite Salafist protests and the assassination of two left-wing politicians, however, Tunisia avoided the military take-over that occurred under similar circumstances in Egypt. Instead, the main political actors chose negotiation and compromise: The Ennahda government resigned and allowed a caretaker government to organize new elections while the constitution was being finished.[52] In this constitution-drafting process, there were some efforts to rollback women's gains in Tunisia, through the adoption of an approach that would substitute "complementarity" for equality as the nominal ideal in gender relations. Complementarity, which was proposed by Ennahda representatives, made reference to traditional gender roles in the family and women activists were afraid that it would allow different treatment of men and women based on those roles rather than requiring equality. The complementarity proposal was effectively countered by the women on the NCA and their more liberal partners.[53] The Constitution, approved in 2014, includes a strong equality provision in Article 20 and an explicit political parity provision in Article 46: "The state works to attain parity between women and men in elected Assemblies."[54]

In the election in October of 2014, under an electoral law that continued the application of the parity rule, 47 percent of all candidates were women, 12 percent of the party leaders (i.e. the first name on the party list) were women, and women

---

49 See Ibid., 145.
50 See Ibid., 150.
51 See ibid., 150–51.
52 See Valentine Moghadam, "Modernizing Women and Democratization after the Arab Spring." *Journal of North African Studies* 19: 137, 138 (2014).
53 See Shalaby, n. 44 at 174.
54 See Constitution of Tunisia, Art. 20 and 46 (2014), *ConstituteProject*. Available at www .constituteproject.org/constitution/Tunisia_2014?lang=en.

received 31 percent of the seats in parliament as a result.[55] Given the small size of the electoral districts (ranging from four to ten seats each) there is a question about the distribution of women's seats across parties: Since men were at the top of the vast majority of lists, only a party that won at least two seats in a given district would be likely to have a woman elected. Given that only two political parties received more than 5 percent of the popular vote, it is likely that the women members are concentrated in the two largest parties: Nidaa Tounes (a secular, progressive coalition that won the largest number of seats in the election)[56] and Ennahda.[57] This pattern was repeated in the 2018 elections, in which women received 36 percent of the seats in Parliament.[58]

The electoral law was amended in 2016 to require parity in party lists at the local level as well. Indeed, the new law on local elections requires not only that male and female names alternate on the lists but also that a given party must put a woman as the top name on half of the lists it runs across local districts ("horizontal" as well as "vertical" parity.) In May of 2018, the law resulted in a record high of 47 percent representation for women at the local level.[59] The initial government after the 2014 elections included eight women out of twenty-six ministers, including a woman serving as the Minister of Finance.[60] The current cabinet includes three women ministers out of twenty-nine.[61]

There are still important challenges facing women in Tunisia, of course. The economic crisis in the country is hitting women particularly hard: The unemployment rate for women is 10 percentage points higher than for men.[62] And there is growing violence against women.[63] At the same time, the women politicians in Tunisia have managed to achieve some notable successes. For example, the parliament recently passed a comprehensive national law addressing violence against women.[64] And the parliament has also recently repealed the old law that prohibited

[55] See Valentine Moghadam, "Democratization and Women's Political Leadership in North Africa." *Journal of International Affairs* 68: 59, 72 (2014).

[56] See Moghadam, n. 12 at 205.

[57] See Tunisian Parliamentary Election 2014, Wikipedia. Available at https://en.wikipedia.org/wiki/Tunisian_parliamentary_election,_2014.

[58] See IPU Women in Parliament. Available at http://archive.ipu.org/wmn-e/classif.htm.

[59] See "Historic Leap in Tunisia: Women Make Up 47 Per cent of Local Government," *UNWomen News*, Monday, Aug. 27, 2018. Available at www.unwomen.org/en/news/stories/2018/8/feature-tunisian-women-in-local-elections.

[60] See "Chahed Nominates Women and Youth to New Tunisia Government," DW. Available at www.dw.com/en/chahed-nominates-women-and-youth-to-new-tunisia-government/a-19490507.

[61] See Sarah Yerkes and Shannon McKeown, "What Tunisia Can Teach the United States About Women's Equality," Carnegie Endowment for International Peace. November 30, 2018. Available at https://carnegieendowment.org/2018/11/30/what-tunisia-can-teach-united-states-about-women-s-equality-pub-77850.

[62] See Don Duncan, "Women in Tunisia Fighting to Preserve Their Rights by Becoming Skilled Politicians," *CBC NEWS*. October 9, 2016. Available at www.cbc.ca/news/world/Tunisia-women-politics-skills-1.3789082.

[63] Ibid.

[64] See "Tunisia Passes Historic Law to End Violence against Women and Girls," *UNWomen*. Available at www.unwomen.org/en/news/stories/2017/8/news-tunisia-law-on-ending-violence-against-women.

Muslim women from marrying non-Muslim men.[65] These achievements are notable for their outcomes, and for the fact that women's voices were strong enough to get these issues on the legislative agenda.[66] One reason for this effectiveness is that NGOs and women's organizations have focused on providing training to increase women's skills and abilities in politics.[67] Thus, the story of Tunisia seems to be a story of strength building on strength: The real changes in women's status achieved under the system of state feminism provided a foundation for the important guarantees achieved in the democratic constitutional moment and the continuing progress since then.

7.1.3 Jordan

I have suggested that the story of women's political representation in Egypt is one of loss of representation, followed by limited regaining of ground, under conditions of a resurgence of authoritarianism. And the story of women's political representation in Tunisia is one of a strong foundation yielding steady growth in representation, even in the face of challenges. The story of women's political participation in Jordan follows neither of these patterns. It is, instead, a story of slow, incremental improvement under conditions where the political institutions suffer from some fundamental limitations.

The Arab Spring in Jordan did not lead to regime change. Jordan remains a constitutional monarchy in which the lower house of the Parliament is elected, while the upper house and the Prime Minister are appointed by the King.[68] During the protests in Jordan, there was a public call for a change in the Prime Minister and cabinet (which were, in fact, dismissed by the King), but no significant call for an end to the monarchy. But there was anger over economic issues, corruption, and the extent of the King's power. In response, the King created commissions, instituted a national dialogue process, and published a series of papers outlining a path to greater democracy in Jordan. The outcome of this process has been some substantial constitutional and statutory change: a new electoral law and political party law, the creation of a Constitutional Court and an Independent Electoral

---

[65] See "Tunisian Women Free to Marry Non-Muslims," *BBC News*. Available at www.bbc.com/news/world-africa-41278610.

[66] There is good evidence to suggest that women are more likely to focus the agenda on women's issues, even if their male colleagues from similar party backgrounds are as likely to vote for the proposals, once the issues are raised. See "Introduction: Conceptualizing the Impact of Gender Quotas," in *The Impact of Gender Quotas*, ed. Susan Francheschet, Mona Lena Krook, and Jennifer Piscopo. Oxford, 2012. As a result, quotas have led to a significant increase in the introduction of woman-friendly policy proposals, even if they often have failed to alter the outcome of policy debates. See ibid. at 12.

[67] "The Woman Pushing Women into Tunisia's Politics." Available at www.theatlantic.com/business/archive/2016/08/ikram-ben-said-tunisia-women/492242/ .

[68] See Constitution of the Hashemite Kingdom of Jordan (1952, as amended in 2011), Art. 35 and Art. 36. Available at www.constituteproject.org/constitution/Jordan_2011.pdf.

Commission,[69] and constitutional amendments described by their supporters as reductions in the King's power (although that description is contested by opponents.)[70]

In order to understand politics in Jordan, it is necessary to recall that there was an extended period of martial law under the prior King Hussein, from 1967 to 1989, during which no elections were held and political parties were outlawed.[71] After this period, the electoral laws in Jordan were changed regularly – essentially before every new election – in order to limit the power of the Muslim Brotherhood parties and assure the dominance of the traditional power base for the monarchy: the tribes.[72] Perhaps as a result of this history, Jordan has an extremely weak political party system and a culture of politics in which patronage and clan identity are the central elements.[73] Jordanians have a generally low opinion of their Parliament.[74] They tend to believe that corruption is rampant in the government[75] and that the primary role of a representative is to channel government benefits and public services to his constituents.[76]

Against this background, Jordan has been gradually increasing the number of women in political positions. The impetus for this change has come primarily from

[69] In the interests of disclosure: the Center for Constitutional Democracy, which I direct, has been working for the past two years with the Constitutional Court and the Electoral Commission in Jordan. We were not, however, involved in any of the changes discussed in this chapter.

[70] For a description of this process, emphasizing the complicated political divisions within Jordan and also the unifying concern not to be swept up into the chaos of the region, see Curtis R. Ryan, "Five Years after Arab Uprisings: Security Trumps Reform in Jordan," *Washington Post.* Available at www.washingtonpost.com/news/monkey-cage/wp/2016/03/04/five-years-after-arab-uprisings-security-trumps-reforms-in-jordan/?utm_term=.b13c59834720.

[71] See Constitutional History of Jordan, *ConstitutionNet.* Available at www.constitutionnet.org/country/constitutional-history-jordan.

[72] See Catherine Warrick, *Law in the Service of Legitimacy.* Abingdon: Routledge, 2009, 127; Ibtissam al-Attiyat, Musa Shteiwi, and Suleiman Sweiss, "Building Democracy in Jordan: Women's Political Participation, Political Party Life, and Democratic Elections," 19 (2003) IDEA Paper. Available at www.idea.int/es/publications/catalogue/building-democracy-jordan-womens-political-participation-political-party-life.

[73] The patronage and clan aspects of the political culture are shared with many other countries, both in the Arab region and elsewhere in the world, so their roots likely lie in more general dynamics rather than in the specific electoral history of Jordan. See Khaled A. Beydoun, "Fast-Tracking Women into Parliamentary Seats in the Arab World." *Southwestern Journal Of International Law* 17: 63, 90 (2011) (tribalism v. cosmopolitanism as the real clash of civilizations). Nonetheless, the frequent and strategic changes in the electoral laws did not help the process of party consolidation in Jordan.

[74] See "Jordan: Economy Breeds Widespread Dissatisfaction with Government," IRI. June 20, 2016. Available at www.iri.org/resource/jordan-economy-breeds-widespread-dissatisfaction-government.

[75] See Andre Teti, Pamela Abbott, and Francesco Cavatorta, *The Arab Uprisings in Egypt, Jordan and Tunisia: Social, Political and Economic Transformations.* Springer, 2017, 111.

[76] See Alaa Zuhair Rwashdeh, "Jordanian Voters' Criteria of Selection of Members of the Lower House of Representatives in 2013 Elections." *Journal of Sociolegal Research* 4: 295, 317–18 (2013) (almost unanimity across groups based on gender, age, location, and education that the most important factor for voters is whether candidate satisfies people's demands for public services.)

the royal family: Support has come from the King and from the primary state women's policy organ, the Jordanian National Commission on Women, which is led by Princess Basma bint Talal.[77] Since 2003, Jordan has had a quota for the lower house. The original quota reserved six seats for women. This was raised to twelve seats in the 2010 election. One woman won a seat outside the quotas in 2007 and in 2010.[78] The King has also been appointing women to the upper house of the legislature: 15 percent of the Senators were female in 2010. Also in 2010, the gender quota for municipal councils was increased to 25 percent, but most of the women on these councils were appointed until very recently. For example, in 1999, forty-three female candidates ran at the local level; eight won and twenty-five more women were appointed.[79]

The Constitution of Jordan does not include a gender quota. Indeed, the Constitution does not include any guarantee of equality on the basis of sex or gender: The equality provision applies only to discrimination on the basis of race, language, or religion.[80] Nothing was added to the Constitution in the recent reforms to address these issues. But the electoral law was revised after the demonstrations to move to an open list proportional representation system and to increase the reserved seats for women in the lower house to fifteen, out of a total of 130.[81] Despite the fact that Jordan now uses a list PR electoral system, the quota is not a candidate quota, as in Egypt or Tunisia.[82] Instead, the quota functions as a reserved seat system. Women must run as members of party lists, like other candidates, but they do not count

---

[77] See Welbome, n. 42 at 71. There is also some indication that the quota – particularly at the local level – was a response to international pressure. See ibid. 72.

[78] See Abeer Bashier Dababneh, "Jordanian Women's Political Participation: Legislative Status and Structural Challenges." *European Journal of Social Sciences* 27: 213, 216–17 (2012).

[79] Ibid. 217.

[80] See Constitution of Jordan, Chapter 2, Art.6 (1), *ConstituteProject*. Available at www.constitu teproject.org/constitution/Jordan_2011.pdf.

[81] See Law No. 6 of 2016, Law on the Election of the House of Representatives, Art. 8 (B). Available at https://iec.jo/sites/default/files/2ParliamentaryElectionLawMay2016EN.docx%20% 281%29_0.pdf.

[82] Both Egypt and Tunisia use closed party list PR – Egypt also has plurality single member districts, but its PR seats are assigned through a closed list system. Because the lists in Jordan are open, a simple candidate quota would be less effective there. A candidate quota in a closed list system can require the party to place the women in particular positions on the list (such as the rule requiring alternation of men and women in Tunisia.) This sort of rule can make it much more likely that women end up in winnable positions on the lists. But if voters can reorder the list, by choosing to move particular candidates up, then women may end up in unwinnable positions even if the party started by placing them higher. Indeed, there is evidence that open list systems undermine the effectiveness of candidate gender quotas in PR elections. See "Introduction: Conceptualizing the Impact of Gender Quotas," in *The Impact of Gender Quotas*, n. 2 at 7. Jordan's system guarantees a certain number of women will end up in the parliament, but it does so at the cost of treating them as separate from other candidates and undermining the incentives of parties to recruit and support them. See "The Implementation of Quotas: African Experiences," IDEA paper (2004) at 78 (reserved seats take the pressure off political parties to include women as candidates or address the barriers they face.)

toward the maximum number of candidates on the list (i.e. a party can add a woman without losing a slot for a man.) Parties are required to run one woman on each list. A few parties do, of course, run more women as their regular candidates, but women rarely win through the normal open list system. Jordan uses a "best loser" approach to fill the reserved seats: The woman who receives the largest percentage of votes in her district, without actually getting enough votes to win in the open list system, will win the one reserved seat in each governorate.[83] There are also quotas for certain minority groups in Jordan: Christians and Circassians. The women who win outside the gender quota sometimes win as candidates for these other sorts of quota seats.

In the 2016 election, twenty women won seats (five of them outside the gender quota) so that women currently make up 15.4 percent of the House. The new Political Parties law was also revised to require a party to demonstrate that 10 percent of its members are women in order to be licensed.[84] There has been more substantial progress at the local level. In the 2013 local elections, women won 345 of 961 seats (36 percent): fifty-one women won seats through the regular process, in addition to the 25 percent quota.[85] In the most recent local elections in 2017, women won 16 percent of all non-reserved seats on local councils. When the reserved seats are added, women make up a total of 32 percent of the elected members of local councils. In municipal councils (which are a different set of bodies), women won a little over 20 percent of the nonquota seats; when quota seats are added, women will make up roughly 42 percent of the total elected members. At the governorate council level, only 4 women won out of 299 seats (1.3 percent); the thirty-two quota seats will bring the percentage to approximately 11 percent. There will be appointed seats at each level as well and half of those will go to women.[86] There are currently two women in Jordan's cabinet of ministers, out of twenty-eight;[87] the previous high point was five women ministers in 2015.[88]

[83] Each governorate includes several electoral districts. The districts are not equipopulational, so the winner of the quota seat is determined by percentage of votes received rather than number of votes received. There are twelve governorates. The other three quota seats are assigned to the Badia zones that cover the Bedouin territories.

[84] See Embassy of the Hashemite Kingdom of Jordan. Available at http://jordanembassyus.org/politics/women-political-life.

[85] See "Jordanian Women Make Strides in Municipal Elections," *International Republican Institute*, available. Available at www.iri.org/web-story/jordanian-women-make-strides-municipal-elections.

[86] See RASED Analysis on the Representation of Women in Municipal and Governorate Council Elections in 2017. Available at www.hayatcenter.org/uploads/2017/09/20170907131130en.pdf. There has only ever been one woman elected local executive (mayor) in Jordan. See al-Attiyah, n. 72 at 36.

[87] "New Jordanian Government Has Fresh Faces but Same Old Problems," *The National*. June 14, 2018. Available at www.thenational.ae/world/mena/new-jordanian-cabinet-has-fresh-faces-but-same-old-problems-1.740222.

[88] See "New Cabinet Includes Record Five Women Ministers," *Jordan Times*. March 2, 2015. Available at www.jordantimes.com/news/local/new-cabinet-includes-record-five-women-ministers.

There is substantial dissatisfaction with the quota for women in Jordan, but it is difficult to disentangle it from the more general dissatisfaction with the legislature. One concern focuses on the operation of the quota and the particular women who receive seats through it. It has become plain that the quota disadvantages women from urban areas, who are more likely to be feminists and/or have experience in activism on women's issues.[89] The disadvantage arises because a woman in a small electoral district may only need a very small number of votes to get a high percentage of the total, whereas a woman in a large district will need many more votes to achieve a similar percentage. As a result, the women chosen for the quota seats come disproportionally from smaller, more rural districts.[90] There is also a concern that the tribes and Islamist parties are using the quota to increase their seats. Women with support from these groups are more likely to win, but such women are not likely to support feminist reforms.[91]

A second complaint argues that the quota has not been effective because women in the legislature do not enjoy real power.[92] Since the quota has not disrupted the basic power structures, which favor clan-based voting and clientelism, there is little scope for the women legislators to have an impact.[93] As a result, many women's activists see women MPs as "tokens who neglect to promote the aspirations of women through relevant legislation and are preoccupied with securing rents for their constituencies."[94] There is some data to support this generalization: From 2013–15, women MPs in Jordan raised questions on the floor of the legislature on some traditional areas of women's concern, such as health and education, but raised no questions on gender in particular.[95] And it would not be surprising if the women MPs adopted this approach: They have good reason to believe that raising gender equality issues would risk alienating their male colleagues and constituents[96] and that the primary concern of voters is the delivery of services rather than the promotion of policies.[97]

---

[89] See Warrick, n. 72 at 131.

[90] See al-Attiyat, n. 72 at 21.

[91] See Warrick, n. 72 at 131.

[92] See Dina Kiwan, May Farah, Rawan Annan, and Heather Jaber, "Women's Participation and Leadership in Lebanon, Jordan, and Kurdistan Region of Iraq: Moving from Individual to Collective Change," Oxfam Research paper (April 2016). Available at https://policy-practice.oxfam.org.uk/publications/womens-participation-and-leadership-in-lebanon-jordan-and-kurdistan-region-of-i-604070.

[93] See Welborne, n. 42 at 74; Warrick n. 72.

[94] See Welborne, n. 42 at 74.

[95] See Shalaby, n. 28.

[96] See Welborne, n. 42 at 74.

[97] See Alaa Zuhair Rwashdeh, "Jordanian Voters' Criteria of Selection of Members of the Lower House of Representatives in 2013 Elections." *Journal of Sociolegal Research* 4: 295, 317–18 (2013) (almost unanimity across groups based on gender, age, location, and education that the most important factor for voters is whether candidate satisfies people's demands for public services.)

The response to these criticisms has gone in two different directions. Some people in Jordan argue that the quota would work better if the number of women was increased.[98] Others think the focus should be on methods of increasing women's representation other than the quota, such as educational and media programs to address gender stereotypes in the culture more generally.[99] Relatively few people want to abandon the quota, but they are frustrated with its results. Thus, the story of Jordan is a story of consistent but incremental change against a backdrop of democratic institutions with limited efficacy.

All three of these stories support the idea that constitutional change may often represent preservation of underlying constitutional assumptions rather than transformation of them. Each country shows continuity in the approach to women's political representation rather than dramatic change. Nonetheless, starting from situations that were similar in many ways, the three countries have ended up in very different places. The next section will explore some of the differences between the countries that might account for the difference in outcomes.

7.2 THE IMPLEMENTATION OF QUOTAS

In order to understand what is happening across these three case studies, it is useful to follow Krook by distinguishing three sets of factors that affect the implementation and impact of quotas: (1) factors related to the quota's fit within the formal rules of the electoral system; (2) factors related to the impact on the quota of informal rules and practices within the political system; and (3) the interaction of the quota with the norms of the political system.[100] Within each of these categories, several specific issues are highlighted by the three case studies.

7.2.1 *The Formal System*

A quota will only be effective if it fits the electoral system within which it operates.[101] The primary focus in the analysis of this set of factors is on descriptive

---

[98] Ibtissam al Attiyat, Musa Shteiwi, and Suleiman Sweiss, "Building Democracy in Jordan: Women's Political Participation, Political Party Life, and Democratic Elections," at 51–52, IDEA Paper (describing the Jordanian Women's Document, which called for a 30 percent quota and list PR).

[99] Dina Kiwan, n. 92 at 27 (quoting a woman's activist as saying "What good is a quota system when gender-biased attitudes continue to prevail?"); al Attiyat, n. 72 at 6–7 (advocating educational and media reform to help with women's representation).

[100] This framework is borrowed from Mona Lena Krook's important work on quotas. See Mona Lena Krook, *Quotas for Women in Politics: Gender and Candidate Selection Reform Worldwide*. Oxford University Press, 2009 (particularly, chapter 3).

[101] See Stina Laserud and Rita Taphorn, "Designing for Equality: Best- Fit, Medium-Fit and Unfavorable Combinations of Electoral Systems and Gender Quotas," *IDEA*. Available at www.idea.int/publications/catalogue/designing-equality-best-fit-medium-fit-and-non-favourable-combinations.

representation: Does the quota result in a substantial number of women in the parliament and do those women represent the diversity of women within the country? Looking across our three case studies, the relative success of the different quotas can be seen to be related to their fit (or lack thereof) with the formal rules of the electoral system.

In Egypt, for example, the underlying electoral system is a combination of seats assigned through closed party list PR and seats in FPP single member districts. The number of PR seats is only a little more than 1/3 of the number of FPP seats and the quota applied only to the PR seats. So, the first problem with the quota is that it is simply too low: It doesn't reach the vast majority of the seats in the legislature and therefore cannot generate a significant level of representation for women.[102] The second problem is that the quota does not work effectively even for the seats to which it applies. Despite requiring almost 50 percent women's names on the lists, the quota resulted in less than 15 percent women elected to the PR seats. This outcome was caused by (1) the lack of an ordering rule requiring parties to put women in winnable positions on their lists and (2) the small party magnitude of most parties, which led to few parties receiving enough seats to reach the women on their lists. This latter factor also affects the diversity of the women chosen. When combined with the fact that almost 20 percent of the women MPs were appointed by the President, it suggests that the women are unlikely to represent a broad cross-section of the female population: They are likely to be disproportionately drawn from the groups that support the al-Sisi regime.

Similarly, in Jordan, the quota has not been effective in getting a significant and diverse body of women into the legislature. In this case, part of the problem is the electoral system; because it is an open list PR system, no simple candidate quota would be likely to work.[103] The reserved seat system chosen has real drawbacks,

---

[102] The traditional consensus in the literature has been that at least one-third of the seats must be held by women in order to achieve a critical mass that will allow for policy effectiveness. For some critical views on critical mass theory, see Sandra Grey, "Numbers and Beyond: The Relevance of Critical Mass in Gender Research." *Politics & Gender* 2: 492 (2006). In addition, as discussed in Section 7.3, where women make up more than 50 percent of the population, there is a powerful justice argument that roughly half of the legislature should be female. Thus, a quota that is designed in such a way as to guarantee that it cannot generate even 30 percent women legislators does not achieve "significant" representation for women.

[103] There have been calls to move to a closed list PR system in Jordan. This would be the obvious way to try to increase the power and coherence of political parties, which is a central tenet of the King's plan to move toward greater democracy. See Abdullah II ibn al Hussein, "Second Discussion Paper: Making Our Democratic System Work for all Jordanians" (January 16, 2013). ("The key driver of the timeline for this transition [to a PM chosen by the Parliament] is our success in developing national political parties . . ."). But there is a general concern that closed list PR would favor the Muslim Brotherhood-affiliated parties, which are the only ones with strong party machinery and constituent party loyalty. The current system allows people to vote for the specific candidates they choose, who are often clan leaders, running on ad hoc lists that do not represent a party at all. See al- Attiyat, n. 72 at 17 (most members of parliament are independent, elected on the basis of tribe, not political party.)

however. First, it is politically difficult to have a large enough number of reserved seats to create real gender balance. While 50 percent candidate list quotas have become more common globally, the average percentage of reserved seats is 20.9.[104] And Jordan is below this average, having set the number of reserved seats at only 11.5 percent. Second, reserved seats undermine the credibility of women MPs: They do not compete with male politicians for these seats and generally do not have the same types of constituencies and are, therefore, often seen as second-class legislators.[105] Finally, the "best loser" system chosen for filling the quota seats has led to a bias against women running from urban districts, leading to an unrepresentative body of women legislators. Again, the appointment of women to the Senate by the King compounds this problem of lack of diversity, in the same way as the appointment by the President in Egypt.

In Tunisia, on the other hand, the quota fits relatively well within the electoral system and all of the necessary formal rules have been put in place to make it reasonably effective. The system is closed party list PR; the quota is high (50 percent); there are ordering rules requiring alternation of names on the lists; and there is an effective enforcement mechanism (rejection of nonconforming lists.) Indeed, the only problem with the quota in terms of the formal system is that the small district size leads to a lower yield than the quota number (30 percent rather than 50 percent) because women do not head a sufficient number of the lists. The small number of parties receiving more than one seat in a district (and therefore reaching the first woman on their lists) also affects the diversity of women representatives.

The recent proposals for horizontal parity (requiring each party to have a women head half of its district lists) are intended to deal with this problem. This approach will probably be only partly effective: Parties are likely to put women at the top of lists in districts where they expect to get no seats or many seats and to leave men at the top of lists in districts where they expect to get only one seat. The most effective way to correct the problem would be to increase district size so that a significant number of parties receive at least two seats in most districts. But that approach would, of course, have other drawbacks: Creating larger districts reduces local representation. This issue is a good illustration of the way in which quota design is often compromised in order to accommodate other goals for the electoral system.

This comparison confirms a number of the current ideas in the quota literature.[106] First, closed list PR makes quotas more effective. Second, placement/

---

[104] See IDEA Quota Project. Available at www.idea.int/data-tools/data/gender-quotas/reserved-overview.

[105] See Irene Tinker, "Many Paths to Power: Women in Contemporary Asia," in *Promises of Empowerment: Women in Asia and Latin America*, ed. Peter H. Smith, Jennifer L. Troutner, and Christene Huefeldt. Rowland & Littlefield, 2004, 35–59.

[106] See *The Impact of Gender Quotas*, n. 2 at 6 ("Quotas have the greatest impact in countries with proportional representation (PR) electoral systems, particularly when combined with closed party lists and high district magnitudes.")

ordering rules and enforcement are crucial to quota effectiveness. Third, small district and party magnitude can undermine the overall effectiveness of the quota – leading to a significantly smaller percentage of women MPs than the percentage of women required on the lists – and can also reduce the diversity of women elected by concentrating them in a small number of parties. And fourth, women who are appointed by a President or King, rather than elected, are also likely to reduce the descriptive representation of a diverse cross-section of the female population. None of these conclusions are surprising: The experience of these countries simply adds to the body of evidence supporting the conventional wisdom on formal quota design.[107]

7.2.2 *Informal Practices, Social and Political*

In addition to the formal rules of the electoral system, there are a number of informal practices – social and political – that can affect the implementation of quotas. These three case studies highlight the significance of four specific factors within this category: (1) the nature of the political party system, (2) the nature and strength of women's movements, (3) the overall status of women in the society, and (4) the impact of "top-down" forms of support for quotas.

The Political Party System

Weak party systems undermine the effectiveness of quotas in a number of ways. First, in a political context with fragmented and disorganized parties, it is less likely (and sometimes less advisable) to adopt a closed party list PR system, thereby foreclosing the best option from the point of view of the quota. Second, decentralized and disorganized parties make it harder to enforce the quota rules on the party leadership. Third, as discussed previously, a very large number of parties tends to dilute party magnitude, leading to a lack of women representatives from many of the parties. In short, a more stable and more centralized party system tends to improve the effectiveness of quotas.[108]

The significance of this factor is borne out by our case studies, but with an interesting twist. All of the countries discussed here had fragmented and disorganized party systems during the period of the Arab spring because all were still coming out of extended periods during which real party competition was prohibited. The only exceptions to the general state of disorganization, in all three countries, were Islamist parties that had developed substantial on-the-ground networks that could be

---

[107] See Georgina Waylen, *Engendering Transitions: Women's Mobilization. Institutions, and Gender Outcomes.* Oxford University Press, 2007, 111 (in general, the received wisdom about PR, high district magnitude, high party magnitude, and closed lists is right, but some other factors matter too.)

[108] See Joni Lovenduski, "The Dynamics of Gender and Party," in *Women, Gender and Politics: A Reader*, ed. Mona Lena Krook and Sarah Childs. Oxford University Press, 2010, 81 at 85.

mobilized for political purposes. In Egypt and Tunisia, the disorganization and fragmentation of the majority of political parties is illustrated by the enormous number of parties running in the first post-transition elections and by the disproportionate success of the Islamist parties. In Jordan, the disorganization and fragmentation is illustrated by the proliferation of electoral lists that are ad hoc collections of names and do not represent a party at all: They are simply the vehicles for clan or local leaders.[109] The fragmented party system contributed to the ineffectiveness of the quotas in Egypt through diluting party magnitude. In Jordan, the party system has hurt the effectiveness of the quota by: (1) reducing the willingness to adopt closed list PR; (2) leading to the election of women with support from tribes or Islamist parties, who are more easily able to compete effectively but less likely to support woman-friendly policies because of their parties' positions;[110] (3) reducing the power of those women in parliament who are trying to raise a feminist agenda because they are struggling against a patronage based system;[111] and, perhaps most significantly, (4) undermining the public sense of quota effectiveness because of the belief that the legislature in general is dysfunctional.

The interesting twist that arises from our case studies is that this disorganized party structure did not succeed in derailing the quota in Tunisia. By diluting party magnitude, the disorganization did reduce the quota's initial effectiveness, as discussed previously, leading to a preponderance of women from one party in the NCA. But the high level of consensus on the need for a 50 percent quota and the ability of the parties to work together cooperatively – despite histories of animosity and continuing violence – seems to have allowed Tunisia to get through that period without long-term damage to the effectiveness of the quota. Thus, Tunisia suggests that even a disorganized party system may not substantially impair quota effectiveness if there is a consensus on the importance of the quota to women's representation and a willingness to work cooperatively across party lines to keep the system functioning.

Women's Movements

The second aspect of informal practices that affects quota implementation is the strength and coherence of the women's political movement. There is evidence to suggest that the adoption of quotas is made much more likely by the existence of a

---

[109] The Independent Electoral Commission is trying to combat this phenomenon with requirements for a party platform and for party membership across a substantial geographical area. So far, these mechanisms have not succeeding in transforming the party structure in Jordan.

[110] See al Attiyat, n. 72 at 40–41 (tribal support and religious support are two of the most important factors determining success for female candidates.)

[111] Georgina Waylen, *Engendering Transitions: Women's Mobilization, Institutions, and Gender Outcomes.* (Oxford University Press, 2007, 114 ("party cultures that include informal structures of power, clientelism, and factionalism ... have a negative impact on levels of women's representation.")

vibrant and coordinated women's movement.[112] Similarly, the effective implementation of quotas also requires the support of such a movement. In order to contribute
to the effectiveness of quotas, women's organizations need to be independent (i.e. of
the government), have strong connections to and working relationships with political parties, and be capable of united action in support of policy goals.

While women's organizations exist and are working hard in all of the three
countries discussed here, those in Egypt and Jordan are weakened by several
important factors. First, in both countries, the civil society organizations are often
dominated by the official quasi-governmental organization focused on women's
rights: the National Council for Women (NCW) in Egypt and the National
Jordanian Commission on Women (NJCW) in Jordan. In Egypt, the independence
of the other organizations in the women's movement has been seriously threatened
by the growing authoritarianism.[113] And in Jordan, there is a history of division
among women's civil society organizations and a reliance on the NJCW to lead.[114]
In the past, the official government organization in Tunisia was also extremely
powerful, but there was an explosion of women's organizations after the fall of the
Ben Ali regime that has given rise to strong civil society leadership for the women's
movement there since the transition.[115]

Second, the ability of such a diverse and independent movement to act in united
ways in support of policy initiatives is also crucial. This ability has often been absent
in both Jordan and Egypt, where there are histories of personality conflicts.[116] But
the ability of women's groups to mobilize for unified action has been demonstrated
repeatedly in Tunisia – most notably in the response to the "complementarity"
proposals for the Constitution.

And third, a connection to political parties also helps with implementation of
quotas. In Jordan, the weakness of the party system undermines the ability of
women's groups to create regular avenues of cooperation with political parties.
The distrust between women activists and women MPs that grows out of this weak

---

[112] See *The Impact of Quotas*, n. 2 at 5–6.·

[113] See, e.g., Mozn Hassan, "What Has Azza Done? Azza Solimon, a Unique Feminist at Risk,"
Open Democracy. Available at www.opendemocracy.net/north-africa-west-asia/mozn-hassan/
what-has-azza-done-azza-soliman-unique-feminist-at-risk (describing the harassment of a major
feminist figure in 2016 and asserting that "the feminist movement as a whole is facing a severe
clampdown").

[114] See Welborne, n. 42 at 79–80 (describing the central differences between Jordan and Morocco
that have led to a significantly higher level of women's political participation in Morocco,
including the absence of a state-sponsored umbrella organization and unity and collaboration
across diverse women's groups).

[115] See Shalaby, n. 28 at 174.

[116] See Mariz Tadros, The Politics of Mobilising for Gender Justice in Egypt from Mubarak to
Morsi and Beyond, IDS Working paper 442 (April 2014) at 12–13 (divisions among feminist
activists over politics, personality, and religion); Assaf David, "Presence Out, Ideas In: Representation and Socio-Political Change in Jordan," 48 Rep. 295, 298 (2012) (describing mass
resignations from the Union of Women's Committees over personal conflicts.)

system also reduces the ability of women's groups to work effectively within the party structure. In Tunisia, despite some initial uncertainty among women activists about working within political parties, there has been a strong push by women in the movement to participate in parties.[117] In all three countries, women's organizations have recognized the importance of training and encouraging women to run for political office, which is one of the central roles that the women's movement can play in increasing the effectiveness of quotas. But the relative weakness and disunity of independent organizations and their distance from political parties reduces their effectiveness in Jordan and Egypt.

Women's Status

Women's general status in society, particularly in terms of education and economic power, has been identified as a factor in the adoption of quotas.[118] For example, low workforce participation is a cause of political disempowerment.[119] The case studies here suggest that this factor might also affect the implementation of quotas by contributing to a shift in cultural attitudes toward women's leadership.[120] Indeed, the comparison between Tunisia and Jordan suggests some interesting possibilities about the importance of specific aspects of women's status. Both countries enjoy strikingly high rates of women's education, particularly at the tertiary level: Women are more likely to hold college degrees than men in both Tunisia and Jordan.[121] But women's history of employment in Tunisia is dramatically different from in Jordan: Not only are many more women employed in general in Tunisia, but they have become a substantial percentage of the profession from which many politicians are drawn (i.e. lawyers). The comparison between Tunisia and Jordan suggests that higher female employment – at least in certain sectors and over a substantial period of time – might contribute to the successful implementation of the quota, both by providing a ready pool of female political candidates and by increasing the public perception that there are qualified women to hold these positions. This hypothesis

---

[117] See "Tunisia's Female Politicians Prepare to Seize Their Chance in Local Polls," *The Guardian.* May 19, 2015. Available at www.theguardian.com/global-development/2015/may/19/tunisia-female-politicians-woman-local-polls.

[118] See *The Impact of Gender Quotas*, n. 2 at 7.

[119] See Pippa Norris and Ronald Inglehart, "Cultural Obstacles to Equal Representation." *Journal of Democracy* 12 (3): 126 (2001).

[120] See Lindsay J. Benstead, "Explaining Egalitarian Attitudes: The Role of Interests and Exposure," in *Empowering Women after the Arab Spring*, ed. Marwa Shalaby and Valentine M. Mogadam. Palgrave, 2016, 119, at 120 (arguing that attitude change occurs through a shift in interests and exposure, both of which are facilitated by women's employment).

[121] See "Gender Gap Report: Jordan" (more women than men in secondary and tertiary education). Available at http://reports.weforum.org/global-gender-gap-report-2016/economies/?doing_wp_cron=1519504439.5087931156158447265625#economy=JOR; "Gender Gap Report: Tunisia" (same). Available at http://reports.weforum.org/global-gender-gap-report-2016/economies/?doing_wp_cron=1519504439.5087931156158447265625#economy=TUN.

would require more investigation, of course, but it might be helpful in thinking about priorities for policy reforms related to women's employment.

"Top-Down" Quota Policies

Another factor in the informal political practices that has been studied in relation to quotas is the "top-down" imposition of quota policies. A contrast is drawn in the literature between improvements in women's political representation that result from policy change controlled by the government as opposed to those policy changes that arise from grass-roots pressures. The argument in the quota adoption literature is that the quota will do a better job of getting both descriptive and substantive representation for women if it is the result of grass-roots efforts.[122] The question raised here is whether the different vectors of change affect the implementation of the quota.

In all three of the countries discussed here, the initial improvements in women's representation came from a top-down process. In Tunisia and Egypt, these processes took place under authoritarian governments; in Jordan, they occurred under a government moving toward more meaningful democratization. It is still the case in Jordan and Egypt that the government dominates the process of political change, including on the issue of women's political participation. In Tunisia, the historical dominance of the government in the field of women's representation has shifted and the primary impetus now comes from civil society.[123] The shift in leadership from government to civil society contributes to the independence of the women's movement, as discussed in the second factor in this section, and thereby supports effective implementation of quotas. But the historical parallel between all three countries suggests an additional perspective on "top-down" efforts.

It seems plain that the earlier government-led reforms in Tunisia contributed to the different status of women in the country, in terms of education and employment. And, as argued previously, those differences then supported the development of different attitudes toward women that have facilitated both the adoption and the implementation of the gender quotas in the post-transition period.[124] Thus, the case of Tunisia suggests that top-down efforts can contribute to effective representation

---

[122] See e.g. Kristine Goulding, "Unjustifiable Means to Unjustifiable Ends: Delegitimating the Parliamentary Quotas in Tunisia." *al raida* 126–27: 71, 72 (2009) (arguing that quotas are useless under an authoritarian structure because they result only in token women "who do not, and cannot, challenge patriarchal norms.")

[123] There is a Ministry of Women, Family, and Children that provides planning and encouragement, but the functioning multi-party democracy in Tunisia means that it no longer dominates the policy field in the way that it did under Ben Ali. The dominance of the Crown in Jordan and the President in Egypt means that the government remains the leader in policymaking in those countries.

[124] See Samar El-Tasri, "Tunisian Women at a Crossroads: Cooptation or Autonomy?" *Journal of the Middle East Policy Council* XXII (2): Summer 2017. Available at www.mepc.org/tunisian-women-crossroads-cooptation-or-autonomy.

for women, at least where (1) they result in a real change in women's status, particularly with respect to employment, and, (2) after that change has been achieved, they end and allow the leadership on gender equality efforts to shift to grass-roots women's organizations. These two requirements distinguish Tunisia from Egypt and Jordan, so the comparison of these three cases might suggest that "top-down" reforms can be effective under these conditions.[125]

7.2.3 *Norms Relating to Gender Equality*

Finally, it is important to consider the normative frameworks and assumptions that inform people's reactions to quotas, and to the issue of women's representation more generally. The three countries discussed here have very different normative political landscapes. In Egypt, there is strong public approval for the military as an institution, which has facilitated the exercise of political power by the army. And, as noted earlier, Egypt tends to be quite conservative in terms of gender roles. Placing value on military control and on traditional gender roles reduces the importance ascribed to women's political representation. In Tunisia, there has been broader public acceptance of women's ability to wield public power and of their equality more generally. There is also a very strong commitment across a wide range of the political spectrum to multi-party democracy and democratic accountability for the government. These values obviously make it easier to see why representation for half of the population is a pressing issue.

Perhaps the most interesting case is that of Jordan. Jordanian society has, in many ways, embraced women's equality, despite the silence of the Constitution on the subject. At the same time, Jordanians retain conservative attitudes on gender roles in many contexts. But, with respect to quotas, there are two cultural frameworks that probably best explain the approach to implementation. First, there is the general inclination to incrementalism in Jordanian political culture. One of the first things I was taught by our partners in Jordan when we began work there[126] was the

---

[125] But the two conditions do not distinguish Tunisia from countries in Eastern Europe in which women's political representation plummeted after the post-Soviet transitions. Based on the experience of those countries, the literature on quotas has often suggested that "state feminism" is either useless or counterproductive. See Goulding, n. 122 at 72. The case of Tunisia therefore poses an interesting puzzle: Why was there no effective backlash against women's representation in Tunisia as there was in Eastern Europe? What else (besides the conditions mentioned earlier) distinguishes this case where state feminism seems to have had a long-term effect on women's representation from those cases where it has not? This question is beyond the scope of this chapter, but it makes plain the need for comparison beyond any single region in thinking about the conditions necessary for effective quota implementation.

[126] The CCD has been working in Jordan since May of 2017. We have worked on research with the Independent Electoral Commission, presented workshops and seminars for the Constitutional Court, and we are helping the Women's Center at the University of Jordan to develop what they hope will be the first PhD program in women's studies in the Arab world. We have met with Ministers and former Ministers, Members of Parliament, and members of the royal

expression, "Schweh, schweh": little by little, or step by step. Any suggestion for reform in Jordan is likely to be met by this response. The progress on gender quotas has certainly exemplified this approach.[127] Second, there is the general distrust of politicians and political parties mentioned earlier. This distrust is profound among the young, but it is widespread throughout all aspects of Jordanian society. It is difficult to generate enthusiasm and political will for the reform of the quotas when there is a sense that the legislature in which they operate is simply not worth the trouble.

Thus, one of the conclusions I would draw from the comparison of these three countries is that we cannot understand the implementation of quotas without taking account of the general functioning of and respect for the legislature in which the quotas would operate. A dysfunctional and/or disrespected institution will undermine the effectiveness of the quota. The analysis in the previous section suggests that this effect will operate both through informal political practices with which the quota must interact and through normative frameworks and commitments of relevant players. Weakness of the legislature at the level of informal practices will reduce the impact of quota policies on both descriptive and substantive representation. Distrust of and disrespect for the legislature will discourage investment by those who must expend political capital to make the quota work. In short, the efficacy of a quota cannot be assessed independently of the legislature in which it operates.

7.3 THE RELEVANCE OF THEORY: EFFECTIVE TO WHAT END?

The discussion up to this point has proceeded on the assumption that we have a consensus about the goals served by quotas that would allow us to assess efficacy in a coherent way. The literature on quotas has, however, identified a number of different approaches to conceptualizing the goal of a quota. The initial movement for quotas focused on descriptive representation: making sure that the legislature reflected the gender diversity of the population (and perhaps other sorts of diversity that cut across gender categories as well: racial, economic, geographical, etc.) Descriptive representation has, however, rarely been seen as an end in itself; rather, it is a means to certain ends. For example, women need to be present in the legislature in order to have their interests fully represented in the policymaking process. Or women need to be present in order to share their distinctive perspectives and information so that better policy can be made. Both of these latter arguments are about the role the quota can play in perfecting democracy by achieving

family. We have talked to activists of many kinds, traditional tribal leaders, and leaders of political parties. We are, of course, still learning about the country, but we have been privileged to have the chance to learn from a diverse group of people, who have shared their views of their country's current challenges and their hopes for its future.

[127] See Khaled A. Beydoun, "Fast-Tracking Women into Parliamentary Seats in the Arab World." *Southwestern Journal of International Law* 17: 63, 102 (2011).

substantive representation. They simply understand democracy in different ways: in terms of interest group politics or in terms of deliberation toward a public good.[128]

A different set of arguments suggests that the real goal of quotas is not limited to politics at all. This set of arguments sees electoral gender quotas as part of the larger project of dismantling patriarchy. On this understanding, women need to be present in government in order to break down the gendered public/private division that perpetuates the oppression of women across many areas of life.[129] Sometimes this argument takes a relatively tame form: Women in politics will be role models, changing girls' expectations for themselves and expanding the culture to include visions of leadership with a female face.[130] Sometimes the argument takes a more radical form: Exclusion from political/public power is seen as a linchpin and pulling it out will contribute to a radical change in gender relations: gender disestablishment.[131] In both cases, the goal is actually gender equality rather than democracy.

I think there is also a third form of argument for gender quotas that rests neither on democracy nor on gender equality specifically, but on a conception of justice. As I have written elsewhere, I believe that Nancy Fraser's model of justice as parity of participation in (1) material resources, (2) cultural recognition, and (3) representation has great potential as a heuristic for many tasks in constitutional design.[132] This argument is distinct from both of the other two. It starts not from democracy but from justice and sees inequality in participation as a central issue of injustice across many forms of difference, including but not limited to gender. This form of argument can explain many of the evolutions in quota laws over recent years: the move toward a more permanent vision of quotas (the need for justice never goes away); the need for full representation for women, not just a critical mass (because this is not primarily about deliberation or interest representation, but about participation); the development of symmetrical quotas (because men have the same justice claims); and the expansion of quotas into other arenas beyond legislatures (because justice is relevant to social life beyond politics.).[133]

I am not suggesting that either scholars or activists need to choose between these different forms of justification for quotas: Ideally, a quota will contribute to all of these goals. Rather, the point is to highlight the ways in which the specific failures

---

[128] For descriptions of the justifications for gender quotas, see Anne Phillips, *The Politics of Presence: The Political Representation of Gender, Ethnicity and Race*. Oxford University Press, 1995, 57–83; Susan H. Williams, "Equality, Representation and Challenge to Hierarchy: Justifying Electoral Quotas for Women," in *Constituting Equality: Gender Equality and Comparative Constitutional Law*, ed. Susan H. Williams. Cambridge University Press, 2009.

[129] See Ruth Rubio Marin and Will Kymlicka, "Introduction: Toward a New Synthesis," in *Gender Parity and Multicultural Feminism*. Oxford University Press, 2019.

[130] See Phillips, n. 128 at 57–83.

[131] See Ruth Rubio Marin, "The (Dis)Establishment of Gender: Care and Gender Roles in the Family as a Constitutional Matter." *International Journal of Constitutional Law* 13: 787 (2015).

[132] See Susan H. Williams, n. 128.

[133] Ibid.

caused by the underlying dysfunction of the legislature interact with each of these different goals. As described in the analysis in this chapter, a dysfunctional legislature makes it more likely that the quota will fail to achieve either its democratic or its gender disestablishment goal. The democratic goals will be frustrated by the inability of women MPs to effectively raise and get results on policies that serve the interests or reflect the perspectives and values of women. In a legislature oriented around patronage and clan identity, rather than policy, it is more likely that they will experience this frustration. The gender equality goals will be frustrated because the women MPs will not be seen as role models but as parts of a corrupt and ineffective body. The general disrespect for the institution undermines the likelihood that their exercise of public power will help dismantle underlying gender hierarchies. Indeed, the only goal of quotas that is not seriously compromised by the dysfunction of and disrespect for the legislature is the goal of justice: It is unjust for women to lack this representation even if the representative body is deeply flawed.

Thus, an examination of the theory behind gender quotas highlights two points. First, as stated previously, the efficacy of the quota in terms of the goals of democracy and gender equality cannot be assessed independently of the functionality of the body to which it applies. And, second, even for legislatures in which these goals may be frustrated, gender quotas can still be justified by the need for representation as a requirement of justice.

PART III

Institutional Development and the Role of Courts

8

Explaining the Institutional Role of the Colombian Constitutional Court

Diego González[*]

8.1 INTRODUCTION

The Colombian Constitutional Court (hereinafter referred to as the CCC) is widely regarded by experts as one of the best-known and activist courts worldwide.[1] Although created just twenty-five years ago, it has gained a prominent place among the leading constitutional courts of the global south, such as the South African and the Indian Supreme Courts.[2] The CCC rulings have become very well-known, especially because of the types of constitutional rights subject to its jurisdiction, its interpretative methodologies in adjudicating constitutional cases, and the type of remedies usually adopted by the Court. Its work has been very popular and influential in the Spanish-language literature during recent decades and is now taking its own place within the relevant English-language literature.[3]

Let us consider some of the reasons for the court's wide recognition. First, the CCC case law is very rich in rulings regarding the protection of individual liberal rights such as freedom of expression,[4] freedom of religion,[5] the right to privacy,[6]

[*] I would like to express my gratitude to Prof. Tom Ginsburg, Justice Carlos Bernal, and Prof. Leopoldo Ferguson for their rigorous reading of the first drafts of this chapter. All my views shared here are personal rather than institutional. This chapter is the product of academic research and does not represent at all the institutional position of the Constitutional Court.
[1] David Landau, *Beyond Judicial Independence: The Construction of Judicial Power in Colombia.* Doctoral dissertation, Harvard University, Graduate School of Arts & Sciences, 2015.
[2] D. Bonilla Maldonado, ed. *Constitutionalism of the Global South: The Activist Tribunals of India, South Africa, and Colombia.* Cambridge: Cambridge University Press, 2013.
[3] Manuel Cépeda and David Landau, *Colombian Constitutional Law: Leading Cases.* Oxford University Press, 2017.
[4] Decision T-361 of 2009.
[5] Decisions T-327 of 2009 and T-462 of 2005.
[6] Decisions T-212 of 2000 and T-134 of 2005.

reproductive rights,[7] and LGBTI rights[8] but also in social and economic rights enforcement such as health,[9] education,[10] housing,[11] transportation,[12] and so on. The CCC is also very famous for creating or inserting into the domestic legal system some categories of rights such as the very right to human dignity, the right to drinking water, the right to try experimental therapies, the right to household electrical power, the collective rights of indigenous communities, and the rights of victims of the internal armed conflict to truth, justice, and reparations, especially for forcedly displaced people.

Second, CCC case law is also well regarded by experts in relation to its interpretative style. In fact, the CCC has been both open-minded and innovative in introducing or creating certain methodologies with which to adjudicate constitutional cases. Since its earliest work, the CCC has introduced both the European proportionality principle and the American strict scrutiny test to adjudicate cases based on fundamental rights and the equality principle.[13] Moreover, by blending both of these techniques, the CCC has defined its own methodology to interpret and adjudicate fundamental rights.[14] The CCC has also established particular methodologies to (1) introduce the international law of human rights and international humanitarian law into the domestic legal system, granting them constitutional status; (2) scrutinize executive orders enacted by the President at exercising extraordinary powers;[15] (3) adjudicate cases involving multicultural accommodations, resolving tensions between the values of indigenous communities, on the one side, and constitutional principles such as democracy, freedom, and economic liberties, on the other;[16] (4) review, and eventually to declare unconstitutional, constitutional amendments that had been enacted with proper procedures;[17] and (5) examine the regulation of transitional justice,[18] among others.

Third, CCC rulings have more recently been studied by experts because of the types of remedies they have ordered. It has mainly implemented three types of remedies, particularly in the so-called *tutela* jurisdiction: simple, complex, or structural. Simple remedies are the regular orders through which the Court mandates the defendant to act or stop acting to cease the violation of plaintiff's fundamental rights.[19] Complex remedies are ordered by the Court when it identifies that

---

[7]   Decisions C-355 of 2006 and C-182 of 2016.
[8]   Decisions C-075 of 2007 and SU214 of 2016.
[9]   Decision T-760 of 2008.
[10] Decisions T-779 of 2011, T-690 of 2012, T-810 of 2013, T-890 of 2013, and T-247 of 2014.
[11] Decisions T-495 of 1995 and T-754 of 2006.
[12] Decision T-595 of 2002.
[13] Decision C-422 of 2005.
[14] Decision C-880 of 2014.
[15] Decisions C-004 of 1992 and C-295 of 1996.
[16] Decision T-002 of 2012.
[17] Decision C-551 of 2003.
[18] Decisions C-370 of 2006, C-577 of 2014, and C-699 of 2016.
[19] Decision T-420 of 1994.

the very same violation brought by the plaintiff to the Court is affecting a broad number of people who have not brought any *tutela* to the Court, though they are seriously affected. In this case, the Court covers the affected community with the same *tutela* remedy adopted in the case brought to the Court.[20] Finally, structural remedies have rarely been ordered by the Court, only being put in place when it is proved that a generalized and a systematic violation of rights is occurring due to the inexistence or the dysfunctionality of public policies.[21] Structural remedies have been implemented by the Court only in cases related to the prison system, the humanitarian crisis of forced displacement, and the health system, which have been declared as "unconstitutional state of affairs."

Most of the studies approach those subjects mainly from a normative point of view,[22] though some others have explored the CCC rulings from sociolegal[23] and economic[24] perspectives. These studies are predominantly descriptive and draw different conclusions, from suggesting that the Colombian court is an archetype for modeling constitutional courts to regretting the so-called judicial activism of the Court.[25] In any event, for better or worse, the CCC has become the focus of significant scholarly and professional attention all over the world.

Despite this, literature on why this Court became such a central player within the Colombian political system remains very sparse. In fact, the CCC is an active Court of Law, which attempts to address a range of issues from pressing realities related to social justice to complex political decisions such as the ones concerning the peace process and political transitions. Though the impact of its interventions is indeterminate, the CCC is commonly regarded by political actors as "the last word" in both legal and political decisions. Most of the studies share the standard opinion, which suggests that the centrality of the CCC is a consequence of having dysfunctional legislative bodies and weak administrative agencies.[26] According to this view, the CCC gained its predominant role by trying to fill some of the black holes left by the

---

[20] Decisions T-698 of 2010 and SU-011 of 2018.

[21] Decisions T-025 of 2004, T-760 of 2008, A092 of 2008, and T-762 of 2015.

[22] Carlos Bernal Pulido, *The Constitutional Protection of Economic and Social Rights in Latin America: Comparative Constitutional Law in Latin America*, ed. R. Dixon and T. Ginsburg. Cheltenham; Northampton: Edward Elgar Publishing, 2017, 325–42 18; Carlos Bernal Pulido. *The Constitutional Adjudication of Positive Social Rights by Means of the Proportionality Analysis*, Rechtsphilosophie und Grundrechtstheorie, ed. M. Borowski, S. L. Paulson, and J. R. Sieckmann. 2017, 497–521.

[23] César Rodriguez Garavito. "Beyond the Courtroom: The Impact of Judicial Activism on Socioeconomic Rights in Latin America." *Texas Law Review* 89: 1669, 1670–71 (2011). David Evan Landau, *Beyond Judicial Independence: The Construction of Judicial Power in Colombia*. Doctoral dissertation, Harvard University, Graduate School of Arts & Sciences, 2015.

[24] Everaldo Lamprea, "Derechos Fundamentales y Consecuencias Económicas." *Revista de Economía Institucional* 8 (14) Primer Semestre, (2006).

[25] David Landau, "Can the Colombian Model Be Generalized?" Virtual Roundtable. IACL – AIDC.

[26] Rodrigo Uprimny Yepes, "Should Courts Enforce Social Rights? The Experience of the Colombian Constitutional Court," *Dejusticia*, 2017.

political branches, created by either the lack of political will or by dysfunctional public policies.

In my opinion this account is only partially true. Other sets of reasons can help explain why the CCC has developed as it has. In fact, there are at least three arguments that I will consider: historical, normative, and conceptual. The first relates to the history of constitutional supremacy and judicial review in Colombia; the second considers the normative design of the 1991 Constitution as the key factor; the third focuses on the CCC's conception of the Constitution and of its institutional role, as embodied in its case law on the protection of rights.

The aim of this chapter is to present each of these arguments, and by doing so to develop an integrated positive account of why Colombia has such a Constitutional Court, rather than celebrating or criticizing the institution on normative grounds.

8.2 THE HISTORY OF CONSTITUTIONAL SUPREMACY AND JUDICIAL REVIEW IN COLOMBIA

The 1991 Constitution created the Constitutional Court, which is considered to be one of the Constitution's most important innovations. However, the very ideas of constitutional supremacy and judicial review have a long history in the country, dating back to the nineteenth century. Even the Constitution of the *Province of Cundinamarca* (1811),[27] which was the very first provincial Constitution in the land, included a "Protection Senate." This was a judicial body whose mandate was precisely "to protect individuals before any violation or usurpation by any branch of the Government against the Constitution." That institution was replicated in other provincial constitutions such as those of *Tunja* (1811),[28] *Antioquia* (1812),[29] and *Cartagena* (1812).[30]

Following the innovations of these provincial constitutions, all the nineteenth-century Colombian National Constitutions had specific provisions that prescribed the constitutional review of both federal and state legislation. Some of these constitutions stipulated that the federal legislature had the power to declare unconstitutional the laws and the executive orders enacted by the institutions at the state level (1832).[31] Some others replicated this model and added the Supreme Court power to suspend regulations before the legislature decided on its constitutionality (1858).[32] Most strikingly, some others reproduced the very same model and granted the same power to the state legislatures regarding federal regulation (1863).[33] Rather

[27] First provincial Constitution enacted in Colombia. Chapter I. Art. 9.
[28] Section I. Art. 1. 17.
[29] Chapter I. Art. 9.
[30] Chapter I. Art. 9.
[31] Art. 162.
[32] Art. 50.
[33] Arts. 14, 25 and 72.

than the constitutional supremacy, the European principle of parliamentary supremacy was truly the conceptual base for this model.

The 1886 Constitution, which was in force until 1991, explicitly laid down the constitutional supremacy principle.[34] Officially, judicial review of the laws was introduced to the legal system through a constitutional amendment in 1910.[35] Under this constitutional amendment, the Supreme Court of Justice had the power to declare unconstitutional laws and executive orders. Though the Supreme Court exercised this power discretely during the first half of the twentieth century, it potentially familiarized the Colombian political institutions and the citizens with the kind of powers that later on would be assigned to the CCC.[36]

In 1958, 1966, 1968, 1977, and 1984, there were several attempts to create a Constitutional Court in Colombia by the means of constitutional amendments. In fact, the very first drafts of those constitutional amendments submitted to the Congress included the creation of the CCC, though this initiative was not ultimately approved. Singularly, the constitutional amendment of 1968 introduced a Constitutional Chamber into the Colombian Supreme Court of Justice, specialized in drafting opinions on the constitutionality of laws and executive orders, though the final decision was up to the Supreme Court of Justice as a whole.[37]

It is very illustrative that in the 2nd Colloquium on Constitutional Justice in *Iberoamerica*, which took place at *Universidad Externado de Colombia* in 1977, delegates from the United States, Argentina, Chile, Brazil, Colombia, Guatemala, Italy, Mexico, Peru, Uruguay, and Venezuela unanimously concluded that: "Given the specificity and complexity of constitutional interpretation, it requires a body made up by jurists of the highest intellectual, moral and legal capacities to give content to the system of constitutional principles and values (...) Because of its historical evolution, the Colombian case offers the most immediate possibility to create an specialized constitutional jurisdiction in Latin America, that is to say, a Court or Tribunal different from the Supreme Court."[38]

Once the Constitutional Chamber was created in 1968, the Supreme Court of Justice more actively exercised the judicial review power until the proclamation of the new Constitution in 1991. During the 1970s, the Supreme Court of Justice

---

[34] Art. 151. 4.
[35] Legislative Act 3.
[36] Art. 40. *"The Supreme Court of Justice is entrusted with guarding the integrity of the Consti-tution. Consequently, in addition to the faculties conferred upon it by the laws, it will have the following: Decide definitely on the constitutionality of the Legislative Acts that haven been objected as unconstitutional by the Government or on all the laws or decrees accused before it by any citizen as unconstitutional, after hearing the Attorney General of the Nation."*
[37] Legislative Act 1.
[38] Carlos Restrepo. "La jurisdicción Constitucional en Iberoamerica," *II Coloquio Iberoameri-cano de Derecho Constitucional.* Universidad Externado de Colombia. 1984.

surprisingly struck down, for the first time in history, two constitutional amendments under the constitutional replacement doctrine. According to the
Court, the Congress "had to preserve the political identity of the Constitution,"
"cannot alter the constitutional rules to amend the Constitution," and "had no
power to delegate the very competence to amend the Constitution into a
body like a Constituent Assembly, which was not prescribed by the 1886
Constitution."[39]

During the 1980s, the Supreme Court of Justice began to exercise active judicial
review over executive orders enacted by the President under extraordinary powers.
In fact, article 121 of the 1886 Constitution allowed a State of Siege and granted
abundant extraordinary powers to the President.[40] Under this article, Colombia
lived in an almost complete state of siege until 1991. Just to give a clue on this
situation, according to the data collected by Uprimny and Garcia, between 1970 and
1991, Colombia experienced 206 months under state of siege, that is to say, seventeen out of twenty-one years.[41] Though the extraordinary powers had almost been
uncontrolled, during the 1980s the Supreme Court of Justice began to play an active
role at reviewing executive orders enacted by the President at exercising extraordinary powers.[42] In 1987, for instance, the Supreme Court of Justice struck down an
executive order that established the competence of military tribunals to prosecute
and judge civilians.[43]

Overall, these historical factors shed some light on the establishment of the CCC
in the 1991 Constitution and its subsequent central role within the political system.
To summarize, Colombia had a long tradition of constitutional supremacy and
judicial review, dating back to the very first constitutions in the nineteenth century,
so that Colombian institutions and the citizens were familiar with the idea. Second,
the very creation of the CCC had been at stake since 1958, so that debate about this
institution had been commonplace within the political sphere before 1991. The
introduction of the CCC into the political system was one of the most anticipated
innovations of the 1991 Constitution. Third, in the decade just prior to the creation
of the CCC, the Supreme Court of Justice had an active role in controlling constitutional amendments and the extraordinary powers. Undoubtedly, these factors
paved the way for the forthcoming role of the CCC.

---

[39] Colombian Supreme Court of Justice. Decisions of 5 of May of 1978 and 16 of October of 1979.
[40] Art. 121. *"In cases of external war, or internal commotion, the President, after a hearing of the
Council of State and with the signature of all Ministers, may declare public order disturbed and
in a state of siege the entire Republic or part of it."*
[41] Rodrigo Uprimny Yepes, and Mauricio Garcia, "¿Controlando la excepcionalidad permanente
en Colombia? Una defense prudente del control judicial de los estados de excepción?"
Documentos de discusión DJS, 2005.
[42] Ibid.
[43] Colombian Supreme Court of Justice. Decision of 23rd of April of 1987.

8.3 THE NORMATIVE DESIGN OF THE 1991 CONSTITUTION

A second explanatory factor is the normative design of the 1991 Constitution. This section examines how the Constitution itself played a role in empowering the Court, through (1) its normative content and (2) the jurisdiction granted to the CCC.

First, the 1991 Colombian Constitution is a very extensive, principle-oriented, and, at some points, very regulatory document. This is an extensive Constitution, not only because of its 380 articles and 59 original transitory provisions but also because it governs a vast amount of public affairs. It contains principles and rules on the basics of the government,[44] a long list of civil and political rights,[45] socio-economic and collective rights,[46] citizenship and nationality,[47] democratic participation and political parties,[48] the structure of the government,[49] the main public institutions,[50] the processes of governmental decision making,[51] the elections and the electoral system,[52] the organization of the territory,[53] the tax system, economic regime,[54] and the constitutional amendment rules,[55] among others.

The provisions of this Constitution are very principle-oriented. Particularly, the provisions on the rights and the structure of the government, among others, definitely have an "open texture" and, to some extent, are written in a vague language.[56] For example, Article 16 prescribes that "all individuals are entitled to the unrestricted development of their personality," Article 18 provides that "freedom of conscience is guaranteed," Article 70 states that "the State has the obligation to promote and foster access to the culture of all Colombians," and Article 79 stipulates that "Every individual has the right to enjoy a healthy environment." Though those are just random examples, they denote the abstract orientation of the 1991 Constitution, which definitely leaves huge room for constitutional interpretation and lawmaking by the Court in defining the content of those provisions.

Though the 1991 Constitution is principle-oriented, it is also very regulatory, with detailed policies in some areas. This is self-evident in provisions on the processes of governmental decision-making, the elections and the electoral system, the organization of the territory, and the economic regime. Unlike typical constitutional

---

[44] Title I.
[45] Title II, Chapter I.
[46] Title II, Chapter II.
[47] Title II, Chapter III.
[48] Title III, Chapters I and II.
[49] Title IV.
[50] Titles V, VI, VII, and VIII.
[51] Title VI.
[52] Title IX.
[53] Title XI.
[54] Title XII.
[55] Title XIII.
[56] H. L. A. Hart, *The Concept of Law*. Clarendon Law Series (2nd ed.) Oxford: Oxford University Press, 1997. Bertrand Russell, *Vagueness*. London: George Allen & Unwin, 1923.

provisions, some of them seem to be specific components of regulatory statutes. Just to bring up an example, Article 360 prescribes the rules on the distribution of national income related to the exploitation of nonrenewable natural resources. Regulation here is very specific and detailed on the precise percentages, competences, and processes for distribution. These components of the 1991 Constitution had the potential to turn every public policy dispute into a case before the CCC.

Because of the extensive nature of the 1991 Constitution, the CCC has "a lot to care about or to guard"; in other words, the CCC can conceivably have something to say about virtually every political and legal decision. Due to the principle-oriented style of this Constitution, the CCC has a huge space for constitutional interpretation and lawmaking in order to make concrete the abstract constitutional provisions. Given its regulatory character, this practically turns any public policy matter into a constitutional debate, under the scrutiny of the CCC. In sum, the blending of these factors reveals, in my opinion, that the normative design of the 1991 Constitution noticeably propitiated the protagonist role of the CCC.

Second, the CCC has a very wide jurisdiction. Article 241 of the Constitution literally provides that the CCC is "the guardian of the Constitution," and consequently establishes broad mandates for the Court. The CCC has the power to declare unconstitutional multiple and diverse normative bodies such as constitutional amendments,[57] laws,[58] referendums,[59] plebiscites,[60] and executive orders enacted by the President at exercising extraordinary powers,[61] and international treaties implementing laws,[62] among others. Such a comprehensive jurisdiction allows the Court to pronounce the last word on nearly all relevant legal and political decisions in the land.

This jurisdiction has not remained only in the written Constitution. Since its very establishment, the CCC has been very committed to the full exercise of its jurisdiction. Just to illustrate this point, between 1984 and 1991, the Supreme Court of Justice declared unconstitutional just 9 percent of the executive orders enacted by the President under extraordinary powers, whereas, between 1991 and 1996, the CCC did so against 34 percent of those executive orders.[63] This shows that, since its first days, the CCC was "taking its jurisdiction seriously."

Apart from this, the same Article 241 stipulates that the CCC has inherent jurisdiction on the *acción pública de inconstitucionalidad* (hereinafter referred to as the API) and *certiorari* jurisdiction on the *acción de tutela* (hereinafter referred to

---

[57] Art. 241.1.
[58] Art. 241.3.
[59] Art. 241.2.
[60] Art. 241.3.
[61] Art. 241.7.
[62] Art. 241.10. Only the Congress can approve an international treaty by the means of "an approbatory law."
[63] *Ob. Cit.* 39.

as the AT).[64] The API is a petition that can be filed directly by any Colombian citizen before the CCC requesting to declare unconstitutional a law, a constitutional amendment, or a plebiscite.[65] The AT is a petition that any person can submit before any judge to claim protection to any fundamental right jeopardized or violated by any public institution or any other individual.[66] Judges adjudicate these petitions within ten days[67] and the CCC has *certiorari* jurisdiction on every writ of *tutela*.[68] The API had been established in the Colombian legal system since the Legislative Act 3 of 1910, though little exercised before 1991; the AT was inserted in the 1991 Constitution and is commonly considered as its principal innovation.

Since 1992, both the API and the AT have decidedly triggered the role of the CCC in the political system. This is so, in my opinion, for three reasons. First, both the API and the AT move the Constitution closer to the ordinary citizen. Second, both bring about the idea of the Constitution as the supreme binding law in the land. Third, and as a consequence, both the API and the AT serve *prima facie* not only to preserve the constitutional supremacy and to protect rights, respectively, but also to channel social discontent and community expectations about the black holes left by the political branches, either for lack of will or for dysfunctional public policies.[69] Let me elaborate on each of these three points.

First, both the API and the AT bring the Constitution closer to the ordinary citizen. Before 1991, Colombians viewed the Constitution as a matter of high politics, which concerned only the highest political institutions. Both the API and the AT made the Constitution a popular legal document, in the sense that it is in the hands of the citizens.[70] In fact, both the API and the AT are informal petitions, which can be filed easily by any citizen, without an attorney and even verbally before the CCC or any judge of the land, respectively.[71] Though there is some controversy on who are the ones who file the API and AT,[72] and on the convenience of this model, it is unquestionable that both petitions are truly public

---

[64] Art. 241.1,2,3, and 9.

[65] Art. 40.6.

[66] Art. 86.

[67] Ibid.

[68] Art. 241.9.

[69] César Rodríguez and Diana Rodríguez, "Cortes y Cambio Social: Como la Corte Constitucional transformó el desplazamiento forzado en Colombia," *Dejusticia*, 2010.

[70] Mauricio García and Rodrigo Uprimny Yepes, "Corte Constitucional y Emancipación Social," *Dejusticia*, 2010.

[71] Decree 2067 of 1991. Art. 2. Decree 2591 of 1991. Art. 14.

[72] Some argue that API and AT plaintiffs are usually middle-class citizens who actually know about both mechanisms and are aware of being right holders, rather than the most vulnerable people. See David Evan Landau, 2015. Beyond Judicial Independence: The Construction of Judicial Power in Colombia. Doctoral dissertation, Harvard University, Graduate School of Arts & Sciences.

and are in the hands of the citizens, which in turn places the Constitution itself in their hands.[73]

According to the official data published by the CCC, between 1992 and 2017, the CCC approximately decided 242 API per year;[74] according to the 2014 report by the Office of the Ombudsman, each minute an AT petition is submitted before Colombian judges.[75] The Judiciary's data shows that AT petitions represented, by 2015, approximately 32 percent of all the legal cases submitted to the judiciary.[76] Additionally, data collected by the Corporation for Excellence in Justice sheds light on two findings:[77] (1) the AT is the best-known mechanism for accessing the judiciary: 83.7 percent of the people interviewed answered that they know about the AT, whereas 20 percent said they have an idea about other kinds of judicial actions and (2) 65 percent of Colombians have "a favorable opinion" on the AT.

Second, the API and the AT bring about the idea of the Constitution as the supreme binding law in the land. Before 1991, Colombians used to see the Constitution merely as a political document; even more, the rulings of the Supreme Court of Justice were based on the idea that the Constitution was merely a programmatic document rather than a normatively binding one. That is why many petitions were simply disregarded on the basis that the Supreme Court of Justice could not adjudicate legal cases by applying a nonbinding document. After the 1991 Constitution, citizens proved that judges at any level do adjudicate cases by directly applying the Constitution.[78]

In its very first cases, the CCC endorsed this principle, which really validates the binding effect of the Constitution as the supreme law in the land. In judgment T-612 of 1992, the CCC highlighted that "the Constitution is the overriding legal body in the Colombian legal system." In the judgment T-483 of 1992, the CCC stated that "constitutional supremacy implies the enforceability of the Constitution, so all the individuals and the government departments have to obey it." This very idea of constitutional supremacy has remained uniformly as the defining factor of the CCC case law over twenty-seven years.

Third, both the API and the AT are thought of as instruments to raise social needs and community expectations toward the black holes left by the political branches. Year after year, consistently there API and AT petitions are brought claiming labor protection for vulnerable individuals (unionized workers, HIV patients, disable people, etc.), extension of the public health system to cover some treatments or

---

[73] David Landau, "The Reality of Social Rights Enforcement." *Harvard International Law Journal* 53: (1), 190–247 (Winter 2012).

[74] Available at www.corteconstitucional.gov.co.

[75] Office of the Ombudsman. (2014). Report on the Petition of Tutela.

[76] Colombian Superior Council of the Judiciary. Report on the Judiciary to the Congress, 2014–15.

[77] Corporation for Excellence in the Justice. (2013) Trust and Use of the Tutela.

[78] Office of the Ombudsman. (2015). Report on the Petition of Tutela.

medicines, protection of individual rights of inmates, protection of armed conflict victims, equal protection for LGBTI individuals, etc. Those are authentic black holes left by the political branches either because of lack of will or inefficient public policies.

According to the 2016 report of the Office of the Ombudsman, more than 25 percent of the *tutela* petitions request protection to the right to health, whereas more than 30 percent request protection from the administrative agencies in charge of the reparation programs for armed conflict victims.[79] In fact, the health and reparations systems are two of the most troublesome implemented public policies of the Colombian government.[80]

8.4 THE CCCS CONCEPTION OF THE CONSTITUTION AND ITS ROLE

Conceptual reasons explain the relevant CCC role within the political system. These reasons are associated with (1) the CCC conception of the Constitution and (2) the CCC conception of its own institutional role. Those conceptions were adopted by the CCC in 1992, in its very first year of operation.

First, the CCC has mainly understood the 1991 Constitution as aspirational rather than conservative. Sociolegal studies distinguish between aspirational and conservative constitutions.[81] An aspirational Constitution seeks to promote social progress, tries to foster changes in society to overcome the *status quo*, and prescribes how society and institutions should be, rather than how they actually are.[82] A conservative Constitution is not based on the idea of promoting social change, tries to preserve the *status quo*, and basically contains the rules to govern the institutions as they actually are and operate.[83] Whereas the former is usually promulgated in contexts of social and economic discontent, the latter happens to be adopted by "*well ordered societies.*"[84]

Since its very first rulings, the CCC adopted an aspirational concept of the Constitution, and, consequently, has considered it as a set of aspirations that depict the Colombian society as it wants to be. This view is based on the idea that the Constitution is mostly a set of principles "under an ongoing construction progress," which is permanently nurtured and developed by the Court's interpretations and adjudication. In case T-006 of 1992, the CCC concluded that the Constitution's aim

---

[79] Office of the Ombudsman (2015) Report on the Tutela.

[80] Office of the Ombudsman (2016) Report on the Tutela.

[81] Robin West (1993). The Aspirational Constitution. Georgetown University Law Center. Theory Research Paper No. 11-98.

[82] Kim Scheppele, *Aspirational and aversive constitutionalism: the case for studying cross-constitutional influence through negative model.* I.Con. Volume 1, Number 2, 2003, pp. 296–324.

[83] Michael Dorf, *The Aspirational Constitution* (2009). Cornell Law Faculty Publications. Paper. 112.

[84] John Rawls, A *Theory of Justice.* Cambridge, MA: Harvard University Press, 2005.

was to create real opportunities for all members of the community to exercise their rights, so the Constitution prescribes "objectives, goals and action programs that can eventually translate into rights to different economic, social and cultural benefits." Since then, the CCC has asserted that the Constitution's aim "is to achieve social equality so that freedom and full development of life is not only available to a small fraction of the population."

During the 1990s, the CCC predominantly considered the Constitution to be a political program that seeks to adjust the *status quo*. Just as an example, in case T-406 of 1992, the CCC highlighted that "the programmatic nature of the constitutional values [should be understood] as a set of purposes through which one should look at the relations between the rulers and the governed (...) the constitutional values express aims for the future; they are the sight that marks the order of tomorrow." In other words, the CCC considered the Constitution to be the beacon for social and political transformation.

In the CCC case law, this aspirational concept of the Constitution is meant to be "on the shoulders of the judge." Many of the most prominent justices of the CCC in the 1990s firmly considered that the judiciary was not a passive and quiet branch of the government, but a decisive branch in charge of the progressive achievement of the social goals of the Constitution. Since the 1992 case law, the CCC foresaw the judge as a "conveyor of the general interest." For instance, in case T-406 of 1992, the CCC interpreted the new Constitution as a new "political strategy" to achieve protection for rights and "consists of giving priority to the judge, and not to the administration or the legislator, the responsibility for the effectiveness of fundamental rights." In other words, the CCC envisioned its mission as turning the Constitution into reality.

Second, the CCC had a very particular conception of its own institutional role to "guard the Constitution" from early days. The CCC understood its own role both (1) as a transformer and also (2) as a leveler Court of Law. Regardless of its success, the CCC has definitely proclaimed itself as a promoter of transformation of both (a) the legal system and (b) society. In the same way, the CCC has seen its role as a leveler to make visible both (a) the disadvantaged population and (b) ordinary cases, which never before came up before the judiciary. Both as a transformer and as a leveler, the CCC has declared itself a Court of Law, rather than a political actor. Its mission, in its own terms, is to enforce the binding force of the Constitution.

Since the very beginning, the CCC set as one of its main goals the so-called constitutionalization of ordinary law. The most immediate goal of the CCC was precisely to update the Colombian legal system according to the new system of constitutional principles. Since 1992, the CCC has considered its mission "to constitutionalize the entire Colombian legal system and, in this way, make effective the protection of the fundamental rights of the people." The CCC called the rest of the judiciary both to adjudicate cases based directly on the Constitution and to interpret the ordinary law according to the Constitution before applying it.

The "constitutionalization of ordinary law" was also meant to familiarize the rest of the judiciary with a new Constitution. In case T-525 of 1992, the CCC concluded that "it is necessary that judges and courts become aware that when the violation of a fundamental right is raised by means of an AT, the essential and immediate parameter of adjudication and interpretation is the constitutional text and not the ordinary legislation." In case T-596 of 1992, the CCC decided that "to protect a fundamental right effectively, judges and courts should not only confront the case before the ordinary legal order but, above all, before the Constitution."

Apart from transforming the legal system, the CCC acted as an agent of social change. CCC justices in the nineties brought forward the very conception of the Court as an agent to promote social change in order to reach a "fairer state of affairs." In T-006 of 1992, the CCC determined that its institutional role was to "shape the constitutional reality," which means to bring about adjustments in society "for the Constitution to transcend as a mere formal political document."

In case T-406 of 1992, the CCC concluded that its injunctions at adjudicating cases were "means to improve the inter communication between the law and the society," by which society could better adjust itself in order to favor the "achievement of the justice." In other words, the CCC proclaimed itself as the agent to transform Colombian society to a fairer one. In case T-223 of 1992, the CCC pointed out that "an evolutive jurisprudence, open to the knowledge of the social, economic and political conditions of the country and aware of the need to stimulate the progressive and firm establishment of a just order, based on the respect and effectiveness of the rights and guarantees of citizens, is the only compatible with the welfare state."

This conception in the adjudication was remarkably apparent in cases regarding the principle of equality and the right to education. On the one hand, on cases related to the equal protection clause, the CCC pointed out that it had "the duty to determine the real existence of discrimination and, after this, to articulate the most adequate remedy from an economic, an efficient and a principled prospective, appealing if necessary to social solidarity." On the other hand, in the very first cases on education, the CCC markedly opted for a transformative view of this right as an instrument for social change. In case T-429 of 1992, the CCC concluded that "the creation and maintenance of schools can be understood as the realization of the deliberate purpose of not leaving the preparation of future generations to chance and of using appropriate instruments to perpetuate, strengthen and promote those conditions and values that society most esteems . . . the school plays the role of agent of change."

Second, the CCC has allegedly seen itself as a leveler Court of Law. The aspirational conception of the Constitution and the transformative conception of the law decidedly influenced the CCC's agenda setting, by making visible traditionally invisible cases. This is certainly evident in the framework of the *certiorari* jurisdiction on the writ of *tutela*. This jurisdiction gives to the CCC at least two institutional advantages in the political system. On the one hand, to elude certain matters in order to keep the institution apart from "hot topics," which were not related to social transformation, but could bring about real threats to the CCC. This was very important for the CCC in its very first years. For instance, the CCC never picked up a *tutela* case related to the extradition of Colombians, though this was an extremely pressing issue in the eighties, at the Constitutional Assembly sessions and in the nineties. This could be due to the hostile victimization of judges and high public officials related to these kinds of decisions.

On the other hand, the CCC has set itself to permanently tackle issues both sensitive to Colombian society and ignored by the traditional public authorities, even the judiciary. The CCC committed itself to trial "traditionally invisible cases" in two ways. First, the CCC extended constitutional and legal protection to peoples who were mostly excluded from it before 1991. Even more so, the CCC makes them visible to the law. The CCC was the only institutional gateway for cases on the protection of forcedly displaced people, LGBTI, inmates, indigenous peoples, and afro descendants, among others. In case T-523 of 1992, the Court decided that the AT "filled by persons belonging to discriminated or marginalized groups should deserve special consideration, in order to mitigate the inequality that has traditionally accompanied these groups."

Most of those groups of people were totally overlooked by public and private actors before 1991. On the contrary, since its very first cases, the CCC declared the very existence of the obligation in charge of the government and the judiciary "to especially protect [the] disadvantaged population." In case T-533 of 1992, the Court extended that obligation to "any person who is in a manifest weakness situation, due to her economic or health condition." If not for the work of the CCC, they would have also been ignored by the new institutions after the 1991 Constitution.

In some cases, those peoples were directly victimized by the very law and legal institutions supposed to protect them. This was the case for indigenous peoples who were named by the preconstitutional legal order as "savage peoples."[85] For those peoples and other marginalized groups, the CCC considered its own duty "to promote the conditions so that equality is real and effective and measures are adopted in their favor (...) to foster their social integration and to enforce the recognition of their human dignity." Even more so, in the subsequent years, the CCC highlighted that refraining from acting like this would be "to perpetuate or to prolong social imbalances that must be corrected."[86]

Second, the CCC extended constitutional and legal protection to personal spheres of individuals that were usually considered by the law as merely private, without constitutional and public relevance. In fact, from 1992 to 1993, the CCC considered cases on the right of a male student to wear long hair in a catholic high

---

[85] Law 89 of 1890.
[86] Decisions T-762 of 1998 and T-093 of 1997.

school,[87] the right of a female student to use make-up while attending a Christian school,[88] the right of a citizen to ask for the exclusion of her critical and impoverished financial situation from the public database,[89] the right of an inmate to have conjugal visits of her husband,[90] the right to education of a student who was unfairly expelled from school,[91] the right of an indigenous political candidate to campaign on radio in his traditional language,[92] and the right of an old and poor rural couple to walk through the farm of a wealthy farmer in order to reach public transport in an easier way, among many others.[93] Before the 1991 Constitution, it was truly unthinkable to file petitions related to such cases before the judiciary, much less before the highest Court in the land.

An example illustrates this point. In case T-494 of 1992, the CCC reversed the Tribunal decision of not delivering labor protection to a domestic worker. Regarding this, the CCC concluded that "not delivering such protection is promoting to make invisible such cases." Even more so, the CCC highlighted that, by ignoring those unseen cases, the judiciary "stimulates and deepens inequality and injustice in social relations, makes economic development inequitable and violates fundamental rights of the human being." Since then, the CCC has considered that "it has the obligation to extend the binding force of fundamental rights to private relations."[94]

The CCC has certainly acted as a leveler as long as it has made visible a series of "ignored cases." Before 1991, those cases were unseen not only because they were sporadic; they were invisible for cultural or political reasons that made them authentic "blind spots" for the legal system. This is why one of the strengths of the CCC has been its ability to make such violations "visible," to integrate them "into the public agenda," and its capacity to unveil them as "public issues" subject to judicial protection, rather than as "private acts" exempted from the control of the judges.

8.5 CCC CASE LAW ON THE PROTECTION OF RIGHTS

The solid CCC case law on the protection of rights explains why the CCC became such a relevant institution in Colombia. In 1992, the CCC paved the way to develop a very rich case law on the judicial enforcement of civil and political rights, social rights, and collective rights. This was possible given that the 1991 Constitution is, by definition, a charter of rights. Apart from a very rich list of civil rights (freedom of

---

[87] Decision T-065 of 1993.
[88] Decision T-524 of 1992.
[89] Decision T-414 of 1992.
[90] Decision T-596 of 1992.
[91] Decision T-065 of 1993.
[92] Decision T-428 of 1992.
[93] Decision T-524 of 1992.
[94] Decision C-587 of 1992.

religion, freedom of thinking, freedom of expression, among others), the Constitution also contains a vast amount of social rights (right to education, right to shelter, right to health, etc.), political rights (right to vote, right to be elected, right to create political parties, etc.), and collective rights (right to a free economic competition, right to administrative morality, right to a healthy environment, etc.) In fact, close to a third of the Constitution is about individual and collective rights.

Reception clauses for international law and the unenumerated rights clause enrich the already large catalogue of rights. Apart from inserting a very ample list of rights, the Constitution contains reception clauses referring to International Law of Human Rights, International Labor Law, and International Humanitarian Law. Articles 53, 93, and 214 of the Constitution incorporate those international covenants and treaties into the domestic legal order, and according to the CCC case law, most of them are part of the "constitutionality block."[95] Article 94 of the Constitution also includes the so-called unenumerated rights clause. This provision states that the enumeration of rights "should not be understood as the negation of others, which being inherent to the human being, are not expressly mentioned" by the Constitution. In the light of this provision, the CCC has protected the rights to human dignity,[96] special labor stability,[97] minimum existential conditions,[98] personal security,[99] drinking water,[100] household electricity,[101] and the right to try experimental health treatments.[102] The CCC became not only the guardian of constitutional rights but also of rights prescribed by international normative instruments and others unenumerated in either international or constitutional texts.

Under that very large catalogue of rights, the CCC developed a rich case law on the judicial enforcement of (1) civil and political rights, (2) social rights, (3), and collective rights since 1992. First, the CCC developed a very solid doctrine on the concept of individual freedom to protect civil and political rights. The CCC stated that the Constitution protects "the general freedom of the human being," that is to say "a very broad scope of freedom for the human being to do or not to do what she considers convenient."[103] This concept of freedom, according to the CCC, implies the individual autonomy to plan and to achieve personal goals, and therefore protects her from external, public, or private interferences on it. Under that concept, the CCC protected academic freedom,[104] freedom of movement,[105] freedom of

---

[95] Decision C-225 of 1995.
[96] Decision T-881 of 2002.
[97] Decision C-710 of 1996.
[98] Decision SU225 of 1998.
[99] Decision T-719 of 2003.
[100] Decision T-733 of 2015.
[101] Decision T-761 of 2015.
[102] Decision T-057 of 2015.
[103] Decision T-222 of 1992.
[104] Decision T-493 of 1992.
[105] Decision T-532 of 1992.

expression,[106] freedom of religion,[107] and economic freedoms[108] in a wide range of cases in 1992.

Second, the CCC reaffirmed that any individual could claim protection of her social rights by means of the AT. This is so because the CCC has asserted that social rights protection is a necessary condition for the protection of individual autonomy.[109] In other words, the satisfaction of social rights is connected to the very protection of civil rights and individual freedoms.[110] Though the CCC acknowledges that the realization of social rights is a matter of politics,[111] it has also declared that it has the power and the duty to handle problems concerning distributive justice when those rights are violated. Under this doctrine, the CCC protected the right to education[112] and the right to health[113] in its 1992 case law.

Finally, the CCC extended protection to collective rights by means of the AT. In fact, the CCC has protected both collective rights and also collectivities since 1992. On the one hand, the CCC handled cases on the right to a healthy environment and the right to access the public water system.[114] On the other hand, the CCC protected indigenous and Afro-Colombian groups as collective right holders rather than a mere sum of individuals.[115]

The year 1992 was decisive for the CCC. In that year, the CCC adopted a doctrine in favor of the judicial protection of individual and collective rights by means of the AT. Apart from the controversies related to this doctrine, its implications, and its outcomes in terms of real protection of rights, it has decidedly contributed to building an image of the CCC as the "guardian of rights" within the Colombian political system.

8.6 CONCLUSIONS

This chapter approaches the question as to *why* the CCC became such a central player within the Colombian political system. The inactivity and lack of will of the political branches are the most obvious reasons with which to explain it. Apart from that, this chapter poses three kinds of arguments to answer the question: (i) historical, (ii) normative, and (iii) conceptual. These are summarized in Table 8.1.

The first contends that the long history of constitutional supremacy and judicial review in Colombia, the recurring political debates about the creation of a

---

[106] Decision T-402 of 1992.
[107] Decision T-403 of 1992.
[108] Decision T-564 of 1992.
[109] Decision T-570 of 1992.
[110] Decision T-406 of 1992.
[111] Decision T-570 of 1992.
[112] Decision T-002 of 1992.
[113] Decision T-406 of 1992.
[114] Ibid.
[115] Decision T 605 of 1992.

TABLE 8.1 *Summary of factors*

Factor	Implications
Historical inheritance	
Constitutional supremacy and judicial review have a long tradition	The political system had familiarity
Several attempts to create a CCC before 1991	The CCC was one of the most "anticipated" innovations of the Constitution
Active judicial review between 1970 and 1980	By 1991, the Colombian political system had become accustomed to the *"activism"* of the Supreme Court
Normative design of the constitution	
Broad mandates	Enables the Court to intervene in a wide range of political and legal decisions
Principle oriented	Leaves huge room for lawmaking
Policy oriented	Turns policy matters into constitutional debates
Acción pública de inconstitucionalidad (API) and *Acción de tutela* (AT)	• Moves the Constitution closer to citizens • Reinforces constitutional supremacy • Channels social discontent and expectations
Self-conception and role of the court	
Aspirational concept of the Constitution	Image of social change
Agent of transformation and equality	• Updating legal order to fit the 1991 Constitution • Including disadvantaged peoples into the public agenda • Unveiling previously invisible cases and issues

constitutional court, and the active role of the Supreme Court of Justice before 1991 paved the way for the CCC's peaceful insertion into the Colombian legal system and determined its protagonist role.

The second holds that the normative design of the Constitution and of the CCC determined the role of this institution. On the one hand, the 1991 Constitution is extensive, principled, and policy-oriented, which in turn enables the Court to intervene on a wide spectrum of political and legal issues and leaves huge space in which to make laws and turn policy matters into constitutional debates. On the other hand, article 241 prescribes broad mandates to the CCC and inserts the API and the AT. Due to both petitions, the CCC has brought the Constitution closer to the citizens, reinforced constitutional supremacy, and channeled social discontent and expectations.

The third argument is based on the CCC case law. It contends that the CCC viewed the Constitution as an aspirational political and normative document, that is to say, as a set of principles aimed to foster changes in society to overcome the *status quo*. Also, the CCC has understood its own role as both transformative and as a leveler. This led the CCC to adopt a doctrine in favor of the extensive judicial protection of individual and collective rights by means of the AT, which has reinforced its image as "the guardian of the rights."

I do not seek to adjudicate among these factors or to attribute a precise weight to each of them. Instead, my aim is to emphasize that the combination of background conditions and the self-conception of the court made the emergence of vigorous rights jurisprudence less surprising than it has sometimes seemed. Together, they helped ensure that the first period of constitutional implementation was one of dramatic change, in a challenging context.

9

Implementing a New Constitution in a Competitive Authoritarian Context

The Case of Kenya

James Thuo Gathii[*]

9.1 INTRODUCTION

Between its independence in 1963 and the inauguration of multi-party politics in 1991, Kenya experienced many years of authoritarian rule. Since 1991, Kenya has held multi-party elections. In 2002, although a united opposition successfully won the Presidency, the elites that lost power in that election quickly regrouped and re-captured the new government in large part by sidelining a large part of the opposition coalition that came together in that election.[1] In 2010, a new Constitution inspired by the Madisonian vision of checks and balances came into force after an overwhelming endorsement in a referendum. This chapter argues that following the 2017 Presidential elections, the Constitution entered its second period. Unlike many Constitutions that die within a year to five years after coming into force, the 2010 Kenyan Constitution is now in its eighth year. It began its life after more than two decades of Constitution making. It was overwhelmingly approved in a referendum as one of the major outcomes of a post-election violence agreement in early 2008. Its implementation in the first five years was largely successful. In particular, it successfully inaugurated a regional system of government in the country. It also introduced a Madisonian design that severely limited presidential power.

The nullification of the Presidential election results in September 2017 by the Supreme Court of Kenya marked the 2010 Constitution's entry into period two. The August 2017 Presidential election was nullified by the Supreme Court for failing to conform to the 2010 Constitution's requirements of a free and fair election. The Supreme Court upheld the repeat election notwithstanding the fact that the opposition coalition, the National Super Alliance (NASA), decided to boycott it.

---

[*] Many thanks to Barry Sullivan, Tom Ginsburg, Alex Tsesis, and Richard Joseph for their comments.

[1] Makau Mutua, *Kenya's Quest for Democracy: Taming Leviathan.* Boulder, CO: Lynne Rienner Publishers, 2008.

The opposition coalition saw the Supreme Court's endorsement of a flawed election as exacerbating the lack of integrity in the electoral system and the officials responsible for conducting elections. NASA had already decided to begin working outside the constitutional framework by deciding not to participate in the repeat election before the Supreme Court endorsed the repeat Presidential election that it boycotted. The fact that NASA at that time decided to work outside the framework of the 2010 Constitution indicated that it had no confidence in its institutional framework for resolving the political and constitutional crisis produced by its boycott of the repeat election. NASA's boycott of the repeat Presidential election of October 2017 was in effect an invitation to renegotiate the 2010 Constitution. Thus, period two of the 2010 Constitution is marked by the fact that it no longer provides clear answers to the contentious politics produced by the predominantly Kikuyu-Kalenjin hold on power of the Jubilee party that has controlled the state since.

On its part, the ruling Jubilee party reneged on the constitutional deal not only by amending the election laws unilaterally but also by using the machinery of the state to undermine the opposition's ability to campaign effectively through intimidation, harassment, use of the police and para-military to quell dissent, and de-registering civil society groups. The Jubilee party has clamped down on the opposition and civil society groups to maintain its dominance. In early 2018 the leader of the NASA opposition agreed to work with the Jubilee government to resolve the crisis that led to the nullification of the presidential election of August 2017 and the boycott of the repeat presidential elections in October 2017. Thus, two electoral cycles since the enactment of the 2010 Constitution have produced Jubilee as a dominant party in Parliament. Rather than play a role in checking the Executive, Parliament has acquiesced to, if not supported, the Executive's muzzling of the press, repressing of civil society groups, and weakening of independent accountability institutions such as the anti-corruption authority and the office of the auditor general. In assessing how the short history of Kenya's 2010 Constitution has shifted from period one to period two, I argue that one has to look at but also beyond the formal rules and institutions the 2010 Constitution created. This means looking at informal sources of influence and power such as the salience of ethnicity and how networks of patronage are preserved or created to forestall state power passing on to new political actors. The requirements of a multi-party system of government in which elections are required to be free and fair contained in the 2010 Constitution unleashed heightened political competition. This competitive environment has accentuated identification based on ethnicity, religion, as well as regional affiliations.[2] Thus, electoral politics in the post-2010 Constitutional order are a major lens through which an appreciation of the extent to which this new constitutional order has been an agent of change or continuity. Using elections as our prism also

---

[2] Benn Eifert, Edward Miguel, and Daniel N. Posner, "Political Competition and Ethnic Identification in Africa." *American Journal of Political Science* 54 (2): 494–510 (2010).

acknowledges that voters and candidates regard elections as important for the distribution of national resources and therefore take them seriously.[3]

How elections are conducted also provides an opportunity to examine the impact of strategies of the leading Presidential contenders and their political parties in the two election cycles on whether or not the aspirations of the 2010 Constitution have been met. By examining this political behavior, particularly the incentive structures that have come to define Kenyan elections as a zero-sum game become visible. After all, electoral victory is a gateway to accessing state resources and the patronage opportunities it opens up, while electoral loss is seen as, and does indeed result in, shutting out losers from these resources and opportunities. This do or die attitude to elections in turn becomes the staging ground for organizing political parties along ethnic lines or ethnic alliances with politicians making appeals to particular ethnic communities to ensure they win and therefore do not get excluded from the resources and opportunities that result from electoral success. An important claim, therefore, made in this chapter is that the significance of formal rules and institutions as provided for in the 2010 Constitution can be best understood through the extent to which informal norms of incumbent party behavior disables their realization.

Elections also provide a good window into whether or not the promises of horizontal and vertical accountability are at play and whether individuals and civil society groups enjoy freedoms such as expression, association, and assembly. In addition, elections are a good moment to examine whether there is free media, whether courts fairly determine disputes, particularly electoral ones, and, importantly, whether Parliament keeps the Executive in check, as well as the extent to which the Executive allows the existence of a vibrant opposition party.

One limit of examining elections and political parties as a lens through which to assess the implementation of the 2010 Constitution is that it zeroes in too sharply on the intra-elite politics of politicians seeking the Presidency. It does not necessarily help to illuminate how the many important goals of the 2010 Constitution such as judicial independence are being pursued, or the extent to which they have been achieved.[4] That is why this chapter also examines how the Jubilee government has used its dominance to undermine the emergence of an impartial and professional bureaucracy, including the police forces. By rewarding officials who do its bidding and punishing those that do not, Kenya's dominant party has played an active role in undermining the institutional framework designed in the 2010 Constitution to keep it accountable.

---

[3] This insight dates to the one-party era in Kenya and is attributable to Joel Barkan, ed. *Legislative Power in Emerging African Democracies.* Boulder, CO: Lynne Rienner Publishers, 2009. Barkan, however, recognized that manipulated elections, particularly during the one-party era, undermined the competitive nature of elections.

[4] But see, James Gathii, *The Contested Empowerment of the Kenyan Judiciary 2010–2015: An Historical Institutional Analysis* (2016). Sheria Publishing House.

Ultimately, this chapter shows that instead of ensuring the liberal guarantees of the 2010 Constitution are protected and safeguarded, the governments in power since its enactment undermined them as part of their strategy of maintaining party and political dominance in the country. In particular, this chapter shows how the Jubilee party's acquisition of political party dominance since 2013 has given it a platform against which to de-legitimate, harass, and weaken the opposition.[5] Other independent institutions have also been deliberately weakened in a manner that has undermined their ability to provide checks on the government in power. In this sense, this chapter shows how authoritarian leaders can withstand the establishment of legal institutions.[6]

I proceed as follows. In Section 9.2, I examine how patronage politics have stymied Parliament's role to check the Executive as envisaged in the Madisonian design of the 2010 Constitution. Section 9.3 examines how the dominant and opposition parties in Kenya have resorted to the Judiciary to resolve election-related cases.

9.2 TESTING THE LIMITS OF THE MADISONIAN DESIGN OF THE 2010 CONSTITUTION: PATRONAGE POLITICS AND PARLIAMENTARY CHECKS ON EXECUTIVE POWER AFTER 2010

The Madisonian design of checks and balances adopted in the 2010 Constitution was necessitated by the legacy of legally unchecked authoritarian Presidents, who could not be replaced by democratic means. Thus, the Presidential system adopted in the 2010 Constitution was a significantly weakened one. It created a system of checks and balances[7] that strengthened the judiciary as an independent institution with the power to review the constitutionality of the conduct of the Executive and Parliament.[8] Parliament was empowered to approve Presidential appointees such as judges and other high-ranking governmental officials that were previously appointed by the President alone. Government ministers are no longer members of parliament.[9] This means cabinet members can no longer use their membership in

---

[5] A frequent refrain of the President is that the opposition leader is a perennial loser, a line the New York Times picked up on in urging him to accept electoral defeat following the 2017 Presidential election.

[6] Tom Ginsburg, *Judicial Review in New Democracies: Constitutional Courts in Asian Cases* (2003) and J. Mark Ramseyer, "The Puzzling (In)dependence of Courts: A Comparative Approach." *Journal of Legal Studies* 23: 721 (1994).

[7] See The Federalist Papers No. 51 noting the separation of powers, an idea built upon the ideas of Montesquieu, In the Spirit of the Laws, 1784.

[8] See The Federalist Papers No. 78 arguing that judges are guardians of the Constitution.

[9] Notably, the Kenyan Parliament's institutionalization had begun prior to the 2010 Constitution, particularly with the establishment of the Parliamentary Service Commission in 2000 that gave Parliament more control over its affairs by shrinking the Executive's formal controls over it such as its legislative calendar, their remuneration, and access to funding to support constituency activities. See Parliamentary Service Act No. 10 of 2000. As a result of these changes, Kenyan

parliament to do the bidding of the government. In addition, cabinet appointments were limited to twenty-two. This requirement reduces the ability of the President to make an unlimited number of cabinet positions, which was characteristic of Kenya's legacy of patronage. In addition, the President no longer has the power to suspend or dissolve Parliament. Parliament was empowered to hold hearings to hold the Executive accountable and to have more control of the budgetary process.[10] Parliament may by two-thirds majorities in both houses override a Presidential veto.[11] The separation of powers adopted in the 2010 Constitution was based on a Madisonian design in which the composition of government is composed of shifting political interests to avoid coalescence. Shifting interests, under the Madisonian framework, means that for government to work, negotiation and compromise are necessary. The requirements of negotiation and compromise in turn prevent majorities from running roughshod over minorities, or that there is a permanent underclass.[12]

In addition to emphasizing the separation of powers in the Madisonian tradition of ensuring that no self-interested faction dominates the affairs of government,[13] another limitation to Presidential authority introduced by the 2010 Constitution was the dispersion of Presidential powers through the creation of at least eight independent bodies charged with powers that were previously exercised by the Executive branch.[14] These are the Auditor General; the Controller of Budgets; the National Police Service Commission; the National Land Commission; the Salaries and Remuneration Commission; the Kenya National Human Rights and Equality Commission; the Independent Elections and Boundaries Commission, and the Commission on the Implementation of the Constitution. These bodies are independent not only because the 2010 Constitution protects their autonomy but also

---

Parliamentarians became some of the best paid in the world in per capita and real terms. They also established a Constituency Development Fund that each Member of Parliament controlled that became a slush fund of sorts for the members to reward their most loyal supporters while dipping into it for their personal needs, including for their campaigns.

[10] In addition, the 2010 Constitution introduced far-reaching reforms to make Parliament a more representative institution and to facilitate its ability to check the Executive. It did so in a number of ways. First, to make Parliament even more representative it introduced a new Chamber, the Senate, to represent the interests of the forty-seven County governments established by the 2010 Constitution. Second, the 2010 Constitution expanded parliamentary membership to include nominated and elected members of parliament representing special groups like women.

[11] Article 115(6) of the 2010 Constitution.

[12] Notably, in footnote 4 of *United States v. Carolene Products*, 304 U.S. 144 (1938), Justice Stone of the United States Supreme Court observed that there might be more exacting scrutiny of some rights under the 14th and also in cases of discrete and insular minorities who have been cut out of the political process.

[13] In Madison's account, the role of separation of powers was to ensure that "ambition must be made to counteract ambition." See James Madison, *The Federalist* No. 51 at 349 (Jacob E. Cooke ed., 1961).

[14] Alexander Hamilton in Federalist No.70, The Executive Department Further Considered, supported a powerful Executive.

because the President's power to appoint their heads is subject to parliamentary approval.

The 2010 Constitution also made changes to the electoral system, particularly through the establishment of an Independent Electoral and Boundaries Commission. The premise of these reforms was to free the electoral system from the direct control of the Executive. Further, the 2010 Constitution entrenched majoritarian provisions for Presidential elections that were designed to encourage inter-ethnic alliances.[15] However, as this chapter will show, the design of these institutions to realize electoral and parliamentary independence from the Executive has not been fully realized. A major reason for this incomplete outcome is that the Jubilee Party, and its predecessor coalition, has continued to be a dominant power through two heavily contested election cycles since the enactment of the 2010 Constitution. The legacy of one-party control over Parliament and individual members of Parliament of the incumbent party in the multi-party era has proved difficult to overcome even with the Madisonian design of the 2010 Constitution.[16]

A major strategy that the Jubilee Alliance in 2013, and later the Jubilee Party in the 2017 election cycle, has deployed to garner electoral success has been through an extensive patronage system to reward key regional supporters and to reward loyal ethnic voting blocks with key national projects. This has been accompanied by a simultaneous process of designating opposition politicians and their regional voting blocks as enemies that the supporters of the Jubilee government should unite against. The Jubilee government has also used state resources to build its capacity as the dominant political party in Parliament, particularly by selecting a very loyal parliamentary leadership team. This in turn means that the dominant party has near total control of the public policy agenda in the country.

As Cherry Gertzel argued in 1970, the weakness of political parties in Kenya is illustrated by the fact that they only come to life during elections.[17] That is still true

---

[15] To win the Presidential candidacy, a candidate must win 50 percent plus one of the vote and at least 25 percent of the votes cast in at least half of Kenya's forty-seven counties as well as a second round of elections if none of the candidates in round one achieves these thresholds. These majoritarian provisions are critical in ethnically divided countries like Kenya to give elected Presidents broad-based legitimacy and public confidence. On the importance of majoritarian provisions in ethnically divided countries, see D. Posner, "The Colonial Origins of Ethnic Cleavages: The Case of Linguistic Divisions in Zambia." *Comparative Politics* 35 (2): 127–46 (2003). In the United States, the electoral college system was seen as a brake on popular government in the same way, perhaps, as in the 2010 Constitution the majoritarian provisions were designed to work.

[16] Ken Opalo, "The Long Road to Parliamentary Institutionalization: The Kenyan Parliament and the 2013 Elections." 8 *Journal of Eastern African Studies* 10: 63–77 (2014).

[17] Cherry Gertzel, *The Politics of Independent Kenya 1963–1968*, at page 31 (1970). Kenya's early political history was one of "disciplining and subordinating the Party to the Government in an attempt to reverse the tradition of decentralized political power that grew with the nationalist movement," ibid. She argues further that "part of Kenya's political inheritance was the strong sense of localism out of which grew the traditional of decentralized political power. Party institutions were consequently weak in organization. The legal and administrative inheritance

in today's competitive electoral environment as it was in the early 1970s, when Kenya was a de facto one party state. In fact, the 2010 Constitution was enacted following post-election violence in early 2008. Further, prior electoral cycles had been followed by violence as a result of rigged or stolen elections. Thus, whether or not a Presidential election candidate opted to pursue legal redress in Court or not as required by the 2010 Constitution has become a real test of whether the 2010 Constitution inaugurated a new electoral environment.[18] Two successive Presidential Election Petitions in the Supreme Court of Kenya since the enactment of the 2010 Constitution have tested the extent to which the 2010 Constitution has succeeded in eliminating electoral authoritarianism – i.e. – whether elections in Kenya promise "a meaningful transfer of national power."[19]

If elections merely legitimate authoritarian regimes, which entrench themselves in power, then the 2010 Constitution has only weakly succeeded in institutionalizing competitive politics. Thus, while formal rules and institutions are playing a more prominent role in the politics of African states[20] and in Kenya in particular,[21] formerly dominant political parties are still finding ways of continuing to dominate national legislatures in the era of multi-party politics.[22] In this sense then, Kenyan Presidential elections in the post-2010 era have been characterized by ruling party dominance. Politics in the post-2010 Constitution period have stifled democratic consolidation as will be more fully explored in this chapter. For this reason,

was very different. It left Kenya with a strong centralized hierarchical machine that had over the years provided an effective counter-balance to localism, the grid that held the country together. Although power might have been decentralized in the national movement, in the Government it had been highly centralized," ibid. at 28.

[18] See Communique Following the Post-Election Meeting of the Heads of International Observation Mission to the 2017 General Elections in Kenya, August 9, 2017. Available at www.comesa.int/wp-content/uploads/2017/08/COMMUNIQUE-BY-IEOMs-post-election-final.pdf (urging restraint by all parties to allow for the transmission of results to the electoral body and for aggrieved parties to pursue remedies through established mechanisms).

[19] http://bostonreview.net/politics/aziz-rana-kenyas-new-electoral-authoritarianism. Larry Diamond refers to regimes like Kenya as pseudo-democracies which are regimes that "have multiple parties and many other constitutional features of electoral democracy but that lack at least one key requirement – an arena of contestation sufficiently fair that the ruling party can be turned out of power," Larry Diamond, 1999b page 15.

[20] Daniel N. Posner and Daniel J. Young, "The Institutionalization of Political Power in Africa." *Journal of Democracy* 18: 126–40 (July 2007). Indeed, Kenya is not anywhere near what B. O. Nwabueze, *Constitutionalism in Emergent States* (1973), claimed accounted for the demise of constitutionalism in Africa: coups; counter-coups; military governments; permanent states of emergency. However, corruption and rigged elections are a feature of Kenyan politics, notwithstanding a written constitution making both illegal.

[21] James Gathii, The Contested Empowerment of Kenya's Judiciary: A Historical Institutional Analysis (2016).

[22] Françoise Bouček, "Electoral and Parliamentary Aspects of Dominant Party Systems," in *Comparing Party System Change*, ed. Paul Pennings and Jan-Erik Lane. London: Routledge, 1998, 103–24.

"democratization through elections"[23] seems an unlikely outcome under the Madisonian framework of the 2010 Constitution. This does not mean that institutions do not matter. However, institutions and formal rules cannot be understood without taking into account the informal rules that operate alongside them. For example, Members of Parliament and regional and ethnic leaders continue to serve as the connection between voters and the Presidency, as was the case in the pre-2010 Constitutional period. This continuing connection in turn facilitates access to the resources of the state for supporters of the President. This is what Richard Sklar referred to as "dual majesty," which is reflected in the persistence of identity-based political mobilization in the era of competitive electoral democracy and the guarantees of modern liberal democratic Constitutions.[24]

In the era of competitive electoral politics, particularly since the enactment of the 2010 Constitution, bottom-up pressure continued to necessitate the creation of political linkages between voters for delivery of goodies from the center. At the same time, Kenya, like other African states, particularly in the era of competitive politics, has continued to engage in coercive control of opposition voters and politicians.[25] In the oneparty era, Joel Barkan referred to this type of politics as competitive authoritarianism.[26] Competitive politics in the post-2010 period have accentuated the need by voters to strengthen their links to their representatives to assure continued access to resources in an era where regime change could mean exclusion from perks. Patronage politics have therefore been a major motivation for excluding opposition political parties from assuming political power, particularly the Presidency.[27]

In short, informal networks and channels between voters and the Presidency, mediated by Members of Parliament, ethnic kingpins, and other intermediaries, are

---

[23] Nicolas van de Walle and Staffan Lindberg, "Opposition Weakness in Africa." *Journal of Democracy* 20: 108–21 (2009).

[24] Richard L. Sklar, "The African Frontier for Political Science," in *Africa and the Disciplines*, ed. R. H. Bates, V. Y. Mudimbe, and J. G. O'Barr. Chicago: University of Chicago Press, 1993, 83. Other scholars that takes seriously the importance of political activities that take place outside formal institutions are Wale Adebanwi and Ebenezer Obadare, *Democracy and Prebendalism in Nigeria: Critical Interpretations* (2013).

[25] Henry Bienen, Kenya: *The Politics of Participation and Control*, (2016).

[26] Joel Barkan, "Advancing Democratization in Africa," in *Africa Policy Beyond the Bush Years: Critical Challenge for the Obama Administration*, ed. Jennifer G. Cooke and J. Stephen Morrison. Washington, DC: Centre for Strategic and International Studies, 2009b.

[27] For a skeptical view of the salience of patronage analysis to explain African politics, see Adebayo Olukoshi, "Economic Crisis, Multipartyism, and Opposition Politics in Contemporary Africa," in *The Politics of Opposition in Contemporary Africa*, ed. Adebayo Olukoshi. Nordic Africa Institute, 1998, 15 (noting in part that "many scholars approach the subject [of African reform] with idealized as opposed to dialectical notions/interpretations of 'Western' democracy and then proceed to catalogue how Africa falls short of the ideal. It does not occur to them to first establish if their idealized notions of democracy exist in the West. Invariably, what we get is the kind of unhelpful duality that celebrates 'social capital' in one context and berates broadly similar relations and networks such as 'neo-patrimonialism' and 'rent-seeking in another.")

key to understanding why some of the features of the Madisonian design adopted in the 2010 Constitution has failed to constrain the power of the governing party to serve all Kenyans equally. At the moment, the government is perceived as primarily serving and rewarding those who vote and support it.[28] This is particularly the case in ethnically homogeneous constituencies where the absence of competitive elections focused the minds of voters on whether they had delivered on their promises.[29] Further, because members of Parliament want to be reelected they have incentives to deliver on their promises. The importance of loyalty to political parties and coalitions is underlined by the fact that it is because of such loyalty that leaders get elected. Political party loyalty therefore is a critical source of political power. Once elected, such leaders are often more beholden to their electorate, and therefore to their political parties, than to advancing the national interest or protecting the functionary power of either the legislative or executive branch as contemplated in the Madisonian design of the 2010 Constitution.[30] Thus, when a political party like Jubilee wins both the presidency and the legislature, the result is a strongly unified government in which the separation of powers contemplated in the Madisonian design disappears.[31]

Voters in ethnically homogeneous opposition constituencies who live in opposition strongholds are more likely to remain aligned with the opposition in order to secure victory in Presidential elections. Since they live in areas that the national government is unlikely to devote a lot of national resources to, they have a large incentive to vote for the opposition without breaking their voting patterns as the road toward opposition victory in Presidential elections. Even more so, elections give hope to opposition political parties and their voters of defeating a dominant party. This is particularly so since the formal rules of the 2010 Constitution provide a constitutional basis for free and fair elections, as well as an equal political playing field for all political parties, as I note at greater length in what follows. Thus, since

---

[28] Under the Madisonian design, the assumption is made that when "a majority is included in a faction, the form of popular government … enables it to sacrifice to its ruling passion or interest both the public good and the rights of other citizens," See James Madison, The Federalist No. 10 at 55 (Henry Cabot Lodge ed., New York, G.P. Putnam's Sons, 1889)

[29] Barkan, Joel D. 1976. "Comment: Further Reassessment of 'Conventional Wisdom'. Political Knowledge and Voting Behavior in Rural Kenya." *American Political Science Review*, 70 (02): 452–455.

[30] For an equivalent argument in the United States, see Daryl J. Levinson and Richard H. Pildes, "Separation of Parties, Not Powers." *Harvard Law Review* 119: 2312, 2316 (2006); See also Stanford Levinson and Jack M. Balkin, "Constitutional Crisis." *University of Pennsylvania Law Review* 157: 732–33 (2009) citing Mark Graber, "Dred Scott and the Problem of Constitutional Evil," 35–36 (2006) to the effect that "the fact that the Constitution requires every member of Congress to be elected locally means that political issues that have strongly regional dimensions may become especially hard to resolve; election-seeking politicians have every incentive to focus on the presumptive interests of their constituents and forego any particular concern about a wider national interest," ibid.

[31] Levinson and Pildes, "Separation of Parties," 2348.

2010, although the opposition controls some levers of power, especially in the devolved units, counties, it has not yet defeated the incumbent President, whose regime had been responsible for massive corruption; stifling of civil society; extra-judicial killings, weakening independent institutions, and police brutality, particularly against opposition leaders and their supporters.

Even when elections do not produce electoral victory for the Presidency, it gives opposition voters the opportunity to repeatedly send vocal critics of the government to Parliament to challenge its authoritarianism.[32] The total effect of these voting patterns is to further consolidate ethnic voting patterns and blocs established under one-party rule rather than establish new ones not based on a patronage system and political linkages between the State and constituencies as an avenue for resource distribution from the State. This type of political competition and largely ethnic mobilization has continued to persist notwithstanding the introduction of an extensive constitutional and legislative framework under the 2010 Constitution for party behavior and discipline that discourages patronage and ethnicity-based political mobilization. This continuation demonstrates the prevalence of informal norms of political behavior established under one-party rule, and the continuing difficulty of fully implementing the promises of political party reform.

To insulate itself against electoral defeat, the Jubilee alliance in the 2013 election, and subsequently the Jubilee Party in the 2017 election cycle, sought dominance through political party coalition building prior to each electoral cycle. Ahead of the 2013 general elections, the United Republican Party of Deputy President William Ruto formed an alliance with President Uhuru Kenyatta's National Alliance. The two parties then brought several parties together in an election alliance. Before the 2017 general elections, the United Republican Party and the National Alliance formed the Jubilee Party, together with ten other smaller parties that agreed to dissolve and join the Jubilee Alliance.[33] By cobbling up a large alliance of parties and crushing small parties out of existence, the ruling party has in two election cycles managed to secure comfortable parliamentary majorities. The ruling party was even more successful in the 2017 election cycle than it was in the 2013 election cycle. Unlike in the 2013 election cycle, the incumbent party required the parties

---

[32] In the current Parliament are members like James Orengo, who has been a vocal critic of the government of the day from the one-party era to the present. In the 2017 election, he won his seat by 98 percent of the vote.

[33] There was to be an eleventh party to comprise the Jubilee Party, the Party of National Unity (PNU), which refused to dissolve ahead of the 2017 election. Its leadership however supported the Jubilee Party. The dissolution was not without controversy as evidenced by suits filed in the High Court and before the Political Parties Dispute Tribunal. See for example, *PNU and another* v. *Registrar of Political Parties and 2 others*. Available at www.capitalfm.co.ke/news/2016/09/registrar-political-parties-barred-dissolving-pnu/ and *R* v. *Registrar of Political Parties & 6 others* Exparte Edward Kings Onyancha (Judicial Review Application 47 of 2017). Available at http://kenyalaw.org/caselaw/cases/view/135472/.

within its coalition to fold, dissolve, and become part of the Jubilee Party.[34] This created more electoral success with its 2013 electoral majority in the National Assembly increasing from 47.85 percent to 49.98 percent in 2017, and from 48.75 percent in the 2013 Senate to 50.74 percent in 2017.[35] This increased degree of disproportionality of Parliamentary seats between the dominant and opposition party in Kenya will likely further reduce legislative checks on executive power.

The formation of the Jubilee Party and the dissolution of many smaller parties that are now part of it means that once elected these Members of Parliament would owe their electoral seats and therefore their allegiance to the ruling party. Having no "institutional cover to act as dissenters,"[36] these Members of Parliament would then be easily coopted to the desires and plans of the ruling party. This has meant that numerically weak opposition parties in Kenya are unable to effectively compete against a dominant party with large majorities in Parliament. This is particularly so because politicians, such as those in the opposition, who fall outside the favor of the State do not have access to its resources and cannot therefore become financial providers for their communities. This strategy of dissolving political parties, even those in the opposition, to merge with a dominant political party dates back to the very first few years of independence in Kenya. Within a year of Kenya's independence in 1963, the ruling party, the Kenya African National Union (KANU), merged with the opposition party, the Kenya African Democratic Union. In 2002, well into the era of Kenya's return to multiparty democracy, KANU again merged with the then main opposition party, the National Democratic Party.[37] Thus, a critical informal mechanism that dominant parties have resorted to in Kenya is seeking the merger of numerically smaller political parties to shore up their dominance and to reduce and fizzle out opposition.[38]

---

[34] The High Court has found that it is not unconstitutional for political parties to merge and in turn create political dominance, in the words of the High Court, "It is good practice for Political Parties to merge or form coalitions to attain political strength and dominance and as long as no law prohibits the practise but in fact that the law encourages them, this Court will not interfere with the right," *John Harun Mwau v. The Independent Electoral and Boundaries Commission & another* (2013) eKLR. Available at http://kenyalaw.org/caselaw/cases/view/91940/.

[35] *The Kenya Gazette* Vol. CXIX- No. 121, August 2017. Available at http://kenyalaw.org/kenya_gazette/gazette/volume/MTUoMw–/Vol.CXIX-No.121 and *The Kenya Gazette* Vol. CXIX-No. 123, August 2017. Available at http://kenyalaw.org/kenya_gazette/gazette/volume/MTU1Nw–/Vol.CXIX-No.123.

[36] Kennedy Opalo, "African Elections: Two Divergent Paths." *Journal of Democracy* 23: 85 (2012). For an early critique of the fragmentation of the Madisonian political system adopted in the United States, see James McGregor Burns, The Deadlock of Democracy: Four-Party Politics in America (1963).

[37] For a brief overview of these early mergers, see *Republic v. Registration of Societies & 5 Others* Ex-Parte Uhuru Kenyatta & 6 Others (2007) eKLR. Available at http://kenyalaw.org/caselaw/cases/view/38945/.

[38] Ahead of the 2017 President election, the opposition formed the National Super Alliance, (NASA), a coalition of four main parties that declined to dissolve themselves into one party.

As a result of being outnumbered in Parliament, the CORD opposition alliance that was put together for the 2013 elections pursued extra-parliamentary options to redraw election rules and institutions in preparation for the 2017 election cycle. It is notable that the CORD opposition alliance resorted to using the referenda provisions of the Constitution to redraw election rules and institutions they argued were biased and implemented in favor of the government, rather than using parliamentary processes. CORD's decision to use extra-parliamentary processes to reform election laws and institutions is also demonstrated by its decision, together with civil society groups, to extensively litigate election rules in the judiciary where they hoped to get a fairer hearing than in Parliament ahead of the 2017 elections. Over thirty election disputes were filed against the Independent Boundaries and Election Commission ahead of the 2017 General Election.

The CORD alliance in the 2013 election cycle found these suits necessary because governments, since the enactment of the 2010 Constitution, had figured out ways of evading restrictions on their power: by using its legislative dominance – in Kenya referred to as the tyranny of numbers – to steamroll its agenda as well as to insulate and protect it against allegations of corruption and abuse of office.[39] In short, since the enactment of the 2010 Constitution, the government in power has used its legislative majorities as well as its ability to distribute patronage and state resources to key supporters and constituencies as an insurance mechanism against being held accountable in Parliament. Deprived of such access to resources and patronage, opposition parties in Kenya have therefore not fared as well as the political parties under the control of incumbent governments both in their organizational and institutional development.[40] This choice to use extra-parliamentary processes questions the resilience of the post-2010 constitutional order, particularly the ability of Parliament to act as a check against Executive abuse of power.[41] This pattern of using extra-parliamentary processes continued in the post-2017 election cycle until the NASA leader, Raila Odinga, decided to work with the President's party in early 2018 to resolve questions such as electoral justice within the framework

The main partners of the NASA coalition are the CORD Alliance, which comprises the following parties, The Orange Democratic Movement; the Orange Democratic Movement-Kenya; the Forum for Restoration of Democracy-Kenya; together with the Wiper Democratic Movement-Kenya, Amani National Congress, and Chama Cha Mashinani. Thus, the NASA alliance had affiliate parties that competed among themselves in the election primaries and again in the general elections. The strategy of the Jubilee Party of dissolving parties avoided this intra-alliance competition. Losers in the primaries were promised positions by the President and Deputy President if the Jubilee Party won the election.

[39] James Gathii, "Assessing Kenya's Constitution Five Years Out," in *Measuring Constitutional Performance*, ed. Tom Ginsburg et al. Cambridge University Press, 2016, 337.

[40] Lise Rakner and Nicolas van de Walle, "Opposition Weakness in Africa." *Journal of Democracy* 20: 109 (2009).

[41] Ken Opalo, "Constitutional Amendment through Popular Initiative: Tentative Lessons from the 'Okoa Kenya' Campaign," January 26, 2016. Available at www.constitutionnet.org/news/constitutional-amendment-through-popular-initiative-tentative-lessons-okoa-kenya-campaign.

created by the 2010 Constitution.[42] Jubilee leadership could have decided to build
bridges with the opposition in March 2018 and abandon their stance against
negotiating reform, because the extra-constitutional processes the opposition was
engaging in such as economic boycotts and street protests were obstructive to
domestic capital accumulation of the Jubilee elite.

To reform the party system, significant changes were introduced by the 2010 Constitution protecting the rights of opposition political parties, requiring political
parties to have a national character[43] and not to engage in violence by, or intimidation of, their members, supporters, opponents, or anyone else. Bribery or corruption
by political parties is also prohibited and they are required not to accept and use
public resources, including public servants, to promote their interest or those of their
candidates in elections. However, Kenya still lacks an institutionalized political party
system in which voters' choices are predominantly based on the policies of the
parties in the election, rather than their appeals that if they do not vote for them,
they will be shut out from access to state resources and the resulting patronage
opportunities.[44] Many of the prohibitions on political party conduct such as bribery
and ethnic mobilization during the elections were openly violated, in the run-up to
both the 2013 and 2017 elections.[45]

Another factor that has weakened opposition political party ability to successfully
contest Presidential power is the rise of independent candidates. The rise of independent candidates in Kenya, particularly in the 2017 General Election, is related to
legislative reforms supported by the incumbent government and its control of
Parliament, requiring candidates who lost in the political party nominations or
primaries not to switch political parties thereafter. Sold as a reform to introduce
party discipline, the effect of this rule in a system with a dominant political party has
been to reduce the discretion of political parties (particularly weaker ones) over
candidate selection.[46] This is because candidates who lost in the primaries overwhelmingly decide to run as independent candidates instead of remaining to

[42] These strategies include the formation of a Peoples' Assembly in Kenya to challenge President
Uhuru's election victory in the repeat Presidential election of October 2017. NASA is pursuing
this strategy through passage of a resolution in support of the Assembly in the County
legislatures in which it has a majority of members. See www.nation.co.ke/news/Nasa-crafts-
People-s-Assembly-motion-as-it-protests-Uhuru-win/1056-4176992-snlsp4z/index.html. Notably,
NASA controls eighteen of forty-seven County Assemblies. Jubilee controls twenty-five County
Assemblies, see www.theeastafrican.co.ke/news/Kenya-ruling-party-to-finally-control-Nairobi-
county-/2558-4055012-q5xevf/index.html.
[43] The 2010 Constitution also proscribed political parties established on the basis of religion,
language, race, ethnicity, gender, or region or promoting hatred on any of these grounds.
[44] Of course, I am not suggesting that voter choices are exclusively defined by narrow ethnic
considerations.
[45] Yash Ghai, "Our Elections Are a Massive Violation of the Constitution," *The Star*, June 2017.
Available at www.the-star.co.ke/news/2017/06/17/our-elections-are-a-massive-violation-of-the-
constitution_c1580060.
[46] Rakner and van de Walle, "Opposition Weakness," 111.

strengthen the party that sponsored their initial primary run. Once elected, independent candidates are very likely to caucus or strike a deal with the dominant party in Parliament, from which they are likely to receive goodies and benefits in return for their support, further weakening opposition party strength in Parliament.[47]

Thus, although the 2010 Constitution largely de-concentrated Presidential power, there has been a re-accretion of this power through legislative dominance. In other words, although the President no longer enjoys exclusive authority to exercise important powers such as the appointment of State officers, because this is now subject to legislative approval, having a legislative majority assures the President's preferences prevail. Elections are therefore a significant opportunity for a Kenyan President to acquire a comfortable Parliamentary majority as an insurance mechanism against being held accountable by an effective opposition.

Weakened legislative checks on Executive power will likely allow a continuation of authoritarian governance in the country. This is precisely why elections in Kenya have come to be regarded as the best chance to tilt governance not only in a more democratic direction but also in a direction acceptable by half the country that has never produced a President nor benefitted in the same way as the other half of the country from the largesse of the State. As a leading critic of the dominant party argued recently:

> Elections in Kenya are always about the sense of exclusion for many communities; the reality of marginalisation including of those in dire poverty, and about moving towards a nation-state from diverse tribal communities. This was not and is not about Raila Odinga. Mr Odinga is simply, at the moment, the symbol of that exclusion, that marginalisation and the desire of many tribes for recognition and respect.[48]

From this perspective, the promises of the 2010 Constitution have not resulted in inclusive governance, particularly in the manner in which national resources are shared. On electoral matters in particular, the values of the 2010 Constitution that encourage consultation, negotiation, and compromise have not changed the dominant party's willingness to run roughshod over the opposition.[49] The Constitution, on this account, has not been an agent of transformation. Rather, it has been an instrument of continuation and entrenchment of the control of the Kenyan state by

[47] Rakner and van de Walle, "Opposition Weakness," 112 (discussing the example of Malawi).
[48] Maina Kiai, "For How Long Will the Kenyans Seeking Inclusion Have to Wait?" *Daily Nation*, August 18, 2017. Available at http://mobile.nation.co.ke/blogs/Kenyans-seeking-inclusion-have-to-wait/1949942-4062454-item-1-10k6j28/index.html.
[49] For example, the opposition unsuccessfully argued in the courts that they had a right to be consulted by the Independent Electoral and Boundaries Commission before it entered into a contract to procure the firm that printed ballot papers, see *Independent Electoral and Boundaries Commission (IEBC) v. National Super Alliance(NASA) Kenya & 6 others* (2017) eKLR. http://kenyalaw.org/caselaw/cases/view/138741/

an alliance dominated by two ethnic groups.[50] Two ethnic groups, the Kikuyu and the Kalenjin, are the only ones among Kenya's forty-seven ethnic groups that have produced a President since Kenya's independence since 1963. Uhuru Kenyatta's victory in the repeat Presidential election of October 2017 made it unlikely that a President will be elected from outside the Kikuyu/Kalenjin alliance in the near future. This is because it is not a secret that the Jubilee Party will in 2022 more likely than not nominate Deputy President William Ruto for the Presidency. If this happens, and the opposition does not find a viable path to victory, that would lock in a Kikuyu–Kalenjin alliance over control of state resources, something the opposition centered on the Luo–Kamba–Luhya ethnic alliance would be shut out from in the foreseeable future.[51]

There is frustration in a large part of the country that supports the opposition that there is no balanced field to pursue the Presidency in the foreseeable future. It seems that in a low-income country with 42 percent of its 44 million population living below the poverty line,[52] consolidating democracy under a Constitution faces particular difficulties when elections do not promise an opposition party representing the aspirations of half of the population that their party leader would be elected President. That is why, toward the end of 2017, threats of secession became a new focal point for the opposition to highlight and contest their exclusion.[53]

The high rates of regional inequalities, which largely show Jubilee Party regions as wealthier and opposition regions as poorer, in large part account for one of the major campaign strategies adopted by the opposition in the 2017 election. By appealing to voters by emphasizing class and ethnic differences and making appeals of economic nationalism – in fact dubbing the election as the *unga* (maize meal, a staple Kenyan food) revolution, opposition politicians sought to convince their supporters that by voting for them there was a real possibility of reversing how national resources are shared. Class, ethnic, and nationalist appeals were also successfully made by weak political parties in Zambia by Michael Sata's Patriotic Front and in Gambia by Laurent Gbabgo's Ivorian Popular Front to unseat incumbents.[54] Such appeals compensate for the weaknesses that opposition parties in Africa face.[55] As noted previously, after boycotting the 2017 repeat Presidential

---

[50] Makau Mutua, *Kenya's Quest for Democracy: Taming Leviathan*. Boulder, CO: Lynne Rienner Publishers, 2008.

[51] Julius Sigei, "Uhuru Win Puts Ruto Firmly on State House Succession Path," *Daily Nation*, August 13, 2017. Available at www.nation.co.ke/news/politics/Uhuru-win-Ruto-State-House-path/1064-4055126-ssgelu/index.html.

[52] UNICEF, "Kenya at a Glance." Available at www.unicef.org/kenya/overview_4616.html. Kenya had over USD 76 Billion GDP in 2016 and has had over 5 percent GDP growth in each of the last two years.

[53] Nic Cheeseman, "Five Things We Learnt about Democracy in Africa," *Daily Nation*, December 27, 2017. Available at www.nation.co.ke/oped/opinion/Five-things-we-learnt-about-democracy-in-Africa-in-2017/440808-4242566-124y9p7z/index.html.

[54] Rakner and van de Walle, "Opposition Weakness," 118.

[55] Ibid. 118.

election, some in the opposition announced a plan to lead a secessionist movement to carve out a new country constituted by opposition strongholds that did not recognize President Uhuru's electoral victory.[56]

Ultimately, the Kenyan experience shows that even when formal Presidential powers are clipped, and greater horizontal and vertical accountability mechanisms are put in place, legislative dominance does not necessarily guarantee the elimination of patron–client politics and even prebendal politics.[57] In this system, Parliament has become the new locus of influence peddling and insulating the Executive from being accountable. Access to state resources, and a national administrative structure to support its campaigns and the organization and mobilization required, gave Uhuru Kenyatta's party Jubilee Coalition in 2013 and Jubilee Party in 2017 a huge advantage over the opposition.[58] For example, following post-election violence in 2013, the Kenyatta government engaged in uneven accountability for post-election violence perpetrators. In other words, "the government negatively sanction[ed] officers who perpetuated violence that harmed the government while rewarding officers who perpetuated violence that was in support of the government's political interests."[59] By engaging in such politicized bureaucratic management of institutions of accountability such as the police, the government has been able to build a loyal police service to serve its interests into the future. This loyalty results from the politicization of rewarding police officers who engage in violence against opposition supporters while punishing those who engage in election violence

---

[56] Rogers Omondi, NASA Leaders Begin Process to Divide Kenya, November 3, 2017. Available at www.kenyans.co.ke/news/24304-nasa-leaders-begin-process-divide-kenya. That plan was put on the backburner after President Uhuru Kenyatta and opposition leader Raila Odinga agreed to work together in early 2018.

[57] N. Van de Walle, "'Meet the New Boss, Same as the Old Boss?' The Evolution of Political Clientelism in Africa" in *Patrons, Clients and Policies: Patterns of Democratic Accountability and Political Competition.* Cambridge University Press, 2003 (defining patronage as "the use of state resources to provide jobs and services to political clienteles" and prebends as "where an individual is given a public office in order for them to gain personal control over state resources."

[58] From this perspective, it becomes clear why President Uhuru Kenyatta opposed the abolition of what was formerly the Provincial administrative system controlled from the center as the 2010 Constitution's mandate of establishing forty-seven independent counties began being rolled out.

[59] Mai Hassan and Thomas O'Mealia, "Uneven Accountability in the wake of Political Violence: Evidence from Kenya's Ashes and Archives." Available at https://sites.lsa.umich.edu/maihassan/wp-content/uploads/sites/412/2016/10/unevenaccountability.pdf. As the authors further explain, "Bureaucratic chiefs whose jurisdictions saw violence against the government's co-ethnic Kikuyus were more likely to be fired from their positions than other chiefs within the same district whose jurisdiction did not see violence. But we find the exact opposite result in areas hit by violence that favored the government: chiefs whose jurisdictions saw Kikuyu-instigated violence against opposition supporters were far less likely to be fired in comparison to other chiefs within the same district whose jurisdiction did not see violence. Our results indicate that the government only viewed officers who misused their authority in service of the opposition, as opposed to all officer who misused their authority, as disloyal, dangerous agents that had to be dismissed," 3.

against government supporters. Bureaucratic management not only of the police force but also the former provincial administrative structures that the government retained even with the establishment of a devolved system of government under the 2010 Constitution is a pervasive feature of how the central government has historically controlled far-flung areas around the country.[60] These officials engage in all sorts of behavior sanctioned by or acquiesced to by the government, including "beating local opposition supporters or preventing them from registering to vote, denying rally permits to opposition candidates."[61] Further, intimidation of low-level government officials perceived to be aligned with the opposition was conducted openly in public meetings by the incumbent President in the 2017 August Presidential cycle.[62] The government also engaged in providing public resources to its strongholds, swing voting areas, and some opposition strongholds in what the opposition termed as bribery.[63] Even after the August 2017 Presidential election was nullified by the Supreme Court, the Jubilee government continued using state resources to publicize its achievements ahead of the repeat election until the High Court intervened.[64] By manipulating bureaucratic processes, the Jubilee coalition has prevented the emergence of an impartial and professional bureaucracy that may be used against it in future should the opposition win an election.

Dominant political parties can therefore more effectively compete for votes than opposition political parties who do not have established access to such organizational and mobilization capabilities or the authority to politicize bureaucratic processes such as rewarding or punishing state officials depending on the roles they play during elections. This in turn undermines the incentives these officials have to exercise their authority fairly and, more importantly, consistently with the Constitution and laws.[65] Instead, these officials exercise their discretion largely in favor of

---

[60] See Cherry Gertzel, *The Politics of Independent Kenya 1963–8*, at page 29 (1970) arguing that "[a]lthough the party machinery could not be used to enhance governmental control and ensure acquiescence in the Government's decisions, the existing civil service machinery could. The bureaucracy was well established, and it was responsible to the Executive. In the case of the Provincial Administration, it offered the government a superb machine that provided a direct chain of command and control from the centre down to the sub-location: it was the centralizing agency that the new Executive needed."

[61] Hassan and O'Mealia, 4.

[62] Elections 2017. President Uhuru Kenyatta Warns Chiefs against Campaigning for the Opposition NASA. *Standard Digital.* August 2017. Available at www.standardmedia.co.ke/elec tions2017/video/2000134788/president-uhuru-kenyatta-warns-chiefs-against-campaigning-for-the-opposition-nasa.

[63] Use of public resources in campaigns is prohibited by Section 14 of the Kenyan Election Offences Act.

[64] Sam Kiplagat. "High Court Stops #GoKDelivers and #JubileeDelivers Adverts." *Daily Nation.* October 2, 2017. Available at www.nation.co.ke/news/High-Court-stops-GoKDelivers-and-Jubi leeDelivers-ads/1056-4121086-tp3c2gz/index.html.

[65] The 2010 Constitution with regard to responsibilities of public officers provides at Article 73(2) (b) that officers should make decisions with "objectivity and impartiality" and should ensure "that decisions are not influenced by nepotism, favouritism, other improper motives or corrupt

government voters and against opposition voters. For this reason, a major claim the opposition made in challenging the 2017 Presidential Election was precisely this abuse and misuse of state resources and state officers, and the growing fusion between the apparatuses of the central government controlled by the Executive, on the one hand, and Parliament, on the other. This fusion in turn means that Parliament adopts the priorities of the ruling party with the consequence that those who did not vote for the ruling party would have no faith in a government that does not take into account the opposition's priorities. Indeed, after the August 2017 General Election, the President is reported to have told Jubilee Party politicians in a Parliamentary Group meeting that he would brook no opposition to his agenda in Parliament. To make his point, he, without consultation of the Parliamentary Group, handpicked the lineup of Parliamentary leadership, which rewarded his most loyal supporters in the previous Parliament and during the campaign[66] while dropping from the lineup the speaker of the previous Senate, who had not fully supported the dominant party's agenda in the previous Parliament or during the campaigns.[67]

It is against the foregoing backdrop that a ruling party, such as Kenya's Jubilee Party, acquires additional power and authority that without checks, such as by independent civil society organizations and opposition parties, becomes the backwater against which its corruption and authoritarianism thrives. The Jubilee Party's clampdown on civil society organizations, including concerted efforts to close them down; intimidation of opposition politicians; the harassment of independent journalists including threatened passage of media restrictive laws; political violence meted against those opposed to the dominant party; and criticism of the judges who make decisions inimical to its interests, are a hallmark of its authoritarian traits. These interventions in the political and electoral environment amount to authoritarian manipulation that influences electoral outcomes alongside popular preferences. If these authoritarian tendencies continue to grow, they are likely to further endanger accountability through competitive democratic elections as well as through horizontal accountability mechanisms such as those in parliament. Ultimately, the promises of strong horizontal accountability mechanisms embodied in the 2010 Constitution will likely be undermined by a Parliament that can hardly be a check on an authoritarian Executive.

---

practices." This provision is part of chapter 6 of the 2010 Constitution, which provides extensive provisions on leadership and integrity.

[66] Wanjohi Githae, "Jubilee Pointmen Lusaka and Teju Set for Key Posts," *Daily Nation*, August 31, 2017. Available at http://mobile.nation.co.ke/news/politics/Tuju–Lusaka-set-for-prime-Jubilee-posts-/3126390-4077542-item-1-0tfr9oz/index.html.

[67] Moses Njagih and Moses Nyamari, "Kenneth Lusaka Favored in Place of Former Senate Speaker Ekwe Ethuro," *Standard Digital*, August 31, 2017. Available at www.standardmedia.co.ke/article/2001253097/kenneth-lusaka-favoured-in-place-of-former-senate-speaker-ekwe-ethuro.

9.3 TESTING THE RESILIENCY OF THE JUDICIARY:
ELECTION DISPUTE RESOLUTION

In the 2007 Presidential election, Raila Odinga urged his supporters to engage in mass action to protest what he believed was a stolen election. Over 1,000 were killed in the violence. It was that violence that set the stage for the enactment of the 2010 Constitution. In the closely contested 2013 Presidential election, the first under the 2010 Constitution, Raila Odinga lost the election by less than a percentage point. He opted to challenge the result in the Supreme Court as required by the 2010 Constitution. Raila Odinga argued that he lost that election unfairly. The Supreme Court declined to accept a 900-page affidavit because it was filed out of time. The rejection of this affidavit on a technicality was seen as unwillingness on the part of the Supreme Court to disrupt the country's stability, which would likely have resulted from nullifying what the opposition argued was a rigged election.[68] In the 2013 Petition, the Supreme Court also overwhelmingly sided with President Uhuru Kenyatta's lawyers on a broad variety of interlocutory applications that Raila Odinga's lawyers filed during the course of the case.[69]

In yet another example of a judiciary hesitant to take the country through electoral uncertainty prior to the 2017 Presidential election, the Court of Appeal reversed a three-judge High Court decision that had ordered Kenya's electoral body to stop the printing of Presidential ballot papers because there had been a constitutional violation.[70] In reversing the High Court decision, the Court of Appeal signaled that the uncertainty that would have been created by postponing the Presidential election was unwarranted. These two decisions signaled to the opposition that the Judiciary was too timid to nullify a Presidential election. Therefore, the opposition's initial hesitancy in resorting to the Judiciary to challenge the August 2017 election result was informed by their past experience.[71] After the August 2017

---

[68] For an excellent analysis, see John Harrington and Ambreena Manji, "Restoring the Leviathan? The Kenyan Supreme Court, Constitutional Transformation and the Presidential Election of 2013." *Journal of Eastern African Studies* 9 (2): 175–92, 2015.

[69] Notably, a new Chief Justice was appointed a couple of years after 2013 Presidential Petition. That new Chief Justice, David Maraga, soon after his appointment met with the 2013 Petitioner (who also became the 2017 Petitioner) to reassure him and other opposition politicians that the Judiciary was ready to determine any election disputes arising from the 2017 General Election fairly. Sam Kiplagat and Patrick Lang'at, "All eyes on CJ David Maraga as Raila Odinga Files Petition." *Daily Nation.* August 18, 2017. Available at www.nation.co.ke/news/CJ-David-Maraga-Kenya-presidential-election-petition/1056-4061974-lbgcatz/index.html.

[70] *Independent Electoral and Boundaries Commission (IEBC) v. National Super Alliance (NASA) Kenya.* Available at http://kenyalaw.org/caselaw/cases/view/138741/ .

[71] John Aglion, "Raila Odinga Calls for UN Analysis of Kenya Presidential Election," *Financial Times,* August 13, 2017. Available at www.ft.com/content/69643ee0-8013-11e7-a4ce-15b2513cb3ff. See also Raila's call on his supporters to boycott going to work on Monday August 14, 2017, *Daily Nation,* "Most Workers Defy Raila Call for Job Boycott." August 14, 2017. Available at www.nation.co.ke/news/politics/Raila-tells-supporters-to-boycott-work-/1064-4056328-nvalcd/index.html and Ibrahim Oruko and Bernard Namunane, "Raila Odinga Mulls

elections, church, business leaders, and many election observers from within and outside Africa also encouraged the opposition NASA alliance to avoid using extra-judicial alternatives such as street protests to contest the election outcome. The NASA opposition eventually agreed to turn to the Courts to challenge the outcome of the August 2017 Presidential election.[72]

In an unprecedented decision, the Supreme Court nullified the 2017 electoral victory of Uhuru Kenyatta's Jubilee Party.[73] The Supreme Court held that the illegalities and irregularities that characterized the Presidential campaign failed to meet the 2010 Constitutional requirements of an election being conducted and administered in a transparent and impartial manner that ensured that the results were accurate and verifiable. The Supreme Court in particular found that the Independent and Electoral Boundaries Commission bangled the electronic trans-mission of the results inconsistently with electoral law.

For the opposition, the nullification renewed confidence in the Judiciary as a viable institution for resolving political disputes that were only otherwise resolvable through other means, such as street protests and picketing, with likely violent outcomes as protestors and picketers, on the one hand, and police, on the other, confront each other on the streets, in neighborhoods, and elsewhere.

However, for the Jubilee Party, the nullification of the election was seen as a judicial coup if not judicial dictatorship.[74] The President referred to judges of the Supreme Court as *wakoras* (crooks or fraudsters).[75] Thus, although the President and Deputy President accepted the nullification of the election,[76] they harshly criticized the judges of the Supreme Court and promised to dress down the judges and reduce the power of the Supreme Court once the repeat election is over.[77]

Next Move After Election Loss," *Daily Nation*, August 14, 2017. Available at www.nation.co.ke/news/Raila-Odinga-Kenya-election-next-move/1056-4056772-15j6h9kz/index.html.

[72] Samwel Owini and Harry Misiko, "See You in Court, Raila Odinga Tells Uhuru Kenyatta." *Daily Nation*, August 16, 2017. Available at www.nation.co.ke/news/Raila-Odingas-Decision-Kenya-Elections-Nasa/1056-4059748-9a5j61/index.html.

[73] *Raila Amolo Odinga & another* v. *Independent Electoral and Boundaries Commission & 2 others* [2017] eKLR. Available at http://kenyalaw.org/caselaw/cases/view/140716/. For detailed analysis of the nullification, see James Gathii, "Explaining the Nullification of the August 2017 Kenyan Presidential Election," forthcoming 2020.

[74] Ibrahim Oruko, "Uhuru Terms Supreme Court Decision as 'coup' by 4 Judges." *Daily Nation*, 2017. Available at www.nation.co.ke/news/Uhuru-terms-ruling-as-coup-judges/1056-4106026-ex7sypz/index.html.

[75] Michael Chege, "Kenya's Electoral Misfire." *Journal of Democracy* 29: 168 (2018).

[76] President Uhuru Kenyatta, Statement on the Supreme Court decision (September 1, 2017), transcript available at www.president.go.ke/2017/09/01/transcript-of-president-uhuru-kenyattas-statement-on-the-supreme-courtdecision/.

[77] BBC News, "Kenya Election: Kenyatta Blasts Court After Vote Annulled." September 1, 2017. Available at www.bbc.com/news/world-africa-41132559 (President states that the government is "keeping an eye" on judges); Maggie Fick and George Obulutsa, "Kenyan Court Scraps Presidential Vote, Kenyatta Calls for Calm, REUTERS." September 1, 2017. Available at www.reuters.com/article/us-kenya-election-court/kenyan-courtscraps-presidential-vote-kenyatta-

By the Fall of 2018, the Jubilee government's threats to dress down the Judiciary came to fruition when a significant portion of the Judiciary's funds in the national budget were slashed.

Notwithstanding these skirmishes between the Judiciary and the Executive, the decision to accept the nullification on the part of President Uhuru Kenyatta was in part because he urged Raila Odinga to take his complaints about the Presidential election to the Supreme Court. Hence, both the Jubilee Party and the NASA coalition ultimately accepted the Supreme Court as the arbiter of disputes surrounding the Presidential election. A lot of informal leverage was put on Raila Odinga by foreign governments, election observers particularly from the United States and the European Union, as well as those within his own coalition who wanted to go to Court, rather than engage in street protests.[78] The eventual decision to use the judicial process served the opposition's goal of exposing how the informal norms of dominant political party control subverted the conduct of a free and fair election. The election Petition laid bare for all to see how the patronage system of the State had been deployed to support the incumbent party in all aspects of the election from voter registration to the campaigns, to the transmission of the results, as well as with regard to the tallying of the votes. The petition also exposed how state resources were mobilized to campaign for the incumbent party; and how this conduct was inimical to the requirements of conducting a free and fair election under the 2010 Constitution.

Following the electoral loss, the NASA opposition coalition exhibited strong independence particularly from international pressures by rejecting their appeal to concede the election and to move on. This included pressure from former US Secretary of State John Kerry, who led the Carter Center's Election observation team, the Secretary General of the United Nations,[79] a group of Western Ambassadors in Kenya, editorials of the largest circulating daily in Kenya,[80] as well as in the *Washington Post*[81] and the *New York*

calls-for-calm-idUSKCN1BC4A5 (President states that Chief Justice should "know he is dealing with the incumbent president").

[78] Samwel Owino and Harry Misiko, "NASA Gives into Pressure over Election Petition Case." *Daily Nation.* August 18, 2017. Available at www.nation.co.ke/news/Splits–observers-pushed-Nasa-to-seek-legal-redress/1056-4061638-ugekvaz/index.html.

[79] Kevin Kelley, "U.N Skirts Raila Odinga's Vote Analysis Call." *Daily Nation*, August 16, 2017. Available at www.nation.co.ke/news/UN-Audit-Kenya-Elections-Raila-Odinga/1056-4058540-u39xwm/index.html.

[80] Macharia Gaitho, "Raila Has an Opportunity to Prove Election Rigging Claims." *Daily Nation.* August 14, 2017. Available at www.nation.co.ke/oped/Opinion/Raila-has-an-opportunity-to-prove-election-rigging-claims/440808-4057580-14gkephz/index.html.

[81] *Washington Post*, "Kenya May Have Had Its Fairest Election Yet. The Winner Shouldn't Tarnish It." August 14, 2017. Available at www.washingtonpost.com/opinions/global-opinions/kenya-may-have-had-its-fairest-election-yet-the-winner-shouldnt-tarnish-it/2017/08/14/505bbdbe-8113-11e7-902a-2a9f2d808496_story.html?utm_term=.933067298843.

Times.[82] There were also reports from election observer teams, including local groups like ELOG,[83] sub-regional ones like EAC,[84] COMESA,[85] and IGAD.[86] Further, there were reports from regional groups like the African Union[87] as well as international observers, including the European Union. Kofi Annan, who led the peacemaking process following the post-election violence in 2008, also praised the election results of the 2017 Presidential Election.[88] In the country, there were vigorous calls by church, businesses, and others for opposition politicians to resort to the "legal process," the "rule of law," and the process laid down by the 2010 Constitution to resolve their dispute about the 2017 Presidential election. This is an important point – that even though Kenya has a dominant political party system, the opposition – at least for the first three months after the repeat presidential election of October 2017, refused to play a role opposition parties in some countries play – that of stabilizing, system-legitimizing, and system maintenance of the dominant party system.[89]

In a demonstration of its resilience as a political party, NASA rejected the findings of these election-monitoring groups and pointed out how the political foundations of the ruling party's incumbency allowed it to influence the election outcome.[90]

[82] "The Real Suspense in Kenya." *New York Times*, August 13, 2017. Available at www.nytimes .com/2017/08/13/opinion/the-real-suspense-in-kenya.html.

[83] Reuters, "Kenya's Poll Monitors Back Official Election Results." August 11, 2017. Available at www.reuters.com/article/us-kenya-election-idUSKBN1AR0SK?il=0.

[84] Edward Rugumayo, Preliminary Statement of the East African Community Election Observer Mission to the 8 August 2017 General Elections in the Republic of Kenya. August 10, 2017. Available at http://eac.int/news-and-media/statements/20170810/east-african-community-elec tion-observer-mission-8-august-2017-general-elections-republic-kenya.

[85] "COMESA lauds Kenya Polls." August 10, 2017. Available at www.comesa.int/comesa-lauds-kenya-for-conducting-peaceful-elections/.

[86] H. E. Hailemariam Desalegn, Statement on the general elections in Kenya. IGAD. August 19, 2017. Available at www.igad.int/press-release/1622-statement-on-the-general-elections-in-kenya-from-the-igad-chair-person.

[87] African Union, Preliminary statement African Union election Observer Mission to the 2017 General Elections in Kenya. August 10, 2017. Available at https://au.int/en/pressreleases/ 20170810/preliminary-statement-african-union-election-observer-mission-2017-general.

[88] Jennifer Anyango, "Former U.N Secretary General Congratulates Uhuru Kenyatta on His Re-Election." *Standard Digital*. August 10, 2017. Available at www.standardmedia.co.ke/article/ 2001251292/kofi-annan-congratulates-uhuru. According to James Orengo, then Senator Elect, speaking for NASA, "Going to the Supreme Court is not an option for us. We have been there and we have been disappointed. The judgement is now out there, in the court of public opinion. I can you, Kenyans always rise up," see Oruko and Namunane, n. 71. Available at www.nation.co.ke/news/Raila-Odinga-Kenya-election-next-move/1056-4056772-15j6h9kz/index .html.

[89] N. L. De Jager, Voice and Accountability in One Party Dominant Systems: A Comparative Case Study of Mexico and South Africa, Doctoral Thesis, University of Pretoria (2009). Available at http://repository.up.ac.za/handle/2263/24736.

[90] Samwel Owino, "NASA Faults Observers for Giving Polls Clean Bill of Health." *Daily Nation.*" August 14, 2017. Available at www.nation.co.ke/news/politics/Nasa-faults-election-observers/1064-4056296-66383lz/index.html.

NASA has also advised its supporters not to tune in to some of the Television broadcasting stations in the country because they had been muzzled, much like the institutions in the country, in a manner that disabled them from fairly reporting on NASA's grievances arising from the 2017 election.[91] The intense internal and external pressure for the opposition to accept the results of the election was justified to avoid a repeat of the post-election violence in early 2008. The potential consequences of mass action or street protests were regarded as likely to be violent and to result in death and destruction. This therefore spurred these extensive calls for the opposition to resort to the processes and institutions laid down in the 2010 Constitution to resolve their Presidential election grievances.

Further, the opposition resisted calls to participate in the repeat Presidential election in October 2010 until all their demands to ensure a free and fair election were met.[92] By refusing to easily acquiesce to such pressure, the opposition did not want to easily give up the opportunity that elections gave it and its supporters – the opportunity to engage in collective protest against a dominant party. In this sense, elections have become a focal point for the opposition to air their grievances, to question the democratic legitimacy and credentials of the dominant party, and even to expose how the dominant party has or may have stolen an election. Scholars have studied how electoral losses resulting from stolen elections become a focal point for coordinating and mobilizing outraged citizens motivated to engage in mass protests against the robbing of their votes, leaving an authoritarian state with at least three choices: first, surrender power, second, crack down on the opposition,[93] or third, disregard the election results and lose power.[94]

The fact that the decision to resort to a judicial process to address their electoral grievances took several days to be made, and was in fact initially rejected, demonstrates the difficulties in building confidence in constitutional processes and institutions. It also reveals the difficulty an opposition that believes an election was stolen yet again has in abandoning protest movements against the electoral outcome. The nullification of the August 2017 Presidential election by the Supreme Court can therefore be regarded as an effort to shore up the credibility of the Judiciary, not

---

[91] Larry Madowo, "#FRONTROW: How I Became the Subject of Another Viral Fake News." *Daily Nation.* August 15, 2017. Available at http://mobile.nation.co.ke/lifestyle/-the-subject-of-another-viral-fake-news/1950774-4058268-item-1-mn9wtoz/index.html.

[92] Rawlings Otieno, "NASA Leader Raila Odinga Declares No Election if Demands Are Not Met." Read more at: www.standardmedia.co.ke/article/2001254356/nasa-leader-raila-odinga-declares-no-election-if-demands-are-not-met," *Standard,* September 13, 2017. Available at www.standardmedia.co.ke/article/2001254356/nasa-leader-raila-odinga-declares-no-election-if-demands-are-not-met.

[93] Andreas Schedler, "The Nested Game of Democratization by Elections." *International Political Science Review* 23: 29–46 (2002).

[94] Mark R. Thompson and Philipp Kuntz, "Stolen Elections: The Case of the Serbian October." *Journal of Democracy* 15: 159–72 (2004) (noting that "A social movement emerging in the wake of a stolen election may be powerful enough to enforce the outcome denied to the people through the ballot box," 161.

merely by demonstrating its independence from the political branches but also winning the acceptance of those in the opposition.

Further, prior to the 2017 election when cases were brought before the Courts in what was a very conflictive electoral environment between a dominant and an opposition party, judges were caught in the crosshairs between the dominant and opposition party as they harangued over the rules of the election. Politicians heavily criticized individual judges in what they perceived were biased decisions.[95] The President criticized the Judiciary in one important case relating to the alleged unconstitutional procurement of ballots for the 2017 Presidential election. Politicians in the government's party made personal attacks on one of the High Court judges, linking his decision perceived to be in favor of the opposition to his marriage to an opposition politician's family.[96] The opposition fared no better when they lost any of the election-related cases they brought ahead of the 2017 election. As a result, judges who had the slightest potential for conflicts arising when they were appointed to a bench dealing with the election cases began recusing themselves from such appointments.[97] Clearly, the criticism the judges suffered had a chilling effect on their willingness to serve in politically charged election-related cases.

9.3.1 *Contests over the Rules of the Election Game*

The Kenyan opposition has not been satisfied with the mere holding of regular multi-party elections even when they did win votes and seats. In addition to participating in each election cycle, the opposition has sought to challenge non-democratic access to power by the dominant political party. They have done so by contesting the lopsided election environment ahead of each electoral cycle because the dominant party has manipulated it to its advantage. Demands for reforms ahead of elections seek to reduce, if not blunt, dominant party manipulation of levers of government to determine the outcome of elections in its favor.[98] Thus we see in

---

[95] *Daily Nation*, "Independence of the Judiciary Cardinal." August 3, 2017. Available at http://mobile.nation.co.ke/blogs/editorial/Independence-of-Judiciary-cardinal-/3112610-4042696-item-1-jm3fx3/index.html and James Aggrey Mwamu, "Leaders Must Not Destroy Judiciary." *Daily Nation*. August 15, 2017. Available at www.nation.co.ke/oped/Opinion/Leaders-must-not-destroy-Judiciary-/440808-4058606-xgr11ukz/index.html.

[96] Andrew Langat, "Jubilee Asks CJ to Drop Justice Odunga from All Poll Cases," *Daily Nation*. August 2, 2016. Available at www.nation.co.ke/news/politics/Jubilee-asks-CJ-to-drop-Justice-Odunga-from-poll-cases-/1064-4041380-15gx6tiz/index.html.

[97] Kamau Muthoni, "Too Hot to Handle? More Judges Quit NASA Suit." *Standard Digital*. August 3, 2017. Available at www.standardmedia.co.ke/article/2001250164/too-hot-to-handle-more-judges-quit-nasa-suit.

[98] Thus, in authoritarian elections, political competition does not occur in an established legal and institutional framework agreed by all parties, but rather an environment that the competing players try to define and redefine to their advantage. George Tsebelis, *Nested Games: Rational Choice in Comparative Politics* (1990) calls these "nested games," in which there is strategic interaction within rules occurring alongside a strategic competition over rules.

every electoral cycle since 1992 the continuity of struggles for reform led by the opposition seeking to unseat an incumbent government, and manipulation of the electoral environment by the incumbent regime.

The run-up to the 2017 Presidential election was also characterized by charges by the opposition that the dominant party intended to use the military to rig the elections. The opposition succeeded in getting assurances from the government that it had no such plans. Major institutional and legislative changes were also undertaken prior to the 2017 Presidential elections to ensure free and fair elections. These changes included the removal of the Commissioners of the Independent and Electoral Boundaries Commission prior to the end of their constitutional terms of office. In addition, over thirty cases litigated a variety of election disputes. These cases culminated in a Court of Appeal decision on the finality of Presidential election results at the constituency level only a couple of days prior to what was seen as a two-horse race between the incumbent President and his challenger Raila Odinga in the August 2017 Presidential elections.[99] By litigating a broad variety of legal provisions relating to the elections, the opposition has engaged in a competitive struggle over the rules of the election.

This struggle of the rules that govern elections reflects the reality that systematic election fraud characterized Kenyan elections even before the inauguration of multi-party democracy in 1991. It is therefore hardly surprising that the opposition in a dominant-party system was interested in ensuring that the rules of the game prevent the conduct of a free and fair election. Opposition parties that face dominant ones like the Jubilee Party seek to strengthen the formal rules of political competition enshrined in large part to deal with the informal sources of incumbent power. This is because informal norms of incumbent party behavior undermine rather than uphold the formal rules of the Constitution. In light of this repeated cycle of promoting or preventing more democratic outcomes, institutions and rules, including those contained in Constitutions, "do not represent stable equilibria, but temporary truces."[100]

9.4 CONCLUSION

The 2010 Constitution of Kenya and the legislative framework that was rolled out to implement it resulted in a weakened presidential system in the Madisonian separation of power system, the contested and uneven but continuing empowerment of the judiciary, as well as a growing regional system of governance. A new legal and institutional framework to discipline political parties so that they can focus on

---

[99] *Independent Electoral & Boundaries Commission v. Maina Kiai, Khelef Khalifa, Tirop Kitur, Attorney-General, Katiba Institute & Coalition for Reforms & Democracy* [2017]. Available at http://kenyalaw.org/caselaw/cases/view/137601/.

[100] Andreas Schedler, "The Logic of Electoral Authoritarianism," in *Electoral Authoritarianism: The Dynamics of Unfree Competition* 12–13 (2006).

developing and implementing policy or be effective opposition parties was also established. Further new electoral institutions and laws to guarantee free and fair elections were established. However, political parties have continued to mobilize their voters by promising allocation of resources from the center. These linkages that Members of Parliament develop to deliver resources from the State make these members dependent on the Executive. This in turn diminishes the ability of Members of Parliament to be truly independent and to act as a check on the Executive. Even more so, since 2013 the Jubilee Party has accumulated majorities in Parliament that insulate the Executive from opposition accountability. The political linkages that elected members of parliament establish with their constituents affect the way in which politics in Kenya is organized. These linkages and their relentless pursuit particularly during elections in turn shape the way in which political institutions in Kenya operate. This larger context therefore shapes how the reforms of the 2010 Constitution should be understood. In particular, this chapter has shown the important influence of political parties and coalitions during election time in constituting governments whose primary loyalty lies with their supporters rather than with preserving the institutional prerogatives of separation of powers of three branches of government in a system of checks and balances contemplated in the 2010 Constitution.

This chapter has argued that the nullification of the Presidential election by the Supreme Court in September 2017 set Kenya's constitutional path in period two. Unlike the hopeful moment after the enactment of the Constitution in 2010, period two has tested the ability of the Jubilee government and the opposition to work within its framework to resolve fundamental political differences. The opposition has often disengaged from Parliament to hold the government accountable and has sought to reform institutions such as the electoral body, which the opposition regards as acting for and on behalf of the government through tactics such as public protests and boycotts. Underlying the pursuit of extra-parliamentary routes to seek accountability is the futility with which the opposition regards using Parliament as an avenue of ensuring horizontal accountability. Kenya lacks elite consensus among its politicians in and out of government to strengthen the independent institutions established by the 2010 Constitution. This lack of consensus on investing in and building strong independent institutions in turn means that these elites cannot make credible commitments to each other, both within and across political, ethnic, and other divides.[101] Ruling party politicians have in particular focused on weakening accountability institutions. The President has used the dominant party in Parliament to make it less able to undertake its role to check the Executive branch. The

---

[101] Ken Opalo, "Constitutional protections of electoral democracy in Africa: A review of key challenges and prospects." *Annual Review of Constitution-Building-Processes*: 2016. International Institute for Democracy and Electoral Assistance. 2016. Available at www.idea.int/sites/default/files/publications/chapters/annual-review-of-constitution-building-processes-2015/annual-review-of-constitution-building processes-2015-chapter-1 pdf.

opposition has more often than not decided not to use Parliament as its main forum to demand legislative and constitutional changes to ensure free and fair elections, for example. A weak Parliament in the context of a history of weak institutions of accountability and nominal separation of powers signals the persistence of vestiges of authoritarianism in an era of increased political competition.

When the Judiciary has exercised its independence to check Parliament and the President for violating the Constitution and the law, the ruling party has reduced judiciary funding and publicly harshly criticized individual judges and the entire judiciary.[102] For the most part, Parliament has also emasculated the anti-corruption authority, making it unable to undertake its oversight role over corrupt offenders, particularly those that hold the highest political offices in the country. The Executive, using Parliament, has also put the Auditor and Controller General under enormous pressure for fearlessly disclosing corruption within the government. By undermining independent institutions, the implementation of the 2010 Constitution has been contested and uneven.[103] As I have argued elsewhere, the judiciary continues to be the one bright beacon of successful transformation.[104] There is no better evidence of this autonomy than the nullification of the August 2017 Presidential election as a result of irregularities and illegalities in the manner it was conducted. Such an unprecedented assertion of judicial power over an incumbent President is already coming at a cost, particularly after major cuts in the Judiciary's budget. This backlash against the Judiciary evidences a primary claim in this chapter. Faithful implementation of a new Constitution is a contested process. So far, it appears that the Judiciary, perhaps unlike Parliament, has a leadership faithful to the rules and values of the 2010 Constitution. However, the independence of the Judiciary will depend in large part on whether Parliament, which is politically dependent on the President, will continue to fund the Judiciary or will choose to starve it of funding as part of a larger effort to undermine its independence. Given that the Judiciary is the only arm of the Government that does not owe its loyalty to the President or the party system, it is not surprising that it has demonstrated a significant and consistent commitment to hold the political branches accountable even though the risks of legislative reversals of judicial independence are not an unlikely possibility. Fortunately, the judiciary enjoys widespread public support and confidence, particularly among civil society groups, in opposition strongholds, and in a large swath of the professional classes. A vigorous opposition and civil society

---

[102] James Gathii, "The Kenyan Judiciary's Accountability to Parliament and to Independent Commissions: 2010–2016," in Jill Ghai (ed.) *Judicial Accountability in the New Constitutional Order*, International Commission of Jurists (Kenya Section), 133 (2016).

[103] Notably, the Jubilee government could not wait for the end of the five-year tenure of the Commission for the Implementation of the Constitution, which played an important role in ensuring the government faithfully implemented the promises of the 2010 Constitution.

[104] James Gathii, *The Contested Empowerment of the Judiciary of Kenya 2010–2015: A Historical Institutional Analysis* (2016).

movement that defends the judiciary when it acts independently and is critical of it when it apparently toes the line of the President and Parliament gives the reforms achieved in the judiciary a measure of insulation from easy reversal even in a Jubilee Party-dominated Parliament. Such contestation is not merely the rough and tumble of politics, but how hard-won gains such as judicial independence must be cultivated and defended to survive political backlash from powerful forces.

PART IV

Authoritarian Transitions

PART IX

Authoritarian Transitions

10

Transformational Authoritarian Constitutions

The Case of Chile

Tom Ginsburg[*]

Can a constitution born in dictatorship serve democracy, or is it inevitably tainted by the circumstances of its birth? This question is a significant one in Chilean politics today. It is also an important question for comparative constitutional lawyers to consider. Chile's Constitution of 1980 represents an important but understudied category of constitutions: those drafted in a dictatorship that survive a transition to democracy. Other prominent examples include the constitutions of Mexico adopted in 1917, Indonesia's of 1945, Turkey's of 1982; Portugal's 1974 document; and Taiwan's Constitution, drafted on the mainland of China in 1947. Less well-known examples include Panama's military-drafted document of 1972 and Guyana's of 1980.[1] I take this opportunity to speculate on the category, and to offer some tentative thoughts on the question Chile has faced in recent years, namely whether or not to replace the document.

Why would democrats retain a constitution set up by dictators? As an initial matter, one might think about this category of countries as being examples of those in which formal constitutional replacement is not correlated with actual 'small-c' constitutional change. In some countries, shifts between democracy and dictatorship tend to be marked by formal constitutional revision and replacement. In others, the two are less tightly linked. My colleagues and I use this observation to argue that constitutional change is a distinct phenomenon from regime change.[2] Chile (Figure 10.1)

---

[*] Many thanks to Javier Couso, David Landau, James Melton, Gabriel Negretto, Pasquino Pasquale, and Jeffrey Staton for helpful comments and discussions, and to Lucas Sierra for the generous invitation to think about Chile. Thanks to Natalia Ginsburg, Suzanne Hillal, and David King for research assistance. I am grateful to my long-time coauthors Zachary Elkins and James Melton for permission to use figures from our joint work.

[1] Table 10.1 has a listing, which includes some ambiguous cases, such as Fujimori's Constitution of 1993, or of constitutions drafted during transitions. Argentina 1853 fits the category notwithstanding major reforms in 1994.

[2] Zachary Elkins, et al. *The Endurance of National Constitutions.* New York: Cambridge University Press, 2009.

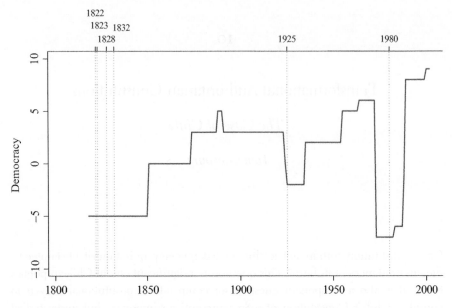

FIGURE 10.1 Constitutional change and regime change in Chile

is a textbook example. It is a country whose history is marked by constitutional stability along with political fluctuation. As such, the 1980 Constitution shares something in common with its predecessors of 1832 and 1925: It has governed over a period of great political change. Indeed, the 1832 Constitution is the seventeenth most enduring out of more than 900 national constitutions adopted since 1789.[3]

There are several possible reasons a country would retain an old constitution. One is that the old constitution must be retained for political reasons – either because it enjoys some legitimacy among the general population or because its erstwhile proponents still retain enough power to block any attempt at replacements. The Mexican and Indonesian cases seem like examples of the former dynamic, in which democratization during the 1990s was not accompanied by a complete constitutional overhaul. In both cases, the Constitution was associated with a significant event – a revolution or a moment of independence – and so retains legitimacy notwithstanding its use by authoritarians. Chile, on the other hand, is a case of retained veto over major change. Political forces associated with the erstwhile military regime played a potential spoiler role for many years after the adoption of the Constitution, and continued to benefit from a set of institutions that endured, including the binomial legislative system, supermajority requirements over certain rules, and *ex ante* review by a constitutional tribunal.

[3] The 1980 Constitution is already older than more than two-thirds of those of the other countries of the world. Data on file with the Comparative Constitutions Project.

This chapter seeks to contribute to some important debates in comparative constitutional law. Notably, there has been increasing attention to the role of constitutions in authoritarian regimes. It is common to characterize constitutions in dictatorships as mere shams or embodying "constitutions without constitutionalism."[4] Following this line of thought, one might think that constitutions are inherently democratic institutions and that authoritarian constitutions are epiphenomenal. But recent work has revealed that, in contrast to a simplistic view of constitutions in dictatorships as being shams, they have an array of sophisticated functions that help regimes to accomplish certain goals, such as committing to property rights, coordinating among the ruling elite, or communicating to the subjects of the constitution about the regime's goals and policies.[5] These functions might actually extend authoritarian rule.[6] Such constitutions also sometimes have in them latent features, which can serve to undermine authoritarian rule or can emerge as tools of coordination when it is close to failing. Understanding the logic of the Pinochet constitution helps to enrich this literature.

The chapter is organized as follows. We first consider the general category of transformational authoritarian constitutions, those designed in dictatorships to guide and constrain a return to democracy. We demonstrate that, in form, these constitutions are fairly similar to those found in democracies, with the addition of special minority veto provisions. We then go on to examine the Chilean case, as it serves as perhaps a paradigm example of this type, but it is not the only one. Next, we consider the question of whether constitutions ought to be amended or replaced, and if the latter, whether replacement should be achieved through a constituent assembly, legislature, or another modality. Finally, we discuss some evidence on the roles of courts and the public in constitutional reform.

10.1 TRANSFORMATIONAL AUTHORITARIAN CONSTITUTIONS AS A CATEGORY

What is an authoritarian constitution? As Zach Elkins, James Melton, and I argue elsewhere, the question is trickier than it first appears.[7] One might think that a constitution is authoritarian if it governs an authoritarian regime, and democratic if

---

[4] David Law and Mila Versteeg "Sham Constitutions." *California Law Review* 101 (Summer 2013); H. W. O. Okoth-Okendo, "Constitutions without Constitutionalism: Reflections on an African Political Paradox," in *Constitutionalism and Democracy: Transitions in the Contemporary World*, ed. Douglas Greenberg, Stanley Katz, and Melanie Beth Oliviero et al. New York: Oxford University Press, 1993, 65–85.

[5] Tom Ginsburg and Alberto Simpser (eds.) *Constitutions in Authoritarian Regimes.* New York: Cambridge University Press, 2014.

[6] Michael Albertus and Victor Menaldo, "The Political Economy of Autocratic Constitutions," in *Constitutions in Authoritarian Regimes*, ed. Tom Ginsburg and Alberto Simpser. New York: Cambridge University Press, 2014.

[7] Zachary Elkins et al., "The Content of Authoritarian Constitutions," in *Constitutions in Authoritarian Regimes*, ed. Tom Ginsburg and Alberto Simpser. New York: Cambridge University Press, 2014

it governs a democratic one. In this sense, constitution-type is congruent with regime type. But this defines away the category that Chile represents. We know that constitutional choices have long legacies, and changing them is costly. We also know that democrats and authoritarian regimes can sometimes exist sequentially even under the same constitution.[8] Thus, we might miss an important subcategory of cases of authoritarian legacies if we simply define a constitution as changing when the political system changes. Constitutional change, as we argue, is different from political regime change, though in many cases the two are tightly linked.[9]

Is a constitution "authoritarian" if it began its life under an authoritarian situation but evolved to reflect, ultimately, many of the document's formally democratic promises? We need to consider whether constitutions that are designed to evolve might somehow form their own subcategory. That is the approach we take here. "Transformational" constitutions are those that are designed to facilitate regime change, even if gradual.

Following Elkins et al., we begin by simply characterizing a constitution as authoritarian if drafted in a year in which the country is coded as authoritarian, and democratic if it is drafted in a year of democracy.[10] We use a binary coding, following much of the literature in comparative politics.[11] Using these criteria and drawing on the Comparative Constitutions Project database on constitutions of independent nation states since 1789, we see that the vast majority of these documents were drafted by authoritarian regimes. As Figure 10.2[12] indicates, 695 of the 846 historical constitutional systems for which we have data on regime type would be considered authoritarian.[13] And, although we are in an "age of democracy," some 56 percent of constitutions currently in force were drafted by dictators.[14]

Using these criteria, we might believe that the number of transitional authoritarian documents was high indeed. Table 10.1 lists current constitutions in force in democracies that were drafted by authoritarians. In some cases, their drafters were monarchs or revolutionaries. Few seem to reflect the Chilean model in which a military regime sought to entrench a certain set of limits that would guide and

---

[8] After this chapter was complete, Michael Albertus and Victor Menaldo published *Authoritarianism and the Elite Origins of Democracy*. New York: Cambridge University Press, 2018, which makes the general argument that democratization often results from inter-elite negotiations that lead to protecting elite interests in a democratic era. Their argument is consistent with that made in this chapter.

[9] Elkins et al., n. 2.

[10] Elkins et al., n. 7.

[11] The characterization draws from the Unified Democracy Scores. *See* Daniel Pemstein et al., "Democratic Compromise: A Latent Variable Analysis of Ten Measures of Regime Type." *Political Analysis* 18 (4): 426–49 (2010); Elkins et al., n. 7, describes our measure. See also Albertus and Menaldo, n. 8.

[12] Drawn from Elkins et al., n. 7.

[13] The universe of constitutional systems from 1789 to 2008 numbers 911; we have regime type data for 846 of these.

[14] Elkins et al., n. 7, at 145–46.

TABLE 10.1 *List of current constitutions born in dictatorship that evolve to democracy*

Argentina 1853	India 1949	Pakistan 2002
Belgium 1831	Indonesia 1959	Panama 1972
Benin 1990	Japan 1946	Peru 1993
Cape Verde 1980	Liberia 1986	Samoa 1962
Chile 1980	Mexico 1917	Sao Tome & Principe 1975
El Salvador 1983	Micronesia 1981	Seychelles 1993
Georgia 1995	Netherlands 1815	Taiwan 1947
Ghana 1992	Nicaragua 1987	Turkey 1982
Guyana 1980	Norway 1814	

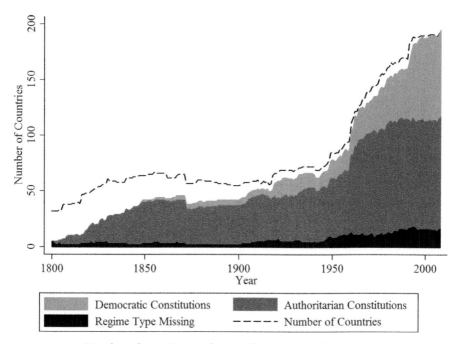

FIGURE 10.2 Number of constitutions born authoritarian or democratic
Universe: 907 constitutions promulgated in independent states from 1800 to 2008

constrain a return to electoral politics, though Turkey 1982 is an important analogue to which we will return.

Figure 10.3[15] provides some sense of the distribution of constitutions based on these criteria over time. The large dark gray area in the middle captures the set of authoritarian documents that remain authoritarian – and in some sense might be considered a pure type. If the countries governed by these documents switched to democracy, they would replace the constitution as well. The smaller light gray area

[15] Also drawn from Elkins et al., n. 7.

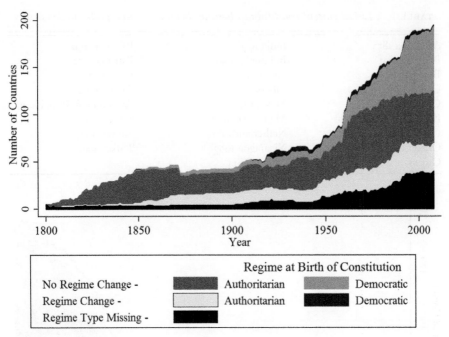

FIGURE 10.3 Number of constitutions born authoritarian or democratic by subsequent regime change
Universe: 907 constitutions promulgated in independent states from 1800 to 2008.
Key: Constitutions that are "born democratic with no regime change" are those that were promulgated in a democratic setting and spent their entire history in a democratic setting. Those "born democratic with regime change" were promulgated in a democracy but lived under authoritarianism as well. And so on.

below these "pure" authoritarian constitutions represents those that were written by authoritarian leaders but survived a transition to democracy at some point in their lifespan. Although this smaller group makes up only 10 percent of historical constitutions, nearly 20 percent of constitutions in force today are of this variety (as listed in Table 10.1). Admittedly, this crude list includes cases – such as Ghana and Japan – that were in the process of democratizing when the constitution was produced. Still, the category is worthy of further investigation.

Assuming that this group forms a coherent category, what are the criteria that distinguish a transformational authoritarian constitution? As an ideal type, I propose the following as essential criteria: (1) the constitution is explicitly framed as helping to structure a return to electoral democracy, after a period that may or may not be specified; (2) the constitution reflects certain policy goals designed to be permanent, that is, to constrain the future democratic regime; and (3) the constitution provides for an enforcement mechanism to ensure that both these goals are met. In other words, the transformational authoritarian constitution acknowledges the superiority of popular sovereignty and seeks to transfer power to democrats, but only subject to certain limitations. Further, there is some mechanism to guarantee these limits.

The 1982 Constitution of Turkey provides a nice paradigmatic example.[16] Turkey has a long tradition of electoral politics but has also experienced periodic bouts of military rule. As Goldenziel notes, the Venice Commission calls Turkey a "tutelary democracy," in which democracy is bounded by an alliance of the military, bureaucracy and courts.[17] In the 1960s, the Kemalist elite that had run Turkey for decades established a Constitutional Court, in part to protect the core values of secularism from reversal by religious parties. As those parties increased in popularity, the Court repeatedly disbanded them and also engaged in a long series of battles with the elected branches of government.[18]

The 1982 Constitution, adopted during one of the periods of direct military rule, illustrates many of the themes of transformational authoritarianism. It was in form a democratic document, calling for elections. Like many military-adopted documents, it speaks of the essential role of the military in saving the nation, but also speaks in a democratic register: democracy is mentioned five times. It reaffirms the values of republicanism and secularism as foundational principles that are unamendable. But it also set up clear mechanisms to limit democratic politics. These included the National Security Council, which served as a check on and supplement to the civilian cabinet.[19] Furthermore, the Constitution featured a low threshold to declaring a state of exception that could be extended indefinitely. Most prominently, the Turkish Constitutional Court played an important role in enforcing the strictures of the 1982 constitution, providing a strict boundary on democratic politics. The Court, and the judiciary more broadly, served to slow down Turkey's democratic transition at several crucial junctures.[20] To provide only one example, in 2008, the Constitutional Court ruled that properly enacted constitutional amendments overturning the ban on wearing a headscarf at state universities were themselves unconstitutional. It also sought to ban the country's ruling political party, the Justice and Development Party (AKP), for violating principles of secularism.

Beginning in 2003, a series of amendments were passed to try to reform the constitution to reflect the electoral rise of the populist AKP and its leader Recep

[16] See Jill Goldenziel, "Veiled Political Questions: Islamic Dress, Constitutionalism and the Ascendance of Courts." *American Journal of Comparative Law* 61: 36–37 (2013); Turkuler Isiksel, "Between Text and Context: Turkey's Tradition of Authoritarian Constitutionalism." *International Journal of Constitutional Law* 11: 702–26 (Summer 2013).

[17] Goldenziel, "Veiled Political Questions," p. 35, n. 143, citing Ergun Ozbudun, European Commission for Democracy through Law (Venice Commission), Civilian Control of the Military: Why and What? (2007), available at www.venice.coe.int/docs/2007/CDL-DEM (2007)005-e.pdf.

[18] Gunes Tezcur, "Judicial Activism in Perilous Times: The Turkey Case." *Law & Society Review* 305–36 (2009).

[19] Isiksel, n. 12, at 717.

[20] See Asli Bali, "The Perils of Judicial Independence: Constitutional Transition and the Turkish Example." *Virginia Journal of International Law* 52: 235–320 (2013).

Tayyip Erdoğan. These amendments eventually created an executive presidency
that Erdoğan has used to consolidate his power and dismantle many of the constraints that the 1982 Constitution had placed on politics. Yet the legacy of the
document turned out to be difficult to escape. As the AKP has replaced one form of
authoritarianism with another, it has used some of the very same instrumentalities as
the military. As Isiksel notes, "authoritarian constitutionalism encourages challen-
gers to develop the same bad habits as the old guard."[21]

Other examples might include several of Thailand's twenty constitutions adopted
since 1932. Thailand has been a uniquely unstable constitutional environment, as
government has oscillated between corrupt civilians and military authoritarians.
Military governments in Thailand, at least since the 1970s, have as a formal matter
accepted the moral superiority of democracy, but have occasionally stepped in to
remove particular leaders or clear a situation of gridlock. After a coup, the military
now seems to routinely promise a return to civilian rule but also has drafted constitutions which differ on one crucial point from their civilian counterparts: ensuring a
nonelected upper house.[22] This reflects the military-bureaucratic distrust of elected
politicians, and allows a veto on change by ensuring that some appointed actors will
have a say on policy.

Closer to home, the Panama Constitution of 1972, promulgated by General Omar
Torrijos following his 1968 coup, designated him as Maximum Leader of the
Panamanian Revolution, with extraordinary powers to last for six years.[23] These
powers expired in 1978, and, under US pressure, the National Assembly passed a
series of amendments calling for a return to democratic processes over the next
several years. Formally, the Constitution remains in force today, having survived the
rise and fall of strongman Manuel Noriega.

Transformational authoritarian constitutions bear some relation to the species of
transitional constitutionalism, as described by Teitel.[24] But they differ in that, unlike
those documents that focus on reckoning with the past, transformational authoritarian constitutions are typically designed to *insulate* the designers from any future
justice. The various mechanisms found in the 1980 Constitution here in Chile
provide a paradigm example: the category of *leyes*, requiring a 4/7 majority of the
legislature to adopt or amend; the Constitutional Court; the binomial election
system; and the guarantees of impunity for the military leaders. The binomial
system, in particular, helped guarantee the political right an ongoing stake in

[21] Isiksel, n. 16, at 72.5.
[22] Tom Ginsburg, "Constitutional Afterlife: The Continuing Impact of Thailand's Postpolitical Constitution." *International Journal of Constitutional Law* 7: 83–105 (2009).
[23] Constitution of Panama. art. 277.
[24] Ruti Teitel, *Transitional Justice*. New York: Oxford University Press, 2000; Ruti Teitel, "Transitional Justice and the Transformation of Constitutionalism," in *the Comparative Constitutional Law Handbook*, ed. Rosalind Dixon and Tom Ginsburg. Cheltenham: Edward Elgar Publishing, 2011.

politics. The binomial system provides seats for the top two vote-getters in any given district, so that a large minority party can be overrepresented. Tellingly, it dates back to a model developed in Poland under the Jaruzelski regime, when the Solidarity movement was on the rise, and would surely have won any free and fair election. Its effect was to assign a legislative seat to what would have been the runner-up in each district under first-past-the-post voting.

Transformational authoritarian documents may be transformational with regard to regime type, but not with regard to accountability for past crimes. While transitional constitutionalism as defined by Teitel focuses on coming to terms with the past, the transformational authoritarian document obfuscates the past and prohibits close examination of it. Amnesty is the key feature here. The logic is that without guarantees of a future role and some immunity for the transformational authoritarian, democratic transition is impossible in the first place. In this sense, they form a kind of counter-category to Teitel's transitional constitutionalism. Instead of dealing with the past to protect the future, they protect the past *from* the future.

From a normative point of view, transformational authoritarian constitutions remind us that entrenchment is a two-edged sword. While democratic theorists celebrate entrenchment as helping to make democratic self-rule possible, it may also serve to limit the scope of that self-rule in situations when one must bargain with an old regime.[25] Entrenchment, as Professor Isiksel puts it, can "foreclose institutional innovation, adaptation, and learning, magnifying the inadequacies, imperfections, and even injustices of the norm in question."[26] Using the technology of constitutionalism to slow down political processes is a move that goes back at least to the American founding fathers, but the ends to which this tool is deployed are as myriad as constitution-making circumstances.[27]

In a recent coauthored chapter, my colleagues Zachary Elkins, James Melton, and I provide some descriptive evidence about this category of cases and how they are distinct from "pure" authoritarian constitutions.[28] We conduct regression analyses concerning the content of the written constitution, measuring (1) the differences between democratic and authoritarian constitutions and (2) the differences between authoritarian constitutions that experience a transition to democracy and those that do not. We also include several variables to control for factors that are generally associated with the contents of a constitution (region; the country's previous constitution type; and era of drafting). The analysis shows that authoritarian constitutions that eventually shift to democracy look much more like democratic constitutions than like "pure" authoritarians. On several dimensions – rights, judicial independence, detail – authoritarian constitutions that do experience a

---

[25] Isiksel, n. 16, at 708.
[26] Ibid.
[27] See Albertus and Menaldo, n. 8.
[28] Elkins et al., n. 7.

transition to democracy at some point during their lifespan are no different in substance than constitutions written by democrats, at least in terms of the constitutional attributes we analyzed.

Transformational authoritarian constitutions, then, are closer to democratic constitutions than one might expect. And in this sense, they differ systematically from "pure" authoritarian constitutions. Our evidence provides some support for the observation of Levitsky and Way that the formal institutions of their category of "electoral authoritarians" are similar to those of democracies. But we introduce a temporal dimension into the analysis: We expect to see specific institutions to control politics downstream, and so government across time is a key feature of our category.

10.2 CHILE'S CASE

Chile seems to fit this paradigm well. The drafting of the Constitution began in earnest soon after the 1973 Coup. Initially, an advisory committee of legal scholars was tasked with writing the first draft. This committee is generally known as the "Comisión Ortúzar" after its President, the legal scholar Enrique Ortúzar. The draft then went to the Council of State, which was an advisory organ within the government and chaired by Jorge Allesandri, a former President who had lost the 1970 election to Salvador Allende. The body also included a former head of the Supreme Court, senior bureaucrats and academics, and former military commanders. Finally, the draft went to the junta itself, which made some minor modifications over the course of a month, including giving more power to the National Security Council. Thus the 1980 Constitution was a largely technocratic document, with the political right playing a major role. It was eventually put before the public in a referendum on September 11, 1980 (the seventh anniversary of the coup d'état), under conditions of a state of emergency, and approved by two-thirds of voters.

General Pinochet's junta drafted the 1980 constitution with an eye to returning power to democratic forces through an orderly transition.[29] This Constitution entrenched property rights (a major concern of the Chilean right), banned communist parties, gave the military a de facto veto through the power to appoint senators, and set up, among other institutions, a Constitutional Tribunal with power to engage in a pre-promulgation review of legislation as a check on the conduct of future actors. But in many other respects, the Chilean Constitution seems fairly democratic in form. It contains 43 rights from an index of 116 analyzed by the Comparative Constitutions Project, which is 16 more rights than its predecessor constitution of 1925, and 11 more than the mean for all constitutions. It provides for

---

[29] See discussion in Albertus and Menaldo, n. 8, at 210–11 & 230–36. They argue that Pinochet and the military sought to empower their supporters, and were not blind followers of neoliberalism as is sometimes argued.

elections after a period of time. And it provides for judicial independence, among other features associated with electoral democracy. The distinguishing features of the 1980 Constitution are those that regulate time and process rather than substance.

Analysts report that the Chilean judiciary as a whole played a generally regressive role in democratization. In the first place, under the myth of maintaining an apolitical role, judges sought to avoid interfering with the dictatorship.[30] Next, for the first decade after Pinochet, they were mostly an obstacle to political change and served to enforce the constitutional bargain of an amnesty for the dictators and strong entrenchment of property rights. They acted to block judicial reforms as well, maintaining hierarchical control over lower court judges under the Supreme Court. Finally, in the early 2000s Chilean judges began to overturn the amnesty laws that had been the basis of Pinochet's transition from power. The courts were an effective downstream enforcer of the amnesty for a long time. They were thus a crucial mechanism of the transformational authoritarian constitution, a guarantor.

At the same time, legal institutions did play a role in constraining the junta. Robert Barros' important study of the Constitutional Tribunal argues that the country's tradition of legality served to make legal institutions an attractive solution to internal coordination problems within the regime.[31] During the first few years of its existence, the Constitutional Tribunal was compliant and duly blessed the dictates of the regime as constitutional.[32] However, in September 1985, the Court issued a ruling that had profound downstream implications for the structure of political competition. The Constitution required that a plebiscite would be held to approve or reject the first civilian president, to be nominated by the military. The relevant organic constitutional law proposed that this referendum be overseen by an ad hoc electoral court. The Tribunal, however, held that the plebiscite required full structure of electoral oversight, including lists of voters and independent countering. This reduced the military's ability to rig the plebiscite.

This was to a large degree a constitution-reinforcing decision. It induced the opposition to participate rather than boycott the plebiscite. The military, in turn, may have been disappointed in the decision, but having invested in the entire structure of the constitutional scheme, may have been reluctant to dismiss it out of hand. Further, the military acquiesced in these rulings in part because it was not unified internally.[33] The court then followed this with a series of decisions in which the junta was required to allow a fair structure of the political process, including free and equal access to the media and rules on political organizations.[34] The process

---

[30] Jill Hilbink, *Judges Beyond Politics in Democracy and Dictatorship: Lessons from Chile*. New York: Cambridge University Press, 2007.

[31] Robert Barros, *The Constitutionalism and Dictatorship: Pinochet, the Junta, and the 1980 Constitution*. Cambridge University Press, 2002.

[32] Ibid. 213.

[33] Ibid. 216.

[34] Ibid. 214.

constrained the junta that had set it up. The opposition eventually won the plebiscite, shocking Pinochet and paving the way for a return to democracy. This illustrates how courts, even in dictatorships, can exercise some autonomy and allow gains by opposition forces. The guarantor institution was a genuine commitment device, restraining both dictators and democrats.

10.3 EVOLUTION OR REVOLUTION? TRANSFORMING THE TRANSFORMATIONAL CONSTITUTION TODAY

All constitutions need to adjust over time, as the world itself changes. New political coalitions and social movements arise; new economic circumstances occur; and the international environment is constantly transforming. It is thus impossible to imagine that any constitution could be completely stable.

There are, of course, several different modalities of constitutional change. Constitutions can be replaced entirely: this occurs far more frequently than one might expect. Constitutions can change through formal amendments, and this might seem to be the most obvious one.[35] Far more frequently, constitutions are transformed through interpretation by courts and other political actors, as the text remains the same but meaning changes; in some cases this may even involve unintended shifts in practice or meaning.[36]

Chile's Constitution has been modified twelve times since 1989, changing more than one hundred articles. Initial reforms sought to entrench military prerogatives on the eve of the return to democracy, and minor modifications continued in the 1990s. Then in 2005, President Ricardo Lagos pushed for and obtained major modifications to the 1980 Constitution. These largely ended the authoritarian enclaves, and many believe this reform marked the end of the democratization process. Lagos himself liked to present it as a complete replacement, although it is counted as an amendment using the criteria developed by my colleagues and I at the Comparative Constitutions Project. Among other things, the 2005 reform reduced the powers of the National Security Council, ended the role of nonelected Senators, and transformed the appointment mechanisms of the Constitutional Tribunal.[37] Later reforms in 2013 ended the binomial system.

In 2013, after winning a huge landslide, President Michele Bachelet promised an effort to write a new constitution for the country. It would not only update the

---

[35] Our study shows that 92 percent of historic constitutions, and all of those in force today, include some amendment procedure. Data on file with authors.

[36] Georg Jellinek, *Verfassungsänderung und Verfassungswandlung* (Häring 1906), recently revived in the interesting work of Julian Arato. See e.g. Julian Arato, "Treaty Interpretation and Constitutional Transformations," *Yale Journal of International Law* 38: 289–357 (2013); Julian Arato, "Constitutional Transformation in the ECtHR: Strausbourg's Expansive Recourse to External Rules of International Law," *Brooklyn Journal of International Law* 37: 349–88 (2012).

[37] One can examine the debates over this reform at www.bcn.cl/historiadelaley/nc/historia-de-la-ley/6131/.

document to meet demands for a social democracy in the twenty-first century but it would also mark an important symbolic turning point, removing the stain of the 1980 Constitution's authoritarian birth. Chile could start over. The constitutional order would no longer be tainted as the "fruit of the poisoned vine." Bachelet's team initiated a program of small-scale constitutional reform discussions, engaging hundreds of thousands of citizens in the process of envisioning what Chile needed going forward. However, her project sputtered, as a corruption scandal hindered her administration, and the political right blocked reforms.

Regardless of the failed attempt to replace the constitution entirely, it is worth asking whether and when such efforts are a good idea. One might, at the simplest level, treat these different modes of constitutional change as pure substitutes. That is, one could simply choose between replacing the constitution all at once and replacing it through a series of amendments in which the formal continuity is retained but the text changes completely. We know, after all, that constitutions can be radically transformed through amendments. Argentina's Constitution of 1853 remains nominally in force today, though it is unrecognizable in many ways. To take some examples from my own country, California passed 130 amendments to its state constitution in 1966; South Carolina passed 200 between 1971 and 1973. The text of these documents today bears little resemblance to that as initially adopted.

Furthermore, we also know that even constitutional changes marked by formal ruptures may conceal a good deal of continuity. Legacies persist and constitutions can have an afterlife even if they are fully replaced. There is, as my colleagues and I have shown in our 2009 book, remarkable serial similarity in the contents of constitutional texts within a single country.[38] Using measures of dyadic similarity, in which we can compare any two constitutional texts, over time within various countries, we show that constitutions adopted within a country's history tend to be more similar to each other than to a constitution picked at random from the entire set of world constitutions. In short, the distinction between replacement and amendment may not be as stark as one might imagine or hope.

So are amendment and replacement indeed pure substitutes? The question is both conceptual and empirical. Conceptually, the question goes to whether there is indeed a kind of identity in the lifespan of a constitution, so that there is continuity in the object under consideration. It has something in common with philosophers' notions of the continuity of a human life. As William Parfit asks, if a surgeon, over a long period of time, takes part of a human brain out and replaces it with an exact replica, and so proceeds until none of the original tissue remained, would it still be the same brain?[39] Parfit uses the point to argue that physical continuity is not necessary for the continuation of human identity, and philosophers have used this

---

[38] Taken from Elkins et al., *The Endurance of National Constitutions*.

[39] Derek Parfit, *Reasons and Persons*. New York: Oxford University Press, 1984. 474.

as a departure for theorizing about issues of human life or death.[40] By analogy, if one amends every provision in a constitution, one at a time, over a sequence of years, is it the same constitution?

Whatever one's view of the philosophy of mind, I think the answer is yes in regard to constitutions. My answer is perhaps more empirically grounded than conceptually. Constitutions, like human bodies, are systems of institutions that work together, and affect the subsequent courses of action. Constitutions shape the political environment, which produces particular actors in a position to subsequently modify the rules of the game. One must treat them as biographies and not simply as static moments. Thus, changing each piece over several years would still lead to a continuity of constitutional identity.

Empirically, our 2009 study observes that there seem to be significant costs to constitutional replacement. We find that various goods such as growth, democracy, and peaceful conflict resolution increase with the age of constitutions, on average.[41] While causality is tricky to disentangle, there are reasons to think that formal continuity may matter for various indicia of success – legitimacy, institutional functioning, and the production of public goods.

As an aside, I note also that the assumption that the circumstances of drafting will inevitably and permanently taint the subsequent document has some relation to normative concepts of original intent. Scholars of American constitutional law, debate – endlessly – the appropriate role of the founders' intent in interpreting the constitution today, more than two centuries later. Originalists focus on the public meaning at the time of the founding, while Living Constitutionalists emphasize the continuous process of recreating the constitution in each era.[42] If we can fundamentally adjust a text written under very different circumstances, constitutional transformation is possible, and we should not worry so much about the circumstances of the founding. The identity that we share with the founders may have symbolic power, but it need not have legal power.

All this, however, does not mean that it is desirable to keep the old constitution in all circumstances. Surely, in some contexts, the taint associated with a constitution's birth is sufficiently powerful that replacement is desirable. Let us briefly canvass arguments for revolution and evolution in such circumstances.

10.3.1 *The Case for Revolution, or Half-Revolution*

When should an entirely new constitution be written? Clearly, doing so marks a large symbolic break that may be desirable in some cases, particularly after radical

---

[40] Jeff McMahan, *The Ethics of Killing: Problems at the Margins of Life.* New York: Oxford University Press, 2002.

[41] Elkins et al., n. 2.

[42] David Strauss, *The Living Constitution.* New York: Oxford University Press, 2010.

political change. Roughly one in five transitions, either from democracy to dictatorship or the other way around, is marked by the adoption of a new constitution. These regime changes lead to a quest for a new founding moment to orient subsequent political activity.

Furthermore, regime change is thus neither a sufficient or necessary condition for constitutional change. Sometimes even very stable regimes adopt a new constitution: Sweden completely rewrote its constitution in 1974, both to consolidate a large number of amendments that had taken place since the previous version had been adopted in 1809, and to institute a unicameral as opposed to bicameral parliament. This might be seen as a more technical project, without obvious symbolic predicate. But nevertheless, it shows that crisis is not a prerequisite for constitutional replacement.

Much work in recent years has emphasized the importance of constitutional identity.[43] This line of work emphasizes the role of the constitution in defining the people, in grappling with the past, and in articulating a vision for the future. Constitution-making processes can provide an opportunity to engage the population in a deliberative project that can have important salutary effects on the polity. For this reason, it has become a norm for the drafting of new constitutions in restructuring states that the population be widely consulted, and typically also have the role of approving the constitution. The constitution-making project can help to cement the nation's sense of itself.

Drawing on Hegel and Lacan, Michel Rosenfeld describes a three-stage process of incorporating the past.[44] First comes the phase of pure negation, which involves a total repudiation of the past; the constitution is aversive of its history.[45] Next, though, there is the recognition that every nation has a past. Constitutional identity cannot be formed in a vacuum, and so the constitution-making project must identify and select some elements of identity from the past that were initially discarded. The third stage is the negation of the negation, which involves the restructuring of these elements into a coherent whole.

This project of reforming the past through constitution-making has its attractions. For Chile today, negating the negation would involve not regression to a pre-Pinochet reality but the incorporation of the diffuse elements of its recent political history into a coherent whole. And such breaks can be accomplished while retaining

---

[43] Donald Kommers, et al., *American Constitutional Law: Essays, Cases, and Comparative Notes*. Maryland: Rowman & Littlefield Publishers, Inc., 2009; Michel Rosenfeld, *The Identity of the Constitutional Subject: Selfhood, Citizenship, Culture, and Community*. New York: Routledge, 2009; Gary Jacobsohn, *Constitutional Identity*. Cambridge, MA: Harvard University Press, 2010; Chaihark Hahm and Sung Ho Kim, *Making We the People: Democratic Constitutional Founding in Postwar Japan and South Korea*. New York: Cambridge University Press, 2015.

[44] Michel Rosenfeld, *The Identity of the Constitutional Subject: Selfhood, Citizenship, Culture, and Community*. New York: Routledge, 2009.

[45] *See also* Kim Scheppele, "A Constitution between Past and Future." *William & Mary Law Review* 49: 1389 (2008).

legal continuity with the past. Andrew Arato, for example, has formulated a model of "post sovereign" constitution-making in which the creation of the new order after the fall of dictators is accomplished within the bounds of the previous constitution, even if that document is normatively and historically tainted.[46] An old constitution can facilitate the birth of a new dawn, simply by grounding the constitution-making process.

These then are the arguments for a new constitution for Chile today. The symbolism of the past, the technical flaws of an oft-amended document, and the specific constraints on majoritarianism provided by the legacies of authoritarian rule all argue for a new beginning, which can be done by invoking the constituent authority.

10.3.2 *The Case for Evolution*

Edmund Burke once wrote that a "government which governs well has the legitimate claim to the obedience of its citizens, even it was illegitimate in origin."[47] In a Burkean vein, proponents of evolution emphasize the virtues of gradual change in constitutions. A general way to approach the problem is of costs and benefits. Constitutional change is costly and total revision is even costlier. It takes time and energy to engage in the deliberation required for amendment. Furthermore, there are risks to total amendment. This is because changing many institutions opens up much more deliberative space; more issues can be negotiated, and ultimate outcomes are more uncertain. The greater the scope of the bargain, the more difficult it is to complete, and the less predictable *ex ante*. Thus, one might argue in a Burkean vein, it is best to proceed by changing institutions one at a time through constitutional amendment.

There are some prominent examples of constitutional evolution away from authoritarian regimes. Indonesia is a very important example that has received too little attention in the literature.[48] More than a decade and a half after the fall of Suharto, Indonesia is widely regarded as a successful example of democratization. This was achieved through two rounds of amendments of the Constitution of 1945, which retained important symbolic legitimacy associated with the country's independence. Indonesia is a very diverse country that faced several secessionist movements, as well as a legacy of decades of military rule, when Suharto was forced from

---

[46] Andrew Arato, *Constitution-Making under Occupation: The Politics of Imposed Revolution in Iraq*. New York: Columbia University Press, 2009, 5–7. Arato distinguishes between legality and legitimacy. For example, the US Constitution was created through a legal rupture, but continuous legitimacy. The Japanese postwar constitution was created with a rupture in legitimacy for many, but legal continuity.

[47] Francis Canavan, "The Relevance of the Burke-Paine Controversy to American Political Thought." *Revolutionary Politics* 69: 163–76 (1987).

[48] Donald Horowitz, *Constitutional Change and Democracy in Indonesia*. New York: Cambridge University Press, 2013.

power in 1988. The country might thus be seen to have unfavorable odds at constitutional transition. Rather than form a new constitution with a sharp break, Indonesia chose to adopt four rounds of constitutional amendments between 1999 and 2002. These completely transformed the political system. The process defied conventional wisdom in many ways. First, Indonesia held elections before initiating constitutional changes and then allowed the legislature, rather than a constituent assembly, to carry out the work. Second, the amendment process was driven by insiders, with members of Suharto's own political party playing key roles. Through a combination of happenstance, luck, and clever institutional design, Indonesia translated its elaborate and complex system of social cleavages into a multiparty system. When the process was ready to spin out of control with the impeachment of Abdurrahman Wahid in 2001, the country responded by creating a constitutional court to adjudicate such disputes in the future. This represented a crucial institutional adjustment.

In Taiwan, too, the constitutional reforms of the 1990s and early 2000s represented a gradual set of reforms that dealt with many of the legacies of authoritarian rule. Before the democratic transition, Taiwan was governed by a one-party regime that had been elected on the mainland in the late 1940s. This group held power over a population of native-born Taiwanese, who were bitterly repressed. When democratization began in earnest under Taiwan-born President Lee Teng-hui in the late 1980s, a major constraint was the People's Republic of China, which might have viewed a new constitution as a declaration of independence and cause for aggression. Thus, the democrats proceeded with a series of constitutional amendments that profoundly transformed both the governance structure and the country's constitutional court, which in turn helped to clear away many of the legacies of authoritarian rule. All this was accomplished gradually, without provoking either internal or external enemies to spoil the process.

In short, at least some anecdotal evidence suggests that radical reform is not necessary to effectuate profound change in a political system, and that a constitutional scheme that governs a dictatorship can indeed survive to democracy. Evolution has been the mode in Chile to date, including at two major junctures in 1989 (Law 18.825 amended fifty-four provisions), as well as 1997 (twenty-one provisions changed in three separate amendments) and 2005 (twelve amendments and more than fifty provisions changed). Again, all this does not mean that evolution is the mandatory strategy. Rather, it means that it is a viable option.

10.4 HOW TO REFORM? CONSTITUENT ASSEMBLY VS. LEGISLATURE

Constituent assemblies and legislatures are two of the most common modalities of constitutional reform. In a 2009 study, we found that of some 400 constitutional design processes, constituent assemblies were employed in 143 cases, usually as sole actor.[49] But there are many variations and few consistent practices. Many hybrids exist.

India's constituent assembly, for example, decided to act as an ordinary legislature prior to the adoption of the constitution in 1949. This is an example of what the literature calls a constituent legislating assembly, simultaneously conducting the day-to-day legislative affairs of an ordinary legislature while also continuing to function as a constituent assembly. Another example comes from Panama, whose constitution promulgated in March of 1946 stipulated that the Constituent National Assembly convert itself into the Legislative Assembly with members serving until September 30, 1948. El Salvador's constituent assembly made the same move in 1983.

Much of the debate in the literature has followed Jon Elster's pathbreaking work in which he argues that ordinary legislatures should not draft constitutions.[50] Elster divides motives in constitution-making into three: reasons, passions, and interests. Although he recognizes that all have their role to play, he thinks the optimal design of a constitution-making process will maximize the role of reason relative to self-interest and popular passions. Legislatures, he suggests, are inferior to special constituent assemblies that are engaged solely in constitution-making. This is because, he thinks, legislatures are more likely to engage in institutional aggrandizement, are less likely to be focused on the task, and are more likely to be victim to path-dependencies in which the ordinary legislative level influences the "higher" constitutional level. Another claim is that legislative bodies will put too much detail into the document, as they fail to distinguish between higher order norms and ordinary policy. Brazil's 1988 constitution is held up as a poster child for this claim.[51]

My coauthors and I have produced a pair of papers interrogating these assumptions. We found that, notwithstanding Elster's intuitions, there were few systematic differences between those constitutions that were produced by legislatures and assemblies.[52] We did find evidence of institutional aggrandizement in constitutions drafted in processes dominated by the executive, which was another of Elster's conjectures. As between the legislature and an assembly, however, there were no differences in terms of length, legislative power, or the number of rights.

[49] Tom Ginsburg, Zachary Elkins, and Justin Blount, "Does the Process of Constitution-Making Matter?" *Annual Review of Law and Social Science* 5: 201–24 (2009).
[50] "To reduce the scope for institutional interest, constitutions ought to be written by specially convened assemblies and not by bodies that also serve as ordinary legislatures. Nor should legislators be given a central place in ratification." Jon Elster (ed.) *Deliberative Democracy.* Cambridge: Cambridge University Press, 1998, 117. Elster has retained this view in his recent work: Jon Elster, *Securities against Misrule.* New York: Cambridge University Press, 2013, chapter four.
[51] Keith Rosenn, "Brazil's New Constitution: An Exercise in Transient Constitutionalism for a Transitional Society." *American Journal of Comparative Law* 38: 773, 775–77 (1990).
[52] Justin Blount, Zachary Elkins, and Tom Ginsburg, "Citizen as Founder: Public Participation in Constitutional Approval." *Temple Law Review* 81 (Summer 2009); Ginsburg, Elkins, and Blount, n. 49.

Constituent assemblies imply the exercise of the *pouvoir constituent*, and so in some circumstances may go beyond their instructions to freely exercise constitution-making power. In Latin America, the doctrine of the constituent power is sometimes held to be very large indeed. David Landau has argued that the use of constituent assemblies in Venezuela and Bolivia was highly problematic because of the risk that assemblies will ignore any upstream constraints that have been put on the process.[53] The river can jump the banks. For example, in Venezuela in 1999, Comandante Hugo Chavez seized control of the constituent assembly to consolidate control over all independent institutions, including the Supreme Court that briefly resisted his power grab. He rigged the voting rules so that, with 60 percent of the vote, his party obtained 95 percent of the seats in the Assembly. And he did this with no legal continuity – the prior constitution had not provided for a constituent assembly. Eventually, the Court, using the doctrine of the "original constituent power," blessed his move. While it tried to put limits on the exercise of this power, Chavez ignored these, and eventually packed the Court, leading one scholar to characterize the Court as having "sign[ed] its own death warrant."[54]

The constituent assembly in Bolivia did remain within the constraints, but only after violent protests that risked tearing the country apart. Evo Morales' party tried to invoke the original constituent power. Bolivia's effort was induced by an attempt to include long-excluded forces in Bolivian society, but was also a highly polarized process in a weakly institutionalized environment. At one point, violent riots erupted, leading to three deaths and hundreds of injuries. This reminds us that constitution-making is not always an opportunity for consensus but can involve moments of political trauma. As Landau argues, precisely because constituent assemblies may be seen as engaged in higher lawmaking, they can sometimes be difficult to constrain.

This is not to say that constituent assemblies are always destabilizing by any means. Colombia's experience in 1991 was one in which, in the face of a fading pact and new insurgent parties, a constituent assembly was elected, but no party dominated. The Assembly served as a vehicle to restructure Colombian politics into a more competitive system.[55] But it does suggest that simple predictions of results based on the choice between constituent assembly and legislature are hard to make.

Another possibility for Chile to consider is a national conference to discuss the framework of constitutional reform, without necessarily producing a specific text. These are bodies that are separate from the ordinary legislature, and not reliant on it for authority. They can also be quite large. For example, Mali's national conference held in 1991 had approximately 1,800 delegates. To the extent that larger delegations may produce more broadly representative and/or inclusive membership, it may

---

[53] David Landau, "Constitution-Making Gone Wrong." *Alabama Law Review* 64: 923–80 (2013).
[54] Ibid. 948.
[55] Ibid. 962.

reduce any risk of institutional self-dealing. Widner's analysis suggests that such conferences are more adept at incorporating large swaths of civil society in the constitutional design process than are ordinary legislatures.[56]

There are few set rules for the design of a national conference. It may be used to generate new ideas, to provide suggestions, or even binding decisions on subsequent decision-makers. In the Chilean context it might allow for broad input from many social forces, without the potentially harmful consequences of alienating the existing political parties and institutions, which by and large are functioning admirably well. We turn to this risk next.

10.4.1 *The Roles of Parties and Electoral Systems*

The Venezuelan and Bolivian cases represented instances in which the constituent assembly was called because of shifts in the party system. Long-established pacts were beginning to break down, and insurgent parties representing new constituencies were on the rise. This meant that constitution-making was easily politicized, and political conflicts that might be considered to be within the realm of ordinary politics escalated to the constitutional level. The party system interacted with constitution-making to foreclose the possibilities of calm deliberation.

In other cases, political parties can play a positive role in constitutional reform. One danger to avoid, however, is the temptation to bypass the political party system. The Icelandic experience is one in which parties ended up blocking a radical initiative from below.[57] Iceland's remarkable experiment began with the severe financial crisis of 2008, in which the country's banking system collapsed. In the aftermath, a groundswell of support for constitutional change led to the overwhelming passage of a parliamentary statute to guide the process. Next was the convening of a randomly drawn group of 950 citizens to generate ideas for constitutional reform. Then, in the fall of 2010, twenty-five ordinary Icelanders were elected from a field of over 500 to serve on a constitutional council that would formulate a new constitution. The councilors sought wide participation, and Icelanders were able to follow the council's decisions and contribute suggestions through the Internet using a Facebook page. There was an iterated process of drafts and comments, which led to some changes in the proposed draft. It is unlikely the general public has ever had such direct involvement in constitution-making.

The final draft produced by the commission greatly expanded direct democracy, allowing the public to be involved in ongoing governance. It included affirmation of the one-person, one-vote principle, with a complicated electoral system. The draft

---

[56] Jennifer Widner, "Constitution Writing and Conflict Resolution." *Commonwealth Journal of International Affairs* 94: 503–18 (2005).

[57] Tom Ginsburg, "Iceland: End of the Constitutional Saga," I-CONnect Blog, April 2013. Available at www.iconnectblog.com/2013/04/iceland-end-of-the-constitutional-saga.

also, controversially, provided that the country's natural resources are the property of the state, available for short-term license but not for sale to private parties. This provision sought to effectively reverse the country's privatization of fishing licenses in the early 1990s, a process that some said had restored the vigor of the fishing industry but also contributed to growing disparities in wealth.

The draft was the basis of a referendum in October 2012 that was supportive of the proposed changes. Under the current constitution, amendment requires a vote in two successive parliaments, so the public's views were merely advisory. But the momentum suggested that a rare example of successful bottom-up demands for constitutional change might be at hand.

The action then shifted to the parliament to develop a final bill. That's where things got tricky. The opposition Progressive and Independence Parties began to attack the proposals with vigor; the Council of Europe's Venice Commission issued a report that identified a number of concerns in the draft; and the parliament began tinkering with the Bill. The parliament passed a bill without the key provisions from the citizen's draft, while raising the threshold for constitutional changes in the next parliament to two-thirds of parliament plus 40 percent of the popular vote. This was done in the shadow of upcoming elections that many expect the opposition expected to win.

In short, political parties, if stable, cannot be bypassed by the amendment process. To do so is to risk derailment at a further stage. Only in situations in which the existing political order is completely discredited can the strategy of bypassing politicians be effective.

10.4.2 *Role of Courts as Guardians*

Courts can play an important role as guardians of the constitution-making process. They form an example of an upstream constraint. Obviously, this option is most available when the courts have a good track record and are trusted by the actors in the political process.

The most famous example of judicial protection of the constitution-making process is that of the Constitutional Court of South Africa during the period of the Interim Constitution (1993–96). That constitution had laid out a set of basic principles to guide the drafting of the ultimate constitution by the constituent assembly. But the final constitution had to be certified by the Constitutional Court as conforming to the list of Constitutional Principles laid out in the earlier draft. The principles included both general concepts and also specific provisions that mattered to particular parties such as cultural self-determination and regional decentralization. In the event, the Constitutional Court rejected several provisions of the Constitution, as requested by several of the main political parties.[58] The Court

---

[58] The National Party and the Democratic Party voted for the Constitution, but challenged certification of certain points. The Inkatha Freedom Party also challenged the document.

provided guidance as to how to revise the text to conform to the Principles. After a revision, the Court engaged in a second round of certification, and approved the draft. Interestingly, the Court had a role in certifying provincial constitutions, and rejected one of them, that of KwaZulu Natal.

Another example occurred in Kenya. During the long period of Kenya's constitutional evolution from the one-party Moi regime in the first decade of this century, the Courts played some role. From 2001 to 2005, a series of drafts were produced by a drafting conference and then by parliament. There was little agreement on such basics as the type of government. In 2004, the Kenyan High Court decision in *Timothy Njoya & Others* v. *CKRC and the National Constitutional Conference* held that the constitution could not be replaced without a referendum. The ordinary amendment process included in Section 47 of the Constitution allowed for amendments, but not a complete replacement. In other words, one had to go back to the well of the pouvoir constituent in order to move forward with reforms of a certain scale. This is consistent with a distinction found in some constitutions between amendment and revision, which implies a larger scale of change.

The Colombian Constitutional Court made a similar move. The Constitution allows the Court to review amendments for procedure, including whether they are issued by a competent authority. The Court used this power to create a doctrine wherein amendments can be distinguished from replacements, which no authority has the power to effectuate. The Court thus set itself up as a guardian, ensuring that no amendment exceed a certain undefined scope.

More generally, constitutional courts have become quite active in policing constitutional amendments, sometimes on substantive grounds and sometimes on procedural grounds. Some Constitutional Courts (beginning with India's) have developed an idea that certain amendments cannot be made because they would change the fundamental structure of a constitution – while not about certifying the initial document, it is an example of how a court could hold that a constitution is unconstitutional.

In other states where the constitution contains different procedures for a "total revision" and a "partial revision" of the constitution, such as Austria or Nicaragua, courts sometimes declare themselves competent to define the distinction. Even without textual support, some courts have generated the distinction. For example, in South Korea, deciding that the Government could not fulfill a campaign promise to move the capital city, the court spoke in terms of an unwritten "customary constitution," which could not be changed without a public referendum. In this case, the court was cloaking its power grab (inventing an unwritten text that only it could see) by saying that it could be overcome with a certain level of political support.

The provisions included those on federal balance of power and that the Bill of Rights was not sufficiently entrenched.

In the Icelandic example described in the previous section, the parliamentary bill authorizing the "citizens' constitution," drafted in the aftermath of the financial crisis, called for, among other things, the election of twenty-five citizens to serve as a Constitutional Commission. The country's Supreme Court, however, invalidated the election. The parliament decided to appoint all of the elected members, so it was of little consequence. Another negative example occurred in Egypt in June 2012, when the Egyptian Supreme Constitutional Court dissolved the People's Assembly. The threat of further action by the country's courts is what prompted president Morsi to ram through his ill-fated constitution in late November.

Whether all of this is democratic or not is not our immediate concern. The conceptual point is that, whether or not they are authorized, courts often emerge as the policemen in constitutional reform processes. And this means that they are a potential modality to be considered in designing a constitutional reform process.

There is another role for courts in constitutional change, one that is so obvious as to be almost invisible. Courts modify the constitution through constitutional interpretation. Thus, if a political system believes that there are problems that need to be addressed, empowering the courts is a potential mechanism, though an unpredictable one. For example, Mexico's constitution has recently been amended to allow the courts to treat the rules of any treaty to which Mexico is a party – including human rights treaties – as superior to domestic law. This means that the normative basis of the constitution has been dramatically expanded. While beyond the scope of this article to address, one possibility for Chile is to reform the jurisdiction of the Constitutional Tribunal so as to encourage it to take a more aggressive role in *ex post*, as opposed to *ex ante*, constitutional review. Many countries in the region have reformed their systems of *amparo* to reflect the modern trend toward greater judicial protection of rights. There is no obvious reason why Chile should be an exception.

10.4.3 *Role of the People*

We conclude with some comments on the role of the people in constitutional reform. There has been a significant trend toward including the public in constitutional design. Indeed, some have argued that the right to participate in constitutional design has the status of a norm of international law.[59] Public participation comes at many phases in the constitutional design process. The public can be consulted in the process of formulating ideas for constitutional reform; it can monitor the drafting process; and it can also play a role in ratifying the final product through a public referendum.

---

[59] Vivien Hart, "Democratic Constitution Making (U.S. Institute of Peace, Special Report No. 107, 2003)." Available at ww.usip.org/pubs/specialreports/sr107.html; Thomas Franck and Arun Thiruvengadam, "Norms of International Law Related to the Constitution-Making Process," in *Framing the State in Times of Transition: Case Studies in Constitution-making* 3, ed. Laurel E. Miller, US Institute of Peace Press, 2010.

Such roles can make a real difference and serve as an important downstream constraint on the process. For example, in some cases, we observe public rejection of constitutional drafts: Kenya's Wako draft was rejected in a public referendum in 2005, and a draft constitution in the Seychelles failed to reach the 60 percent support threshold in 1992. In each case, these rejections led to renewed attempts at constitution-making that were more inclusive, and were ultimately successful.

Chile's public is politically informed and generally fairly well educated. In this sense, there is no theoretical reason why the public cannot play an important role in adopting a new constitution for itself. It is probably advisable, then, that any effort to reform the Constitution of Chile includes the voice of the public at the final stage, or very close thereto.

10.5 CONCLUSION

Chile's experience epitomizes what we have characterized as transformational authoritarian constitutionalism, in which the constitution is explicitly designed to return to popular rule but entrenches certain policy goals beyond democratic decision-making, and provides genuine institutional mechanisms to enforce these limits. It is a genuine form of constitutionalism, including the essential elements of entrenchment and constraint of both rulers and ruled. It is an explicitly temporary arrangement, which even the founders must realize has the potential to decay over time.[60] But, believing in the merits of their policy preferences, the founders seem to think the limitations will eventually become so internalized by the population as to be self-enforcing. In this sense, these are optimistic documents.

In many ways, the 1980 Constitution of Chile has served its purpose, however defined. It successfully entrenched major policy priorities of the military regime, while also facilitating a major political transition, and has secured a strong market economy. Though too slow for proponents of democratic reform, the transition has been accomplished without violence, with most amendments having secured the political support of the inheritors of the 1973 coup.

During the last decade, there have been calls for change, reflecting the completely different context of Chile today. Such calls are quite natural and should be addressed. How to do so is a major question. My suggestion is that the comparative literature sheds little light on the precise modality by which reform is accomplished, whether through constituent assembly or legislature. We can say, however, that there are other possibilities that should be considered. A national conference on constitutional reform might be a first step; the last step should include broad participation through constitutional referendum. And the drafting process in between ought to include the existing political parties, as they cannot be avoided in any case.

[60] *See* Ozan Varol, "Temporary Constitutions." *California Law Review* 102 (2014).

Authoritarian Straitjacket or Vehicle for Democratic Transition?

The Risky Struggle to Change Myanmar's Constitution

Melissa Crouch[1]

11.1 INTRODUCTION

Since the referendum that nominally approved the 2008 Constitution, scholars of comparative politics have sought to understand and explain Myanmar's political transition after decades of seemingly indefatigable military rule.[2] There has been less scholarly focus on the politics of constitutional reform in Myanmar. This chapter advocates taking law seriously in authoritarian regimes and builds on a line of scholarship that examines the role of courts and constitutions in these regimes.[3] Contributing to the theme of this volume on implementing new constitutions, I consider the challenges to the 2008 Constitution in its first period of implementation. In exploring the options for constitutional reform by democratic actors, I emphasize the risks these options entail.

There is a paradox in a country like Myanmar where a constitution drafted under authoritarian rule facilitates a political transition. The Constitution can be understood as a "transformative authoritarian constitution," which Ginsburg argues is a

[1] I would like to thank Theunis Roux for comments on an early version of this chapter, as well as Dan Slater and other participants of the workshop in Chicago.
[2] See, for example, Kyaw Yin Hlaing, "Power and Factional Struggles in Post-independence Burmese Governments." *Journal of Southeast Asian Studies* 39 (1): 149 (2008); Ian Holliday, "Myanmar in 2012: Toward a Normal State." *Asian Survey* 53 (1): 93–100 (2013); Lee Jones (2013) "Explaining Myanmar's Regime Transition: The Periphery Is Central," *Democratization*, 1–23; Dan Slater, "The Elements of Surprise: Assessing Burma's Double-edged détente." *South East Asia Research* 22 (2): 171–82 (2014). Marco Bünte, "Burma's Transition to Quasi-Military Rule: From Rulers to Guardians?" *Armed Forces & Society* 40 (4): 742–64 (2014).
[3] See for example Tom Ginsburg and Tamir Moustafa (eds.) *Rule by Law: The Politics of Courts in Authoritarian Regimes.* Cambridge University Press, 2008; Tom Ginsburg and Albert Simpers (eds.) *Constitutions in Authoritarian Regimes.* Cambridge University Press, 2014; Tamir Moustafa, "Law and Courts in Authoritarian Regimes." *Annual Review of Law and Social Sciences* 10: 281–99 (2014); Robert Barros, *Constitutionalism and Dictatorship: Pinochet, the Junta and the 1980 Constitution.* Cambridge University Press, 2002; David Landau "Abusive Constitutionalism." *UC Davis Law Review* 47: 189–260: (2013–14).

subtype of authoritarian constitutions that can be seen at work in a range of countries from Chile to Taiwan.[4] Ginsburg finds evidence to suggest that such constitutions may lead to democratic transformation. However, this finding should not cause us to dismiss the very real risks to democratic actors who seek to change a constitution in its first period since transition from direct military rule. By its very nature, a transformative constitution is not designed to allow substantial change in the future, and any change that is permitted is likely to be highly contained and controlled. I assume that the risks associated with changing a constitution during the first period of implementation after a transition from direct military rule are higher than in later stages, and that the risks to change a transformative authoritarian constitution are higher than the risks to change a democratic constitution, at least if fundamental change is being considered. In this respect, I focus on constitutional change and risk-taking during the first period, and particularly under authoritarian constitutions.

The potential risks are related to the different strategies available to pro-democratic actors who seek greater social and political transformation through constitutional change in Myanmar. I suggest there are three main strategies: to draft a new constitution, amend the constitution formally, or attempt informal amendment. These options are potentially open to both pro-democratic[5] actors, such as the National League for Democracy (NLD), and undemocratic actors, such as the military. The least likely option, given present political conditions in Myanmar, is revolution and the drafting of a new constitution. The reason this is near impossible is because the 2008 Constitution was designed as a permanent and lasting structure that conditions and limits politics in the new regime. There is little political space or tolerance toward efforts to draft a new constitution.

Another option is for pro-democratic actors to push for formal constitutional amendment through the required procedure under the 2008 Constitution. This option means that pro-democratic actors must subject themselves to the authority of the Constitution and the specific requirements it mandates for change. The third option for constitutional change is for pro-democratic actors to make efforts toward informal constitutional amendment. While there may be many ways in which informal constitutional change takes place, I focus on two means of informal amendment: by the legislature passing a law that empowers the administration to do something that does not appear to fit within the existing constitutional order; and judicial interpretation as a means of informal amendment. I seek to show that both

---

[4] Tom Ginsburg, Fruit of the Poisoned Vine? Some Comparative Observations on Chile's Constitution, *Centro de Estudios Públicos* (CEP), Santiago de Chile (2014).
[5] In this chapter, I use a thin definition of "democratic actors" – i.e. those who advocate for an elected government. This thin definition of democratic actors means that they are not necessarily advocates of liberal ideas of rights or equality, as we will see in the case of the NLD and prevailing views toward the Rohingya.

formal and informal amendment of Myanmar's Constitution during this first period has attracted certain risks.

In the first part of my chapter I explain why we are still in the first period of Myanmar's Constitution and I introduce the contours of Myanmar's 2008 Constitution that are designed to endure. I then consider three different strategies that have been used to try to change the 2008 Constitution – formal constitutional amendment proposals; judicial interpretation in the Constitutional Tribunal; and legislative innovation with the Office of the State Counsellor. I identify the various risks pro-democratic actors have suffered for these actions as a result of seeking change in this first period. I conclude by suggesting that it is necessary to keep in mind the risks to local actors who push for constitutional change in the first period of transitional regimes.

11.2 THE FIRST PERIOD OF THE 2008 CONSTITUTION

The first presidential election held at the beginning of 2011 marked the initiation of a new political and legal system in Myanmar. This system is regulated and framed by the 2008 Constitution. My approach in this chapter to the study of Myanmar's Constitution is intentionally qualitative and based on extensive field research. The need to base the study of constitutional law and politics in Myanmar on ground up studies of Burmese language texts, understood within the wider social and political context, is critical.[6]

In keeping with the theme of this volume, Myanmar remains in this critical "first period" of the Constitution. Any of the possible approaches to defining the first period, as identified by Ginsburg and Huq, suggest that Myanmar remains in this first period. Their first approach is to define the first period within the general hazard rate of constitutions. Clearly, Myanmar's 2008 Constitution has outlasted the average constitution beyond the first year or even five years. However, since the drafters clearly intended the Constitution to last far beyond this average, other measures of the first period are more relevant.

The second approach to the first period is to identify a key institutional event, such as free and fair elections. Many observers credit 2015 as the first free and fair elections, although as I show later in this chapter it is questionable whether we should in fact consider this the first free and fair election when over one million people were disenfranchised in the process. At any rate, most scholars of democratic consolidation would agree that a minimum of two successive elections must be held

---

[6] This is particularly the case because the Burmese version is declared to be the *only* authoritative version, and the English language translation of the 2008 Constitution is inaccurate and inconsistent. This creates a potential problem for text-based case studies of Myanmar's Constitution that presume the accuracy of the English language translation of the Constitution.

before consolidation, or that crucial first period, has taken place. This is not yet the case in Myanmar.

The third approach to defining the "first period" is by asking whether the constitution-drafters are still involved in governance. In brief, the National Convention was held from 1993–97 and 2004–7. Representatives were chosen by the military, although initially some of these were members who had been democratically elected in the 1990 elections. There are both high and low profile actors from the military and ethnic groups who were involved in the National Convention of the 1990s–2000s and who remain involved in government today. These political elites are well-known and include former President Thein Sein, the Chief Justice of the Supreme Court, and the former Speaker and chairperson of the Legal Affairs and Special Cases Assessment Commission, Shwe Mann. But it also includes other characters, such as former representatives of ethnic nationalities at the National Convention, some of whom are now Ministers for National Races Affairs. There also remain a cast of characters behind the scenes, including General Than Shwe, who led the prior military regime. In this regard, the first period of the Constitution continues under the influence of constitution-drafters.

The fourth approach is to measure the "first period" as the time when habits and shared understandings about the Constitution are solidified. As I will show, the high level of contestation over the Constitution and efforts for constitutional change suggest that this process of embedding shared accepted understandings has not yet taken place.

Finally, and perhaps most relevant to Myanmar, the first period can be defined as the time when the policy issues that constitution-makers sought to address via the Constitution are resolved. There are a range of policy issues that Myanmar's Constitution targets that have been resolved. The goal of ensuring that the military retains a prominent role in national governance has been secured by the Constitution. The Constitution has facilitated a return to party politics and achieved the goal of ending one-party socialist rule or rule without political parties. The Constitution has also solved the problem of a minimum level of political inclusion for both ethnic political parties and democratic parties, who can now compete in elections. The Constitution plays a role in reinforcing the principle of a market economy, which achieves the goal of shifting away from a socialist economy.

However, the Constitution has failed at this juncture to address one major policy goal: the end to several decades of armed conflict and the creation of a durable nationwide peace agreement. Despite the ceasefire agreements of the 1990s and new constitutional arrangements to recognize select ethnic groups, war has continued. The need for a national ceasefire process was not anticipated by the constitution-drafters. The new national ceasefire process commenced in 2012, and by 2015 the National Ceasefire Agreement was signed by eight of fifteen groups. However, all invited armed groups have not yet signed the agreement, and even if this does occur it may then lead to increased demands for constitutional change. What is clear is that on any approach, Myanmar remains within the first period of its Constitution. I suggest that the possibility of changing the Constitution during this first period remains low, and that the risks to actors of trying to do so are relatively high.

This is because many of the core features of the Constitution are designed for permanence. The Constitution centralizes and affirms the role of the military in the governance of the country. This is evident from the first chapter on Basic Principles, where the military is given prime position in the future political system and is central to the objectives of protecting national unity, maintaining territorial unity, and guaranteeing the sovereignty of the nation. These principles mirror the previous slogans of the former military regime, upgrading them from military slogans to constitutional principle. The chapter on Basic Principles subverts the very idea usually associated with constitutional principles, as it is used to entrench military governance.[7] The chapter on Basic Principles is explicitly required to guide the legislature in its role in drafting laws, and also the courts in their role in interpreting both the Constitution and other laws.[8]

It is within this context of military governance that the rest of the political system needs to be viewed. While the Constitution does establish a bi-cameral union parliament, 25 percent of the seats are unelected and constitutionally reserved for the military. What is more, the military has adopted a deliberate practice of rotating military officers, so that they are not in parliament long enough to build connections with, be influenced by, or form allegiances with other political actors such as the NLD or ethnic political parties. The NLD has protested against this practice, arguing that at the very least military officers appointed to parliament should be required to serve the full five-year term rather than being subject to constant rotations. These complaints have been ignored.

The reservation of 25 percent of parliamentary seats does not enable the military to block legislative proposals. But the reserved seating system does ensure that the military members of parliament can infiltrate and monitor democratically elected members of parliament, as well as participate in various high-level appointments. For example, the military members of parliament, along with the upper house and lower house, each appoint a candidate for the positions of president and vice-presidents. This means that, at the very least, the military members of parliament get to appoint a vice-president. In addition, the constitutional amendment clause requires more than 75 percent approval in parliament, giving the military members of parliament veto power over any future constitutional amendment proposal.

The next indication of the dominance of the military over the most important and influential areas of government administration is the designation of three important

---

[7] This is contrary to the usual focus in comparative constitutional studies on Fundamental or Basic Principles in democracies such as the Indian and Irish Constitutions.

[8] For a detailed discussion see Melissa Crouch, *The Constitution of Myanmar: A Contextual Analysis*. Oxford: Hart Publishing, 2019.

Ministries – Home Affairs, Defence, Border Affairs – who are recommended by the Commander-in-Chief of the President. There are several reasons these ministerial positions are important. The Ministry of Border Affairs has historically been used by the military to control and contain areas on the territorial periphery of the country that are more prone to ethnic armed insurgencies. The Ministry of Home Affairs supervises the police, and so the line between the military and the police is blurred. The Ministry of Home Affairs also supervised the General Administration Department (GAD), which is the government administration at the state and region level. In December 2018 this changed, with the GAD now responsible to the Ministers Office of the Union of Myanmar. The Ministry of Defence is in full control of all aspects of the army, navy, and air force, and is not subordinate to the executive. The Constitution also creates a National Defence and Security Council, in which military officers or military appointees hold a majority of the seats. Although the president has the power to call a meeting of the Council, he must the consult the Council on any decision to declare a state of emergency.

Despite the military's pervasive role, the Constitution still offers significant, highly centralized powers to any party that can win a majority of seats in the union parliament, as the NLD did in 2015. The Constitution introduces a President as the head of state. The President does have the power to appoint many key political, administrative, and judicial posts. The election of the heads (known as "chief ministers") of the fourteen states and regions is not a democratic or direct election, but remains the decision of the President. This stunts any independence that the states/regions might have and limits future possibilities for decentralization or federalism. The appointment and accountability structure means that the President has significant control over some aspects of the civilian dimension of the political system. However, the President and the government of the day are entirely dependent on the military for security and for its cooperation in the implementation of policy through the administration.

The Constitution does provide for an upper house (Amyotha Hluttaw) with ethnic representation, but in the end the will of the more numerous lower house (Pyithu Hluttaw) prevails in any decisions made by the Pyidaungsu Hluttaw (Union Parliament) sitting jointly. The Constitution includes a chapter on duties and rights that positions duties as more important and conceptually prior to rights.[9] This chapter is hedged by qualifications and in practice has delivered no practical benefits or protections for individuals. Despite the reintroduction of the constitutional writs and the potential to use these remedies for the enforcement of individual rights, the writs applications have largely been stymied in the court system.

The outcome of the 2008 Constitution is to introduce a highly centralized and militarized regime. In addition to limitations on elections, Myanmar's contemporary

---

[9]   See further Crouch, The Constitution of Myanmar: A Contextual Analysis, chapter 9.

political regime is animated by other tensions common to authoritarian regimes. Pro-democratic actors still face significant threats to their personal safety. Limited forms of opposition are now permitted, such as the formation of political parties and unions. Yet the situation remains precarious for democratic actors – particularly student activists and journalists – who remain targets of surveillance, harassment, punishment, and detention. There also remains rampant abuse of state resources through the opaque nature of state-owned enterprises, the omnipotent presence of major military-run corporations, and the cartels of cronies in natural resources such as jade, rubies, oil, and gas. Land claims and complaints of land grabbing remain among the top concerns of abuse of state power. This is all the more pressing given that a large percentage of the population depends on agriculture for their livelihood. Further, Myanmar remains plagued by media restrictions. In 2012, media restrictions were lifted, censorship regulations were removed, and papers were allowed to publish daily (rather than weekly). Yet practical restrictions remain, and this is evident in the frequency with which journalists and editors are found in contempt of court or face politicised criminal charges. In 2018 two Reuters journalists were convicted by a court for investigating a massacre in Rakhine State.

Understanding the system that the 2008 Constitution puts in place and the privileges it grants to the military enables us to better appreciate how the prospect of constitutional change may be perceived as a threat. Constitutional change threatens the centrality of the military in governance, politics, security, and the administration. It threatens the military with the potential loss of its immunity under the existing Constitution. It also threatens to deny or limit the military's ability to engineer a constitutional takeover, as justified in the extensive emergency powers chapter, if or when needed. In order to mitigate the perception of these threats, I suggest that the NLD chose formal constitutional amendment to demonstrate its willingness to work within the current system.

11.3 FORMAL CONSTITUTIONAL CHANGE IN THE FIRST PERIOD

Formal constitutional change is a means of working *within* the system for social and political change. It requires actors to demonstrate a sense of commitment to and recognition of the existing political and legal order, regardless of how it came into existence. This was particularly difficult for the NLD and other parties who won seats in the 1990 elections but were later told by the military that the election was to appoint a Constituent Assembly to draft a new constitution, rather than an election for a new and democratic Parliament. The NLD held out until they finally agreed to run in the 2012 bi-elections. In doing so, the NLD demonstrates that it is willing to work within the boundaries of the Constitution. Reinforcing this approach, the NLD has shown that it is willing to go through the arduous constitutional amendment requirements as set out in the Constitution. In doing so, the NLD's proposals were largely ignored, and instead the bills submitted to parliament contained a range of proposed amendments that would instead have reinforced regime interests. Attempts to formally amend the Constitution in the first period have come attached with certain risks for democratic actors.

The official process to initiate formal constitutional amendment began in 2013 after the NLD and 88 Generation had campaigned widely on the issue. In 2013, a Constitutional Review Committee was established by parliament. The Committee was responsible for proposing constitutional amendments to promote peace, national unity, and democratic reforms in Myanmar. The Committee consisted of existing members of parliament. Most were from the USDP (the civilian political party most closely aligned with the military), ethnic-based political parties, or the military itself. All of these members of parliament (except for the military officers) were elected in the 2010 elections, which were not considered to be free and fair. The Committee did include seven NLD members, who were elected in the 2012 by-election, which was considered to be free and fair.

In advocating for formal amendment, the NLD first organized a series of peaceful demonstrations as well as education campaigns across the country. In late 2013, the public was given the opportunity to make written submissions to the Committee. The NLD's formal submission emphasized democracy, federalism, and civilian control over the military. I discuss its proposal here in order to contrast it with the Committee's 2014 Report and with the 2015 proposed bill for amendment. The NLD sought to emphasize that the Union should be identified as a federal Union. The NLD's proposal aimed to reinforce the principle of democracy by removing the word "disciplined," which currently qualifies the principles (i.e. "disciplined democracy"). This emphasis was related to its proposal to remove the role of the military from politics and remove its influence over any political appointments. This included removing military members of parliament, and removing the military's power to appoint a vice-president and other ministerial positions. This was highly controversial, although in its submission the NLD admitted this may need to be done gradually. They also suggested reforms to separate the military from the police.

The NLD proposed limits on executive power. They suggested that the term of office of the President and Vice-presidents should be limited to just one term. Rather than leave many decisions within the sole power of the president, the NLD suggested balancing the power of the President by requiring him or her to make certain decisions together with the Speakers of the upper and lower houses. The NLD proposed to bring all cabinet positions (President, Vice-President, and all Ministers) back into parliament, and allow them to retain their status as an active member of a political party. It also proposed that only elected representatives can be appointed as Ministers (currently unelected persons can be appointed to these positions). The NLD sought to change the balance of power in the National Security and Defence Council by adding in the Speakers of the upper and lower house as members, which would mean that the government of the day, rather than the military, would have a majority on the council.

In terms of central–local relations, the NLD proposed to change the balance of power and reporting lines slightly at the subnational level. Instead of the Ministers of State/Region Hluttaws being responsible to the President, they suggested that the Minister be responsible to the Chief Minister. The Chief Minister would be appointed by a majority of votes of the Ministers of that state/region parliament.

Regarding the courts, there were several key changes proposed. The NLD wanted to change the centralized judicial appointment processes so that the Chief Justice of the Supreme Court, together with Chief Ministers of the States/Regions, appointed the High Court judges (instead of the President). They also wanted the Supreme Court to be the highest court (i.e. the courts martial would be subordinate to it), and they proposed to abolish the Constitutional Tribunal and give these powers to the Supreme Court. In terms of individual rights, the main change was a proposal to make the Basic Principles in chapter 1 judicially enforceable (they are currently unenforceable in a court), because they felt this would better protect individual rights.

The NLD wanted to change the constitutional amendment provision so that proposals could be approved by a two-thirds vote of civilian members of parliament in the Pyidaungsu Hluttaw (i.e. excluding military members from the vote). They also wanted to delete section 59f (to allow Suu Kyi to be elected as president) and amend section 59d so that a presidential candidate did not have to have military experience.

The Constitutional Amendment Committee received a large number of submissions but the recommendations in these submissions were not made public. In January 2014, the Committee released its report, yet it failed to identify any proposals for constitutional amendment. The Report adopted an "anti-change" tone and was emphatic that some provisions of the Constitution *should not* be amended. The most controversial aspect was the report's reference to key aspects of the Constitution that should not be amended, based on a petition signed by 106,102 people (which was presumed to be organized by the USDP and military). These recommendations ran directly contrary to the NLD's main proposals for change. The petition recommended that three key aspects of the Constitution be *retained*: the role of the military in politics, the prohibition on presidential candidates holding foreign citizenship in section 59f, and section 436 on the process for amendment that gives veto power to the military. This was the first major sign that the NLD's efforts at formal constitutional amendment would not only fail to be put to parliament but lead to constitutional regression.

In mid-2015 two bills were finally proposed in parliament, one containing provisions that required both parliamentary approval and a nationwide referendum, and the other bill that only required approval by more than 75 percent in parliament. The main proposal that did address concerns raised by the NLD but did not go far enough was the extent to which the President should have control over appointments and responsibilities of state/region parliaments. The system is highly centralized, and democratic actors wanted to decentralize power to an extent. The NLD's proposal for Chief Ministers to be appointed by a vote in the State/Region parliament was not accepted. Instead, the proposed bill suggested that the Union Parliament should decide together with the President on the appointment of the Chief Ministers of the States and Regions (rather than the President alone).

On the courts, the proposed bill would have led to undemocratic reforms by suggesting five-year terms for judges of the Supreme Court and High Courts. This would change the current system of retirement at a set age to instead effectively tie judges to the term of the government. The proposal did not agree with changes to the appointment process for judges as the NLD had suggested, but instead allowed the Speakers of the upper and lower house to decide together with the president on certain appointments. This was another minor concession to balance the power of the President with that of parliament. The proposed bill sought to retain the Constitutional Tribunal, which the NLD had wanted abolished.

Regarding the proposal to amend constitutional provisions, the NLD's suggestions again were ignored. For provisions that also require a constitutional referendum, it was proposed that the constitution require more than half of those who voted to agree (rather than half of all eligible voters). This proposal also failed to receive approval.

There were only two proposed amendments that were actually approved by parliament, and neither is centrally directed at democratic transformation. The first was to change the wording of section 59(d) on presidential requirements, so that a president must be familiar with "defence" matters rather than "military" affairs. This distinction between defence/military is subtle, and suggests that a presidential candidate does not actually have to come from the military. To be fully approved, this provision requires a referendum to be held, which has not occurred to date. The only other proposal that was approved and did not require a referendum was the clarification of legislative and taxation powers as set out in the Schedules to the Constitution. The proposal clarified the ability of the fourteen States and Regions to collect income tax, customs duties and stamp duty, and levies on services (tourism, hotels, private schools, and private hospitals) and resources including oil, gas, mining, and gems. Combined with a decision in which the Tribunal declined to interpret the legislative schedules and instead deferred a question of inconsistency between the schedules to the Parliament, the constitutional amendments suggest that the Constitutional Tribunal does not have power to interpret the schedules to the Constitution and instead the Union Parliament must clarify or expand the list via formal amendment. This appears to be based on a misunderstanding that legislative power in the Constitution can only be clarified or changed by the parliament, rather than interpreted by the Tribunal. In this way, formal amendment detracted further from the power of the Tribunal as a check on parliament.

The outcome of the 2015 proposals for amendment suggests that the NLD's strategic choice to pursue formal constitutional amendment during the first period has backfired. Many individuals have faced *personal risks* such as being arrested and tried for criminal offences for their efforts in demonstrating or protesting in favor of constitutional change. Efforts toward formal constitutional amendment have *reinforced limits* on democratic reform, rather than open up greater social and political transformation. The NLD's proposals for formal constitutional amendment failed to even be reflected in the bills submitted to parliament. In addition, the Committee's first report reinforced central elements of the Constitution that favor military interests, and the contents of the bills proposed in parliament affirm the interests of a highly centralized and militarized political system.

On January 29, 2019, on the second commemoration of the political assassination of lawyer U Ko Ni, the NLD initiated a process of constitutional amendment in the legislature. The military displayed its opposition to this initiative by refusing to vote on the legislative proposal to form the committee. The Committee was formed in February 2019 with forty-five members, and this process remained ongoing at the time of writing. One of the biggest issues that has dominated discussion is whether to amend section 261 to allow Chief Ministers at the subnational level to be appointed directly. However, it is unclear whether the legislature will be able to agree on any proposal for amendment, given that the military has expressed its strong disapproval of the process. While the NLD's efforts to formally amend the Constitution demonstrate it is still trying to work within the limits of the 2008 Constitution, this approach remains risky and there is no indication they will be able to amend the Constitution before the 2020 elections.

11.4 JUDICIAL INTERPRETATION AS CONSTITUTIONAL CHANGE

Aside from formal constitutional change, there is a range of ways that actors may seek informal constitutional change during the first period of the Constitution. For pro-democratic actors, judicial interpretation may provide an opportunity to work around the initial or original intentions of the drafters of the constitution. The courts are potentially a means to push for a new or more expansive interpretation in light of changing social and political circumstances. The potential risk is that if pro-democratic opposition forces do not take up the opportunity that judicial interpretation presents, then the courts may instead be used by regime forces to bolster their existing position. In Myanmar, it is pro-military forces, that is, the USDP, military officers, and to a lesser extent some ethnic political parties, that have been willing to use the courts to seek informal change through judicial interpretation. I identify how the failure of pro-democratic forces such as the NLD to take up the opportunity that judicial interpretation offers has instead allowed room for regime forces to take full advantage of the courts to bolster their existing constitutional position.

This is exemplified in the mass disenfranchisement of temporary identity card holders (once known as "white cards") prior to the historic 2015 elections in Myanmar. In a country going through a transition from authoritarian rule, there is inevitable controversy over who is a citizen of the state and how the rules of citizenship are determined.[10] The issue of citizenship and who can vote remains a heated debate in Myanmar and relates to racialized ideas of citizenship.[11] Although the general international perception is that the 2015 elections in Myanmar were the first free and fair elections for over fifty years, there remained significant limitations. Pro-regime forces used the Constitutional Tribunal to support its agenda of disenfranchising over 1.3 million people who held temporary identity cards, most of whom are Rohingya Muslims.

In 2015, the Citizenship Case before the Constitutional Tribunal raised the issue of the right to vote in the Constitution.[12] The question before the Tribunal was not whether legislation had *failed* to protect the constitutional right to vote and to be elected, but rather whether it had gone beyond the legal scope of the constitutional right. In effect, the applicants were seeking to *restrict* the constitutional right to vote and to be elected to parliament, in order to deny temporary identity card holders (many of whom are Muslim) from enjoying this right. The Tribunal case came in the wake of several years of violence, discrimination, and efforts to marginalize and exclude the Rohingya and Muslims more broadly, as well as attempts to discredit the NLD by painting them as a "pro-Muslim" political party. Although Myanmar is a Buddhist-majority country, it has a Muslim population of 4 percent according to the 2014 census. An additional 1.3 million Muslims were not recorded in the census. Myanmar does, however, have a history of Muslim political participation. In the 2010 election and 2012 bi-election temporary identity card holders were able to vote and to run in the elections.[13] Three Muslim candidates were successful in winning seats in elections during this period. The political parties that these members of parliament represent have never been based on an Islamist ideology and do not advocate for the institutionalization of Islamic law.[14] However, from 2011 to 2015, the three Rohingya members of parliament in northern Rakhine State were questioned over their citizenship status and hounded out of parliament.

This effort coincided with the rise of radical Buddhism and the ensuing violence against Muslims in Myanmar.[15] This has been a critical issue since 2012, when large-scale conflict broke out in northern Rakhine State and spread to many major towns

[10] Juan J Linz and Alfred Stephan, *Problems of Democratic Transition and Consolidation: Southern Europe, South America, and Post-Communist Europe.* Baltimore: Johns Hopkins University Press, 1996, 28.
[11] See Ian Holliday, "Addressing Myanmar's Citizenship Crisis." *Journal of Contemporary Asia* 44 (3): 404–21 (2014); and, Nick Cheesman, ("How in Myanmar 'National Races' Came to Surpass Citizenship and Exclude Rohingya." *Journal of Contemporary Asia* 47 (3): 461–83 (2017).
[12] Constitutional Court Decision, Citizenship Case 2015.
[13] Nicholas Farrelly, "Muslim Political Participation in Myanmar," in *Islam and the State in Myanmar,* ed. M. Crouch. Oxford University Press, 2016.
[14] Melissa Crouch, "Myanmar's Muslim Mosaic and the Politics of Belonging," in *Islam and the State in Myanmar,* ed. M. Crouch. Oxford University Press, 2016.
[15] Nyi Nyi Kyaw, "Islamophobia in Buddhist Myanmar: The 969 Movement and Anti-Muslim Violence," in *Islam and the State in Myanmar,* ed. M. Crouch. Oxford University Press, 2016.

across Myanmar.[16] While the initial targets in Rakhine State were largely Rohingya Muslims, the conflicts that broke out in other parts of Myanmar targeted Muslim communities more broadly. In short, by 2014, this led to overt anti-Muslim campaigns and attempts to smear the NLD in the lead up to the 2015 elections for being perceived as "pro-Muslim." In 2014, the President issued a notification requiring all temporary identity card holders to hand in their cards. In late 2014, parliament amended several electoral laws so that temporary identity card holders – many of whom are Muslim and from Rakhine State (who may identify as Rohingya) – could not vote or run for elections. In 2015, a law was passed in parliament to set out the process for a referendum on constitutional amendment, although it *did* allow white card holders to vote.[17]

As a result, an application was brought to the Constitutional Tribunal challenging the provision by arguing that it was unconstitutional to allow white card holders to vote in a referendum. The case was brought by Dr. Aye Maung, an ethnic Rakhine Buddhist and leader of the Arakan National Party, and other members of the Amoytha Hluttaw (the Upper House). The applicants challenged the provision of the Law on the Constitutional Referendum concerning who could vote in a referendum.[18] The applicants relied on the constitutional provisions on the right to vote and to be elected, and also referred to the process and eligibility of a citizen to vote.[19] They argued that the Constitution did not mention the phrase "temporary identity card holders" but only used the term "citizens," and so under s 198(a) the provision of the law was inconsistent with the Constitution and the Constitution should prevail. The application also referred to the definition of a citizen in the Constitution that limits the concept of "citizen" to a person whose parents were born in Myanmar, or a person who had already been granted citizenship at the time the Constitution came into force.[20] The applicants emphasized the constitutional provision stating that sovereign power resides in citizens,[21] and argued that only citizens should have the right to vote in a referendum on constitutional amendment. Instead of conceiving sovereign power as residing in "the people" in a broad sense, it was argued that sovereign power was restricted to citizens.

The Tribunal noted that the 1982 Citizenship Law allows associate citizens and naturalized citizens to have the same rights as citizens, unless this right is limited by the state. The Tribunal observed that the law does not, however, offer the same rights to temporary card holders. The Tribunal held that the provision of the Law on

[16] For a recent collection of articles on communal violence in Myanmar, see Nick Cheesman, "Interpreting Communal Violence in Myanmar," *Journal of Contemporary Asia* 47 (3), Special Issue (2017).
[17] Law on the Referendum to Amend the 2008 Constitutional of the Union of Myanmar No 2/2015 [in Burmese].
[18] Law on the Constitutional Referendum No 11/2015, s 11(a).
[19] 2008 Constitution, ss 38(a), 369, s 391(a).
[20] 2008 Constitution, s 345.
[21] 2008 Constitution, s 4.

the Constitutional Referendum was invalid because it was inconsistent with the provisions on the right to vote in the Constitution.

The Tribunal's decision contributed to the disenfranchisement of over one million people. White card holders were explicitly denied the right to vote in an election and denied the right to run for political office. While it was not just the Tribunal decision that triggered this legislative reversal against electoral rights for individuals with white cards, it was one more justification for the parliament to pass legislative amendments to the electoral laws. This demonstrates that the right to vote in the 2008 Constitution is a fragile and highly contingent right.[22] Major conflict in Rakhine State continued in 2016–17 and led to the mass displacement of Rohingya, with over one million now living in camps in Bangladesh. The 2020 elections, if they go ahead in Rakhine State, are likely to perpetuate the exclusion of the Rohingya. The 2015 court case is an instance of constitutional change for illiberal means, that is, the exclusion of a particular group from the right to vote that reinforces regime interests.[23]

11.5 LEGISLATIVE REFORM AS INFORMAL CONSTITUTIONAL CHANGE

Another type of informal constitutional change that has occurred in Myanmar is change through legislative reform and executive action. Although the NLD has failed to formally amend the Constitution to date, it has been able to effect informal constitutional change in the creation of a de facto leader for the government. I focus on the example of the legislative creation of the Office of the State Counsellor created under the NLD.[24] This example demonstrates that pro-democratic forces may seek informal constitutional amendment to get around provisions of the Constitution that do not allow them to rule directly in the way they want. I will show that this is a high-risk option in the first period, particularly when informal constitutional change is perceived to be an underhanded means of changing the Constitution.

In early 2016, as the NLD was poised to take over government, there was clearly overwhelming public support for Aung San Suu Kyi to lead the country. The question that the NLD had to resolve was how this could be constitutionally justified. At first, a prominent lawyer and legal advisor to the NLD, U Ko Ni, argued

---

[22] This is important to note, as some quantitative comparative constitutional law studies argue that Myanmar is an example of a Constitution where the right to vote is fully protected and upheld. The reality of mass disenfranchisement, the social pressure not to vote for Muslims, and the absence of elections in areas of ongoing conflict show otherwise.

[23] I leave aside the issue of whether the NLD agreed that white card holders should not be allowed to vote, but this does raise the question of how proposals for constitutional change are affected when those who claim to be democratic actors hold illiberal views.

[24] There are other examples, such as actions that Suu Kyi took while chair of the ad hoc Rule of Law Committee in parliament, which were not within the remit of the legislative committee and could be perceived as informal constitutional change.

that the parliament could appoint Suu Kyi as president if parliament first *suspended* section 59(f) of the Constitution (the provision that is regarded as barring Suu Kyi from becoming president). This option was risky and did not have a clear constitutional basis.

An alternative option advocated by U Ko Ni was a law to establish a new and unprecedented executive position. The first law proposed by the NLD government was for the creation of the position of State Counsellor.[25] This option was justified based on the constitutional power of parliament to pass laws, and the power of the President to delegate executive power to anyone he chose. In this way, it could be argued that the law did not betray the constitutional text. Yet the military members of parliament were under no illusion that this reform amounted to constitutional change and threatened the system they had created. They raised objections in parliament and at one point there were indications that the military members of parliament may challenge the constitutionality of the State Counsellor law in the Constitutional Tribunal, although this has not occurred to date. Their objections were ignored and the law was passed by the majority NLD government.

The State Counsellor's Office is an innovative use of legal text to achieve the goal of Suu Kyi serving as leader of the government.[26] There are several reasons why this innovation can be understood as informal constitutional change. This legislative reform enabled Suu Kyi to become the de facto leader of the government and to the international community, the de facto leader of the country. The creation of the State Counsellor role readjusted the way people understand the role of the President in Myanmar, giving the President a more symbolic and ceremonial function. The State Counsellor draws attention and authority away from the Office of the President.[27] The Office of the State Counsellor is specific to Suu Kyi, so no other person can occupy this office unless the law is changed. The stated purpose of the role of the State Counsellor is to foster a market economy, to enhance democracy, to promote peace and development, and to work toward federalism. The goals of building a market economy and promoting peace and development are consistent with the wording and intentions of the 2008 Constitution. However, the goal of fostering democracy may be at odds with the 2008 Constitution's more qualified version of "disciplined democracy"; and the goal of working toward a federal system is arguably inconsistent with the 2008 Constitution, which does not explicitly claim to uphold federalism as a fundamental principle.

The State Counsellor has appropriated and adopted many leadership functions that may otherwise have been undertaken by the president. The law requires the State Counsellor to make recommendations and report to the Union Parliament,

---

[25] Law 26/2016 on the Office of the State Counsellor.

[26] This can also be understood as a constitutional workaround, see Mark Tushnet, "Constitutional Workarounds." *Texas Law Review* 87 (7): 1499 (2009).

[27] See further, Crouch, *The Constitution of Myanmar: A Contextual Analysis*, chapter 6.

and in doing so to work within the existing Constitution. In this role, Aung San Suu Kyi has established and spearheaded the new 21st Century Panglong Peace Process (a reference to the 1947 Panglong Agreement orchestrated by her father General Aung San). She is the chairperson of the Union Peace Dialogue Joint Committee that facilitates and manages the ongoing peace talks. She also occasionally issues announcements, such as granting an amnesty for political prisoners, which is a task former President Thein Sein previously undertook. She is the chairperson of the Central Committee on the Implementation of Peace, Stability and Development of Rakhine State. She plays a significant role in international relations, meeting with foreign ambassadors and other foreign dignitaries, although she also wears the hat of Minister of Foreign Affairs and Minister of the President's Office. It is not always clear which capacity she is acting in. Further, the international community sees Suu Kyi, rather than the President, as the leader of Myanmar. An example is the response of the international community in August 2017, when they called upon Suu Kyi to speak out in support of the Rohingya and to acknowledge and address the grave humanitarian crisis. The international community implored the President, U Htin Kyaw, to speak out in support of human rights on this issue.

The angst and controversy that the Office of State Counsellor has attracted has come at a great price to the NLD. On January 30, 2017, U Ko Ni, the lawyer mentioned earlier who was considered to be one of the architects of the State Counsellor law, was brutally assassinated. Despite his ordinary background as a traditional civil and criminal law lawyer,[28] he had taken the risk of speaking out against the undemocratic elements of the Constitution and to advocate for the constitutionality of Suu Kyi's position as State Counsellor. There were no doubt multiple reasons for his death – U Ko Ni was also a Muslim and he had been outspoken on other controversial law reforms such as the need for a hate speech law. He had also spoken about the need to draft a new constitution. Yet his role in the creation of the Office of State Counsellor was certainly one of the reasons for his assassination. The trial against the four accused (two of whom who are former military officers) ended in death sentences for two of the accused, although the fifth accused and mastermind remains at large. On the first anniversary of U Ko Ni's death in 2018, a small group dared to protest in support of the accused, threatening to harm the judge if they were convicted. On the second anniversary of Ko Ni's death, the NLD submitted its proposal to the legislature to form a committee to amend the Constitution. Myanmar lost its most articulate lawyer on constitutional reform, a tragic and untimely loss for efforts at democratic transformation.

In the first period, the costs of informal constitutional amendment via legislative reform and executive action may be high, particularly if legislative change is

---

[28] On the career paths of legal professionals in Myanmar, see Melissa Crouch, "Myanmar: Law as a Desirable and Dangerous Profession," in *Lawyers in Society* (2nd ed, two volumes), ed. Richard Abel. Hart Publishing, 2019.

perceived to be an underhanded means of constitutional change. The death of U Ko Ni also suggests a highly targeted campaign against those most visibly involved in advocating for constitutional change.[29] U Ko Ni was first a lawyer, and his death was a warning to legal advocates involved in constitutional and rights reform to back down. U Ko Ni was affiliated with the NLD and pro-democratic actors, and so his death was a warning to them and a stark reminder that the NLD government is extremely vulnerable without the protection of the police or military. The third group U Ko Ni represented in a symbolic sense was minorities, both Muslims but also other ethnic groups or non-Buddhists. His death was aimed at silencing those seeking to advocate for greater equality in constitutional reform.

11.6 CONCLUSION

Myanmar's Constitution remains in its crucial "first period." The possibility of substantially changing the Constitution during this first period remains low, and the risks of trying to do so are relatively high. This is because constitutions drafted under authoritarian rule that facilitate a new political era are often designed to endure. My chapter has focused specifically on the strategies being employed in Myanmar by democratic actors to try to change the Constitution. The option of drafting a new constitution remains unrealistic in Myanmar's political climate. Instead, I identified that the main strategies pro-democratic actors have pursued are formal amendment or informal constitutional change.

Formal constitutional amendment under the new Constitution means that the NLD and other pro-democratic actors have to submit to the authority of the Constitution and work to achieve the required approval threshold it mandates for change. In doing so, they face a strategic dilemma, and despite running for office on a program of constitutional reform, have only put forward a series of limited proposals. Yet the outcome of that process reinforced the limits of democratic reform. The NLD was unable to obtain sufficient support for its proposals. It then had to watch as the Committee Report identified three issues that are off-limits in terms of amendment. In 2015 a range of undemocratic proposals were put forward in the bills to parliament. The Report and the subsequent proposals reaffirmed the Constitution's core commitments to military governance. People who advocate for change, particularly on the off-limits topics such as the section 436 amendment formula, face challenges ahead. The NLD is unlikely to get the approval rate it needs to amend the Constitution in its first term (2016–21).

Having failed at formal constitutional change, the NLD, once in government, has engaged in *informal* constitutional amendment through the creation of the Office of

---

[29] On how authoritarian Leviathans with the capability of punishing their opponents in a targeted and pinpointed fashion, see Dan Slater, *Ordering Power: Contentious Politics and Authoritarian Leviathans in Southeast Asia.* Cambridge University Press, 2000, 17.

State Counsellor. The military's opposition to this legislative reform made clear that they perceived this as an inappropriate means of constitutional change in this first period. The NLD has ultimately paid a high price for the creation of the Office of State Counsellor with the assassination of prominent lawyer U Ko Ni. The option of informal constitutional change through the Constitutional Tribunal represents untapped potential for democratic actors in Myanmar. Given that the NLD appointed all nine Tribunal members (who serve five-year terms), now is a better time than any to use this mechanism. I suggest that the NLD's failure to use the Constitutional Tribunal while in opposition (2012–16) left the courts wide open for use by regime supporters, as illustrated in the Citizenship Case.

I have drawn attention to the risks that these strategies may entail. Attempts at constitutional change during the first period may attract a range of risks including *personal* risks, such as the risk of arrest, torture, disappearance, or death (as in the case of the students mentioned at the beginning of the chapter); *institutional* risks such as the surveillance or deregistration of a political party; or the risks may be *political*, that is, a decline in public support and a loss of votes in a future election. The risks of constitutional change are heightened during the first period, particularly if it is a transformative authoritarian constitution that protects the interests of the former authoritarian regime.

In this chapter, I have suggested that we need to pay attention to the potential *risks* that pro-democratic actors may be exposed to if they seek to change a constitution during the first period of a transition from authoritarian rule. This focus on risk-taking in constitutional change is an area ripe for further comparative study.

The Ethiopian Constitution and Ethnic Federalism

Daniel Abebe[*]

12.1 INTRODUCTION

Much has been written about Ethiopia's more than two-decade experiment with ethnic federalism and scholars are still asking the same questions: Is ethnic federalism good or bad for Ethiopia? What can be done to address its weaknesses today or was it a flawed model from the beginning? Will it lead to Ethiopia's collapse? The answers to these questions can be usefully described as coming from consequentialist or constitutionalist perspectives. From the consequentialist view, ethnic federalism reinforces and deepens ethnic differences, dilutes a shared national identity or membership in a broader political community, and leads to separatism, which will eventually result in the dissolution of Ethiopia. Ethnic federalism is thus undesirable. At the same time, ethnic federalism is preferred to the forced integration of different ethnic groups, the suppression of group rights, and the absence of ethnocultural justice, all of which will lead to ethnic conflict and, of course, the dissolution of Ethiopia. On this type of consequentialist account, ethnic federalism is desirable.

Similarly, from one constitutionalist perspective, greater fidelity to the terms of the Ethiopian Constitution, combined with some adjustments to the relationship between the Federal government and the provinces, will make ethnic federalism successful in Ethiopia. Others respond that the extant Constitution is fundamentally unsuitable for ethnic federalism because the Federal government has the formal authority and institutional capacity to strongly influence policy in the provinces. On this telling, the Constitution is either part of the solution or the primary problem. Whatever the perspective, no clear consensus exists on how to answer critical questions about the merits of ethnic federalism in Ethiopia.

[*] I would like to thank Chelsea Munoz-Patchen for excellent research assistance, and I am pleased to acknowledge the support of the George J. Phocas Fund at the University of Chicago. All errors are mine.

In this chapter, I approach the question of ethnic federalism in Ethiopia from a different perspective, one that considers ethnic federalism as an institutional design mechanism to balance the tension between the transformational and preservative elements of the Ethiopian Constitution of 1994 ("the Constitution"). Rather than asking whether ethnic federalism is good for Ethiopia, I examine ethnic federalism as a concession to the populace by the ruling elite – the drafters of the Constitution – to preserve their control of the Ethiopian government. To make some progress on this complicated inquiry, I consider the self-interest of the architects of the Constitution and their immediate and long-term goals, and describe the Constitution's founding context. Although the Constitution was transformational at its inception, ethnic federalism was likely the most attractive preservative institutional design mechanism for the ruling elite to maintain power, placate much larger ethnic groups, and buy time to establish a strong Federal government. The tension between the Constitution's transformational and preservative character became most clear during the multi-ethnic, multiparty election of 2005, when the ruling elite engaged in fraud and violence to manipulate results and maintain power. This institutional juncture or inflection point may very well mark the end of the first period of Ethiopian constitutionalism, a period when the transformational character of the Ethiopian Constitution appeared to be in ascendance.

If the Constitution's embrace of ethnic federalism is actually a concession to preserve the power of the ruling elite, the relevant question is whether ethnic federalism has been an effective tool to achieve that goal. To be clear, I am not evaluating ethnic federalism generally or its strategic use as a tool to maintain power, and I don't take a position on its merits as a normative matter. The chapter simply considers ethnic federalism from a preservative, accommodationist perspective consistent with the incentive structure of the ruling elite. At the time of this writing, Ethiopia is arguably entering into a distinctive period of constitutionalism under the leadership of Abiy Ahmed, who became Prime Minister on April 2, 2018. Although Prime Minister Ahmed's first year in power has been well received – more in Section 12.5 – it is too soon to determine whether his new policies mark a return to the period of transformational constitutionalism that likely ended in 2005. As a consequence, this chapter will focus on the policies and practice of ethnic federalism after the adoption of the Ethiopian Constitution of 1994.

12.2 ETHIOPIA AND ITS CONSTITUTION

The Ethiopian Constitution of 1994 is both transformative and preservative in character, and Ethiopia's lived experience with ethnic federalism surfaces this core tension. The founders created a Constitution that is aspirational in its formal devolution of power to subnational units – constitution-making – yet accommodationist in the post-ratification constitutional practice. Ethnic federalism, I suggest, is the vehicle through which the Constitution attempted to create a new political and social order without fundamentally changing the power, influence, and dominance of the governing elite. Before developing this claim, it is useful to provide a very brief summary of Ethiopia's modern history and the key components of the Constitution.

Background. The Federal Democratic Republic of Ethiopia ("Ethiopia") is a landlocked[1] east African country with a population of 105 million people, 80 percent of whom live in rural areas and work in agriculture.[2] Ethiopia has approximately thirteen major ethnic groups[3] – of which nine are formally recognized in the Constitution of 1994[4] – at least eighty ethnic groups overall, and eighty-eight different languages are spoken in the country.[5] The Constitution designates Amharic as the working language of the Federal government. Amharic is also one of the two most widely spoken languages in Ethiopia, along with Oromo, and at least 60 percent of Ethiopians speak one of the two languages.[6]

For over a millennium, Ethiopia had a long and relatively continuous history of dynastic rule, ending with the reign of Emperor Haile Selassie in 1974. Ethiopia was subsequently governed by a communist regime led by Mengistu Hailemariam until 1991, when a coalition of rebel forces toppled the government and installed a new dictatorship under the leadership of Prime Minister Meles Zenawi. Zenawi died in office in 2012 and was succeeded by Hailemariam Desalegn as Prime Minister of Ethiopia. Desalegn resigned on February 15, 2018,[7] and Abiy Ahmed was named Prime Minister on April 2, 2018.

Constitutional History and Structure. Over the last eighty years, Ethiopia has had four constitutions, each known by their respective dates of ratification: 1931, 1955, 1987, and, most relevant for this chapter, 1994.[8] Before discussing the Constitution,[9] it is helpful to situate its creation in the broader politics of that era. Consideration of the historical context sheds light on the Constitution's transformational and preservative elements and the importance of ethnic federalism to the populace and ruling elite.

Very briefly, the Constitution was drafted and ratified after two major events in modern Ethiopian history: the 1991 collapse of the "Derg," the regime led by Mengistu Hailemariam (referenced earlier); and the 1993 independence of Eritrea,

[1]   Ethiopia shares a border with Eritrea, Sudan, South Sudan, Djibouti, Somalia, and Kenya.
[2]   *World Factbook: Ethiopia*, Central Intelligence Agency January 17, 2018. Available at www.cia
      .gov/library/publications/the-world-factbook/geos/et.html (last visited January 22, 2018).
[3]   Ibid.
[4]   Constitution of the Federal Democratic Republic of Ethiopia, art. 47(1) (1994).
[5]   *Ethiopia*, Ethnologue: Languages of the World. Available at www.ethnologue.com/country/
      ET (last visited January 22, 2018).
[6]   Central Intelligence Agency, n. 2.
[7]   BBC, "Who Will Be Ethiopia's Next Prime Minister?," *BBC News*. March 16, 2018. Available
      at www.bbc.com/news/world-africa-43414557.
[8]   Bereket Habte Selassie, "Self-Determination in Principle and Practice: The Ethiopian-Eritrean
      Experience." *Columbia Human Rights Law Review* 29: 91,125 (1997).
[9]   For a broader discussion, see John M. Cohen, "'Ethnic Federalism' in Ethiopia." *Northeast
      African Studies* 2: 157 (1995).

which had been internationally recognized as part of a federation with Ethiopia after World War II.[10] The drafters of the Constitution were members of the Ethiopian People's Revolutionary Democratic Front (EPRDF),[11] which at the time was a coalition or umbrella party led by the Tigrayan People's Liberation Front (TPLF),[12] the group that coordinated with the Eritrean Liberation Front (ELF)[13] to overthrow the communist regime.[14] The EPRDF also included now defunct parties that, at the time, claimed to represent the two largest ethnic groups in Ethiopia by population, the Oromo (34 percent) and Amhara (27 percent) peoples, but the EPRDF was effectively controlled by a smaller ethnic group, the Tigrayan people (6 percent).[15] Since 1991, the EPRDF has governed Ethiopia, and Prime Ministers Zenawi, Desalegn, and Ahmed have all served as Chairman of the EPRDF. As I discuss in Section 12.4, the interests and incentives of the political forces during the drafting of the Constitution (and over time) are key to assessing the transformational and preservative impact of the Constitution.

In 1994, Ethiopia ratified a Constitution based on ethnic federalism, with nine ethnic-based autonomous administrative units or "States," each exercising substantial authority within their respective regions. By way of structure, the Constitution consists of 12 Chapters and 106 Articles, of which 39 describe the organization and structure of the Ethiopian state; 28 enshrine the fundamental rights of all Ethiopians; and 7 enumerate Ethiopia's national policy objectives for purposes of national defense, foreign affairs, economics, and other areas.[16] The remaining Articles are described as "General" or "Miscellaneous" provisions, describing the national flag, the national anthem, basic tax policy, and other items.[17] Most relevant for this Chapter, Article 8 allocates all sovereign powers to the "nations, nationalities and peoples" of Ethiopia, defined in Article 39(5) as:

> People who have or share large measure of a common culture or similar customs, mutual intelligibility of language, belief in a common or related identities, a

[10] The history of Ethiopia's relationship with Eritrea is long and contested. For an introduction, see Selassie, "Self-Determination in Principle and Practice," 91.
[11] *Ethiopian People's Revolutionary Democratic Front*, Terrorism Research & Analysis Consortium. Available at www.trackingterrorism.org/group/ethiopian-peoples-revolutionary-democratic-front-eprdf (last visited January 23, 2018).
[12] *Tigray People's Liberation Front*, Terrorism Research & Analysis Consortium Available at. www.trackingterrorism.org/group/tigray-peoples-liberation-front-tplf (last visited January 23, 2018).
[13] *Eritrean Liberation Front*, Terrorism Research & Analysis Consortium. Available at www.trackingterrorism.org/group/tigray-peoples-liberation-front-tplf (last visited January 23, 2018).
[14] Selassie, "Self-Determination in Principle and Practice," 91, 118–19.
[15] Lovise Aalen, "Ethnic Federalism and Self-Determination for Nationalities in a Semi-Authoritarian State: The Case of Ethiopia." *International Journal on Minority & Group Rights* 13: 243, 245 (2006); Cohen, "'Ethnic Federalism' in Ethiopia," 157, 158. Central Intelligence Agency, n. 2.
[16] Constitution of the Federal Democratic Republic of Ethiopia (1994).
[17] Ibid.

common psychological make-up, and who inhabit an identifiable, predominantly contiguous territory.[18]

The Constitution formally recognizes nine ethnic States within Ethiopia but also provides that the "nations, nationalities, and peoples" within each State have the right to create their own States through a specified process.[19] In addition to the fundamental rights outlined in the Constitution, the "nations, nationalities, and peoples" of Ethiopia have "an unconditional right to self-determination, including a right to secession … a full measure of self-government [and a right] to equitable representation in state and Federal governments."[20] Such powers necessary to self-government include the power to create a state, collect taxes, enforce the law, administer land, and supervise the police force. Residual powers not allocated to the Federal government or jointly to the Federal government and the States are reserved to the States.[21] Finally, the "nations, nationalities, and peoples" in States have the right to speak their own language, preserve their culture, and teach their history.[22]

The Constitution is unique because "nations, nationalities and peoples" are granted the right to self-determination and secession.[23] It is noteworthy that the right is seemingly granted to "nations, nationalities and peoples" instead of States, which might complicate the exercise of this right as "nations, nationalities and peoples" are harder to define and less clearly delineated than States.[24] Article 39(4) describes the procedures for secession:

(a) When a demand for secession has been approved by a two-thirds majority of the members of the Legislative Council of the Nation, Nationality or People Concerned;

---

[18] Ibid. art. 39 ¶ 5; Jon Abbink, "Ethnicity and Constitutionalism in Contemporary Ethiopia." *Journal of African Law* 41: 159, 166 (1997).

[19] Constitution of the Federal Democratic Republic of Ethiopia, art. 47 (1–3) (1994).

[20] Ibid. art. 39(1, 3); Aalen, "Ethnic Federalism and Self-Determination," 243.

[21] *Constitution of the Federal Democratic Republic of Ethiopia*, art. 47(2), 52(1–2) (1994); Aalen, "Ethnic Federalism and Self-Determination," 243; Tsegaye Regassa, "Learning to Live with Conflicts: Federalism as a Tool of Conflict Management in Ethiopia – An Overview." *Mizan Law Review* 4: 52, 91–92 (2010).

[22] Constitution of the Federal Democratic Republic of Ethiopia, art. 39(2) (1994); Aalen, "Ethnic Federalism and Self-Determination," 243 (citing article 5(1) as well, which gives all languages equal status).

[23] Modern federalist democracies, including those with formally recognized ethnolinguistic units like Switzerland, Belgium, and Canada, do not recognize unilateral secession, and Ethiopia is virtually unique in this regard. Alem Habtu, "Multiethnic Federalism in Ethiopia: A Study of the Secession Clause in the Constitution." *Publius* 35: 313, 317 (2005). Regassa, "Learning to Live with Conflicts," 52, 93–94.

[24] Constitution of the Federal Democratic Republic of Ethiopia, art. 39(1) (1994); Abbink, "Ethnicity and Constitutionalism in Contemporary Ethiopia," 159, 167.

(b) When the Federal Government has organized a referendum which must take place within three years from the time it received the concerned council's decision for secession;
(c) When the demand for secession is supported by majority vote in the referendum;
(d) When the Federal Government will have transferred its powers to the council of the Nation, Nationality or People who has voted to secede; and
(e) When the division of assets is affected in a manner prescribed by law.[25]

The right to secession is unilateral and unconditional, and neither requires approval by other States or the Federal government nor a specific justification for its exercise.[26] The Federal government's only recourse to prevent secession is to attempt a negotiated resolution with the relevant "nations, nationalities and peoples" during the three-year "cooling off" period after secession has been demanded but prior to the required referendum.[27]

12.3 ETHNIC FEDERALISM IN ETHIOPIA

Consideration of the transformational and preservative character of the Constitution requires an assessment of ethnic federalism as a design mechanism and an evaluation of its impact on Ethiopian society. The constitutional devolution of decision-making authority from the center to the various subnational units is unprecedented and transformational in Ethiopian history but, at the same time, the actual implementation and practice of ethnic federalism might still accommodate the interests of the ruling elite. This section briefly describes and summarizes the extant literature on Ethiopia's version of ethnic federalism.

12.3.1 *Ethnic Federalism and the Dissolution of Ethiopia*

The Perils of Ethnic Federalism. For many scholars, Ethiopia's constitutionalized version of ethnic federalism, with its focus on nations, nationalities, and peoples; creation of States along purely ethnic lines; and use of ethnicity as the key component for political participation;[28] will lead to greater instability, more ethnic conflict,

---

[25] Constitution of the Federal Democratic Republic of Ethiopia, art. 39(4) (1994).
[26] Habtu, "Multiethnic Federalism in Ethiopia," 313, 327–28; Legesse Tigabu Mengie, "Federalism as an Instrument for Unity and the Protection of Minorities: A Comparative Overview: Ethiopia, India and the US." *Mizan Law Review* 10: 265, 284–85 (2016).
[27] Habtu, "Multiethnic Federalism in Ethiopia," 313, 329.
[28] Lovise Aalen, "Ethnic Federalism and Self-Determination for Nationalities in a Semi-Authoritarian State," 243, 261 (describing how the current constitution does not allow "citizens to register with mixed or pan Ethiopian identity"); Mengie, "Federalism as an Instrument for Unity and the Protection of Minorities," 265, 273. ("Thus, mere citizenship does not enable

and the proliferation of secessionist movements.[29] Ethnic federalism entrenches difference while simultaneously creating and reinforcing purportedly "primordial" ethnic divisions that may not be fixed or even pre-date the labeling.[30] The concretization of ethnic identities hinders the ability of different groups to integrate and develop national identities, and may lead to ethnic conflict and the eventual dissolution the nation.[31] From this perspective, the Constitution exacerbates the problem of tribalism.[32]

Some scholars contend that Ethiopia still has a strong national identity,[33] but worry that the identity might erode as individuals are encouraged to think of

citizens to actively participate in politics if they are not members of the ethnic group of a region"); Legesse Tigabu Mengie, "Ethnic Federalism and Conflict in Ethiopia: What Lessons Can Other Jurisdictions Draw?" *African Journal of International & Comparative Law* 23: 462, 468 (2015).

[29] Alemante G. Selassie, "Ethnic Federalism: Its Promise and Pitfalls for Africa." *Yale Journal of International Law* 28: 51, 95–96 (2003). Selassie notes that strengthening these group rights may lead to a "loss of self-identity and individual rights." Ibid. 73.

[30] "The conventional view on ethnicity in social science research today is that it is a constructed phenomenon, based on the selection of cultural markers and mobilized as a political force in the struggle for political power and resources," alternatively, it has been seen as "naturally inborn fixed, and stable" under the primordialist view. Aalen, "Ethnic Federalism and Self-Determination," 243, 246–47; Abbink, "Ethnicity and Constitutionalism in Contemporary Ethiopia," 159, 160–61, 172; Charles E. Ehrlich, "Ethnicity and Constitutional Reform: The Case of Ethiopia." *ILSA Journal of International & Comparative Law* 6: 51, 61 (1999); Minasse Haile, "The New Ethiopian Constitution: Its Impact upon Unity, Human Rights and Development." *Suffolk Transnational Law Review* 20: 1, 4 (1996); Mengie, "Ethnic Federalism and Conflict in Ethiopia," 462, 469 (describing how the creation of ethnic states has led to the breakup of historic ties, trade routes, and migration flows between different groups).

[31] Aalen, "Ethnic Federalism and Self-Determination for Nationalities in a Semi-Authoritarian State," 243, 256; Selassie, "Ethnic Federalism: Its Promise and Pitfalls for Africa," 51, 86. Selassie says that once this happens it becomes hard to foster "cooperation, sharing and mutual solidarity among groups," for example getting substates to cooperate for national unity or sacrifice for the sake of other groups, as occurred in Yugoslavia's failure.

[32] Abbink, "Ethnicity and Constitutionalism in Contemporary Ethiopia." 159, 174 (suggesting that ethnocentrism may result as the ethnic focus is combined with the reproduction of inequalities and economic problems at the state level); Haile, "The New Ethiopian Constitution," 1, 4. But see T. S. Twibell, "Ethiopian Constitutional Law: The Future of the Ethiopian Government and the New Constitution's Ability to Overcome Ethiopia's Problems." *Loyola L.A. International & Comparative Law Journal* 21: 399, 463–66 (1999) (defending the Ethiopian Constitution as a useful document that will be better applied as it ages and society progresses, and noting how "ethnically blind" constitutions are not necessarily better).

[33] Aalen, "Ethnic Federalism and Self-Determination," 243, 255–56; Abbink, "Ethnicity and Constitutionalism in Contemporary Ethiopia," 159, 173 (describing how Ethiopia never went through a modern phase with a nation state project, solid industrialism and mass consumption, and media, though Ethiopians do have shared fears of past exploitation and "violent inclusion.") The Ethiopian identity includes common historical, religious, and social ties, including fighting off foreign invasions, the early adoption of Christianity, plough agriculture, imperial rule, and written language, and existing as a state for millennia. Though much of this identity is strongly linked to the dominant Amhara ethnic group. Haile, "The New Ethiopian Constitution," 1, 22; Mengie, "Federalism as an Instrument for Unity and the Protection of Minorities," 265, 287–88; Selassie, "Ethnic Federalism," 51, 61.

themselves as a member of a specific ethnic group or State, rather than as an Ethiopian citizen.[34] Highlighting ethnic differences through the Constitution and the political process – instead of letting them fade – "encourages aggressive ethnic identification and separatism ... and exacerbates ethnic distrust and social discord."[35] It also incentivizes each State to pursue its own parochial interests strictly defined on ethnic lines. To this point, land disputes between pastoralists and farmers have been sometimes labeled as "ethnic disputes," along with land grabs, land evictions, and suggestions of ethnic cleansing that some fear could worsen.[36]

Right to Secession. The right to self-determination and secession was likely included to gain the support of different ethnic groups for the Constitution, though there may be ideological reasons for its inclusion as well.[37] Many scholars, however, view the right to secession as a perilous feature of Ethiopian constitutionalism that might inadvertently facilitate the dissolution of the country.[38] Since the Constitution formally recognizes separate ethnic identities; devolves power to States created along ethnic lines; and grants nations, nationalities, and peoples broad authority within their States, ethnic federalism seems like an invitation to secede.[39] A constitution that strengthens ethnic identities and weakens a core national identity

---

[34] Aalen, "Ethnic Federalism and Self-Determination," 243, 247; Mengie, "Ethnic Federalism and Conflict in Ethiopia: What Lessons Can Other Jurisdictions Draw?" 462, 464; Mengie, "Federalism as an Instrument for Unity and the Protection of Minorities," 265, 273, 287.

[35] Selassie, "Ethnic Federalism," 51, 95–96. Selassie also notes that it may also become increasingly difficult to convince a state that it should adopt a policy that may negatively affect it, but is good for another state or the common interest.. see Aalen, "Ethnic Federalism and Self-Determination," 243, 261; Haile, "The New Ethiopian Constitution," 1, 14–16 (citing the struggles rooted in Nigeria's 1960 Constitution, which divided the country into tribal regions and was run by tribal political parties); Selassie, "Self-Determination in Principle and Practice," 91, 139.

[36] Aalen, "Ethnic Federalism and Self-Determination," 243, 259 (2006); Mengie, "Ethnic Federalism and Conflict in Ethiopia: What Lessons Can Other Jurisdictions Draw?" 462, 472–73.

[37] Abbink, "Ethnicity and Constitutionalism in Contemporary Ethiopia," 159, 167 (describing the secession right as a holdover from socialist-communist thinking as extreme self-determination); Habtu, "Multiethnic Federalism in Ethiopia," 313, 324, 326–27, 334. Those not in favor included The Worker's Party of Ethiopia, elite Amharas, and other pan-Ethiopianists. Ibid. at 325. The right to secession was given to every Union Republic in the Soviet Constitution of 1936, though this right was not as complete as the Ethiopian right to secession since the Soviet Constitution of 1977 required lower bodies to comply with the decisions of higher bodies like the Central government. Haile, "The New Ethiopian Constitution," 1, 32–33; Tsegaye Regassa, "Comparative Relevance of the Ethiopian Federal System to other African Politics of the Horn: First Thoughts on the Possibility of 'Exporting' Multi-ethnic Federalism." *Bahir Dar University Journal of Law* 1: 5, 31 (2010).

[38] Ehrlich, "Ethnicity and Constitutional Reform: The Case of Ethiopia," 51, 62.

[39] John McGarry and Brendan O'Leary, "Must Pluri-national Federations Fail?" *Ethnopolitics* 8: 5, 6 (2009) (describing how plurinational federations make it easier to secede, as ethnic groups already have a distinct territory and a bureaucratic system, and are more likely to be recognized under international law). McGarry and O'Leary also review the popular American view that ethno-national federalism heightens group consciousness and leads to state breakup. Selassie, "Ethnic Federalism," 51, 87; Ehrlich, "Ethnicity and Constitutional Reform," 51, 61–62.

might, on the margin, encourage ethnic groups to seek independence.[40] The former Soviet Union, Yugoslavia, and Czechoslovakia are examples of the claim that "rival citizenships cannot exist – at least not for a long time – in the same political space" and that the emotional force of ethnic citizenship will likely carry the day.[41] Scholars with this view argue that a stable and long-lasting federalist model cannot be built on ethnicity, but requires engendering loyalty to the state.[42]

In theory, the inclusion of a right to secession and self-determination might lead to strategic behavior among States who can leverage the potential exercise of the right as a threat to extract benefits from the Federal government.[43] In practice, however, scholars contend that completing the constitutional procedures required to exercise the right to secession will be difficult.[44] Ethiopia has banned several nationalistic liberation groups and organizations and deployed the federal army to prevent groups like the Oromo Liberation Front (OLF) from encouraging people to seek self-determination.[45] Although the Ethiopian government has characterized these groups as seeking secession through violence, it appears unlikely the Federal government would permit secession, even through constitutional processes. And in many cases, exercising the right to secede is almost infeasible for very small ethnic groups.[46]

Conflicts within States. Ethnic federalism has also led to ethnic conflicts within States.[47] This is perhaps unsurprising since ethnic States do not perfectly correspond with malleable ethnic identities, many Ethiopians have multiple ethnicities, and

---

[40] Cohen, "'Ethnic Federalism' in Ethiopia," 157, 168; Ehrlich, "Ethnicity and Constitutional Reform," 51, 53, 71. (describing the Constitution as creating divisions and eliminating a stable unifying force). See Haile, "The New Ethiopian Constitution," 1, 16–19 (describing the breakup of the Soviet Union after the fall of the communist dictatorship, and the success of India's federal constitution supported by strong unifying forces and judicial review); Mengie, "Federalism as an Instrument for Unity and the Protection of Minorities," 265, 273 (2016); Regassa, "Learning to Live with Conflicts," 52, 57, 63.

[41] Selassie, "Ethnic Federalism," 51, 88.

[42] Abbink, "Ethnicity and Constitutionalism in Contemporary Ethiopia," 159, 173 (suggesting integration and compromise at the national level would have been better); Ehrlich, "Ethnicity and Constitutional Reform," 51, 60; Regassa, "Learning to Live with Conflicts," 52, 71.

[43] Paul H. Brietzke, "Ethiopia's 'Leap in the Dark': Federalism and Self-Determination in the New Constitution." *Journal of African Law* 39: 19, 32 (1995); Haile, "The New Ethiopian Constitution," 1, 34 (citing Cass R. Sunstein, "Constitutionalism and Secession." *University of Chicago Law Review* 58: 633 (1991)).

[44] Abbink, "Ethnicity and Constitutionalism in Contemporary Ethiopia," 159, 167; Cohen, "Ethnic Federalism," 157, 166.

[45] Aalen, "Ethnic Federalism and Self-Determination for Nationalities in a Semi-Authoritarian State," 243, 257 n. 15; Habtu, "Multiethnic Federalism in Ethiopia," 313, 329.

[46] Brietzke, "Ethiopia's 'Leap in the Dark'," 19, 32; Habtu, "Multiethnic Federalism in Ethiopia," 313, 328.

[47] Aalen, "Ethnic Federalism and Self-Determination for Nationalities in a Semi-Authoritarian State," 243, 257 (believing minority concerns will be dealt with at the local level by being granted special zones or districts within larger ethnic states).

Ethiopia has many more ethnic groups and tribal affiliations than States.[48] When ethnic minorities within States attempt to vindicate their rights to self-determination, conflict sometimes ensues,[49] presenting an intractable problem for the least populous ethnic groups. As some have noted, if it is infeasible to provide a contiguous State for all ethnic groups, Ethiopia's recognition of group rights based on ethnic territorial autonomy is problematic.[50] The right to secede from a State or a district within a State is not usually recognized by the relevant governmental unit and may not be possible for the smallest ethnic groups.[51] In this example, the States – not the Federal government – are the administrative units refusing to recognize the rights of minorities and failing to provide any recourse.[52] Even if the States were to

[48] Ibid. at 243, 247; Abbink, "Ethnicity and Constitutionalism in Contemporary Ethiopia," 159, 171; Mengie, "Federalism as an Instrument for Unity and the Protection of Minorities," 265, 276; Margaret Moore, "Sub-State Nationalism and International Law." *Michigan Journal of International Law* 25: 1319, 1326 (2004).

[49] Ibid. at 1319, 1328–29. Moore discusses nonterritorial autonomy, which may be safer and more peaceable, though less satisfying to minority groups, and likely serve to ease assimilation. If nonterritorial autonomy is paired with power-sharing models it may be more effective; Haile, "The New Ethiopian Constitution," 1, 11 (1996); Mengie, "Federalism as an Instrument for Unity and the Protection of Minorities," 265, 289 (suggesting that frustrated minorities may seek to splinter off into their own states); Selassie, "Self-Determination in Principle and Practice," 91, 96 (1997). Recent Disputes within Ethiopia include:

> a) an intensified quest for self-definition and distinct identity intent on securing local self-rule to get more resources, power, and opportunities; b) border disputes between and within states; c) competition for federal grant and subsidy; d) quest for having one's language given a co-equal status as a federal working language; e) competition for access to and authority over federal, state, and local capital cities; f) conflict over mistrust about one's lot with/in a state or in the country; g) the quest for a more robust minority rights regime, especially right to representation; etc.

Regassa, "Learning to Live with Conflicts," 52, 98.

[50] Aalen, "Ethnic Federalism and Self-Determination," 243, 257; Mengie, "Federalism as an Instrument for Unity and the Protection of Minorities," 265, 273, 277, 288.

[51] Constitution of the Federal Democratic Republic of Ethiopia, art. 47(2) (1994), Aalen, "Ethnic Federalism and Self-Determination," 243, 258 (2006); Habtu, "Multiethnic Federalism in Ethiopia," 313, 328 (describing how under the constitution groups can seek out its own district, zone, or regional state and some difficulties in exercising these rights); Selassie, "Ethnic Federalism," 51, 65; Christopher Van der Beken, "Federalism, Local Government and Minority Protection in Ethiopia: Opportunities and Challenges." *Journal of African Law* 59: 150, 162–65 (2015). It is worth noting that all but the Harar regional state in Ethiopia have allowed local ethnic governments to be established within the state with self-governance similar to a regional state, though there are still questions as to how much autonomy actually exists in these smaller districts.

[52] Haile, "The New Ethiopian Constitution," 1, 11–12, 52; Alemante G. Selassie has even suggested that ethno-national federalism is at odds with the international right of nondiscrimination, as inevitably an ethnic group is given sovereign powers and thus can exclude minority groups or shape a regional government such that it is discriminatory to other groups. Selassie, "Ethnic Federalism," 51, 93–94. Selassie also feels it infringes international norms of free movement and choice of residence by pressuring citizens to live in the appropriate region. Van der Beken, "Federalism, Local Government and Minority Protection in Ethiopia," 177.

create districts for smaller groups,[53] conflict might persist because fixed administrative boundaries and fluid ethnic identities will not always match. Given these
challenges, ethnic disputes regarding recognition, self-rule, autonomy, and minority
rights are often shifted by States to other States or districts.[54] A final complication
involves Addis Ababa and Dire Dawa, two self-governed, non-ethnic administrative
units with multi-ethnic populations.[55] These two cities are located within ethnic
States, leading to conflicts over jurisdiction and governmental authority.[56] Overall,
from this perspective ethnic federalism generates ethnic conflict; undermines the
development of a strong Ethiopian national identity and a broad Ethiopian cultural
and political community; and weakens the foundation of the country.

12.3.2 *Ethnic Federalism and Stability in Ethiopia*

The Benefits of Ethnic Federalism. John McGarry and Brendan O'Leary argue that
most plurinational state failures occur because of the forced integration of different
ethnic groups and associated restrictions on group autonomy.[57] On this account,
ethnic conflicts derive from attempts to eliminate ethnic differences, normalize
group identities, and suppress the rights of ethnic groups.[58] Instead of trying to forge
a single national identity, states should formally recognize ethnic diversity by
granting ethnic groups autonomy (with the aim of reducing ethnic conflict).[59]

---

[53] Ibid. at 150, 162–65.

[54] Regassa, "Learning to Live with Conflicts," 52, 100.

[55] Constitution of the Federal Democratic Republic of Ethiopia, art. 49 (1994); Abbink, "Ethnicity and Constitutionalism in Contemporary Ethiopia," 159, 171–72.

[56] Ibid. at 171–72 (stating that this conflict includes the cities having no political voice within the
broader region); Mengie, "Federalism as an Instrument for Unity and the Protection of
Minorities," 265, 276. There were protests around August 2016 in part inspired by the Oromos
complaining that they had been excluded in the country's political process and from the
economic development of the capital Addis Ababa, which is in their state. BBC, "What Is
Behind Ethiopia's Wave of Protests?" *BBC News.* August 22, 2016. Available at www.bbc.com/
news/world-africa-36940906. Other disputes have happened as the government has recognized
and de-ethnicized certain cities without approval of local ethnic groups. Aalen, "Ethnic
Federalism and Self-Determination," 243, 260.

[57] McGarry and O'Leary, "Must Pluri-national Federations Fail?" 5, 9, 11 (suggesting most state
breakups occurred in federations created and held together by nondemocratic centralist states
without judicial review and in a time of restriction of autonomy). Some of these factors may
apply to Ethiopia to some degree. The authors review many other factors that may help or hurt
the continuing existence of a plurinational federation, including consociational practices
granting minority groups autonomy, and providing proportional and meaningful representation
for groups in the national government. Others have suggested that the idea that multi-ethnic
nations breed conflict is a base-rate fallacy. James Habyarimana, Macartan Humphreys, Daniel
Posner, and Jeremy Weinstein, "Is Ethnic Conflict Inevitable: Parting Ways over Nationalism
and Separatism." *Foreign Affairs* 87: 138, 138–39.

[58] Adeno Addis, "Cultural Integrity and Political Unity: The Politics of Language in Multilingual
States." *Arizona State Law Journal* 33: 719, 725, 769 (2001).

[59] McGarry and O'Leary, "Must Pluri-national Federations Fail?" 5; Moore, "Sub-State Nationalism and International Law," 1319, 1337 (citing John McGarry, *Federal Political Systems and*

Ethiopia's Constitution reflects this approach by accommodating ethnic diversity and "ethno-cultural justice" through group rights, ethnic-based self-government, and the right to self-determination and secession.[60]

In practice, the Federal government has permitted the States and ethnic groups to speak their own languages, maintain their own cultures, develop their own educational systems, teach their own historical narratives, and choose their own local leaders.[61] To focus on one factor, the right to use one's language in education and administration is perhaps most important.[62] It strengthens group identities and allows meaningful participation in political and cultural life.[63]

Over the last few years, the devolution of authority to States and districts appears to have led to an increase in education spending and enrollment, partially closing the gap between rural and urban areas.[64] Some speculate that the opportunity to attend school in one's local language increases both the acceptance of education and enrollment,[65] though concerns about education quality and dropout rates

National Minorities, in Handbook of Federal Countries 437 (Ann L. Griffiths ed., 2002); Selassie, "Ethnic Federalism," 51, 61; Stefan Wolff, "Conflict Management in Divided Societies: The Many Uses of Territorial Self-Governance." *International Journal on Minority & Group Rights* 20: 27, 29 (2013); Twibell, "Ethiopian Constitutional Law,"399, 457–58; Some have suggested that blaming ethnonational-federalism is incorrect and that the problems Ethiopia has faced are rooted in "a history of highly centralized authority, great poverty, [ ] civil conflict, and unfamiliarity with democratic culture," 457 (citing U.S. Dep't of State, *Ethiopia Country Report on Human Rights Practices* (1997)).

[60] Regassa, "Comparative Relevance of the Ethiopian Federal System to other African Politics of the Horn," 5, 7, 31, 33. "Ethno-cultural justice includes equality, non-discrimination on ethnic and religious basis, the right to one's identity, language, culture, way of life, the right to one's history (and one's narrative of history), the right to self-administration within one's territory, the right to self-determination including and up to (conditional) secession," 97. Multi-ethnic federalism is suited to handle conflicts over "ethno-cultural justice minority rights, border disputes, identity-related disputes, disputes over local self-rule," 99; Selassie, "Ethnic Federalism," 51, 57, 64; Selassie, "Self-Determination in Principle and Practice," 91, 139–41 (describing how many communities may be appeased through community recognition and feel this government is an improvement); Twibell, "Ethiopian Constitutional Law," 399, 453.

[61] Habtu, "Multiethnic Federalism in Ethiopia," 313, 335 (stating that the system has dampened ethnic oppression, increased autonomy, and potentially increased interethnic harmony and respect); Aalen, "Ethnic Federalism and Self-Determination," 243, 256; Selassie, "Ethnic Federalism," 51, 66–67 n. 29, 70 (suggesting that building ethnic communities is beneficial because it gives people a sense of belonging while noting that that fostering ethnic equality was a Leninist tactic to "dissipate ethnic antagonisms and encourage ethnic groups to come together."); Twibell, "Ethiopian Constitutional Law," 399, 456–57.

[62] See generally Addis, "Cultural Integrity and Political Unity," 719 (discussing in detail the importance of language and culture and situating these issues in liberal cosmopolitanism). Addis also discusses how important a language is to cultural identity, meaning, and communicating experience, 727.

[63] Ibid. 723–24.

[64] Petra Zimmerman-Steinhart and Yakob Bekele, "The Implications of Federalism and Decentralization on Socioeconomic Conditions in Ethiopia." *Potchefstroom Electoral Law Journal* 15: 89, 101–2 (2012).

[65] Ibid. 103.

persist.[66] Relatedly, Ethiopia has seen dropping mortality rates for infants and children under five, along with increased per capita expenditures, higher total expenditures, and better access to basic healthcare facilities.[67]

Challenges of Ethiopian Ethnic Federalism. Whatever the constitutional guarantees, to be effective ethnic groups in the States must feel that they can actually exercise power, work productively with the Federal government, and resolve ethnic conflicts peacefully.[68] The Constitution's grant of autonomy to the States has been undermined by State reliance on funding from the Federal government and by requirements to meet national standards in health, education, and development.[69] The Federal government also controls much of Ethiopia's financial resources and determines the country's development initiatives, which can be used to favor certain ethnic groups and States.[70] Similarly, some have argued that the Constitution's right to culture and history is nothing more than permission to use local languages in education, and they question whether ethnicity is a foil to maintain a certain social and political organization.[71] In fact, one significant consequence of prioritizing the use of local languages in each State is that Amharic, the working language of the Federal government, is not taught in all States.[72] The relative absence of a common language weakens ties between Ethiopians in different States and creates obstacles to the formation of a shared national identity and political community.[73] It especially disadvantages smaller minority groups – whose languages are not spoken widely – as they are sometimes forced to learn Amharic outside of the State's school system (if at all).[74]

The upshot is that Ethiopia appears to have both a powerful but unrepresentative Federal government and a Constitution that seemingly delegates substantial powers

[66] Ibid.

[67] Ibid. 104–5, 108–9.

[68] Regassa, "Learning to Live with Conflicts," 52, 54, 70, 76 (suggesting conflicts may be inevitable but ethnonational federalism will maintain pluralism and manage conflicts); Wolff, "Conflict Management in Divided Societies," 27, 49–50. Contra Aalen, "Ethnic Federalism and Self-Determination," 243, 260 (voicing concerns that in actuality groups are not being appeased by democracy but are being oppressed by the ruling group).

[69] Constitution of the Federal Democratic Republic of Ethiopia, art. 51, ¶ 3 (1994). Aalen, "Ethnic Federalism and Self-Determination," 243, 248; Cohen, "'Ethnic Federalism' in Ethiopia," 157, 171–72 (describing that if the central government dominates revenue collection and budgeting, states will be hindered from performing the tasks assigned to them and that this appears likely to happen since about 85–90 percent of revenue collected is federal).

[70] Brietzke, "Ethiopia's 'Leap in the Dark'," 19, 29; Selassie, "Ethnic Federalism," 51, 80.

[71] Abbink, "Ethnicity and Constitutionalism in Contemporary Ethiopia," 159, 161.

[72] Ehrlich, "Ethnicity and Constitutional Reform," 51, 63.

[73] Addis, "Cultural Integrity and Political Unity," 719, 768.

[74] Abbink, "Ethnicity and Constitutionalism in Contemporary Ethiopia," 159, 172 (noting that city dwellers' children within a minority state will also be disadvantaged by not learning Amharic in school); Addis, "Cultural Integrity and Political Unity," 719, 725, 775; Ehrlich, "Ethnicity and Constitutional Reform," 51, 63; Haile, "The New Ethiopian Constitution," 1, 36–39; Moore, "Sub-State Nationalism and International Law," 1319, 1327; Selassie, "Ethnic Federalism," 51, 75.

to the States, creating dual sovereigns with seemingly unlimited and unchecked authority.[75] The Federal government and the States have overlapping authority in some areas without a formal mechanism to resolve competing claims in the event of a conflict.[76] For some, the Constitution reads more like an international treaty between nations or a confederation, and the States are largely free to determine their own powers and political organization.[77] In contrast, others argue that the only thing keeping the "unconstrained" States in check is the immense power of the Federal government.[78]

Making Ethiopian Ethnic Federalism Work. In light of these challenges, scholars have offered several correctives to improve Ethiopia's version of ethnic federalism. Alemante Selassie proposes the use of a single language for official activities at the Federal and the State level to create unity and efficient governance, while still allowing the States to teach and use minority languages without restriction.[79] In his view, Ethiopia should organize the States equally by population or economic resources, or subdivide ethnic groups within the existing federal structure.[80] More ambitiously, Alem Habtu argues that Ethiopia should expand democratic representation by permitting real political competition and opening the ruling EPRDF to other ethnic groups.[81] Legesse Mengie goes even further and claims that Ethiopia should reverse the policy of ethnic federalism and restore the historic provincial system.[82] Still others have suggested some version of "non-territorial" autonomy to address challenges for underrepresented ethnic groups within administrative

---

[75] Cohen, "'Ethnic Federalism' in Ethiopia," 157, 165; Haile, "The New Ethiopian Constitution," 1, 20, 46, 55. Haile suggests the failure to provide for judicial or other constitutional control was likely rooted in the former Soviet Union's rejection of the idea because it believed that the legislature which was elected by the people "should not be controlled by extra-parliamentary bodies," 59; Mengie, "Federalism as an Instrument for Unity and the Protection of Minorities," 265, 287.

[76] Haile, "The New Ethiopian Constitution," 1, 20, 46, 55; Mengie, "Federalism as an Instrument for Unity and the Protection of Minorities," 265, 268–69 (noting there appears to be a slight supremacy of the federal government in the Constitution).

[77] Abbink, "Ethnicity and Constitutionalism in Contemporary Ethiopia," 159, 167; Brietzke, "Ethiopia's 'Leap in the Dark'," 19, 33; Cohen, "'Ethnic Federalism' in Ethiopia," 157, 158; Ehrlich, "Ethnicity and Constitutional Reform," 51, 62.

[78] Ehrlich, "Ethnicity and Constitutional Reform," 51, 62.

[79] Selassie, "Ethnic Federalism," 51, 101. But compare Addis, "Cultural Integrity and Political Unity," 719, 737–45 (claiming that a system based on negative rights may lead to the potential disappearance of languages).

[80] Selassie, "Ethnic Federalism," 51, 97–100, 103. Dividing states by economic resources is attractive for avoiding contentious transfers of wealth between subunits, and creating small poor minority states. Ibid. 103–4.

[81] Habtu, "Multiethnic Federalism in Ethiopia," 313, 334.

[82] Mengie, "Federalism as an Instrument for Unity and the Protection of Minorities," 265, 288–89.

regions, or for ethnic groups outside of a particular region but impacted by that region's policy decisions.[83]

The Constitution's ethnic federalism model is a significant departure from earlier Ethiopian constitutions and governance structures – in that limited sense, it is transformational – but the extant literature focuses more on its suitability for Ethiopia, rather than on its aspirational or preservative characteristics. As this very brief survey of the literature suggests, ethnic federalism may or may not be the appropriate governance structure for Ethiopia depending on one's assumptions about its impact on ethnic conflict, identity formation, and the long-term viability of the country. Similarly, the Constitution may or may not require modifications (or wholesale change), with proposed adjustments ranging from new language policies and membership rules for political parties, to some form of non-territorial ethnic autonomy or non-ethnic federalism. The States are either too weak or too powerful, while the Federal government is dominant yet lacks meaningful authority. All of this may be true (or not) but it doesn't tell us whether to view the Constitution as a transformational document to create a new political order or a preservative instrument to lock-in the interests of the ruling elite.

12.4 THE CONSTITUTION AND ETHNIC FEDERALISM: A PRESERVATIVE CONCESSION?

Is the Constitution fundamentally transformational or preservative? Can we learn anything from the period between its ratification and the most significant multi-ethnic, multiparty elections of 2005? The Constitution is best viewed along a continuum, and it clearly has both transformational and preservative components. But the interests of the Constitution's drafters – the ruling elites – and the political context of the Constitution's drafting provide some guidance on where to situate the Constitution along the continuum. Eleven years of post-ratification implementation provides the outline of a first period of Ethiopian constitutionalism and marks a meaningful inflection point; the moment when the tension between the transformational and preservative characteristics of Ethiopian constitutional practice became most salient.

Consider the following. You are the leader of an ethnic party that accounts for 6 percent of your country's population, and you have been aligned with another ethnic party that has been engaged in an armed independence struggle for some fifty

---

[83] John Coakley, "Approaches to the Resolution of Ethnic Conflict: The Strategy of Non-Territorial Autonomy." *International Political Science Review* 15: 297 (1994). Coakley notes that this arrangement may not be satisfactory as groups may prefer territoriality, police, military, and true autonomy, whereas with non-territorial autonomy groups are at least partially assimilated into the nation, but are granted a political voice at the national level and some degree of control over their affairs, 299–300, 311; Van der Beken, "Federalism, Local Government and Minority Protection in Ethiopia," 172–73.

years against your country's government. The regime in power has driven your country's economy into the ground, engaged in gross human rights violations, and presided over multiple famines, among other catastrophes. Suddenly, the armed struggle succeeds and the regime collapses, leaving you in *de facto* control of the state.

Soon after, your brothers in arms secede from your country, leaving it landlocked, poor, and economically mismanaged after years of war. You and your ethnic party have been in control of the levers of the state for less than two years and, since your party represents only 6 percent of the population, you lack the legitimacy and the functional capacity to govern. If your primary goals are to maintain control of the state, win the support (or at least the acquiescence) of the remaining 94 percent of the population, enrich your ethnic group, and build a long-term structure for governance, what would you do? You could call for open and free elections, but you might lose. You could try to form a highly centralized dictatorship with no devolution of power to the 94 percent, but the majority might coalesce to remove you. And given your country's recent history, it might not be peaceful. What options are left?

This over simplified and highly stylized example is intended to help unpack the ruling elite's potential set of goals, incentives, and options during the creation, drafting, and ratification of the Constitution. With this in mind, imagine that the Constitution's drafters want to entrench and preserve their power, while still providing a concession to those seeking transformational change. If this framing is even reasonably accurate, a constitution based on ethnic federalism satisfies many of these objectives. It allows a small ethnic group to remain in power; satiates the demand of many ethnic groups to be free from ethnic oppression, speak their languages, and celebrate their cultures; ensures that the financial resources of the Federal government are available to support favored groups; and allows the small ruling elite to establish an infrastructure for long-term rule. On this telling, the Constitution is more preservative than transformational, and the post-ratification constitutional practice, especially the Federal government's handling of the 2005 elections, seems consistent with this conclusion. This is, of course, a theory but evidence exists to sustain it.

Entrenching TPLF Power. Since the Constitution was created primarily by the TPLF, a group that represents a very small minority of the population, some question the Constitution's legitimacy.[84] One claim is that the TPLF and the broader EPRDF specifically adopted ethnic federalism to maintain power consistent

[84] Haile, "The New Ethiopian Constitution," 1, 44 (noting that the TPLF had been recognized as a third world communist insurgency that opportunistically claimed it was converting to democracy to gain acceptance by the west); Mengie, "Federalism as an Instrument for Unity and the Protection of Minorities," 265, 292 (citing Lovise Aalen, *Ethnic Federalism in a Dominant Party State: The Ethiopian Experience 1991–2000*, Report R.2 Chr. Michelsen Institute Development Studies and Human Rights 114 (2002)).

with Stalinist ideology, which views ethnic groups as an advantageous way to organize people if led by a strong vanguard party.[85] Unsurprisingly, many Ethiopians still feel the TPLF is monopolizing political power for their own benefit as they continue to dominate the political process.[86]

For example, the Constitution has no federal system of checks and balances to prevent the Federal government or the States from violating the rights of Ethiopian citizens within their respective jurisdictions.[87] The Constitution grants the power of review to the House of Federation – sometimes referred to as the Federal Council – a small body consisting of representatives from different "nations, nationalities and peoples."[88] Although it might appear to allow the many "nations, nationalities and peoples" to interpret the Constitution and account for political and cultural factors, it is a small body of indirectly elected, non-experts, who lack accountability and are often tied to the Federal executive branch.[89] The House of Federation is the upper chamber of the Parliament of Ethiopia.

Beyond the power of review, the House of Federation is the primary form of representation at the federal level for Ethiopia's ethnic groups and has at least one

[85] Aalen, "Ethnic Federalism and Self-Determination," 243, 245–46. See Ibid. 250 for further discussion on methods of EPRDF governmental dominance. Aalen also describes how the EPRDF's goal of liberation has shifted to administrative efficiency over time. Ibid. 259. Brietzke, "Ethiopia's 'Leap in the Dark'," 19, 27 (describing how many Ethiopians see the federalist model as a divide-and-rule tactic and that the states do not have the capability to serve as genuine federal units); Ehrlich, "Ethnicity and Constitutional Reform," 51, 53 (claiming the constitutional model has primarily served to uphold Tigrayan power); Habtu, "Multiethnic Federalism in Ethiopia," 313, 314(describing concerns that self-determination is not truly a commitment of the government and sees the one party state leading the country); Haile, "The New Ethiopian Constitution," 1, 43 (describing the TPLF's desire to maintain power as a minority of only 9.7 percent of the population by using divide and rule methods).

[86] Aalen, "Ethnic Federalism and Self-Determination," 243, 250 (noting during Constitutional development the TPLF had military control so no real opposition could be mounted against the "federal bargain"); Ehrlich, "Ethnicity and Constitutional Reform," 51, 62.

[87] Aalen, "Ethnic Federalism and Self-Determination," 243, 249; Abbink, "Ethnicity and Constitutionalism in Contemporary Ethiopia," 159, 170; Haile, "The New Ethiopian Constitution," 1, 27–31.

[88] Mengie, "Federalism as an Instrument for Unity and the Protection of Minorities," 265, 292.

[89] Aalen, "Ethnic Federalism and Self-Determination," 243, 249; Yonatan Tesfaye Fessha, "Judicial Review and Democracy: A Normative Discourse on the (Novel) Ethiopian Approach to Constitutional Review." *African Journal of International & Comparative Law* 14: 53, 70–72, 75, 78 (2006) (noting that members of the House of Federation in practice are often appointed by state councils, not by a vote by the people, and most members of the House are not independent but members of the executive branch, state government, or state council and are without the necessary expertise to decide constitutional issues). In practice as of 2006, twenty-three cases had been brought, mostly by individuals and not referred through the court system. The vast majority has been dismissed and only five have been decided. The decisions of the House are not published, 80, 80 n. 96, 97; Habtu, "Multiethnic Federalism in Ethiopia," 313, 330; Haile, "The New Ethiopian Constitution," 1, 25–30; Mengie, "Federalism as an Instrument for Unity and the Protection of Minorities," 265, 293; Twibell, "Ethiopian Constitutional Law,"399, 448–49 (stating that this indirectly elected body, which can deny *certiorari* for constitutional review, has political influence and weakens the constitution).

representative from each group, along with an additional representative for each one million people.[90] In 2005, twelve ethnic groups lacked representation in this body,[91] though there have been changes more recently. Some States send only representatives of one preferred ethnic group even if other ethnic groups with populations over one million are present in the State.[92] When the House of Federation does act, the "representative" body has no legislative authority and can only "'settle disputes' between member States, and interpret and contribute to amending the Constitution."[93]

The more important lower chamber – the House of People's Representatives – has broad, formal decision-making authority and is dominated by the EPRDF, making Ethiopia a "de facto single party system."[94] As a consequence, the EPRDF controls the legislature, judiciary, and executive, along with the military, and has been unwilling to share power democratically.[95] The best known example is the EPRDF's conduct during the 2005 multiparty elections. During the initial campaign, opposition parties operated relatively freely and were given television airtime.[96] However, once the EPRDF determined that the opposition parties were gaining popularity and had a real chance to win the election, then-Prime Minister Meles Zenawi "declared a month long ban on demonstrations and out-door meetings" immediately prior to Election Day.[97] During this period, "more than a hundred protesters were killed and tens of thousands of opposition members and supporters were detained" and charged with "treason, inciting violence, and planning to commit genocide."[98] Unsurprisingly, the EPRDF "won" the 2005 election by showing its willingness to undermine democratic processes to retain power.[99]

---

[90] Mengie, "Federalism as an Instrument for Unity and the Protection of Minorities," 265, 278 (explaining that some even find proportional representation inequitable since it leads to the domination of large ethnic groups rather than equal representation for each group).

[91] Habtu, "Multiethnic Federalism in Ethiopia," 313, 330.

[92] Ibid.

[93] Abbink, "Ethnicity and Constitutionalism in Contemporary Ethiopia," 159, 168; Haile, "The New Ethiopian Constitution," 1, 25–26.

[94] Mengie, "Federalism as an Instrument for Unity and the Protection of Minorities," 265, 277–79, 295; Van der Beken, "Federalism, Local Government and Minority Protection in Ethiopia," 150, 158.

[95] Mengie, "Federalism as an Instrument for Unity and the Protection of Minorities," 265, 276, 283.

[96] Mengie, "Ethnic Federalism and Conflict in Ethiopia: What Lessons Can Other Jurisdictions Draw?" 462, 470.

[97] Aalen, "Ethnic Federalism and Self-Determination," 243, 252.

[98] Ibid.

[99] Ibid. 255. But Compare Brietzke, "Ethiopia's 'Leap in the Dark'," 19, 21 (describing early electoral dominance by the EPRDF in part because of their perceived power but also because opposition groups fail to challenge them, voter apathy, and poorly designed and implemented electoral laws). Brietzke does suggest advocating for more competition within the government, transparency, a free press, and free voting etc., to create civil society and legitimacy for the government. Ibid. 36. Cohen, "'Ethnic Federalism' in Ethiopia," 157, 162 (describing how opposition parties boycotted initial elections due to disputes about the new government).

The 2010 and 2015 elections were non-events, marked with boycotts, low voter turnout and occasional protests that generated a strong response from the Federal government. Ethnic federalism in Ethiopia, on this view, is "continuing dictatorial rule by another name."[100]

Apart from the electoral process, the EPRDF took steps to ensure that the Federal government could maintain control over various resources and prevent any one State from controlling any vital commodity. To that end, States were drawn without regard to size, governance capacity, or economic resources, leading to skepticism about whether such a structure can facilitate development across the country.[101] The EPRDF's decision to ignore these factors likely exacerbates natural resource and human capital disparities since wealthier States are not required to share their resources with poorer States[102] (and redistribution through taxation is infeasible). Resources and human capital will likely stay in one State, so competition among States is minimized.[103] As a consequence, poorer and more conflict-prone States have fallen behind on development metrics.[104]

Finally, the Constitution vests ownership of land and natural resources in "the [Federal government] and the people of Ethiopia" as "a common property" that "shall not be subject to sale or to other means of exchange."[105] In theory, this might prevent the growth of a landless class and reduce inequality.[106] At the same time, it could allow the Federal government to confiscate or appropriate private land for projects in resource-rich areas, which may stunt investment and development in economically beneficial projects.[107]

---

[100] Aalen, "Ethnic Federalism and Self-Determination," 243, 243–44.
[101] Abbink, "Ethnicity and Constitutionalism in Contemporary Ethiopia," 159, 168.
[102] Cohen, "'Ethnic Federalism' in Ethiopia," 157, 169; Selassie, "Ethnic Federalism," 51, 91–92. Selassie also says this was a problem in Yugoslavia where relatively wealthy ethnic states resented having to help relatively poor ethnic states. *Id.* at 92.
[103] Cohen, "'Ethnic Federalism' in Ethiopia," 157, 168; Selassie, "Ethnic Federalism," 51, 89–90. Selassie gives examples in Nigeria and India where certain ethnic groups were barred from economic activity. Ibid. 90–91.
[104] Abbink, "Ethnicity and Constitutionalism in Contemporary Ethiopia," 159, 173; Zimmerman-Steinhart and Bekele, "The Implications of Federalism and Decentralization on Socioeconomic Conditions in Ethiopia." 89, 111, 113 (describing how some regions are falling behind on generally improving education and healthcare metrics due to capacity deficits and political instability).
[105] Constitution of the Federal Democratic Republic of Ethiopia, art. 40(3) (1994).
[106] Abbink, "Ethnicity and Constitutionalism in Contemporary Ethiopia," 159, 169.
[107] Ibid. 69–70; Haile, "The New Ethiopian Constitution," 1, 66–69 (discussing the failures of the Ethiopian constitution in the realm of property rights); Selassie, "Ethnic Federalism," 51, 81 (mentioning that this may be problematic for state-level development since the central government owns the land, and local governments likely know local needs and conditions better than the national government).

12.5 CONCLUSION

This Chapter highlights the transformational and preservative character of the Ethiopian constitutional practice by examining ethnic federalism from the perspective of the Constitution's drafters. Given a set of constraints, should we view Ethiopia's ethno-federalist Constitution as an aspirational document or a means to an end? Since 1994, the EPRDF (and TPLF) has maintained power and facilitated peaceful intra-party leadership transitions in 2012 and 2018. According to the World Bank, Ethiopia has enjoyed a 10.5 percent growth rate between 2005 and 2015,[108] providing the Federal government with revenue to assuage ethnic States. Ethiopia continues to improve on various health, education, and mortality metrics, and the country has not been at war since the cessation of hostilities with Eritrea in 2000. While the EPRDF engages in human rights violations, refuses to tolerate free elections, and still severely restricts the press, its human rights record is, perhaps unbelievably, still better than the record of gross human rights violations and war crimes committed by the Mengistu Hailemariam regime that preceded it (albeit an extraordinarily low baseline). Given the goals, incentives, and constraints of the EPRDF and its allies, constitutionalized ethnic federalism has likely been an effective means to an end for twenty-five years.

Has the EPRDF's ethnic federalism model run its course? On February 15, 2018, Prime Minister Desalegn finally resigned after the deaths of hundreds of anti-government and anti-EPRDF protesters in the Amhara and Oromo States in 2016.[109] His successor as Prime Minister, Abiy Ahmed,[110] is the son of a Muslim Oromo father and a Christian Amhara mother and speaks Oromo, Amharic, Tigrinya, and English, making him a uniquely popular choice among the largest ethnic groups in Ethiopia.[111] In one year alone, Prime Minister Ahmed made peace with Eritrea, freed imprisoned journalists, and engaged opposition groups,[112] and his first cabinet was 50 percent female, with women appointed to key posts including the Ministry of Defense and the Ministry of Trade and Industry.[113] Still, when his

[108] *The World Bank in Ethiopia,* The World Bank. Available at www.worldbank.org/en/country/ethiopia/overview (last visited February 1, 2018).
[109] "Ethiopia PM Hailemariam Desalegn in Surprise Resignation." Available at www.bbc.com/news/world-africa-43073285 (last visited August 1, 2018).
[110] Prime Minister Ahmed comes from the Oromo Democratic Party, one of the parties within the EPRDF ruling elite. "Has Abiy Ahmed Turned Ethiopia into a One-Man Show?" Available at www.aljazeera.com/indepth/features/abiy-ahmed-turned-ethiopia-man-show-190401222240311.html (last visited May 5, 2019).
[111] "Abiy Ahmed: Ethiopia's Prime Minister." Available at www.bbc.com/news/world-africa-43567007 (last visited August 1, 2018).
[112] "The next year will test whether Abiy Ahmed is Ethiopia's best hope for stability." Available at https://qz.com/africa/1590323/ethiopia-prime-minister-abiy-ahmed-marks-one-year-in-office/ (last visited May 5, 2019).
[113] "Ethiopia's new 50% women cabinet isn't just bold – it's smart." Available at https://qz.com/africa/1426110/ethiopias-new-cabinet-is-50-women/ (last visited May 5, 2019).

honeymoon period eventually ends, Prime Minister Ahmed will have to decide whether his regime is more interested in open elections and democratic rule or the continuation of EPRDF one-party rule. In other words, will the beginning of the second period of Ethiopian constitutionalism bring transformational change in the form of democratic governance, or will it continue down the path of preservative concessions? Only time will tell.

Index